MECCAN OPENINGS

A PILGRIM'S GUIDE TO DIVINE SECRETS

Shaykh Nazim Adil al-Haqqani
Shaykh Muhammad Hisham Kabbani
Hajjah Amina Adil
Shaykh Nour Mohamad Kabbani

INSTITUTE FOR SPIRITUAL & CULTURAL ADVANCEMENT

Library of Congress Publication Control Number: 2022941662
ISBN: 978-1-938058-65-3

Library of Congress Cataloging-in-Publication Data Forthcoming.

Published and Distributed by:
Institute for Spiritual and Cultural Advancement

17195 Silver Parkway, #401
Fenton, MI 48430 USA
Tel: (810) 593-1222
Email: staff@naqshbandi.org
Web: www.naqshbandi.org

بسم الله الرحمن الرحيم

وَأَذِّن فِى ٱلنَّاسِ بِٱلْحَجِّ يَأْتُوكَ رِجَالًا وَعَلَىٰ كُلِّ ضَامِرٍ يَأْتِينَ مِن كُلِّ فَجٍّ عَمِيقٍ

And proclaim unto Mankind the pilgrimage.
They will come to you on foot and on every lean camel from
every distant path. (Sūratu 'l-Ḥajj, 22:27)

الْحَاجُّ وَالْعُمَّارُ وَفْدُ اللَّهِ إِنْ دَعَوْهُ أجابَهمْ وإِنِ استَغفروهُ غفرَ لهمْ

The pilgrims who perform Hajj and 'Umrah are Allah's delegation. If they supplicate to Him, He will respond to them, and if they ask Him for forgiveness, He will forgive them. (Ibn Mājah from Abū Hurayrah ﷺ)

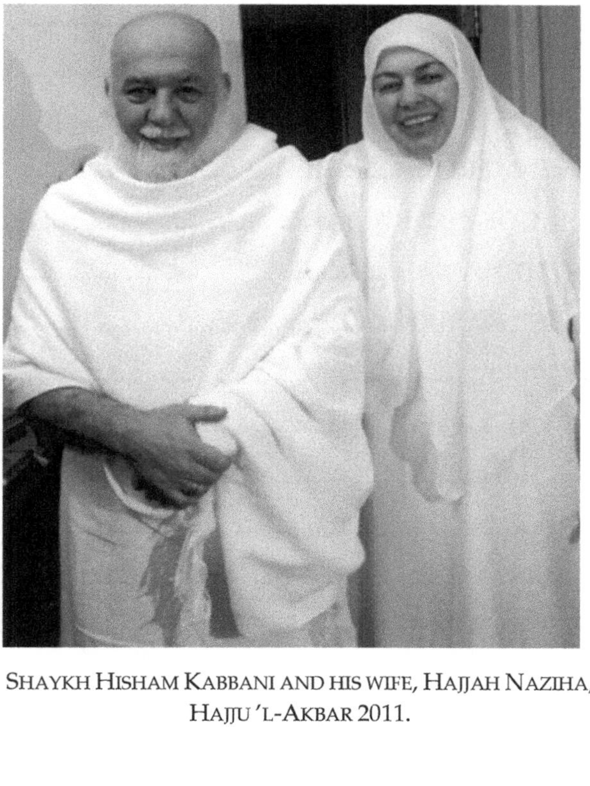

Shaykh Hisham Kabbani and his wife, Hajjah Naziha,
Hajju 'l-Akbar 2011.

CONTENTS

Publisher's Notes

References from the Quran and the hadith (holy traditions) are most commonly italicized and offset. References from the Quran are noted in parenthesis, i.e. (3:127), indicating the third chapter, verse 127. References from hadith are attributed to their transmitter, i.e. Bukhārī, Muslim, Āhmad, etc. Quotes from other sources are offset without italics.

Dates of events are characterized as "AH/CE," which infers "after Hijrah (migration)" on which the Islamic calendar is based, and "Christian Era," respectively.

Muslims around the world typically offer praise upon speaking, hearing, or reading the name "Allah" and any of the Islamic names of God. Muslims also offer salutation and/or invoke blessing upon speaking, hearing or reading the names of Prophet Muhammad, other prophets, his family, his companions, and saints. We have applied the following international standards, using Arabic calligraphy and lettering:

﷾ *subḥānahu wa taʿālā* (Glorified and Exalted), after the proper name of God, "*Allah*" in Arabic.

ﷺ *ṣall-Allāhu ʿalayhi wa sallam* (God's blessings and greetings of peace be upon him) following the names of the Prophet.

عليه السلام *ʿalayhi 's-salām* (peace be upon him) following the names of other prophets, angels, and Khiḍr.

عليها السلام *ʿalayhā 's-salām* (peace be upon her) following the name of Mary, Mother of Jesus.

رضي الله عنه/رضي الله عنها *radī-Allahu ʿanhu/ʿanhā* (may God be pleased with him/her) following the name of a male or female companion of the Prophet.

ق *qaddas-Allāhu sirrah* (may God sanctify his secret) following the name of a saint.

TRANSLITERATION

Transliteration is provided in the glossaries and in the section on the spiritual practices to facilitate correct pronunciation and is based on the following system:

Symbol	Transliteration	Symbol	Transliteration	Vowels:	
ء	ʼ	ط	ṭ	Long	
ب	b	ظ	ẓ	آ ى	ā
ت	t	ع	ʻ	و	ū
ث	th	غ	gh	ى	ī
ج	j	ف	f	Short	
ح	ḥ	ق	q	◌َ	a
خ	kh	ك	k	◌ُ	u
د	d	ل	l	◌ِ	i
ذ	dh	م	m		
ر	r	ن	n		
ز	z	ه	h		
س	s	و	w		
ش	sh	ى	y		
ص	ṣ	ة	ah; at		
ض	ḍ	ال	al-/’l-		

About the Authors

Shaykh Muhammad Nazim Adil al-Haqqani

Although there are no longer prophets upon the earth, the Most Merciful Lord did not leave His servants without inspired teachers and guides. One such teacher, a shaykh or *murshid* of the Naqshbandi Sufi Order, is Shaykh Nazim Adil al-Haqqani. A descendant not only of the holy Prophet Muhammad (peace and blessings be upon him) but also of the great Sufi masters, ʿAbd al-Qādir Jīlānī and Jalāluddin Rūmī, Shaykh Nazim was gifted from earliest childhood with an extraordinary spiritual personality. Bringing over eighty years of experience in the Sufi Path to bear, Shaykh Nazim focuses his profound and practical insight on the everyday travails confronting humankind in the 21st-century.

Most teachers, lecturers, professors and scholars, when they speak, address the minds of their listeners, attempting to provoke new thought patterns, impart fresh information and describe what they know. However, the Sufi masters speak "from the heart to the heart." For this reason, the shaykh's students are energized by his words, which directly address their desires and deepest needs with spiritual nourishment. Under the heavenly manifestations that accompany the shaykh's simple but pithy words, those seeking realities are showered with holy impressions, whose mere touch sets the heart afire with Divine Love.

Shaykh Nazim studied Classical Arabic and Islamic Jurisprudence (*fiqh*) in Istanbul, Turkey under Jamāluddīn al-Lāsūnī (d. 1955 CE/1375 AH) and received an *ijāza* (permission to teach) in these subjects from him. He was initiated in Naqshbandi Sufism by Sulaymān Arzarūmī (d. 1948 CE/1368 AH), who eventually directed him to Damascus, Syria, to continue his studies with his destined shaykh. He left Istanbul and arrived in Syria in 1944.

Shaykh Nazim continued his *Sharīʿah* studies in Aleppo, Hama, and Homs in Syria. In Homs, he studied at the *madrasa* adjoining the burial shrine and mosque of Muhammad's companion, Khālid ibn al-Walīd. There, he received further *ijāzas* in Ḥanafī jurisprudence (*fiqh*) from Muhammad ʿAlī ʿAyūn as-Sūd and ʿAbdul Jalīl Murād.

Following the end of the unrest in the region due to World War II, Shaykh Nazim was able to enter Damascus in 1945. There, he met Shaykh ʿAbdAllāh Fā'izi ad-Dāghestānī, from whom he took the oath of allegiance (*bayʿah*). Shaykh ʿAbdAllāh trained him well in Naqshbandi Sufi path, putting him through numerous seclusions. Shaykh Nazim followed Shaykh ʿAbdAllāh as his primary spiritual guide (*murshid*) until his passing in 1973 when Shaykh Nazim received his spiritual successorship (*khilāfa*).

In 1974, Shaykh Nazim began to visit Western Europe, traveling every year to London, England, for the month of Ramadan. He gained a large following of spiritual seekers from Western Europe and North America, many of whom converted to Islam after encountering his teaching. From 1980, his lectures on Islam and Sufism were published in English and other European languages Shaykh Nazim's transnational appeal was facilitated by his ability to speak English, Turkish, Arabic, and Greek.

In his later years, Shaykh Nazim was regularly recognized among the world's fifty most influential Muslims in the annual publication, *The 500 Most Influential Muslims in the World*. Notable students and followers of Shaykh Nazim include John G. Bennett, the British author on spirituality.

SHAYKH MUHAMMAD HISHAM KABBANI

World-renowned religious scholar Shaykh Muhammad Hisham Kabbani is featured in the ground-breaking book published by Georgetown University, *The 500 Most Influential Muslims in the World*. For decades, he has promoted traditional Islamic principles of peace, tolerance, love, compassion and brotherhood, while rigorously opposing extremism in all its forms. He hails from a respected family of traditional Islamic scholars, which includes the former head of the Association of Muslim Scholars of Lebanon and the present grand mufti (highest Islamic religious authority) of Lebanon.

Shaykh Kabbani is highly trained, both as a western scientist and as an Islamic scholar. He received a Bachelor's degree in Chemistry and later studied medicine. Under the instruction of Shaykh ʿAbdAllāh ad-Dāghestānī of Damascus (d. 1973), he holds a degree in Islamic Divine Law. Shaykh Muhammad Nazim Adil al-Haqqani, world leader of the

Naqshbandī-Ḥaqqānī Sufi Order, authorized him to teach and counsel students in Sufism.

In his long-standing effort to promote a better understanding of traditional Islam, in February 2010, Shaykh Kabbani hosted HRH Charles, the Prince of Wales at a cultural event at the revered Old Trafford Stadium in Manchester, U.K. He has hosted two international conferences in the U.S., and regional conferences on a host of contemporary issues that attracted moderate Muslim scholars from Asia, the Far East, Middle East, Africa, U.K. and Eastern Europe. His counsel is sought by media outlets, academics, policymakers and government leaders.

For thirty years, Shaykh Kabbani has consistently promoted peaceful cooperation among people of all beliefs. Since the early 1990s, he launched numerous endeavors to bring moderate Muslims into the mainstream. Often at great personal risk, including a '*fatwā*' condemning him issued by ISIS, Shaykh Kabbani has been instrumental in awakening Muslim social consciousness regarding the religious duty to stand firm against extremism and terrorism, for the benefit of all. His bright, hopeful outlook, with a goal to honor and serve all humanity has helped millions understand the difference between moderate mainstream Muslims and minority extremist sects.

In the United States, Shaykh Kabbani serves as Chairman, Islamic Supreme Council of America; Founder, Naqshbandi Sufi Order of America; As-Sunnah Foundation of America. In the United Kingdom, Shaykh Kabbani is an advisor to Sufi Muslim Council, which consults to the British government on public policy and social and religious issues.

Among over 30 titles by Shaykh Kabbani include: *The Importance of Prophet Muhammad in Our Daily Life*, *Classical Islam and the Naqshbandi Sufi Tradition*, and *Remembrance of God Liturgy of the Sufi Naqshbandi Masters.*

HAJJAH AMINA ADIL

The late Hajjah Amina Adil, renowned author and lecturer, was a spiritual advisor for more than thirty years, devoting herself to helping people of all walks of life better understand Islam and Sufism. In addition, she played a pivotal role in helping Muslim women understand and apply the many distinguishing rights God Almighty set forth for women in the Islamic faith.

Hajjah Amina studied under many scholars of the Middle East and Turkey, including Grandshaykh ʿAbdAllāh ad-Dāghestānī an-Naqshbandi, among others.

Married for fifty years to Shaykh Muhammad Nazim Adil al- Haqqani, the spiritual head of the Naqshbandi-Haqqani Sufi Order, Hajjah Amina traveled the world. A scholar of *Sharīʿah* in her own right, she had thousands of students throughout North and South America, Europe, the Middle and Far East, Southeast and Central Asia, and Africa.

Hajjah Amina, a direct descendant of Prophet Muhammad ﷺ was born in Russia's Kazan Province during the early Communist era. As a child, she made the dangerous emigration from Russia to Turkey during a time when Muslims were being persecuted and killed. After more than a year and with Communist officials in deadly pursuit, the family was able, miraculously, to make their way to Turkey. After some years there they moved to Mt. Qasyūn, a high mountain overlooking Damascus, Syria. There they were fortunate to come under the guidance of the renowned spiritual guide Grandshaykh ʿAbdAllāh al-Fā'iz ad-Dāghestānī ق who took particular care in overseeing Hajjah Amina's religious and spiritual development. Under Grandshaykh ʿAbdAllah she studied *Taṣawwuf* (Sufism – Islamic spirituality) and she studied Fiqh (Islamic Jurisprudence) under such notable scholars as Shaykh Ṣāliḥ Farfūr of Syria and Shaykh Mukhtār ʿAlaily, then Secretary General of Religious Affairs of Lebanon.

Hajjah Amina Adil married the Grand Shaykh of the Naqshbandi Sufi Order, Shaykh Muhammad Nazim Adil with whom she lived for over fifty years. In addition to her own four children, sixteen grandchildren, and six great-grandchildren, she raised and nurtured with love and wisdom the thousands of students and visitors who would descend yearly upon the humble house of the Shaykh in Cyprus.

Not one to spend time in idle talk, Hajjah Amina taught the art of servanthood by serving the Shaykh and his guests tirelessly with good humor, cooking every day for everyone. She taught respect for all God's gifts by never wasting anything and using and reusing everything. She taught worship by following faithfully *Sharīʿah* and Sunnah and maintaining her Sufi practices. She taught patience, kindness, respect and hard work by her daily example. As a scholar, she passed on to new generations from her vast knowledge stories of the prophets and saints, stories used to teach wisdom since the beginning of time.

Hajjah Amina, passed from this earthly life in 2004. Hajjah Amina spent the last years of her life in the village of Lefke, in northern (Turkish) Cyprus in a comfortable "old world" farm house with a spacious garden. There she used to receive thousands of visitors every year from every corner the world. She would often accompany Shaykh Nazim on his official visits to other countries and had been a keynote speaker at numerous conferences on Islam and Muslim women.

SHAYKH NOUR MOHAMAD KABBANI

Dr. Nour Kabbani was born in Beirut in 1971, where he was raised by his parents, As-Sayyid Shaykh Hisham Kabbani and Hajjah Naziha Adil Kabbani, respective deputy and daughter of the late As-Sayyid Shaykh Muhammad Nazim Adil an-Naqshbandi (d. 2014), Chief Scholar of Ḥanafī Fiqh in Turkey and founder of the Naqshbandi-Haqqani Sufi Order.

At an early age Dr. Nour began attending his grandfather's lectures on the Islamic Sciences of Fiqh (*Sharīʿah*), *ʿAqīdah* (Doctrine), and *Akhlāq* (Islamic Ethics). He also studied under his father, a scholar of Shafiʿī *Fiqh* and Ashaʿrī *ʿAqīdah*. With the special *du`a* of renowned Naqshbandi Shaykh, ʿAbdAllāh al-Fā'iz ad-Dāghestānī ق of Damascus, he trained under as-Sayyid Shaykh Nazim ق and became proficient in commentary of the Holy-Qur`an and hadith, specifically the doctrine of *Āhl as-Sunnah wa 'l-Jamaʿah.*

Dr. Nour acquired his M.D. in Istanbul, Turkey, and after moving to New York City, completed his residency at Colombia University, St. Luke's Roosevelt Hospital.

Since moving to America, Dr. Nour continued his Islamic education two-to-three months each year in Cyprus, where he studied deeper aspects of the Islamic Sciences under his noble grandfather, Shaykh Nazim, who authorized him to give *khuṭbahs,* lectures and lead *dhikr* (meditation). Shaykh Nour's talks reflect the nurturing wisdom of his illustrious teachers who have brought Islam to hundreds of thousands of converts and revitalized the faith of millions of Muslims around the world.

Due to his unique life experience and noble lineage, Western audiences in particular resonate with his advice, which they find practical and spiritually uplifting. In the US, Dr. Nour has addressed groups in Los Angeles, Houston, Dallas, Chicago, Michigan, New York, New Jersey, and Metro Washington DC. In Canada, his tours of Montreal, Ottawa and London were highly successful. Since 2015, his UK tours have attracted a strong youth following, much like when his beloved grandfather first toured England in the mid-1970s.

FOREWORD

Shaykh Muhammad Nazim Adil al-Haqqani ق

SHAYKH NAZIM ADIL AL-HAQQANI WITH HIS WIFE, HAJJAH AMINA ADIL.

Aʿūdhu billāhi min ash-Shayṭāni 'r-rajīm

Bismillāhi 'r-Raḥmāni 'r-Raḥīm

Today *ḥujjāj al-kirām*, the honored pilgrims, turned their faces towards the Kaʿbat al-Muʿazzamah, supplicating, "*Labbayk*, here I am (my Lord)!" They are going. May we be with them *Inshā-Allāh* and may we get relief. Noble pilgrims are turning towards Kaʿbat al-Muʿazzamah.

مَا شَاءَ اللّٰهُ كَانَ ، وَمَا لَمْ يَشَأْ لَمْ يَكُنْ .

Mashā Allāhu kān wa mā lam yashā' lam yakun.

What Allah wills is and what He does not will is not.

May Allah ﷻ include us together with them. Let us say: *Bismillāhi 'r-Raḥmāni 'r-Raḥīm! Bismillāhi 'r-Raḥmāni 'r-Raḥīm*! *Bismillāh ash-Sharīf* opens the doors to all goodness. May we have a share of it, too. Welcome to these beautiful days. May we reach them, too. May our fellows, our children reach them, as it is a great honor.

Go ahead, O Lovers of Shāh Mardan! Let us drink from the favors of these holy days. Every day has its own favor. There are twelve months, each with its own favor. This is Dhul-Qaʿdah and Dhul-Ḥijjah is approaching. May we reach it with goodness and health! May we reach it with the noble pilgrims. Welcome, O Lovers of Shāh Mardan! May our burdens be gone! May relief come upon us! May our day be blessed! May we be clean inside and outside.

Angels descend from Heavens and angels ascend from Earth. The honored pilgrims turned towards Kaʿbat al-Muʿazzamah, supplicating, "*Labbayk*! – We are here!" Let it be. May we be dressed in the adornment of honor. Let us say, "*Bismillāhi 'r-Raḥmāni 'r-Raḥīm,*" as this is the dress of honor. The dress of honor for the Sons of Ādam is "*Bismillāhi 'r-Raḥmāni 'r-Raḥīm.*"

O our Lord, Our *Subḥān*, our Sulṭān! While the *ḥujjāj al-kirām* are turning towards Kaʿbat al-Muʿazzamah, may we turn as well, may we get relief, may we open up and may our souls be filled with relief. May Allah, *dhul jalāli wa 'l-jamāli wa 'l-kamāl*, include us as well; may He include us among those turning towards the Kaʿbah. May descending mercy come upon us, too. May our way be the Way of Truth. May it be the relieving way. Let us say "*Bismillāhi 'r-Raḥmāni 'r-Raḥīm.*" O our Lord, may we remember Your Glorious Names. May we find strength and may we be dressed in majesty.

What shall we do? Who is destined to go will go.

إنّما الأعْمَالُ بالنّيّة،

Innamā 'l-ʿamālu bi 'n-nīyyāt

Every action is according to (its) intention.[1]

Everyone's deeds are according to their intentions, so make good intentions. What is our intention? Servanthood to Janab al-Mawla, to Allah Almighty. What are we created for? For servanthood to our Lord, for revering our Lord. May our day be happy, may it be beautiful! Janab al-Mawla says, "Ask from Me! All your wishes will be accepted; We don't turn away the wishes of Our Servant. We are giving!"

How many people from the nation of Muhammad ﷺ ran towards the Kaʿbat al-Muʿazzamah! They said, "*Labbayk! Labbayk, yā Rabbī*! O our Lord, we are running for Your Command. Give us strength on the way of worshipping You!" What shall we ask from our Lord? We ask for strength and health to run for worshipping Him.

Whoever reveres Kaʿbat al-Muʿazzamah will be revered. Whoever respects Kaʿbat al-Muʿazzamah will find respect; he will find glory, honor and strength. O our Lord, we are Your weak servants. May our Mawla who strengthens weak servants, who gives strength to weak servants on the way of worshipping Him, give us strength, too. May He give honor.

Ask for honor! We ask for honor from our Lord. O our Lord, our *Subḥān*, our Sulṭān! Dress us in the beautiful adornments You dress the *ḥujjāj al-kirām* at the Kaʿbat al-Muʿazzamah. Dress us in the adornment of honor in which You dress the *ḥujjāj al-kirām, yā Rabb*! May the one saying "Allāh!" today drink the wine of love, O my Lord! May we be among those saying "Allah!" How beautiful are those saying "Allāh!"

Go ahead, O Shāh Mardan! The field is yours. Welcome! Let us drink the wine of love. May our souls be revived; may our love increase. All the prophets walked around Kaʿbat al-Muʿazzamah, built by Prophet Ibrāhīm ﷺ. They said, "O our Lord, we came to circumambulate this House of Yours! And we ask to be filled with Your love. Grant us good servanthood!"

O my Lord! O our Lord! *Innamā 'l-ʿamālu bi 'n-nīyyāt,* the deeds of a man are according to his intentions. Keep your intention right and don't fear, don't be afraid.

---

[1] Bukhārī.

Allāhu Allāh! Allāhu Allāh! Allāhu Rabbī, mā lī siwāhu.

Hū! Allāhu Allāh!

مَا شَاء الله كَان، وَمَا لَم يَشَأ لَم يَكُن

Mashā Allāhu kān wa mā lam yashā' lam yakun.

What Allah wills is and what He does not will is not.

Kaʿbat al-Muʿazzamah is 5,000 years old, is it not? It has been open for 5,000 years. It is open for the servants of the nation of Muhammad ﷺ, not only for the Prophet Ibrāhīm ﵇. It is open for all of the nation of Muhammad! Ask, "Dress us in the adornment of mercy, *yā Rabbī*!" All prophets were calling, "Let us go, too. Let us visit!"

How beautiful! How beautiful it is to walk around the Kaʿbah. How nice it is to run towards our Lord. How beautiful it is to run towards the command of our Lord. It removes all worries! If the world was without the Kaʿbah, what value would it have? What is the value of the world, if there were no Kaʿbah? Allah ﷻ says, "It is *Baytu 'Llāh,* the House of Allah!" *Allāhu Allāh!*

> *Labbayk Allāhumma labbayk! Labbayka lā sharīka laka labbayk!*
> *Inna 'l-ḥamda wa 'n-niʿmata laka wa 'l-mulk, lā sharīka lak!*
> Here I am, O Lord, You have no partner. Here I am.
> For You the praise, the favor, the dominion. You have no partner!

So much has come and gone from this world. So many lovers have come and left this world. They cried and asked, "We want to see it, too." May those saying "Allah!" today drink the wine of love. Say "Allah!" All prophets, from the beginning, all of them said "Allah!" They called for Allah.

O our Lord, may the supplication of Your Glorious Names continue in our hearts, *yā Rabbī.*

> *Allāhu Allāh! Allāhu Allāh! Allāhu Rabbī, mā lī siwāhu, Hū!*

Let us wake up and say, "*Allāh! Allāh, jalla jalāluhu, jallat ʿaẓamatuhu wa lā ilāha ghayruhu*!" Let us say, "My Lord!" Our Lord is Allah. Our glory is with saying, "Allah!" Let us ask for it.

O Lovers! O those surrendering their souls to their Lord! What do you live for? What is the value of life if you don't say "Allah"? If they don't say "Allah," they are worthless rubbish. Let us say "Allah, *yā Hū*!" What sufferings lovers have gone through and what they have asked for from their Lord!

Ilāhī anta Rabbī! Ilāhī anta maṭlūbī! Ilāhī anta maqṣūdī!

You are our Lord! You are our desire! You are our goal!

O our Lord, may our souls expand, may we be glad. May we be loaded with the relief of the bliss of Your Love, *yā Rabbī*! May we get relief! May we find relief when we say "Allah!" May Allah, who raises the sun, give us the light of faith and love. Let us say, "Allāh, Allāh, Allāh!" Whoever does not say "Allah!" is dead. Who says "Allāh!" is alive. Let us be alive, let us be clean!

Hū! Allāhu Allāh! Mashā Allāhu kān wa mā lam yashā' lam yakun.

What Allah ﷻ wants happens, what He doesn't want won't happen.

Let us ask from our Mawla so that He gives from His Love. May our Mawla revive us with love. All prophets said "Allāh!" and they were filled; they got loaded with Divine Love and became full of it. If they don't say "Allāh!" what's their benefit? Rubbish.

O Allah, the One raising the sun every day! How beautiful, how beautiful! Let us say "Allāh!" and let us run towards Allah ﷻ. How beautiful! Don't run towards *dunyā*; run towards Allah ﷻ!

Our souls are under Your Command, *yā Rabbī*! They are sacrificed on Your Way, *yā Rabbī*. May we live for Your Love, *yā Rabbī*.

Allāhu Allāh! Allāhu Allāh! Allāhu Rabbī, mā lī siwāhu, Hū!

Hū! This is the task of the day, saying, "*Hū*!" saying, "*Allah Hū*!"

O lovers of Shāh Mardan! May we open, may we be loaded with relief. May Allah Almighty fill those walking around the Kaʿbah with relief. Ask for relief from Janab al-Ḥaqq, the Lord Almighty, don't ask for sadness. He created us, and He created us beautiful. He made us busy with supplication and reason. What should our task be? Let it be saying, "Allah, O our Lord!"

Go ahead, O Shāh Mardan. May our hearts be glad together with you. May our hearts be relieved. O our Lord. Let us say, "*Yā Hū*!"

Shukr to Allah ﷻ for letting us reach this day. Our Mawla can make us reach even better than this. He removes all sadness from our hearts. He gives relief. May those saying "Allāh!" enter the Rose Garden of Paradise. May those saying "Allāh!" today enter it. Say "Allāh!" and don't fear.

What shall we do? Slowly, slowly, slowly. It's not easy. It's not easy to be filled with the Divine Love. It's not easy to walk around the Kaʿbah with that love. It's not easy to say "Allāh!" with that love. May our hearts be filled with Divine Love.

Allāhu Allāh! Allāhu Allāh! Allāhu Rabbī, mā lī sīwāhu, Hū! Illa Hū!

Hū, our Lord. *Bismillāhi 'r-Raḥmāni 'r-Raḥīm*. What shall we do? They made us say a few words on these holy days. May our hearts open and be glad. May they be filled with relief. May our day be good. May our deeds be good. May our way be honored!

Al-Fātiḥah.

PREFACE

Shaykh Nour Mohamad Kabbani

DR. NOUR KABBANI WITH HIS FATHER, SHAYKH HISHAM KABBANI AT MASJID AN-NABAWI, ʿUMRAH 2018.

Aʿūdhu billāhi min ash-Shayṭāni 'r-rajīm. Bismillāhi 'r-Raḥmāni 'r-Raḥīm.

Alḥamdulillāhi Rabbi 'l-ʿĀlamīn, wa 'ṣ-ṣalātu wa 's-salāmu ʿalā ashrafi 'l-mursalīn, Sayyīdinā wa Nabīyyīnā Muhammadin wa ʿalā ālihi wa ṣaḥbihi ajmaʿīn, wa man tabiʿahum bi iḥsānin ilā yawmi 'd-dīn.

Let's speak a little bit about Sayyīdinā Ibrāhīm ﷺ, Allah's Intimate Friend, *Khalīlu 'Llāh*. It was Hajj, and Sayyīdinā Ibrāhīm ﷺ raised the foundations of the House of God. What did Allah ﷻ say? *Astaʿīdhu billāh*:

إِنَّ أَوَّلَ بَيْتٍ وُضِعَ لِلنَّاسِ لَلَّذِي بِبَكَّةَ مُبَارَكًا وَهُدًى لِّلْعَالَمِينَ

Indeed, the first House (of worship) established for Mankind was that at Bakkah (Mecca), full of blessing and a guidance for the worlds. [2]

فِيهِ آيَاتٌ بَيِّنَاتٌ مَّقَامُ إِبْرَاهِيمَ وَمَن دَخَلَهُ كَانَ آمِنًا وَلِلَّهِ عَلَى النَّاسِ حِجُّ
الْبَيْتِ مَنِ اسْتَطَاعَ إِلَيْهِ سَبِيلًا وَمَن كَفَرَ فَإِنَّ اللَّهَ غَنِيٌّ عَنِ الْعَالَمِينَ

In it are Signs Manifest, (for example), the Station of Abraham. Whoever enters it attains security. Pilgrimage there is a duty men owe to Allah, those who can afford the journey, but if any deny faith, Allah stands not in need of any of His creatures.[3]

Allah ﷻ is saying, "O Muhammad ﷺ! Know that the first House put for people on Earth was the Kaʿbah, in Bakkah[4]. Tell the nations of Jewish people that objected." The Jewish tribes of Madina were upset asking the Prophet ﷺ, "Why did you change the direction of prayer from Jerusalem, which was the initial *Qiblah* before Kaʿbah! All *Anbīyā*, prophets, were in that Holy Land, so why did you change your *Qiblah*?" According to Īmām as-Suyūṭī in his *tafsīr*, *Ad-Durr al-Manthūr*, this *āyah* came down when the Jewish people of Madina commented on the shifting of the *Qiblah* and Allah ﷻ said to Prophet Muhammad ﷺ, "Tell them: No, not *Baytu 'l-Maqdis*, but Kaʿbah was the first Heavenly House put for people on Earth."

What is there? We want to go to the Kaʿbah, but what is in it? What is in Mecca that all of us want to go there and perform our Hajj? Allah ﷻ explains that we escape to His Mercy. You take yourself out from this *dunyā*, out of work, you take yourself out of your family, too, because sometimes family can be a problem. You take yourself out of yourself, which has a problem with all the thoughts that come in your head. You

---

[2] Sūrat Āli ʿImrān, 3:96.

[3] Sūrat Āli-ʿImrān, 3:97.

[4] Ancient name for Mecca.

dive into the stories of the Qur'an of the pious ones and the prophets, and you try to find a happy, peaceful way. He says, "*Indeed, the first House of Worship established for Mankind was that at Bakkah (Mecca), full of blessing.*" There is *barakah* there. When we go to Ka'bah, it's not only four walls, but there is also *bi bakkata mubārakan*, a lot of benefit, goodness (*khayr*) for us there, for those who visit! *Wa hudan*, and there is guidance there *li 'l-'alamīn*, to everyone, *fīhi āyātun bayyināt*, and there are clear signs at Maqām Ibrāhīm, the Station of Abraham. We love Sayyīdinā Ibrāhīm, he is our father:

$$مِلَّةَ أَبِيكُمْ إِبْرَاهِيمَ هُوَ سَمَّاكُمُ الْمُسْلِمِينَ$$

(It is) the religion of your father, Ibrāhīm. Allah named you 'Muslims'.[5]

Allah is saying in the Holy Qur'an, *millata abīkum Ibrāhīm*, "On the way, the religion of your father, Ibrāhīm." *Hūwa sammākumu 'l-muslimūn*, "He called you Muslims and your religion is of your father, Ibrāhīm." It is an honor for us that our father is Sayyīdinā Ibrāhīm. We all go to Maqām Ibrāhīm, we do our *ṭawāf* and pray two *raka'ats*, *alḥamdulillāh*, but what really is Maqām Ibrāhīm? Is it only an encasement behind which you stand and pray or is it something else? Maqām Ibrāhīm, the Station of Abraham. What level did Sayyīdinā Ibrāhīm reach? Because he is our father, we also have to follow his footsteps, which are only in Islam, for he was Muslim.

CHARACTERISTICS OF SAYYĪDINĀ IBRĀHĪM:

1) HE WAS GENEROUS IN THE WAY OF ALLAH

Sayyīdinā Ibrāhīm was a very wealthy person and he used his wealth in the Way of Allah. He honored his guests by being very generous to his people; he gave them from his knowledge, *'ilm*, and from his wealth. By being generous, he gained a higher level of *Īmān*, because Allah said:

$$الَّذِينَ يُقِيمُونَ الصَّلَاةَ وَمِمَّا رَزَقْنَاهُمْ يُنْفِقُونَ$$

---

[5] Sūratu 'l-Ḥajj, 22:78.

The ones who establish prayer, and from what We have provided them, they spend.[6]

So Sayyīdinā Ibrāhīm ﷺ spent from what Allah ﷻ gave him, and that was the level of his *Īmān*.

2) He Sought Allah's Guidance and Asked for a Helper

As Allah ﷻ said in the Holy Qur'an:

وَقَالَ إِنِّى ذَاهِبٌ إِلَىٰ رَبِّى سَيَهْدِينِ رَبِّ هَبْ لِى مِنَ الصَّالِحِينَ فَبَشَّرْنَاهُ بِغُلَامٍ حَلِيمٍ

He said, "Indeed I am going toward my Lord, who will guide me. O my Lord! Send me someone from among the righteous." So, We gave him good tidings of a forbearing boy.[7]

Nimrud, the tyrant of that time, threw Prophet Ibrāhīm ﷺ in the fire and Allah ﷻ saved him. After he was saved, he said to his people, *innī dhāhibun ilā Rabbī*, "I am going to my Lord." Sayyīdinā Ibrāhīm ﷺ was seeking the Way, that's why he said, *sa-yahdīni*, "Surely, my Lord will guide me to the way. I am going to my Lord!" But where is "the way"? *Sa-yahdīni*, "He will guide me. I am sure He will guide me." He invoked the Lord in *duʿā*, saying, *Rabbī hab lī min aṣ-ṣāliḥīn*, "O my Lord, give me someone from the pious ones to help me find my way to You!"

He wanted guidance and he asked for support from the pious ones as helpers to help him find the way. You need a helper to help you find the way; you cannot find it by yourself. Even Sayyīdinā Mūsā ﷺ asked for help. From whom? He asked Allah ﷻ for help from Sayyīdinā Hārūn (Aaron) ﷺ, did he not? He asked Allah ﷻ, "I need a helper. Give me someone that will help me in my mission." So Sayyīdinā Ibrāhīm ﷺ asked for a helper and that was his son, Sayyīdinā Ismaʿīl ﷺ. Allah ﷻ said, "We gave him the guidance of *ghulāmin ḥalīm*," a young man who is *ḥalīm*, forbearing, very tolerant. *'Ḥalīm'* is the one who doesn't rush things. When something bad happens to them, it doesn't shake them from the

---

[6] Sūratu 'l-Anfāl, 8:3.

[7] Sūratu 'ṣ-Ṣāffāt, 37:99-101.

inside, they are stable; if someone hurts them, they are patient. Allah ﷻ gave him *ghulāmin ḥalīm*, a tolerant boy, some say at 10 years old, others 15, but he was a young boy. That was the age when he was with Sayyīdinā Ibrāhīm ﷺ, a time when he could walk with him and help him in his chores.

3) HE HAD SUPERIOR MANNERS AND OBEYED *SHARĪʿAH*

Sayyīdinā Ibrāhīm ﷺ said, "O my son, I see in the dream that I am slaughtering you."

فَلَمَّا بَلَغَ مَعَهُ السَّعْيَ قَالَ يَا بُنَيَّ إِنِّي أَرَىٰ فِي الْمَنَامِ أَنِّي أَذْبَحُكَ فَانْظُرْ مَاذَا تَرَىٰ

And when (his son) was old enough to walk with him, (Ibrāhīm) said, "O my dear son, I have seen in a dream that I must sacrifice you. So, look what you think?[8]

Look at the *adab* of Sayyīdinā Ibrāhīm ﷺ and his compliance with *Sharīʿah*! He was asking Sayyīdinā Ismaʿīl's ﷺ *shūrā'*, counsel, saying, "O my boy! I am seeing in the dream that I am slaughtering you; consult with me. *F'anẓur*, look into this thing. What do you think about it?" That is why, when we have to do something, we must make *mashwara*, consult others. Sayyīdinā Ibrāhīm ﷺ consulted a boy, his son. So sometimes we can consult sons or daughters if something pertains to them, as in this example when Sayyīdinā Ismaʿīl ﷺ was going to be slaughtered and his father asked, "What is your opinion?"

قَالَ يَا أَبَتِ افْعَلْ مَا تُؤْمَرُ سَتَجِدُنِي إِنْ شَاءَ اللَّهُ مِنَ الصَّابِرِينَ

He said, "O my father! Do that which you are commanded. Allah willing, you shall find me of the steadfast."[9]

Sayyīdinā Ismaʿīl ﷺ said, "O my father, do it!" Look at his *Īmān*! What 10-year-old boy will tell his father, "Yes father, please slaughter me! What are you waiting for, do what you are ordered, don't hesitate! *Satajidunī*

[8] Sūratu 'ṣ-Ṣāffāt, 37:102.

[9] Sūratu 'ṣ-Ṣāffāt, 37:102.

Inshā-Allāhu min aṣ-ṣābirīn, by Allah's Will, you will find me patient." Even Sayyīdinā Isma'īl ﷺ asked for Allah's help, he said, "*Inshā-Allāh*!"

إِيَّاكَ نَعْبُدُ وإِيَّاكَ نَسْتَعِينُ

You (alone) do we worship, and You (alone) we ask for help.[10]

He is saying, "O my Lord, I obey Your order for me to be slaughtered, but I seek help from You, *Inshā-Allāh*."

4) HE SURRENDERED HIS SON, HIS WEALTH AND HIMSELF TO ALLAH ﷻ

Since both Sayyīdinā Ibrāhīm ﷺ surrendered his son, Sayyīdinā Isma'īl ﷺ to Allah ﷻ, and Sayyīdinā Isma'īl ﷺ also surrendered himself to Allah ﷻ Allah ﷻ accepted their intentions.

فَلَمَّا أَسْلَمَا وَتَلَّهُ لِلْجَبِينِ

Then, when they had both surrendered (to Allah) and he had flung him down upon his face.[11]

They became so pure and took themselves out of the equation. If we were going to be slaughtered, we would ask ourselves a hundred times, "What am I throwing myself into?" How many of us say, "What am I getting into? I am getting involved in this thing, what is this?" No submission, but Sayyīdinā Ibrāhīm ﷺ and his son became very, very obedient to Allah Almighty's Order. Then Allah ﷻ said, "O Ibrāhīm! You have fulfilled the dream and made it become a reality."

وَنَادَيْنَاهُ أَنْ يَا إِبْرَاهِيمُ قَدْ صَدَّقْتَ الرُّؤْيَا إِنَّا كَذَٰلِكَ نَجْزِى الْمُحْسِنِينَ

We called unto him: O Abraham! You have fulfilled the vision." Indeed, We thus reward the doers of good.[12]

What did Sayyīdinā Ibrāhīm do? He offered his son as a sacrifice to Allah ﷻ, Who accepted the sacrifice based on his *nīyyah*, intention:

---

[10] Sūratu 'l-Fātiḥah, 1:4.

[11] Sūratu 'ṣ-Ṣāffāt, 37:103.

[12] Sūratu 'ṣ-Ṣāffāt, 37:104-105.

إنّما الأعْمَالُ بالنِّيّةِ،

The Prophet ﷺ said, "Verily, actions are by intentions."[13]

Sayyīdinā Ibrāhīm ﷺ demonstrated his intention, *nīyyah,* when he took up the knife and put the child on the rock in Mina to slaughter him. He tried to cut his son's neck once, then twice, then three times, but the knife did not cut! That is against the laws of physics. He showed the *nīyyah,* he fulfilled the action, but Allah ﷻ did not give permission for the boy to die. Allah ﷻ said, "I accepted your intention, and your action, so it is as if you slaughtered your child, but We are going to spare him for you."

إِنَّ هَٰذَا لَهُوَ الْبَلَاءُ الْمُبِينُ وَفَدَيْنَاهُ بِذِبْحٍ عَظِيمٍ وَتَرَكْنَا عَلَيْهِ فِي الْآخِرِينَ

Indeed, this was a clear test and We ransomed him with a great sacrifice, and We left (this blessing) for him among generations (to come) in later times.[14]

We are talking about Sayyīdinā Ibrāhīm's *maqām,* station, and let's test ourselves as to where we are in comparison. Allah ﷻ continues in the verse:

سَلَامٌ عَلَىٰ إِبْرَاهِيمَ كَذَٰلِكَ نَجْزِي الْمُحْسِنِينَ إِنَّهُ مِنْ عِبَادِنَا الْمُؤْمِنِينَ

Peace be unto Ibrāhīm! Thus, indeed do We reward those who do right, for he was one of Our believing servants.[15]

Allah ﷻ witnessed that he was from the *mu'min* servants and Allah's witnessing is Absolute Truth, *Ḥaqq*. That reality came true for Sayyīdinā Ibrāhīm ﷺ, because Allah ﷻ said, "You are a *mu'min.*" So Sayyīdinā Ibrāhīm's station is the Station of *Īmān*. He is a *mu'min* as Allah ﷻ is saying, but what did he do? One, he gave up his wealth in the Way of God, *fī sabīlillāh,* from what he owned of *māl,* money. Second, he gave up his son, part of his family, in the Way of Allah. And what was the third thing? Did he give up himself, too? Yes, as he was thrown in the fire by Nimrud, he accepted it as Allah's Will and submitted. Why? Because

---

[13] Bukhārī and Muslim.

[14] Sūratu 'ṣ-Ṣāffāt, 37:106-108.

[15] Sūratu 'ṣ-Ṣāffāt, 37:109-112.

when Jibrīl 🕮 came to rescue Sayyīdinā Ibrāhīm 🕮 and asked him, "Do you have anything to tell me?" Sayyīdinā Ibrāhīm 🕮 answered, "Do you know, I accept the decree of my Lord." He gave himself up when he knew he was going into the fire to die. So, he gave up his wealth, his son and himself: <u>that is the Station of Sayyīdinā Ibrāhīm 🕮</u>!

Did anyone of us reach that? Everyone can check himself, but did any group of people reach that station this year? Yes. We all know about it: the *ḥajjis* that died in Mina. They gave from their money in the Way of Allah 🕮 to reach Ka'bah; they gave up their families in the Way of Allah by leaving their families behind; and they gave themselves up in the Way of Allah 🕮 because they were going to do Hajj. They gave from their money in the Way of Allah 🕮 to reach Ka'bah; they gave up their families in the Way of Allah by leaving their families behind; and they gave themselves up in the Way of Allah 🕮 because they were going to do Hajj. So those who died in Mina are true *mu'mins*.

Why were they there to begin with? For Allah 🕮! And we know when we go for Hajj, something may happen that we may die. In the past, it was certain *ḥajjis* would die, because before there were planes, trains or cars, they used to go on foot, by camel or horse or some other animal, and they went to their neighbors and say, *hakkini helal et*, which means, "If I did something wrong to you, please forgive me." That was the practice of the old *ḥajjis*: they asked forgiveness from their families, because they did not know if they would return alive. This shows they were giving themselves up in the Way of Allah 🕮.

The *hajjis* that died in Mina died fully *mu'min*, as witnessed by Allah 🕮 to Sayyīdinā Ibrāhīm 🕮, who gave up his wealth, his son and himself. The *ḥajjis* gave up their families to go on Hajj. Sayyīdinā Ibrāhīm 🕮 accepted he would burn in that fire and asked for no help except from Allah 🕮. "*Ḥasbīyy Allāhu wa ni'ma 'l-wakīl!* Allah is sufficient for me and the best of Helpers," was the only thing he said when he was thrown in the fire. "I don't need Jibrīl 🕮, I don't need anyone else, I need only my Lord!" *Ḥasbīyy Allāhu wa ni'ma 'l-wakīl*, Allah is enough for me."

قُلْنَا يَا نَارُ كُونِى بَرْدًا وَسَلَامًا عَلَى إِبْرَاهِيمَ

O fire! Be cool and peaceful on Ibrāhīm.[16]

Allah ﷻ hears, Allah is not deaf, *Astaghfirullāh*. We don't have to shout for Allah ﷻ hears you even if you whisper to yourself in the slightest way; even when an idea comes to your mind, Allah hears it and knows it. So Sayyīdinā Ibrāhīm ﷺ was ready to give up himself, and Allah ﷻ said, "This deed is from My *mu'min* servant." The *hajjis* that passed away in Mina this year are from the true *mu'min* servants, they went as *shahīd*, martyrs.

We ask Allah ﷻ to make us from the *mu'min* servants, from the ones that bring Muslims and *mu'mins* together, that make the people to wake up to read Holy Qur'an and Hadith.

May Allah ﷻ unite us, as we have more in common than differences: we all pray to the same Lord, face the same Kaʿbah, follow the same Prophet ﷺ, love the Sahabah ؓ and the Holy Family of the Prophet ﷺ, and we all love to read Qur'an and Hadith. There is more in common between *mu'mins* around the world than there are differences. We ask Allah ﷻ to forgive all the *mu'mins* and all Muslims.

---

[16] Sūratu 'l-Anbīyā, 21:69.

أعوذ بالله من الشيطان الرجيم

بسم الله الرحمن الرحيم

INTRODUCTION

Aʿūdhu billāhi min ash-Shayṭāni 'r-rajīm.
Bismillāhi 'r-Raḥmāni 'r-Raḥīm.
Nawaytu 'l-arbāʿīn,
nawaytu 'l-ʿitikāf,
nawaytu 'l-khalwa,
nawaytu 'l-ʿuzla,
nawaytu 'r-riyāḍa,
nawaytu 's-sulūk,
lillāhi taʿālā fī hādhā 'l-masjid.

I seek refuge in Allah from Satan, the Rejected.
In the Name of Allah, the Merciful,
the Compassionate.
I intend the forty (days of seclusion);
I intend reclusion in the mosque,
I intend withdrawal, I intend isolation,
I intend discipline (of the ego); I intend wayfaring
in God's Path for the sake of God,
in this mosque.

أَطِيعُواْ اللّهَ وَأَطِيعُواْ الرَّسُولَ وَأُوْلِي الأَمْرِ مِنكُمْ

Obey Allah, obey the Prophet,
and obey those in authority among you.
(Sūratu 'n-Nisā', 4:59)

Hajj: An Honor Granted to Us by Our Lord

Shaykh Muhammad Hisham Kabbani

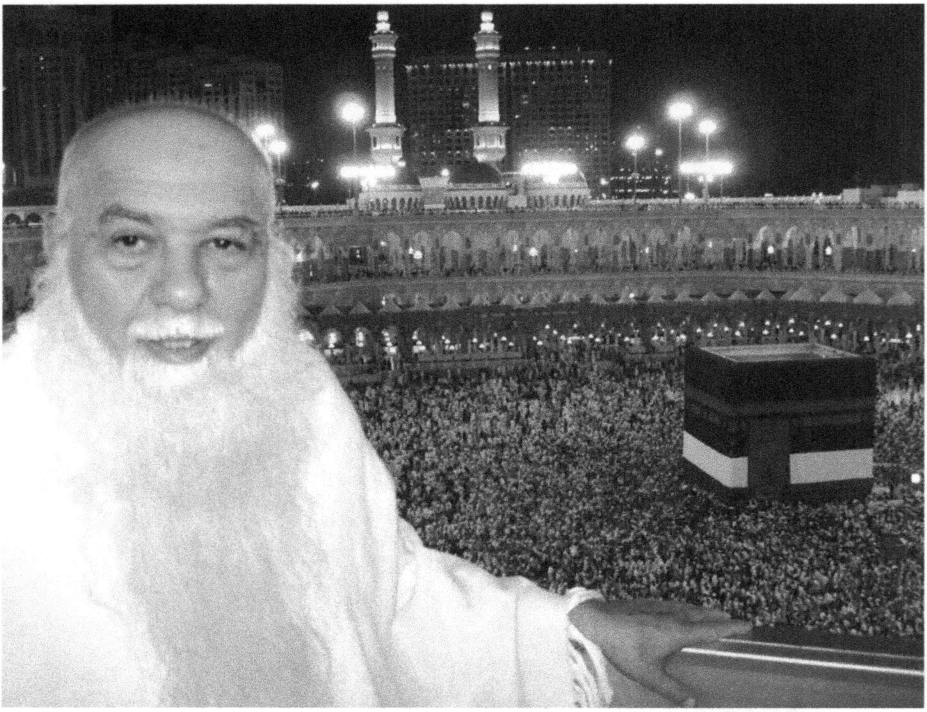

SHAYKH HISHAM KABBANI IN MASJID AL-HARAM, HAJJ AL-AKBAR 2011.

O Muslims, O Believers! Allah ﷻ has dressed us and perfected us from heavenly honor, as He said in the Holy Qur'an:

وَلَقَدْ كَرَّمْنَا بَنِي آدَمَ

We have honored the Children of Ādam."[17]

He honored the Children of Ādam above all Creation, and He honored some by choosing them to be from *Ummat an-Nabī* ﷺ:

[17] Sūratu 'l-Isrā', 17:70.

كُنتُمْ خَيْرَ أُمَّةٍ أُخْرِجَتْ لِلنَّاسِ تَأْمُرُونَ بِالْمَعْرُوفِ وَتَنْهَوْنَ عَنِ الْمُنكَرِ

You are the best Ummah of Mankind, enjoining what is right, preventing what is forbidden.[18]

We are now in the time of Hajj. It is Allah's ﷻ honor towards us to perform Hajj at least once in our lifetime, for whoever can afford it health-wise and financially. He ﷻ has granted Hajj once a year for more than 1400 years, and every Hajj has its own unique taste! There is no resemblance between one Hajj and another. Whatever Allah ﷻ sends from the manifestations of His Beautiful Names and Attributes on one Hajj He does not send again on the following Hajj but sends more.

So, Hajj is like a rainbow displaying all kinds of different colors, each one giving you a different taste. If you examine that rainbow with a magnifier, you will see even more colors all of which increase your joy. Hajj is thus like a rainbow displaying different manifestations of Allah's Beautiful Names and Attributes. Each year that goes by receives more manifestations over what came the previous year, all the way from the time of the Prophet ﷺ up to the year you go for Hajj.

Allah ﷻ is generous and whatever He sends, He does not take back. Therefore, what He gave before is still there. The rainbows of manifestations that Allah ﷻ sent on people making Hajj 1400 years ago is still there from that time, and you receive them cumulatively from each preceding year, along with those of the year you perform Hajj!

The manifestation of this year is going to have a different taste from those that happened in prior years.

This does not mean that you will only receive the blessings manifested with your presence at Hajj in this year or that those who went last year, or another year are deprived. No. Rather it means who goes for Hajj receives the accumulated manifestation of all preceding years' Hajj as this *dunyā* is moving quickly towards a heavenly change that will bring the power of Heavens to restore peace and happiness on Earth!

---

[18] Sūrat Āli-ʿImrān, 3:110.

DO NOT DELAY AN OBLIGATION

There are many people who did not perform Hajj. I ask them, "Why don't you go on Hajj?" They say, "It is still early; we are waiting, as there is a long time ahead of us!"

What if you die tomorrow? Allah ﷻ will ask, "Why did you not do Hajj when you were young and had the power?" Can you say, "I will make Hajj next year"? You may die. Do not postpone any *Sharīʿah* order as we are responsible to fulfill it. Do not postpone any *Sharīʿah* order as we are responsible to fulfill it. Allah ﷻ will judge us according to *Sharīʿah*. Only after that will He manifest His mercy on us according to *Ḥaqīqah*.

فَمَن يَعْمَلْ مِثْقَالَ ذَرَّةٍ خَيْرًا يَرَهُ وَمَن يَعْمَلْ مِثْقَالَ ذَرَّةٍ شَرًّا يَرَهُ

Whosoever has done an atom's weight of good shall see it, and whosoever has done an atom's weight of evil shall see it.[19]

That is the *ḥukm*, judgment of *Sharīʿah*: this one to Paradise, the other to Hellfire. So, in order to avoid that, you have to follow *Sharīʿah*. On the other hand, there is judgement through His Mercy: Allah ﷻ will forgive you and love you. So, what you do in spirituality is different from what you do in *Sharīʿah*. You must fulfill the obligations of *Sharīʿah*, but it is up to you to follow the path of spirituality. If you want to be dressed in heavenly mercy, fulfill both *Sharīʿah* and *Ṭarīqah*! So, Allah ﷻ is inviting us to His House. Do we say, "No, we won't go"? We go! Everyone who goes there has been invited. Those who are able must visit the House of Allah ﷻ:

وَلِلَّهِ عَلَى النَّاسِ حِجُّ الْبَيْتِ مَنِ اسْتَطَاعَ إِلَيْهِ سَبِيلًا

Pilgrimage to the House is a duty men owe to Allah, those who can afford the journey.[20]

---

[19] Sūratu 'l-Zalzalah, 99:7-8.

[20] Sūrat Āli-ʿImrān, 3:97.

A YOUNG SHAYKH HISHAM KABBANI IN *IHRĀM* DURING HAJJ.

If you are able, do it when you are young and do not delay it, but if you cannot, Allah ﷻ will forgive you. As soon as you appear in front of the Holy Kaʿbah, your 'picture' is taken and on the Day of Judgment you come up with that picture saying, "*Yā Rabbī*! I was invited to Your House. Where are you going to put me, in Hellfire? I came to Your Home." When someone knocks on your door in *dunyā*, do you open it or do you lie and say, "Go away, there is no such person here!" Even if you knock at a door, that person will feel bad if he doesn't open his door for you; and not only that, but he will also feed you and send you with what you like to take, and you will take it and go. Allah ﷻ made that possible for us, saying, "I put My House in *dunyā*, as I am Merciful. I want you to visit!"

What is better than visiting Allah's House? Today people visit Spain, Italy, the Eiffel Tower, the leaning Tower of Pisa. They say, "I am busy, I am busy." What are you busy with? "I have to go to visit Europe." Why don't you say, "I'm busy, I'm going to visit *Baytu 'Llāh*, Allah's House!" What is better, Europe, America, Malaysia, Indonesia, the Sub-continent, Southeast Asia, Africa? No, the direction of every Muslim is to reach the House of Allah ﷻ!

Regarding *ʿUmrah*, the Prophet ﷺ said in a Hadith:

الْعُمْرَةُ إِلَى الْعُمْرَةِ كَفَّارَةٌ لِمَا بَيْنَهُمَا

From one ʿUmrah to another is expiation for the sins committed between them.[21]

[21] Bukhārī and Muslim.

So, if you do *'Umrah* today and after one year you do another *'Umrah*, whatever sins you committed in between them is forgiven! Even if you do an *'Umrah* today and you do another *'Umrah* after thirty years, all your sins in between are going to be *mukaffarah*, waived. So, it is also good to do *'Umrah*, as Allah ﷻ will reward and forgive everything in between two *'Umrahs*.

وَالْحَجُّ الْمَبْرُورُ لَيْسَ لَهُ جَزَاءٌ إِلاَّ الْجَنَّةُ

> *And the reward of Hajj Mabrūr [a Hajj accepted by Allah] is nothing except Paradise.*[22]

As for Hajj, no one knows what Allah ﷻ will give from His Heavenly Rewards, and not even an angel knows that! *"Laysa lahu jazā"* means whatever you think Allah ﷻ gives is not enough, He gives more! He keeps giving for the one who is doing Hajj.

EVEN BREATHING IS CONSIDERED A PRAYER THERE!

The Prophet ﷺ said in a *Hadith ash-Sharīf*:

عَنْ النَّبِيِّ ﷺقَال : صَلَاةٍ فِى مَسْجِدِى هَذَا أَفْضَلُ مِنْ لْفِ صَلَاةٍ يمَا سِوَاهُ مِنْ الْمَسَاجِدِ إِلَّا الْمَسْجِدَ الْحَرَامِ ، وَصَلاَةٌ فِى الْمَسْجِدِ الْحَرَامِ أَفْضَلُ مِنْ صَلَاةٍ فِى مَسْجِدِى هَذَا بِمِائَةِ صَلَاة ، '

> *One prayer in my mosque is better than one thousand prayers elsewhere, except Masjid al-Ḥarām, and one prayer in Masjid al-Ḥarām is better than one hundred thousand prayers elsewhere.*[23]

---

[22] Bukhārī.

[23] Sunan Ibn Mājah.

SHAYKH HISHAM MAKING *ṬAWĀF*, 'UMRAH 2020.

The hadith of the Prophet ﷺ is that any prayer made in Madinatu 'l-Munawwarah is worth 10,000 prayers made elsewhere, and in Mecca it is 100,000 prayers. That also means, any breath or movement is considered a prayer in Madinah and Mecca; they will be rewarded as prayers, not as some scholars say, "only the prayers." If you have missed any prayers, then go there and pray; it will be as if you have completed all your missed prayers, and more! You must still make up your missed prayers, but Allah ﷻ is *Arḥamu 'r-Rāḥimīn,* the Most Merciful of those who show mercy. If you go to Mecca and pray there, Allah ﷻ will give your due rights; you will get all the rewards, because you took all that difficult way to reach Mecca and Madinah, and that's why Allah ﷻ gives a lot.

So, I recommend doing Hajj when you are young, not when you are old, sitting in a wheelchair where they have to push you. Go when you are young!

النَّفَقَةُ فِى الْحَجِّ كَالنَّفَقَةِ فِى سَبِيلِ اللّٰهِ بِسَبْعِ مِائَةِ ضِعْفٍ

The Prophet ﷺ said, "Whatever you spend of money in Hajj is like money spent in the Way of Allah multiplied by seven hundred."[24]

WHAT IS THE PURPOSE OF HAJJ?

Grandshaykh ʿAbdAllah ad-Dāghestānī ق once asked a question: "Why do human beings go for Hajj?" Why do we go for Hajj? To obey Allah's ﷻ order! That is Hajj! Those who are going there, their intention must be to fulfill what Allah ﷻ has ordered them to do. Some people go early, some go late, but all go to stand on the Plain of ʿArafat:

قال النبى ﷺ: "الحجُ عرفةُ."

As the Prophet ﷺ said: "Hajj is ʿArafat."[25]

So, standing on the Mount of ʿArafat means you have accepted to obey Allah ﷻ!

Allah ﷻ knows Hajj is not easy; it is a difficult journey. However, the explanations of the principles of Hajj in the different schools of thought, from Ḥanafī, Mālikī, Shafiʿi to Ḥanbalī makes it easy. They took from the *Aḥadīth* of the Prophet ﷺ of when he gave his companions ؓ instructions to reduce the difficulty of Hajj during the *Ḥajjat al-Wadaʿ*, the Farewell Pilgrimage.

عَنْ أَنَسٍ، عَنِ النَّبِيِّ ﷺ قَالَ " يَسِّرُوا وَلاَ تُعَسِّرُوا، وَبَشِّرُوا وَلاَ تُنَفِّرُوا".

The Prophet ﷺ once said: Make things easy and don't make them difficult and give good tidings and don't push people away."[26]

Why make things difficult on people? You see their capacity is unable to fulfill something, yet you push them to do it? They cannot do it! There are many people today that look at a mistake from you. Why push them so hard? Are we *maʿṣūm*, infallible? No, we are not *maʿṣūm*.

---

[24] Sunan Ahmad from Burayda ؓ.

[25] Sunan at-Tirmidhī.

[26] Sahīh Bukhārī from Anas ؓ.

I will relay some examples of how the Prophet ﷺ made the performance of Hajj easy for people with various needs.

One day Sayyīdinā ʿAbbās ؓ came to the Prophet ﷺ, saying, "Yā Rasūlullāh! I have to give water to the pilgrims in Mecca, but I cannot stay for three days in Mina. What should I do?" The Prophet ﷺ said, "Yes, you have a good excuse. Throw your stones on the first day of Mina and go back to Mecca or stay in Mecca during the four days of Hajj."[27]

In another example, a group of shepherds came to the Prophet ﷺ and said, "We have to look after the flocks of sheep for *Āhlu 'l-Islam* to do *zabiha,* so we cannot go to Mina." The Prophet ﷺ said, "Yes, stay in Mecca."

One day, someone came to the Prophet ﷺ and said, *"Yā Rasūlullāh*! There are too many principles to follow in Islam and it's becoming very heavy on me. I can't fulfill all the requirements."

For instance, when you go for Hajj, they tell you, "You cannot throw pebbles at the *Jamarāt*, which represent Satan's temptations, at a certain time (before *Ẓuhr*, for example)—it has to be after *Ẓuhr*." They ignore the fact that the wise scholars of Islam gave a ruling saying you can do it, because "necessity waives the forbidden." So, even if it is forbidden, you can do it (if it is a must), as Allah ﷻ is saying, "I am lifting the prohibition in this instance." It is a principle in Islam, so you cannot say, "Don't do it." With all these millions of people, how many people will die if all of them go at once to stone the *Jamarāt*? That is why they say, "Do it or delay it, and either is accepted."

عَنْ عَبْدِ اللَّهِ بْنِ بُسْرٍ ؓ أَنَّ رَجُلاً، قَالَ يَا رَسُولَ اللَّهِ إِنَّ شَرَائِعَ الإِسْلاَمِ قَدْ كَثُرَتْ عَلَىَّ فَأَخْبِرْنِى بِشَىْءٍ أَتَشَبَّثُ بِهِ . قَالَ " لاَ يَزَالُ لِسَانُكَ رَطْبًا مِنْ ذِكْرِ اللَّهِ "

A man said, "Yā Rasūlullāh, there are too many Islamic rules, and I cannot do all of them. Give me something easy to hold onto!" The Prophet ﷺ said, "Keep your tongue moist with dhikrullāh."[28]

---

[27] Bukhārī.

[28] Tirmidhī.

It means, "Remember Allah ﷻ by keeping your tongue moving in *dhikrullāh*," which means to not backbite. You cannot stop making sins by backbiting? Then make your tongue say, "Allah!" or *"lā ilāha illa 'Llāh*!" or whatever *tasbīḥ* you want. These are examples to show that Hajj does not have to be difficult. However, it is also not so easy for a different reason: we are moving towards the Last Days, because the Prophet ﷺ said:

يَأتِى عَلَىَ النَّاسِ زَمَانٌ الصَّابِرُ فِيهِم عَلَىَ دِينِهِ كَالقَابِضِ عَلَىَ الجَمَرِ

There will come a time upon the people when the one who patiently holding fast to his religion will be like one holding a burning coal in their hand.[29]

Nowadays, it is not easy to afford to go from far countries for Hajj; it is so expensive and difficult. It is not like you are there, or that you take a one-hour flight to be in Mecca and Madinah. The hassle of traveling and of more and more people making Hajj is making it become more difficult, but as is often said:

لَا رَاحَة فِى الدِين

(There is) no rest in religion.

It means that you must always struggle, especially if you are young and strong and can fulfill all the principles, without observing only the easiest ones.

STORY: A CARRIER OF BURDENS

Once I was with Shaykh Nazim ق carrying the burden of a lot of Cypriot pilgrims—men and women 60 years and older. You have to carry them, like one woman who could not walk, once said, "Carry me!" Just like that he used to bring them, as he liked difficulties. It was a very tough Hajj with Shaykh Nazim ق, as they carry burdens. One time they wanted to move from one place to another, going and coming. One lady, 80 years of age, was pulling behind her not only a suitcase, but a trolley! They had a duffel bag on the trolley and inside the bag was an old stove with

[29] Tirmidhī.

kerosene inside it! She said, "I don't want to lose it and I want to go to that masjid and come back." She wanted to bring it with her, so Shaykh Nazim ق carried that to the masjid and came back! Mawlana ق was patient, very patient.

Pious Travelers of the Past

Shaykh Muhammad Hisham Kabbani

MAWLANA SHAYKH NAZIM (MIDDLE), SHAYKH HISHAM (RIGHT) AND HIS BROTHER, SHAYKH ADNAN (LEFT) IN *IHRĀM*, HAJJ IN THE 60S.

LEAVING *DUNYĀ* FOR *ĀKHIRAH*

From the Signs of the Last Days, time will contract. Imagine one-hundred years ago or less, people used to travel on foot to perform Hajj. Walking in the desert or on a caravan, they would spend one year to reach Mecca and Madinah. Today you go by plane, and you say you are tired.

In the past, before the pilgrims departed, they would call everyone in their family, their neighbors and friends to say goodbye, as the one going does not know if he will return, if he will die there or not. Their families would tell them, "If you come back alive, we will be very happy, but if you die, may Allah ﷻ bless you!" It means, they were looking at death when going on Hajj, which was a minimum of two-year travel, one year going and one year coming back. So, for everyone going for Hajj, the intention must be that you are leaving *dunyā* to go for *Ākhirah*, the Next Life. When you enter prayer five times a day, it is as if you are entering Heavens, because you are directing your face to *Baytu 'Llāh*, the House of Allah ﷻ, which is directly below *Bayt al-Maʿmūr*, the original House in the Fourth Heaven. As the Prophet ﷺ said, "*The coolness of my eyes lies in prayer*," because that is when he is in the Divine Presence!

There once was a *Walī* in Central Asia who went for Hajj. Every step he took, he would stop and pray two *rakaʿats*. It took him seven years to reach Madinatu 'l-Munawwarah! He had no provisions with him; he went carrying only the love of Allah ﷻ and the Prophet ﷺ in his heart, and Allah ﷻ used to provide him food whenever he was hungry.

Where is our level of *Īmān* compared to such people? Today they tell you, "It is difficult to go," or "I will go after I reach seventy years of age." Speak with people today and ask them, "Do you have energy?" They will say, "We are feeling weak, tired, depressed with no energy." In the time of the Prophet ﷺ, *Ummat an-Nabī* was very energetic; they walked everywhere, as there were no cars, trucks, or airplanes.

I heard from some people who met one man who walked to Mecca to perform Hajj, not too long ago, and for every step he took forward he stopped and prayed two *rakaʿats* until he reached Makkatu 'l-Mukarramah, and then died there. We say we are worshippers, but who can do that? We say we prayed *Ṣalātu 'ẓ-Ẓuhr* and *Ṣalātu 'l-ʿAsr*, but that is for you, and even so, you prayed it with laziness!

Shaykh Nazim's ق own paternal grandfather, As-Sayyid Yesilbas Ḥusayn al-Qādirī al-Qubruṣī ق, who for forty years took care of the burial chamber of Umm Ḥirām bint al-Milḥān, the maternal aunt of the Prophet ﷺ, performed Hajj four times on foot! After he passed away, he was buried outside the resting place of Umm Ḥirām in Cyprus.

SHAYKH NAZIM'S PATERNAL GRANDFATHER SHAYKH YESILBAS HUSAYN AL-QĀDIRĪ AL-QUBRUṢĪ ق.

May Allah ﷻ forgive us and bless us and give us a straightforward way to reach our destination. This cannot be done except by following a guide. *Alḥamdulillāh* that Allah ﷻ has connected us to a guide who can take us to the holy presence of the Prophet ﷺ.

Make *ṣalāwāt* on the Prophet ﷺ and you will get there; that is the fastest way to reach! *Ṣallū ʿalā ʾn-Nabī* ﷺ! Why do you want to make a long travel? *Yā Sayyīdī, yā Rasūlullāh, yā Raḥmatan li ʾl-ʿālamīn! Yā Shafīʿ al-mudhnibīn*! We have come to the presence of *Awlīyāullāh*! May they present us to the presence of the Prophet ﷺ clean and pure.

STORY: SHAYKH ʿABDALLĀH AD-DĀGHESTĀNĪ'S STATION

One day, Shaykh Sharafuddīn ad-Dāghestānī ق was sitting in a meeting of big masters in a remote place far outside the city. As Grandshaykh ʿAbdAllāh ق, still a teenager at that time, was on his way to meet them, Shaykh Sharafuddīn ق said:

> My son ʿAbdAllāh Effendi has reached a level where no one has set foot yet, not myself, nor all the Golden Chain masters. He is only 18 and I am 60, yet he has reached a level that is higher than mine and all the Golden Chain Masters that have passed away. If I am going to send him a child of seven years to tell him, "Your Shaykh is ordering you to direct yourself to Mecca for pilgrimage," from Daghestan, here in the middle of Russia, without coming and asking me for confirmation whether this is true or not, he will immediately think, "Who is making that child speak? My shaykh has to know even before I know. Otherwise, how have I accepted him as a shaykh and yet represent him as not knowing anything? If my shaykh doesn't know, who will know?" He will immediately believe the child and without going back to his house to tell his mother or his wife that he wants to go to pilgrimage, without taking any clothes, money, or food, he will direct himself to Mecca, which is 10,000 miles away, walking, without asking anything! He will know the order comes from me and will simply change the direction of his walk.

This is the Station of *Waḥdatu ʾl-afʿal*, unification of actions, deeds and words, where you must see everything as coming from Allah ﷻ. This is a higher level in Sufi knowledge. You cannot see people doing anything anymore, but you must consider them instruments in the hands of Allah ﷻ. If Shaykh Nazim ق came to you and said, "Go to Mecca," you will say, "Okay, my shaykh, but I must buy a ticket, and I have to see if my wife gives me permission..." In the Naqshbandi Order you cannot do all this. You must move immediately!

Belief in the Unseen

Shaykh Nazim Adil al-Haqqani

HOLY KAʿBAH JUST BEFORE MAGHRIB, HAJJ AL-AKBAR 2011.

Everyone who took this way, started by believing in the Unseen. They said, "There is a Kaʿbah over there, walk and see if you reach the glorious Kaʿbah!" In the old times they went to the desert. The camels and *ḥujjāj* passed through the desert, sinking into the sand up to their knees, believing in the Kaʿbah that they didn't see. They passed through the desert with love. Finally, they would find the Kaʿbah.

Now our way is also like that. We walk by believing in the Unseen. That's why we are obliged to believe in the Unseen. If it were already visible, there would be no need to say, "Believe in this." You should believe here and go into the desert. You'll pass those deserts and find the Kaʿbah. You'll be the guest of the Lord of the Kaʿbah.

Anyone who has hope will go to the Kaʿbah. Whoever cuts the road to the Kaʿbah, Allah ﷻ will cut his life! They will be judged as unbelievers.

Allah ﷻ orders everyone who has financial and physical power, to go and visit the Kaʿbah. No one can set conditions. When you do, you'll be judged as an unbeliever. It isn't an easy matter. We believe in the Unseen. We have peace inside that we will reach what we believe day by day. That's why a believer thinks of the day he will reach Allah ﷻ and feels an endless peace that the unbeliever is deprived of. We will meet Allah ﷻ! We are going to Allah ﷻ! We are going to Allah ﷻ! We are approaching day by day!

Hajj is *Dhikrullāh*

Shaykh Muhammad Hisham Kabbani

Those who did not go for Hajj must prepare to go today, tomorrow, or next year, but make your intention and prepare to go. The Prophet ﷺ said to the Sahabah رضي الله عنهم:

مَا الْعَمَلُ فِى أَيَّامِ الْعَشْرِ أَفْضَلَ مِنَ الْعَمَلِ فِى هَذِهِ ". قَالُوا وَلاَ الْجِهَادُ قَالَ " وَلاَ الْجِهَادُ، إِلاَّ رَجُلٌ خَرَجَ يُخَاطِرُ بِنَفْسِهِ وَمَالِهِ فَلَمْ يَرْجِعْ بِشَىْءٍ ".

> *"No good deeds done on other days are superior to those done on these (first ten days of Dhul-Hijjah)." Then some companions of the Prophet ﷺ said, "Not even jihād?" He replied, "Not even jihād, except that of a man who does it by putting himself and his property in danger (for Allah's sake) and does not return with any of those things."*[30]

It means, the ten days of Dhul-Hijjah are more important than that, during which we must try to do *dhikr* as much as possible, such as, "*Ḥasbunā 'Llāh Rabbunā 'Llāh,*" or "*lā ilāha illa 'Llāh,*" or whatever comes to the heart.

Allah ﷻ will be very happy with those who are making a lot of *dhikr* and shows them to His Angels, saying, "Look how happy I am with them!" All deeds, prayers, fasting, *Zakāt*, Hajj, *Shahādah*, everything you do that reminds you of Allah ﷻ is *dhikrullāh*. These actions are only decreed for the sake of *dhikrullāh*; these constitutions and orders are there for the purpose of *dhikrullāh*! Saying "*alḥamdulillāh*" is *dhikrullāh*! The one addicted to *dhikrullāh* will enter Paradise laughing because of no *hisāb*. His mind is already with Allah ﷻ, not in *dunyā,* so he is not seeing anything else; he is only loving Allah ﷻ, and that one does not need to walk on *Ṣirāṭ al-Mustaqīm,* the Straight Path, as he is already there. So *dhikrullāh* is a safety net for us to enter Paradise.

---

[30] Bukhārī.

اتْلُ مَا أُوحِيَ إِلَيْكَ مِنَ الْكِتَابِ وَأَقِمِ الصَّلَاةَ إِنَّ الصَّلَاةَ تَنْهَى عَنِ
الْفَحْشَاءِ وَالْمُنكَرِ وَلَذِكْرُ اللَّهِ أَكْبَرُ وَاللَّهُ يَعْلَمُ مَا تَصْنَعُونَ

Recite what is sent of the Book by inspiration to you and establish regular prayer, for prayer restrains from shameful and unjust deeds. And remembrance of Allah is the greatest (thing in life) without doubt. And Allah knows the (deeds) you do.[31]

"Read what has been revealed to you from the Book and establish the prayer!" Reading the Holy Qur'an and beginning your prayer is *dhikrullāh*. When you enter into prayer, what do you say? "*Allāhu Akbar*," which means, "*Yā Rabbī*, I'm sorry for the way I'm doing my prayer, as it is not to Your Honor. My ego, my bad *ʿamal* is blended with my prayer and it doesn't befit You, so please forgive me. You are *Allāhu Akbar*, You are the Greatest, no one can reach You, *yā Rabbī*! I did not praise You as You deserve." Then according to the Ḥanafī School, you say:

سُبْحانَكَ اللَّهُمَّ وَبِحَمْدِكَ، وَتَبارَكَ اسْمُكَ، وَتَعالَى جَدُّكَ، وَلاَ إِلَهَ غَيْرُكَ

Subḥānak allāhumma wa bi ḥamdika wa tabāraka 'smuka wa taʿālā jadduka wa lā ilāha ghayruk.

Glory is to You O Allah, and praise. Blessed is Your Name and Exalted is Your Majesty. There is none worthy of worship but You.

You are making *tasbīḥ* and *ḥamd,* and saying, "Your Name be blessed!" In the Shafiʿī School, you say:

إِنِّى وَجَّهْتُ وَجْهِىَ لِلَّذِى فَطَرَ السَّمَاوَاتِ وَالأَرْضَ حَنِيفًا وَمَا أَنَاْ مِنَ
الْمُشْرِكِينَ

For me, I have set my face, firmly and truly, towards Him Who created the Heavens and the Earth, and never shall I give partners to Allah.[32]

---

[31] Sūratu 'l-ʿAnkabūt, 29:45.

[32] Sūratu 'l-Anʿam, 6:79.

إِنَّ صَلَاتِى وَنُسُكِى وَمَحْيَاىَ وَمَمَاتِى لِلّٰهِ رَبِّ الْعَالَمِينَ اَ شَرِيكَ لَهُ

وَبِذَٰلِكَ أُمِرْتُ وَأَنَا أَوَّلُ الْمُسْلِمِينَ

Truly, my prayer and my service of sacrifice, my life and my death, are (all) for Allah, the Cherisher of the Worlds in whose divinity none has a share: for thus have I been bidden, and I shall (always) be foremost among those who surrender themselves unto Him.[33]

This *duʿā* also has *Tawḥīd* in it, it has Hajj in it: "I directed my face to the One Who created Heavens and Earth and I am not from the *mushriks* that associate someone with You," and "All my prayers and all my *nusuk*," meaning, the different rituals of Hajj, "are all for Allah!" Making *ṭawāf, saʿī,* going to ʿArafat, coming to Mina, Muzdalifah, and going back to Mecca, all of these are *nusukī*. "My life and my death are in Your Hand, *yā Rabbī,* and I am from the Muslims." This is the *duʿā* of Sayyīdinā Ibrāhīm ﷷ.

That is why Sayyidah ʿĀ'ishā ﵂ mentioned in a *saḥīḥ* hadith that the Prophet ﷺ said:

إِنَّمَا جُعِلَ الطَّوَافُ بِالْبَيْتِ وَبَيْنَ الصَّفَا وَالْمَرْوَةِ وَرَمْىُ الْجِمَارِ لِإِقَامَةِ ذِكْرِ اللهِ

Going around the Kaʿbah, running between Ṣafā and Marwa and stoning of the pillars are meant for Dhikrullāh, the remembrance of Allah.[34]

The *ṭawāf*—to circumambulate around the Kaʿbah—has been ordered for every person who enters the Meccan Sanctuary (al-Ḥaram al-Makkī). If a person lives outside of Mecca, in Jeddah for example, he has to do *Ṭawāf al-Qudūm,* the Circumambulation of Arrival, once he enters into Mecca. *Saʿī,* the running between Ṣafā and Marwa is also a ritual that must be performed by Allah's order. Those on *ʿUmrah* are obliged to do *saʿī* between Ṣafā and Marwa, while those on Hajj are obligated to perform many other rituals, including pelting the *Jamarāt*. So, all these *nusuk*, rituals, are considered forms of *dhikrullāh*. Even throwing stones at the

---

33 Sūratu 'l-Anʿam, 6:162-163.

34 Abū Dāwūd and Tirmidhī.

devil is from *dhikrullāh*. You are stoning Shayṭān, but you are saying, *Riḍan li 'r-Raḥmān, raghman li 'sh-shayṭān*, "(This is for) Allah, the Most Merciful to be happy with us and for Shayṭān to be down!" to reject Shayṭān and for *Ḥaqq*, the Divine Truth to rise up. *Sa'ī*, the running between Ṣafā and Marwa involves reading many kinds of *du'ā* that the Prophet ﷺ used to recite, and thus is *dhikrullāh*. *Ṭawāf* around the Ka'bah, going to Mina, going to 'Arafat, going to Muzdalifah are all forms of *dhikrullāh*. All the principles of Hajj are forms of *dhikrullāh*.

REVELATION OF AL-FĀTIḤAH IN MECCA AND MADINAH

So, Allah ﷻ said in the Holy Qur'an, "Establish the prayer (*ṣalāt*)," and He ﷻ said to His Prophet ﷺ in a Hadith *Qudsī*:

أَنَا جَلِيْسُ مَنْ ذَكَرَنِى

I sit with the one who remembers Me.[35]

So, you begin your *ṣalāt*, prayer with *dhikrullāh* by showing *tawḥīd*, as Īmām Abū Hanifa ؓ mentioned. Then, you recite Sūrat al-Fātiḥah, because now you are clean: your tongue, your smell, your breath and your heart are clean to read Sūrat al-Fātiḥah. You cannot read the Holy

[35] Hadith Qudsī. Āḥmad, Bayhaqī.

Qur'an unless you are clean, as it is Allah's Words, especially Sūrat al-Fātiḥah, which contains the secret of the Holy Qur'an.

The entire Qur'an was revealed all at once by Sayyīdinā Jibrīl ﷺ, and then in verses, over a period of 23 years, except the Fātiḥah, which was revealed twice: first in Makkatu 'l-Mukarramah, then in Madinatu 'l-Munawwarah. What was the wisdom behind this?

Sūrat al-Fātiḥah was revealed in Mecca, for the House of Allah ﷻ and to praise Sayyīdinā Muhammad ﷺ and lift him up. The Fātiḥah is the heart of the Holy Qur'an, so when it was revealed in Mecca, all angels came to the Prophet ﷺ for him to get the blessings of that *Sūrah* with all the manifestations that it carries. The Fātiḥah was revealed a second time in Madinatu 'l-Munawwarah for the blessings of Madinah to be dressed on the Prophet ﷺ. So, anyone who visits Madinah will receive all those blessings with which the Prophet ﷺ was dressed.

Good tidings for us that Allah ﷻ obliged us to recite the Fātiḥah in every *raka'at* of the five daily prayers, without which our prayers would not be accepted. If you don't read any other *Sūrah* or *āyah* after the Fātiḥah, your prayer will still be accepted, but you cannot leave out the Fātiḥah. Sūrat al-Fātiḥah is a secret given to the Prophet ﷺ.

الْفَاتِحَةُ لِمَا قُرِئَتْ لَهُ

For that reason, the Prophet ﷺ said, "The Fātiḥah is for what it is read."[36]

So, in *ṣalāt* there is *dhikrullāh,* in Hajj there is *dhikrullāh,* in visiting the Prophet ﷺ in Madinah there is *dhikrullāh* and in making *ṣalāwāt* and praying there is *dhikrullāh*. Therefore, all of Islam is built on remembering Allah ﷻ!

[36] Īmām Bayhaqī's Sh'ub al-Īmān.

The Reward of Hajj Is in Every Perfect Prayer

Shaykh Muhammad Hisham Kabbani

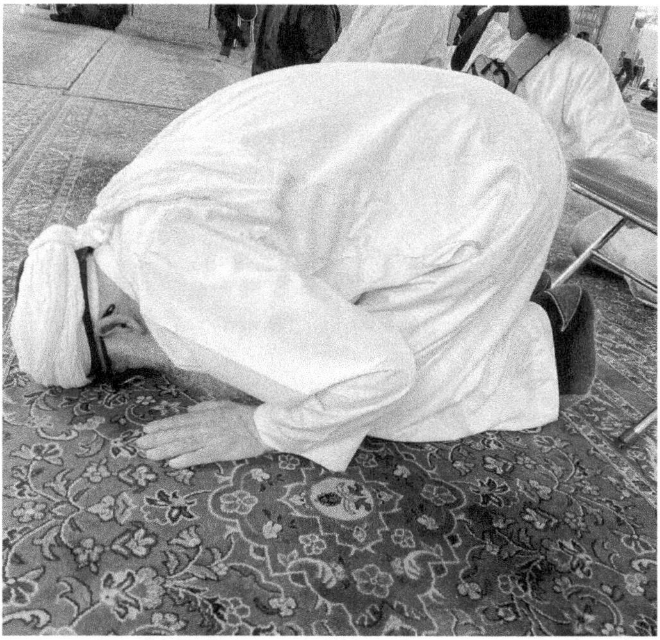

SHAYKH HISHAM KABBANI MAKING *SAJDA* IN THE HOLY RAWDAH, `UMRAH 2020.

Allah ﷻ ordered us to perform the Five Pillars of Islam and to make *ṣalāwāt* on the Prophet ﷺ. As we are taught in the Holy Qur'an, Allah ﷻ ordered His Angels to make *ṣalāwāt* on the Prophet ﷺ, which means the obligation of angels is *ṣalāt ʿalā an-Nabī* ﷺ; they do not need to follow the Five Pillars, as they are already clean, so Allah ﷻ gave them something else. We human beings, however, were not only ordered to make *ṣalāwāt* on the Prophet ﷺ, but we were also given the Five Pillars: *Shahādah, ṣalāt, siyām, zakāt* and Hajj, so that they cleanse and polish us, presenting us clean to Allah ﷻ.

Why did *ṣalāt ʿalā an-Nabī* ﷺ come at the end of the *ṣalāt*, prayers and not at the beginning? That is because Allah ﷻ likes His Servant to be clean when he makes *ṣalāwāt* on the Prophet ﷺ, because when you pray, you are performing all Five Pillars of Islam.

So, prayer (*ṣalāt*) combines all obligations of Islam: *Shahādah* (Testimony of Faith) in *at-Tahīyyāt, Ṣalāt* (prayer) by praying, *Zakāt* (charity) by devoting your time to Allah ﷻ and leaving *dunyā, ṣawm* (fasting) by not eating or drinking during the prayer, and Hajj by directing your face towards the *Qiblah*, which is *Kaʿbatu 'Llāh*. During *ṣalāt* you turn your face to Ka'bah every time. Do not think Allah ﷻ is not going to reward you! He will reward you according to His Greatness and will make each of your prayers equal to a Hajj if it is perfect. And if you really focus on the Ka'bah when you are praying, you can actually see it!

In each prayer, different dresses come with everything included: *Shahādah, Ṣalāt, Zakāt, Ṣiyām* and Hajj. That is why the Prophet ﷺ mentioned and insisted that you teach your children to pray when they are seven years old, and that is why it is so important.

عَنْ جَابِرٍ، أَنَّ النَّبِيَّ صلى الله عليه وسلم قَالَ " بَيْنَ الْكُفْرِ وَالإِيمَانِ تَرْكُ الصَّلاَةِ "

The Prophet ﷺ said, "Between unbelief and faith is to leave prayers."[37]

If you leave your prayers or don't pray regularly, you are between *kufr* and *Īmān*, and if you leave it completely you are on the side of *kufr*. Allah ﷻ prepared all these dresses for you on the Day of Promises, when He asked everyone, *alastu bi-rabbikum,* "Am I not your Lord?" and, "Who am I and who are you?" We said, "You are our Lord, and we are Your Servants," and we promised to fulfill all religious obligations. Allah ﷻ rewarded everyone, because at that time they said, "Yes." So, He gave them heavenly dresses and we came to *dunyā* wearing them. However, some pray some do not pray, and some are in-between: sometimes they pray and sometimes they do not.

An example of this is if someone says, "I have a trust of one thousand golden coins that I will give here to this place that has one thousand people," then each of the people get one coin. However, if their numbers diminish and they are only one-hundred people, Allah will give ten coins to each because His generosity never diminishes. So, with all these dresses of stations and states that we were granted on the Day of Promises, because most people are now doing less than they promised, whoever is fulfilling his promise will get double and triple the reward as it is distributed to fewer people!

---

[37] *Jamī' at-Tirmidhī.*

STORY: BEHIND THE FIVE DAILY PRAYERS

Allah ﷻ gave us five prayers equal to fifty prayers! When Allah ﷻ brought the Prophet ﷺ on *Miʿrāj*, Ascension, he went to the Seven Heavens and the Divine Presence, where Allah ﷻ ordered his Ummah to pray fifty prayers daily:

فَفَرَضَ اللَّهُ عَلَى أُمَّتِي خَمْسِينَ صَلاَةً، فَرَجَعْتُ بِذَلِكَ حَتَّى مَرَرْتُ عَلَى مُوسَى فَقَالَ مَا فَرَضَ اللَّهُ لَكَ عَلَى أُمَّتِكَ قُلْتُ فَرَضَ خَمْسِينَ صَلاَةً. قَالَ فَارْجِعْ إِلَى رَبِّكَ، فَإِنَّ أُمَّتَكَ لاَ تُطِيقُ ذَلِكَ. فَرَاجَعْتُ فَوَضَعَ شَطْرَهَا، فَرَجَعْتُ إِلَى مُوسَى قُلْتُ وَضَعَ شَطْرَهَا. فَقَالَ رَاجِعْ رَبَّكَ، فَإِنَّ أُمَّتَكَ لاَ تُطِيقُ، فَرَاجَعْتُ فَوَضَعَ شَطْرَهَا، فَرَجَعْتُ إِلَيْهِ فَقَالَ ارْجِعْ إِلَى رَبِّكَ، فَإِنَّ أُمَّتَكَ لاَ تُطِيقُ ذَلِكَ، فَرَاجَعْتُهُ. فَقَالَ هِيَ خَمْسٌ وَهْيَ خَمْسُونَ، لاَ يُبَدَّلُ الْقَوْلُ لَدَيَّ. فَرَجَعْتُ إِلَى مُوسَى فَقَالَ رَاجِعْ رَبَّكَ. فَقُلْتُ اسْتَحْيَيْتُ مِنْ رَبِّي.

The Prophet ﷺ said, "Then Allah enjoined fifty prayers on my followers. When I returned with this order of Allah, I passed by Moses who asked me, 'What has Allah enjoined on your followers?' I replied, 'He has enjoined fifty prayers on them.' Moses said, 'Go back to your Lord (and appeal for reduction) for your followers will not be able to bear it.' So, I went back to Allah and requested for reduction, and He reduced it to half. When I passed by Moses again and informed him about it, he said, 'Go back to your Lord as your followers will not be able to bear it.' So, I returned to Allah and requested for further reduction and half of it was reduced. I again passed by Moses, and he said to me, 'Return to your Lord, for your followers will not be able to bear it. So, I returned to Allah, and He said, 'These are five prayers and they are all (equal to) fifty (in reward) for My Word does not change!' I returned to Moses, and he told me to go back once again. I replied, 'Now I feel shy of asking my Lord again.' "[38]

So, we have been assigned the *ṣalāt*, five daily prayers, but we are not completing them. The prayer is a physical reminder for us that we will be judged. That is why you must not miss your prayers, as Allah ﷻ will not be happy. Those who miss them must redo them as soon as they remember, or else judgment is in Allah's Hands!

In *Ākhirah*, what is the punishment for those who do not pray all their prayers? Those who miss their prayers will have to make them up in *Jahannam*. However, many prayers they have missed, they must pray. I do not want to say too much, because people will get worried and afraid, but these are reminders to keep your contract with Allah ﷻ! May Allah forgive them.

Anything Allah ﷻ asks you to do, do not ask 'why?' If there is no benefit, then Allah ﷻ will not put that on you. Why did Allah ﷻ put these obligations on you? In order for you to receive the Manifestations of Allah's Beautiful Names and Attributes on Judgment Day. If you are not prepared by praying, you are not able to receive them and you will be put to the side. If you are under that Light, you are safe. If not, then you have a problem. Praying is an opportunity, which will not be repeated. May Allah ﷻ grant us intercession of the Prophet ﷺ to be saved or else we will fall apart.

EVERY HAJJ HAS A UNIQUE TASTE

Every moment has its unique specialty and taste. That is why we are ordered to perform the five prayers, because every prayer has a taste, a different manifestation. The first prayer might be a manifestation from the First Heaven, the second prayer from the Second Heaven, and the third prayer from the Third Heaven, and so forth.

Fajr prayer has a certain taste, because its manifestation is different at night, and Ẓuhr, ʿAsr, Maghrib and ʿIshā prayers all have a different taste. As the Prophet ﷺ said, "The best time for me between Allah's Hands is when I am in prayer." When you say "*Allāhu Akbar*!" you are

---

[38] Bukhārī.

there, not on this prayer carpet! It is a heavenly, angelic place where you are worshipping, near everything heavenly, and you will feel that taste. When they take that veil from your eyes, you can see everything! So, you must be in the right moment and right place, because at that moment a Heavenly Presence will come.

Similarly, each Hajj has a different taste, and this year's Hajj (2011) has its own taste. I performed many different pilgrimages and ‘Umrahs from the 1960s to 1990 when I came to the U.S., and each Hajj had a different taste. Be happy that this year you are going and will get that taste. *Inshā-Allāh*, Allah ﷻ will give us the taste that He gave to the Sahabah ؓ when they went with the Prophet ﷺ on *Ḥijjat al-Wada‘*. May Allah ﷻ give us a long, happy, healthy life and may we go healthy and return healthy with heavenly wealth.

"My *Qiblah* is the House of Allah, My *Īmām* is the Messenger of Allah ﷺ!"

Shaykh Muhammad Hisham Kabbani

I remember whenever Grandshaykh ʿAbdAllah al-Fāʾiz ad-Dāghestānī ق used to stand for prayer, he would make this intention:

نَوَيتُ الأَربَعِين، نَوَيتُ الإعتِكَاف، نَوَيتُ الخَلوَة، نَوَيتُ العُزلَة، نَوَيتُ الرِيَاضَة، نَوَيتُ السُلوك لِلهِ تَعالى فِى هَذا المَسجِد أَن أُصَلِى مُقتَدِيًا بِرَسُولِ الله مُستَقبِلا الكَعبَةُ الشَرِيفَة.

Nawaytu 'l-arbaʿīn, nawaytu 'l-ʿitikāf, nawaytu 'l-khalwah, nawaytu 'l-ʿuzlah, nawaytu 'r-rīyāḍa, nawaytu 's-sulūk, li-Llāhi taʿālā fī hadha 'l-masjid an uṣallīya muqtadīyan bi Rasūlillāh, mustaqbilan al-Kaʿbatu 'sh-Sharīfah.

I intend the Forty Days; I intend retreat; I intend isolation; I intend devotion; I intend discipline, I intend spiritual wayfaring for the sake of Allah Most High, in this place of worship to pray following (behind) the Messenger of Allah ﷺ and facing the Kaʿbah ash-Sharīfah.

So, the Prophet ﷺ himself is your Īmām in the prayer! For example, if your Īmām in the prayer is your shaykh, when he is praying, his Īmām is the Prophet ﷺ, as the Prophet ﷺ said, "I am fresh and alive in my grave."

Today, they say, "Don't make *nīyyah,* just say '*Allāhu Akbar*' and start the prayer, as the intention is already known." So, they are automatically canceling all of these! They say, *An-nīyyatu fi 'l-qalb,* "The intention is in the heart. Why mention it on the tongue? That is a *bida*ʿ!" So, this gives you a hint that when you are praying with the Īmām or by yourself, you must know who your Īmām really is. That is why when we go to Mecca or Madinah, as Grandshaykh ق said, "Pray behind the Īmām, but know that whatever he is, there is another Īmām there, a real Īmām appointed by Sayyīdinā Rasūlullāh ﷺ, but you cannot see him; you only see the one appointed by the people."

SHAYKH HISHAM KABBANI DIRECTING HIS FACE TOWARD THE KA`BAH, HAJJ 2011.

So, you say, "*muqtadīyan bi Rasūlillāh,* (I intend to pray) following behind the Prophet of Allah ﷺ," because he is there! Was he not praying with Sayyīdinā Mūsā عليه السلام when he went on Isrā' wa 'l-Mi'rāj? He said, "I saw Sayyīdinā Mūsā عليه السلام praying in his grave." Why is the Prophet ﷺ not praying in his grave? Is Sayyīdinā Mūsā عليه السلام better than Sayyīdinā Muhammad ﷺ?

So Grandshaykh ق used to start his prayer, saying, "My *Īmām* is Sayyīdinā Muhammad ﷺ."

It is therefore as the Prophet ﷺ said:

إنّما الأعْمَالُ بالنِّيّةِ،

Verily, actions are by intentions.[39]

Is it not better to be praying behind the Prophet ﷺ? When we pray behind an *Īmām*, bad thoughts come and go, so Grandshaykh ق was teaching us the intention, "My *Īmām* is the Prophet ﷺ," and *adaban,* from good manners, we must say, "Our *Īmām* is our shaykh and our shaykh is following the Prophet ﷺ, and we are in front of the Kaʿbah."

نَوَايْتُ اَنْ اُصَلِّيَ لِلّهِ تَعَالَى مُقْتَدِيًا بِمَوْلَانَا الشَيخ نَاظَم وَمُقْتَدِيًا بِرَسُول الله

مُسْتَقْبِلًا اَلْكَعبَةُ الْمشَرَفَة

Nawaytu an uṣallī li 'Llāhi taʿālā muqtadīyan bi Shaykh Nazim wa an uṣallīya muqtadīyan bi Rasūlillāh ﷺ, mustaqbilan al-Kaʿbatu 'l-musharafah.

I intend to pray to Allah Most High, following (behind) our shaykh, Shaykh Nazim ق and following (behind) the Prophet ﷺ, facing the Holy Kaʿbah.

Then, whatever *Īmām* is there, we will be following the Prophet ﷺ through our intention. So, let us now go and pray!

STORY: FOLLOW THE TRUE APPOINTED ĪMĀM

Shaykh Nazim ق once told a story about accepting Allah's Will:

One day, I wanted to go visit the Prophet ﷺ in Madinatu 'l-Munawwarah. I went to the embassy and the employees insisted in not giving me a visa. After they had made it so hard to get one, I read them the Hadith of the Prophet ﷺ, in reverse: rather than, *yassirū wa lā tu-ʿassirū* "Make it easy for people and don't make it difficult," I read, *ʿassirū wa lā tu-yassirū*, "Make it difficult for people and don't make it easy.'"

They said, "O Shaykh, you have reversed the words of the Hadith.'

I said, "No, I have mentioned what you are doing, which is the

[39] Bukhārī and Muslim.

reverse of the Hadith: you have made it difficult for someone to visit the Holy Land, the Divine Kingdoms, *Rawḍah min rīyāḍ al-jannah,* preventing people from attaining the rewards and mercies. You are applying the Hadith in reverse!" They said, "O Shaykh, go by plane, not by car." I said, "My son-in-law lives in Saudi, and I travel with him by car, so why do I need to go by plane?" Then I asked the Prophet ﷺ, "*Yā Rasūlullāh*! They are not giving me a visa and I am not going to go there until they leave."

Grandshaykh ʿAbdAllāh ق also asked from Rasūlullāh ﷺ two things:

1) for the colonialists to leave Sham,

and

2) for those who make Islam difficult on people to leave Hijaz.

Grandshaykh ʿAbdAllah ق said, "A message from Rasūlullāh ﷺ came to me, 'We are going to make the colonialists leave,' and that happened. As for the second request, the response came, 'O Shaykh ʿAbdAllāh! In this time, we did not find for *al-Ḥaramayn ash-Sharīfayn*, the two Holy Places, more suitable people than those who are now in Hijaz because they have the good characteristic that they do not see themselves as higher than others; that bad manner is weak in them.'" This is Rasūlullāh's ﷺ

explanation of why Allah ﷻ allowed Hijaz to be under a certain authority, and that was over forty years ago.

إِن يَمْسَسْكُمْ قَرْحٌ فَقَدْ مَسَّ الْقَوْمَ قَرْحٌ مِّثْلُهُ وَتِلْكَ الأَيَّامُ نُدَاوِلُهَا بَيْنَ النَّاسِ

If misfortune touches you, (know that) similar misfortune has touched (other) people as well, for it is by turns that We allocate to Mankind such days (of fortune and misfortune).[40]

Now they are in there, whereas before there was someone else, and after them will be someone else, so you never know when the days will change. Grandshaykh ق and Shaykh Nazim ق were upset. So, the Prophet ﷺ said, "We found them suitable for this time, because they have the characteristic of pride, *takabbur*, but it is weak. Had someone else been appointed *Īmām* of the Ḥaram, they would be the most selfish and arrogant people of all time and enter the Ḥaram as if they were the king of the world."

Imagine if it was one of us! Mawlana ق says anyone who enters and intends to be the *Īmām* of the *jamaʿah,* the ego will come and show itself. Nowadays they have so many Ramadan series on social media. Everyone is giving a Ramadan talk. They make their hair nice; some even have gel in their hair with no cap on. What suits you, *yā ʿalim,* is to cover your head with *ʿamāmah,* which is the *sunnah* of Rasūlullāh ﷺ! This is the reason they made it hard for Shaykh Nazim ق to get the visa, because he was wearing the *ʿamāmah* (turban). In front of Allah ﷻ and in front of Rasūlullāh ﷺ, you have to wear the *ʿamāmah,* as Allah ﷻ orders:

يَا بَنِي آدَمَ خُذُواْ زِينَتَكُمْ عِندَ كُلِّ مَسْجِدٍ وكُلُواْ وَاشْرَبُواْ وَلاَ تُسْرِفُو

O Children of Ādam! Wear your beautiful apparel at every time and place of prayer, and eat and drink (freely), but do not waste.[41]

Allah says, "Take your decoration in every *masjid,*" not hair gel, but the Islamic decoration! What is better than what the Prophet ﷺ wore? And it

[40] Sūrat Āli-ʿImrān, 3:140.

[41] Sūratu 'l-ʿĀrāf, 7:31.

is confirmed that he wore turbans. Shaykh Nazim ق says, "I went, and I did not wear a scarf like women, but I wore the ʿ *amāmah.*"

Grandshaykh ʿAbdAllāh ق used to pray after the *jamaʿah* in Ḥaram ash-Sharīf. I heard many people say, "We don't pray behind those *imāms,* we wait until they're done and then pray." Initially, Grandshaykh ʿAbdAllāh ق did not pray behind the big *jamaʿah* as he did not want to follow them, until Rasūlullāh ﷺ informed him, "This year we have appointed an *Īmām* from our side who moves in front of the officially appointed *Īmām,* so follow them in their prayer, and don't mind who the visible *Īmām* is, as we have appointed another *Īmām* in front of him." Even the outward *Īmām* is following the invisible one, the spiritual *Īmām* who takes over the whole *jamaʿah,* so we pray with them. He says this is the case in both Ḥarams.

Previously, there was an *Īmām* who was Hafīẓ al-Madinatu 'l-Munawwarah, the Keeper of Madinah, and any *Walī* who wants to enter Madinatu 'l-Munawwarah has to take permission from this *muhafizh,* as he was the original, genuine *Īmām.* In Kaʿbat al-Muʿazzamah and Ḥaram al-Madanī, there is an invisible, appointed *Īmām,* so that those who pray there are not wasting their prayers. When you pray behind anyone there, in reality you are praying behind the real saint appointed by Rasūlullāh ﷺ to lead the *jamaʿah.* They have not left it to this one and that one. In that *masjid,* you must have *walīyu 'Llāh* as *Īmām.*

These are secrets mentioned by Grandshaykh ق in order to keep unity, because imagine if Muslims did not pray behind each other; Shayṭān keeps playing with them! "Don't follow him, don't be friends with them!" No, Muslims must unite, regardless of who is in charge, you must pray together. Grandshaykh ق is saying pray behind the existing *Īmām* in whatever *masjid,* and say, "I am praying behind the original *Īmām* appointed for this congregation," then it doesn't matter who is visibly leading. Grandshaykh ق teaches people unity, not separation or enmity. We must keep the unity and pray behind Muslim *imāms* and make the *nīyyah,* "I am following the real *Īmām, al-Īmām al-ḥaqīqī.*"

The Ultimate Purpose: Allah's Greatest Pleasure

Shaykh Muhammad Hisham Kabbani

إِلَهِى أَنتَ مَقصُودِى وَرَضَاكَ مَطلُوبِى

Ilāhī anta maqsūdī wa riḍāka maṭlūbī.

O Allah, You are my goal and Your Pleasure is what I seek!

For *Awlīyāullāh, Riḍwānu 'Llāh al-Akbar,* Allah's Greatest Pleasure is far better than the Seven Heavens. There is no comparison between the two. For that, there is a *duʿā* of Grandshaykh ق:

اَللَهُمَ أدخِلنَا فِى بَحرِ رِضوَانَك الأَكبَر

Allāhumma adkhilnā fī bahri Riḍwānika 'l-akbar.

O Allah! Immerse us in Your Greatest Ocean of Your Heavenly Pleasure.

The focus of *Awlīyāullāh* is not on Heavens, but rather their goal is to reach Allah's Greatest Pleasure, for Allah ﷻ to be happy with them, a level which every *Walī* tries to reach. If a *Walī* reaches the Seven Heavens, he is not considered to have reached the highest, as he did not yet perfect his worship to attain the Greatest Pleasure of Allah ﷻ on him.

Today, some people only think about how to enter Paradise and they follow what the Prophet ﷺ has mentioned; some follow and some do not. Let us say they all follow. Yes, they will enter Paradise and will be safe from punishment, but they are going to regret if they are in the first, second, third, fourth, fifth, sixth, or seventh Heaven. Although it is the best of what we can get, we will still be regretting why we were not following the real way of Prophet ﷺ that *Awlīyāullāh* took, and they were able to reach Allah's Greatest Pleasure.

That is a level or situation described in the Holy Qur'an that everyone has to ask for: *Yā Rabbī! Let us be resurrected with those You favored from the prophets, the trustworthy, the martyrs and the pious,* as they will be granted from Allah's Light in their level.

وَمَن يُطِعِ اللّهَ وَالرَّسُولَ فَأُوْلَـئِكَ مَعَ الَّذِينَ أَنْعَمَ اللّهُ عَلَيْهِم مِّنَ النَّبِيِّينَ
وَالصِّدِّيقِينَ وَالشُّهَدَاء وَالصَّالِحِينَ وَحَسُنَ أُولَـئِكَ رَفِيقًا

All who obey Allah and the Prophet are in the company of those on whom is the grace of Allah, of the prophets, the steadfast affirmers of Truth, the martyrs, and the righteous. Ah, what a beautiful fellowship.[42]

Allah ﷻ will expose or open to them in that level to

مَا لاَ عَيْنٌ رَأَتْ، وَلاَ أُذُنٌ سَمِعَتْ، وَلاَ خَطَرَ عَلَى قَلْبِ بَشَرٍ

No eye has seen, and no ear heard and never imagined (by mind), nor has it occurred to the human heart.[43]

That is according to the Hadith and *Sharī'ah*, that Allah ﷻ will be seen in Heaven by the Believers, but not in every Paradise; only in *that one* to be with the prophets, the trustworthy, martyrs and saints. In that level, you will be able to see your Lord. Many people might say, "How will we see? Do we see a shape?" No way! Allah ﷻ knows what you will see, but *Awlīyāullāh* said that Allah ﷻ will manifest on you and dress you from His Beautiful Names and Attributes according to your status and achievement in that level. He might dress you from one Name and dress another from a different dress of the same Name. Don't think that every Name has only one dress! Every Name has infinite number of dresses, means of lights, colors and knowledge. He will give some people one, two, three, 10, 50 or 99 names, and those who are in the circle of Sayyīdinā Muhammad ﷺ will be most lucky, which all of us would like to be in!

Allah ﷻ said in the Holy Qur'an:

ٱدْعُونِىٓ أَسْتَجِبْ لَكُمْ

Ask Me and I will give.[44]

---

[42] Sūratu 'n-Nisā', 4:69.

[43] Sahīh Muslim.

[44] Sūratu 'l-Ghāfir, 40:60.

So, all of us are asking:

> *Yā Rabbī, aḥshurna maʿ al-Musṭafā.* O our Lord! Make us to be resurrected with the Prophet ﷺ. You said, 'Ask and I will give,' and You are Al-Karīm, The Generous One; if You promise something, You will give. Who is better than Your Generosity? You are Al-Karīm! *Yā Rabbī,* we are weak servants. We are asking You to put us in the same Heaven that you put Your Beloved Prophet ﷺ, Sayyīdinā Muhammad ﷺ, *wa karram wa ʿaẓẓam,* may he be shown generosity and made greater, and to put us with Sulṭān al-Awlīyā, Sayyīdī Shaykh Muhammad Nazim!

Do you think that will not happen? Today if someone asks you for something you have, do you not give? You give. If this *masjid* is full of walnuts and someone from the road comes and says, "Please give me one," what do you do? You will give him ten! That one takes ten and the next one takes ten and the next one takes ten. That will reduce to the level that they cannot ask any more, but Allah's ﷻ treasures are never (depleting). He is the Creator! Ask Him and you will get, and if you don't ask, you don't get? So, ask, and don't worry. "*Yā Rabbī,* give us!"

We get tired, but Allah ﷻ doesn't get tired. He is not like us, so He keeps giving; You are asking, and He keeps giving. *Awlīyāullāh* know this reality, so they keep asking for their followers, not just followers but for *Ummat an-Nabī* as a whole. They ask Allah ﷻ for more and more.

VISITING THE HOLY LANDS

Visiting the Holy Lands will take us to (the realm of) *Riḍwānu 'Llāh al-Akbar,* Allah's Greatest Pleasure. Shaykh ʿAbdAllāh al-Fā'iz ad-Dāghestānī ق once said that Allah ﷻ has created holy places on Earth, in Heavens, and in this universe, which only Sayyīdinā Muhammad ﷺ and *Awlīyāullāh* can reach and know about.

Everyone knows that the holy places on Earth are Makkatu 'l-Mukarramah, Madinatu 'l-Munawwarah, *ʿalā sākinihā afḍalu 'ṣ-ṣalāti wa 's-salām* (abundant peace be upon the one who resides in it), and Masjid al-Aqsa, as mentioned by the Prophet ﷺ in a Hadith:

لَا تُشَدُّ الرِّحَالُ إِلَّا إِلَى ثَلَاثَةِ مَسَاجِدَ الْمَسْجِدِ الْحَرَامِ وَمَسْجِدِ الرَّسُولِ صَلَّى
اللَّهُ عَلَيْهِ وَسَلَّمَ وَمَسْجِدِ الْأَقْصَى

Do not undertake a religious journey except to three mosques: The Sacred
Mosque in Mecca, the Mosque of the Messenger of Allah, and the
Farthest Mosque in Jerusalem.[45]

He ﷺ said that packing to travel is permissible only for three places that
will be counted as worship; all other worldly places you are visiting are
not a way of nearness to Allah ﷻ. If you want to be near to Allah ﷻ, pack
for these three places: Makkatu 'l-Mukarramah, Madinatu 'l-
Munawwarah and Masjid al-Aqsa. The Prophet ﷺ encouraged people to
visit the Holy Lands, as whoever visits them will receive rewards that no
one can describe.

Scholars know that the Prophet ﷺ has also mentioned many *aḥādīth* about
faḍā'ilu 'sh-Shām ash-Sharīf, the benefits and favors upon the Holy land of
Shām, meaning Damascus. Many people don't know that. The Prophet ﷺ
mentioned that Sayyīdinā Mahdī ؏ will come from Mecca to Madinatu
'l-Munawwarah, and then to Shām ash-Sharīf. There, he will pray Ṣalāt
al-Jumu'ah in Masjid al-Amawī, where Sayyīdinā 'Isa ؏ will descend
from Heavens on the white minaret, leading the people. A lot of Sahabah,
Āhlu 'l-Bayt and the wives of the Prophet ﷺ are (buried) in that holy city.

Therefore, it is highly recommended to visit these important holy places,
that human beings wish to visit, like the people in this gathering.
However, there are people outside who wish to visit the Eiffel Tower, the
Taj Mahal, the Statue of Liberty, or the Pyramids; to them those are holy
places. To us it is Makkatu 'l-Mukarramah, Madinatu 'l-Munawwarah,
Masjid al-Aqsa and Shām ash-Sharīf. So, if you want Allah's Greatest
Pleasure, then visit Makkatu 'l-Mukarramah, Madinatu 'l-Munawwarah
and Masjid al-Aqsa, and Allah ﷻ will be happy with you.

---

[45] *Saḥīḥ Muslim.*

ATTENDING ASSOCIATIONS OF *DHIKRULLĀH*

Grandshaykh ʿAbdAllāh ق once said, "When we sit to do *dhikrullāh,* we are attracting *Riḍwānu 'Llāh al-Akbar,* the manifestation of Allah's Greatest Pleasure. As soon as you sit in a gathering for Allah's Pleasure, the Prophet's pleasure and the pleasure of those (*Awlīyā*) in authority, then Allah's Pleasure will be manifest on everyone." So, in such associations, Allah's Greatest Pleasure is manifest on us, which some people can feel, smell, hear and see.

Ṣuḥbah is also *dhikr*. All of us receive knowledge in equal measures, but not everyone's knowledge is the same. Now I am looking at you and you are looking at me, but we are not knowing what knowledge is manifest on you. That is because we are still blind, deaf and dumb. We don't even feel, as some people who don't feel when they get a stroke; we have a spiritual stroke! So, we are blind, we are not feeling, not seeing and not hearing. That is why teaching is important. We used to do everything possible in order to attend Shaykh Nazim's *ṣuḥbahs*. After *Ṣalāt al-ʿAṣr,* he used to give *ṣuḥbah* from Grandshaykh's notes, teaching from these heavy-duty *ṣuḥbahs*. As you know, there are some heavy-duty (bulletproof) cars that can withstand a bullet, but there are also cars with protection even from rockets being shot at it. These *ṣuḥbahs* are rocket proof!

The *tajallī* in this *ṣuḥbah,* which is *Riḍwānu 'Llāh al-Akbar,* will put us on the railway, on the track, which is what we need. Later we will be in the (train) wagons, but now we have no track; we don't know where we are going and where we are coming from.

EMBARKING ON THE JOURNEY

Aʿūdhu billāhi min ash-Shayṭāni 'r-rajīm.
Bismillāhi 'r-Raḥmāni 'r-Raḥīm.
Nawaytu 'l-arbāʿīn,
nawaytu 'l-ʿitikāf,
nawaytu 'l-khalwa,
nawaytu 'l-ʿuzla,
nawaytu 'r-riyāḍa,
nawaytu 's-sulūk,
lillāhi taʿālā fī hādhā 'l-masjid.
I seek refuge in Allah from Satan, the Rejected.
In the Name of Allah, the Merciful,
the Compassionate.
I intend the forty (days of seclusion);
I intend reclusion in the mosque,
I intend withdrawal, I intend isolation,
I intend discipline (of the ego); I intend wayfaring
in God's Path for the sake of God,
in this mosque.

أَطِيعُواْ اللَّهَ وَأَطِيعُواْ الرَّسُولَ وَأُوْلِي الأَمْرِ مِنكُمْ

Obey Allah, obey the Prophet,
and obey those in authority among you.
(Sūratu 'n-Nisā', 4:59).

First and Foremost: Intention

Shaykh Muhammad Hisham Kabbani

The Prophet ﷺ said in a Hadith:

إنَّما الأعْمالُ بالنِّيّاتِ، وإنَّما لِكُلِّ امْرِئٍ ما نَوَى، فمَن كانَتْ هِجْرَتُهُ إلى دُنْيا يُصِيبُها، أوْ إلى امْرَأَةٍ يَنْكِحُها، فَهِجْرَتُهُ إلى ما هاجَرَ إلَيْهِ

> *Actions are only by intention, and every man shall only have what he intended. Thus, he whose migration was for Allah and His Messenger, his migration was for Allah and His Messenger, and he whose migration was to achieve some worldly benefit or to take a woman in marriage, his migration was for that for which he made migration.*[46]

The Intention for Every Act of Goodness

Awlīyāullāh know the secret of how to raise us higher and higher, even by us doing something very small. The *ʿulamā* teach the Ummah, but they don't have that ability to take a small deed and make it big.

I remember Grandshaykh ʿAbdAllah al-Faʿiz ad-Dāghestānī ق once saying, "When you pray, Allah ﷻ will shower you with such rewards that no one can imagine how big they are! For example, when someone goes to a *masjid*, like *Masjid an-Nabawī* or *Masjid al-Ḥarām*, every step they take walking or riding on a transportation, Allah ﷻ will give them one good deed and remove from them one sin." Even that is in limits!

Grandshaykh ʿAbdAllah al-Faʿiz ad-Dāghestānī ق said, "Allah ﷻ opened His Favor on anyone who makes just the intention (*nīyyah*) to go, even though he did not fulfill it; he will still get the reward as if he went and came back!" From Allah's Mercy in these Last Days, your intention will elevate you where no one knows how high except Allah ﷻ and His Prophet ﷺ.

---

[46] Bukhārī and Muslim.

That is why Grandshaykh ق said, "Every time you pray or do any form of worship or goodness, make your intention to be:

نَوَيتُ اَلأَربَعِين، نَوَيتُ اَلإعتِكَاف، نَوَيتُ اَلخَلوة، نَوَيتُ العُزلَة، نَوَيتُ الرِيَاضَة، نَوَيتُ السُلوك، لِلهِ تَعالَى فِى هَذَا اَلمَسجِد

> *Nawaytu 'l-arbaʿīn, nawaytu 'l-ʿitikāf, nawaytu 'l-khalwah, nawaytu 'l-ʿuzlah, nawaytu 'r-rīyāḍa, nawaytu 's-sulūk, lillāhi ta'ala al-ʿAzhīm fī hadha 'l-masjid.*
> I intend the forty days (seclusion), I intend seclusion (from *dunyā*), I intend to isolate myself (from sin), I intend to adopt discipline (of Ṭarīqah), I intend complete obedience to Allah, The Great, in this place of worship.

The moment you make this intention, it will be as if you sat in seclusion for forty days. Allah ﷻ will reward you so extensively that the angels will not be able to write the rewards down, because the same worship you normally do is now enhanced by your intention. Grandshaykh ق said, "When you combine this intention of making seclusions in *dunyā*, then in *Ākhirah* you will be with those who also made this intention (*Awlīyāullāh*)."

Allah ﷻ wants from you the intention, to show your *nīyyah*, and that is why the Prophet ﷺ said: *Verily, actions are by intentions.*[47]

Any good *ʿamal* you want to do with intention, *Awlīyā* are able to raise you higher, even if you are unable to do it. For example, I read the Qur'an every morning, but today when I wanted to read, a guest came. Later I began to read the Qur'an again and another guest came. I began to read again, but then phone calls interrupted me. These interruptions deprive you of reading, but because your intention was to read the Holy Qur'an, it is written for you that you read it.

---

47 Bukhārī and Muslim.

HAJJ IS WRITTEN FOR YOU WHETHER YOU REACH OR NOT

Therefore, from the moment you leave your house, saying, "I am going for Hajj," Hajj will be written for you, whether you reach or not. If you make the intention to make *Zīyārah* (visitation) to the Prophet ﷺ and prepare all necessary documents, but you take one step out of the house and get involved in an accident, the reward will still be written for you. Similarly, for anyone who steps out with the intention to visit a *masjid*, or to go for *Zīyārah* to the grave of a *Walī*, it is written as him having done so. What do you think then if you are stepping out to visit a living *Walī*? Allah ﷻ will reward you as soon as you step out of your house, as it will immediately be written that you visited him. What if you are visiting Sulṭān al-Awlīyā, Shaykh Nazim Adil al-Haqqani ق? This is an ocean, and we are diving in it! When you go to the ocean, what do you see? What is the color of the ocean? Do you see anything else? To see more, you need to dive into the ocean. Then you will see how everything completely changes into colorful scenery and you will begin to witness nature's beauty as you have never witnessed from the land!

So, we are intending Hajj, 'Umrah and zīyārah to the Holy Prophet ﷺ, unless something prevented us and held us back.

وَعَنْ عَائِشَةَ رَضِيَ اَللَّهُ عَنْهَا قَالَتْ: دَخَلَ اَلنَّبِيُّ ﷺ عَلَى ضُبَاعَةَ بِنْتِ اَلزُّبَيْرِ بْنِ

عَبْدِ اَلْمُطَّلِبِ رَضِيَ اَللَّهُ عَنْهَا, فَقَالَتْ: يَا رَسُولَ اَللَّهِ! إِنِّي أُرِيدُ اَلْحَجَّ, وَأَنَا شَاكِيَةٌ,

فَقَالَ اَلنَّبِيُّ صلى الله عليه وسلم " حُجِّى وَاشْتَرِطِى: أَنَّ مَحَلِّى حَيْثُ حَبَسْتَنِى"

Sayyidah 'Ā'isha ؓ once narrated:

The Prophet of Allah ﷺ went to visit Duba'ah bint az-Zubayr bin 'Abdul Muṭṭalib. She said to him, "O Prophet of Allah! I have made the intention to perform Hajj, but I am suffering from an illness." He ﷺ said to her, "Perform Hajj, but set a condition that you shall be relieved of the iḥrām whenever you are prevented (due to illness, etc.)."[48]

The Prophet ﷺ said that if you are on the road and you made the *nīyyah* (to perform Hajj or 'Umrah), then you must fulfill it, even if something prevented you. However, if you add to the intention an exception, saying, "unless I am prevented," such as lack of money, bad health or family problems, or you can't get the visa, etc., then you are okay with that *nīyyah*, as everything is by intention.

That is a blessed place, and the most important thing is whether or not there is a heavenly invitation for us to go there. No one can go without receiving a heavenly invitation; if it is not written for you to go this year, you will not make the intention. However, because there is a heavenly invitation, we did everything we needed to do from our side, and now if we go or we don't go, we still get the blessings here in this area, because we did everything with the intention of going. Our intention is to go for Hajj: we prepared ourselves, we prepared our horse (transportation), we paid our tickets and prepared our caravan. Now, if for certain reasons you don't go, it will be written as if you went, because "deeds are by intention," and your intention was to migrate to Allah ﷻ and His Prophet ﷺ!

---

[48] Bukhārī and Muslim.

EVERY MOMENT WAITING IS COUNTED AS HAJJ

أَفضَل اَلعِبَادَة، اِنتِظَار اَلفَرَج

The Prophet ﷺ said:

The best of worship is to await an opening (relief) from difficulty.[49]

For example, someone wants to go for Hajj and from his inner self he is saying, "*Inshā-Allāh*, this year I want to go for Hajj." So, until the visa and Hajj time comes, he is worried, thinking, "Am I going or not?" You feel that within you. So *intiẓār al-faraj*, people who are waiting for an opening to go, the Prophet ﷺ said, "It will be considered worship." It is worship. Now you are planning for Hajj and how far is Hajj? *Al-hajju ʿArafah*, Hajj is ʿArafat, it is one day.

When I was living in Hijaz for many years, for us Hajj was so easy, living there in Jeddah, every year you go for Hajj, and every Thursday or Friday you go for *ʿUmrah* because it is easy as you are living there. ʿArafat is on the 9th and on the 8th, you go from Jeddah to Mecca, in your *iḥrām*. Everyone is there. You go and make *Ṭawāf al-Qudūm*, and as you finish the *saʿī* it is the morning of the ninth and you go to ʿArafat, until *Maghrib*. You finish ʿArafat and you go to Muzdalifah; then it is finished, the Hajj is two days. *Al-ḥajju ʿArafah*, "Hajj is ʿArafat" and the most important day and everyone is waiting for that day. Every moment you are waiting for that day to come is a day of Hajj!

STORY: *ṬAYY AZ-ZAMĀN*, FOLDING TIME AND SPACE

Prophets like to travel and *Awlīyāullāh* inherit from them, so they also travel. Shaykh Nazim's ق whole life has been a journey of traveling by body or by soul, as *Awlīyāullāh* can also travel by soul. Many people have seen him, although physically he may not have moved, but in spirit he went somewhere and people who know him have seen him. Allah ﷻ granted *Awlīyāullāh* the powers of *Ṭayy az-Zamān wa 'l-Makān*, the Folding of Time and Space.

One example of this that I can mention took place in the early 1980s when the Prime Minister of Lebanon along with the governor of the city, Ashar

[49] Tirmidhī.

ad-Daya, came to visit Shaykh Nazim ق, who was in our home in Tripoli; after the Israeli invasion of Beirut in 1982, we moved to Tripoli from Beirut and Mawlana normally stayed with me in Lebanon. So, during their visit, they invited Shaykh to go to Hajj. Mawlana said, "This year I am busy and cannot go." Although he made Hajj physically twenty-seven times and I also heard that he made Hajj forty times, that year Mawlana said, "No, I can't, I have no permission." They said, "From whom do you want to take permission, you don't need permission! You are going with the prime minister on the private jet." Mawlana said, "No, my permission is from the Prophet ﷺ, not from anyone else. If he ﷺ gives me permission, I will come. I am not going." He didn't agree to go with them to Hajj, so they left. When you are invited by a prime minister or by the government of Hijaz, you will be given special treatment; it will be a very comfortable Hajj and you may even go inside the Kaʿbah, pray there and wash the inside of the Kaʿbah, but he didn't go and stayed with us.

After the season of Hajj finished, and the governor had returned, he rushed to the house where Shaykh Nazim ق was staying. In front of one-hundred people, while we were watching, he said, "O Shaykh Nazim ق, why did you go with someone else, why didn't you come with me?" We said, "The shaykh did not go on Hajj. For two months he has been here with us, traveling around Lebanon." He said, "No! He was on Hajj. I have witnesses. One day I was making *ṭawāf*, the ritual circumambulation of the Kaʿbah, and Shaykh Nazim ق came to me and said, 'O Ashar, are you here?' I said, 'Yes, my shaykh.' Then he made *ṭawāf* with me. We spent the night together in our hotel in Mecca. He spent the day with us on ʿArafat, in our tent. He spent the night with me in Mina, and he stayed with us in Mina for three days. Then he told me, 'I have to go to Madinah to visit the Prophet ﷺ.'"

As he told this story, we were carefully observing Shaykh Nazim ق, as we knew that he had never left our presence in Lebanon. We saw that unique, hidden smile, as if he meant to say, "That is the power that Allah ﷻ grants to His saints. When they are on His Way, when they reach His Divine Love and His Divine Presence, Allah ﷻ will grant them everything."

When he saw that, the governor said, "O my shaykh, what is this miraculous ability that you showed us? It is incredible. That is something I never saw in all my life. I am a politician, and I rely on my mind and my logic. Yet I must say that you are not an ordinary person, you have superhuman powers. It must be something that Allah Himself has dressed you with!" He kissed the hand of the shaykh and asked him for initiation in the Naqshbandi Order. Whenever Shaykh Nazim ق would visit Lebanon, that governor and the Prime Minister of Lebanon would sit in the shaykh's association. Up until today, their families and many of the Lebanese people are his followers.

We were shocked, but a *Walī* is a *Walī*. If Allah ﷻ wants to give *wilāyah* (sainthood) to someone, He will give, regardless of their actions. What kind of power does Allah ﷻ give to *Awlīyāullāh*? Not everything is by *ʿilm*! Besides your obligations, it is by *ḥusn al-akhlāq*, the best of manners. Shaykh Nazim ق was following in the footsteps of the Prophet ﷺ in good manners, and he went to Hajj without physically moving his body from Lebanon; he was making Hajj there

STORY: THE TWO BROTHERS AND THEIR SINCERE WIVES

There were two real *murīds* who, when they prayed, as soon as they said "*Allāhu Akbar*", they appeared at the Kaʿbah; they both would rise from the floor and appear directly in front of the Kaʿbah. Don't think this is too much, no! For *Awlīyāullāh* this is child's play; anyone who is pious and sincere, who has reached the level of vision can move in *zamān* (time) and *makān* (space)! That is *ṭayy*, when time gets folded for him, and he can move across the border from America to China as if they are one country. With the power of "*Bismillāhi 'r-Raḥmāni 'r-Raḥīm*," you will be able to reach anywhere you wish! This is coming in the time of Mahdī عليه السلام: *Ḥaqīqat at-Ṭayy*, "The Reality of Folding Time and the World." In one second, you will be in another place, and in another moment you may be back where you were. So, with "*Allāhu Akbar*," the first one appeared at the Kaʿbah and the other one held his *jubbah* and appeared with him there.

One day they were sitting together discussing their state, saying, "By Allah's Blessing, by our being patient, we are able to pray our five prayers at the Kaʿbah." The brothers said, "It is because we are patient, pious and sincere that we are able to pray at the Kaʿbah." Their wives, who were sisters, overheard that and didn't like what their husbands said. The wives said to each other, "It is not like that. In fact, our piety is the reason for their success as we are patient with them. We cook, clean, care for the kids and do the laundry." Then the laundry was not like today, where you just throw the clothes in the machine, no! They had to really scrub and clean the clothes and there was no convenience of disposable diapers, they had to boil the nappies to clean them, and if the stain still didn't go, they had to take a brush and scrub, which was half a day's process for only one child! So, they said, "We will teach them a lesson."

That night they prepared the food and said to each other, "Today we will cook with no *ghusl* or *wuḍū*," as they usually either took a shower, made *wuḍū*, and then cooked. They served the nice, warm, delicious bread with the steam still coming from it. Their husbands ate, enjoyed it and thanked Allah for the food, and when it was time to pray, they stood and said "*Allāhu Akbar*" but soon realized they did not move. They were heavy like iron, pulled to the gravity of the earth. They repeated "*Allāhu Akbar*" but were still not able to move. The two sisters said, "Who is more pious? You or us? You cannot move, and do you know why? Because we cooked for you with no *wuḍū* and no *ghusl*. This whole time we have been cooking with the utmost purity and you thought you made that light that moved you to the Kaʿbah!"

Permission is Essential for Safe and Blessed Travel

Shaykh Muhammad Hisham Kabbani

NAQSHBANDI HUJJAJ IN A BUS GOING TO ʿARAFAH, HAJJ AL-AKBAR, 2011.

There are three major life decisions that require permission from a true shaykh, a *Walīu 'Llāh*: marriage, divorce and travel, such as for Hajj.

Grandshaykh ق once said, "I was born without veils; Allah ﷻ gave me the power to see the Preserved Tablets. At age seven, parents of Daghestan used to come to me and ask which girl is suitable to marry their boys. Allah ﷻ gave me the power to see the names on the Preserved Tablets, but I would consult the parents, who sometimes said, 'We want this boy to marry that girl,' and sometimes I would refuse and say, 'No, go and find this one instead.' They would find that person and live happily, as it coincided with the Preserved Tablets."

Some people's actions will not coincide with what is written on the Preserved Tablets, as they have followed their emotions and desires.

What is written there might be different, which is why it is very important to ask the advice of your teacher about these three matters.

Asking permission from the *Walī* for traveling is important, because you do not know if you will come back; when you leave, there is no guarantee you will return safely. So, you have to ask, especially when going for Hajj. The shaykh can look at the Preserved Tablets and see if there is a problem or not in that coming year. He can see if the manifestation of the Beautiful Name ar-Raḥmān is there or *ghufrān*, forgiveness will come or not, and he will take permission on our behalf from the Prophet ﷺ! Otherwise, they will not cover us if anything happens.

Today, if you want to travel, they tell you to buy travel insurance. They say, "If you die you die, but we will pay your inheritors." However, when you take permission from the Prophet ﷺ through your shaykh, they make sure you reach safely. If you take permission from the one representing the shaykh, that representative has to take permission from the one he represents, the living *Walī*. Then that *Walī* will take permission from the Prophet ﷺ, or else they cannot save you if something happens. For example, if a ship is sinking, they make all the possibilities for that ship not to sink. They ask Allah ﷻ through the Prophet ﷺ, as they can see:

يَمْحُو اللّهُ مَا يَشَاء وَيُثْبِتُ وَعِندَهُ أُمُّ الْكِتَابِ

Allah blots out or confirms what He pleases. With Him is the Mother of the Book.[50]

So *Awlīyāullāh* immediately jump in on our behalf to ask the Prophet ﷺ for their students to be saved. Whether it is a sinking ship, or riding a horse in the desert, or going in a car, bus, train or airplane, with all of this technology today, you have to take permission to go. Otherwise, we will not fall into the category to be saved, they pull their hands.

TRAVELING IN THE CARE OF THE *AWLĪYĀ*

Allah ﷻ said in an *āyah*:

ذَلِكَ تَقْدِيرُ الْعَزِيزِ الْعَلِيمِ

---

[50] Sūratu 'r-Raʿd, 13:39.

dhālika taqdīru 'l-ʿazīzi 'l-ʿalīm.

That is the decree of the Exalted in Might, the Knowing.[51]

Allah ﷻ assigned two angels on this *āyah* that if you are in a problem, they will carry you and you will be saved. Remember in Malaysia, when the airplane vanished in the ocean, then sometime later another plane also went into the ocean. Had one of the passengers recited, *"Bismillāhi 'r-Raḥmāni 'r-Raḥīm, dhālika taqdīru 'l-ʿazīzi 'l-ʿalīm,"* Allah ﷻ would have sent the two angels that carried Sayyīdinā Yūnus ﷺ, who was one of the *Mūsābiḥīn,* and the whole ship would have gone up (when the ship crashed and he was swallowed by the whale), but *Awlīyāullāh* did not hear that recitation from anyone or they would have rescued the plane.

So, Grandshaykh ʿAbdAllāh al-Fā'iz ad-Dāghestānī ق ordered us to recite, *"Bismillāhi 'r-Raḥmāni 'r-Raḥīm, dhālika taqdīru 'l-ʿazīzi 'l-ʿalīm"* whenever we travel, by car, train, bus, boat, or airplane. Then, if the plane crashes, you will not be harmed. He ق also said, "If there is a war in any country and the people recite this *āyah,* the war will stop! Even if you are in the middle of an explosion and you recite this, you will be saved." But what to teach people today? They follow so many teachers in so many countries, but it is infinitely better to be with one who is connected.

Alḥamdulillāh, Allah did not leave this *dunyā* without pious people, as it is related in the *tafsīr* of Sūrat al-ʿAraf, there are 124,000 saints standing on the threshold of 124,000 prophets. There are *Awlīyā* about whom the Prophet ﷺ informed us that if you are in a forest and night comes and you cannot get back home, and you begin to feel afraid, call on unseen servants of Allah. They are *Awlīyā, Rijālullāh.* They will come and support you.

Where is the jungle? Everywhere is a jungle; it is not necessary to be in a real jungle. To be around people is a jungle, to be in gatherings is a jungle, because when you have people with different beliefs, minds, actions, behaviors and ideas, it is a jungle of bad and low desires. So, Allah ﷻ gave these *Abdāl* power to go everywhere, because everywhere is a jungle; today there is no place pure on this *dunyā.* You find that *Balad al-Ḥarām,* the Sacred City, is pure in Mecca, in Madinah, in Masjid al-Aqsa and in

---

[51] Sūrat YāSīn, 36:38.

Shām (Damascus). Allah ﷻ gave us these, but still, even in these pure places today people are not behaving correctly. It is a jungle, so they need *Awlīyāullāh,* Abdāl to reach them. They are taking and following orders from Qutbs: "Go here, go there, appear in this place and appear in that place." Sometimes they use normal, physical means and sometimes they use spiritual means. They don't like to show *karamāh,* miracles, they want to show normality to everyone.

Allah ﷻ gave them the power of *sahr 'alā rāḥat an-nās,* to stay up late at night for the comfort of people. If a baby is sick in the hospital, for example, you stay with her all night. Similarly, these *Abdāl* look after everyone through their spiritual means in order to lift up the one who is losing his faith or losing his duties during the day. They reach him and they don't differentiate from one to another, as they have orders to reach everyone in need.

Call on the *Abdāl,* the Substitutes, and there are forty of them, mainly from Sham, Madinah and Mecca. They help as soon as they are called, so call on them! These *Awlīyāullāh* are in five groups: *Budalā, Nujabā, Nuqabā, Awtād,* and *Akhyār.* They are the best of the Ummah; they will guide the Ummah, and they will guide you. Don't depend on yourself because you will not succeed; you will lose yourself, your family, your children, your friends, your brothers, your sisters. You will lose everything and Shayṭān will be sitting, laughing at you, happily watching.

A Hajj Travel Guide

Shaykh Muhammad Hisham Kabbani

SHAYKH HISHAM LOOKING AT A HAJJ GUIDEBOOK AT A BOOKSTORE IN THE HOLY LAND, 'UMRAH 2020.

WE NEED GUIDES TO NAVIGATE THE HOLY CITIES

Today they say, "Don't take a guide." Why not take a guide? The Prophet ﷺ took a guide when migrating from Mecca to Madinah to teach us discipline. He took a guide to Madinah and to the station of *Qāba*

Qawsayni aw Adnā, within Two Bows' Length or less of the Divine Presence, with Jibrīl 🖉 as his guide. Couldn't Allah 🖉 call the Prophet 🖉 to His Presence without sending Jibrīl 🖉? But He put Jibrīl 🖉 there in order for us to learn that we need a guide! After reaching the Seven Heavens, Jibrīl 🖉 stopped and said, "I am not going any further." That meant, "There is no need for me anymore. You needed me so you could show your humbleness, which you achieved. I cannot go further, because I will be burned! Now, go wherever you like!"

That is the humbleness of our Prophet 🖉 who went through the Seven Heavens! The one 🖉 who went into *mi'rāj*, ascension, cannot go from Mecca to Madinah without a guide? Of course, he can! Then why did he need a *dalīl*, a guide? Because he wanted to teach us that you need a teacher, a master, a shaykh to reach the Prophet 🖉; you cannot reach with your barefoot going in the desert. Your feet will burn! You need someone to guide you. This life is worse than the desert. So how can you travel all this distance without a guide, a master, a shaykh? He is showing us that, "If you want to be guided, this is the way of guidance. You need my way; you need to follow my message."

Sayyīdinā Mūsā 🖉 is "*Kalīmullāh*," to whom Allah 🖉 spoke directly, because he didn't need an intermediary. Sayyīdinā Muhammad 🖉 was so humble that he accepted an intermediary; he accepted to take messages from Jibrīl 🖉 to show humbleness, to show us that in our work we need each other. Don't do something without guidance. Don't say, "I don't need a teacher." In reality, the Prophet 🖉 didn't need a teacher, but he took a guide from Mecca to Madinah in order to teach us. Does the one who went to Paradise and to the station of *Qāba Qawsayni aw Adnā* need a guide to go from Mecca to Madinah?

This is to teach us not to raise our heads, as we don't know anything. What we know is a drop from an endless knowledge ocean. Human knowledge, secular and religious, is not a drop in the ocean of Sayyīdinā Muhammad 🖉! It is nothing, because whatever levels of knowledge they reached was like going 100 kilometers high in space, and Sayyīdinā Muhammad 🖉 went beyond space.

So, you need a guide to take you through the alleys and deserts from Mecca to Madinah. Don't we have Madinah and Mecca in our hearts? Yes, we do. We love Mecca and Madinah! They are part of our prayers, as we perform our prayers looking towards Mecca. They are inside, but we need guides to navigate the way, as by ourselves we do not know how to get there. Like when you are sick you need a doctor to navigate through your body; you cannot do it yourself, you need a doctor.

PURIFICATION OF THE SELF REQUIRES A GUIDE

It is mentioned by Shaykh ash-Shaʿrānī ق, who died about 500 years ago and has a big *maqām* in Egypt:

> I took the road of purification of the self by myself, without a shaykh, by reading through the books of scholars from over 1,000 years before, such as Risālat al-Qushayrīyya, Awārif al-Maʿārif, Qūt al-Qulūb by Abī Ṭālib al-Makkī and Īmām Ghazālī's Ihyā ʿUlūm ud-Dīn. I would read from one book and switch to another, as my ego would say, "Drop that one and read another," so I was confused. I used to do according to what I understood. I would do the first and read it, then leave it and go to the second and then to the third. I was like someone who enters a tunnel and doesn't know if they will reach the end or not, as it might have a dead end. Even though I was reading the books, I did not know whether it would take me to a dead end or a way out of the tunnel.

This is the way of the one who has no shaykh: he does not know, as Īmām ash-Shaʿrānī ق said, "I didn't know what to do. Then I took a shaykh as they did, such as Īmām Abū Ḥāmid al-Ghazālī ق," because you don't know if you will get out of the tunnel or not, but the shaykh knows if there is an exit to the tunnel. To take a shaykh is to give you a shortcut, not to go in a maze and not know whether you will exit or not. The shaykh will tell you if you want to go in a maze, "Take this way," and how to get you out the quickest. Anyone who did not take a shaykh will go on this road and will be lost for sure. Whoever is lost in the desert will end his life without reaching the goal. As we say, *Ilāhīyy anta maqṣūdī wa riḍāka maṭlūbī*, "O Allah, You are my goal and Your Pleasure is what I seek!"

It is like someone who says to you that they will take you to Hajj but does not know the way. The example of a shaykh is that he will take you directly to Madinatu 'l-Munawwarah and Makkatu 'l-Mukarramah, not take you somewhere else, leave you there for ten days and then take you to Madinah for only two to three days. What is the benefit of going like that when you need to stay in Madinah longer? At least perform the forty prayers there!

So, Shaykh ash-Shaʿrānī ق said, "It is unacceptable for people to go without a shaykh, as they will not reach anywhere." If a shaykh was not needed, then why did most of the scholars of Islam take a shaykh, such as Ḥujjat al-Islam Īmām Ghazālī ق, ʿIzz ad-Dīn ibn ʿAbdus-Salām ق and Īmām Nawawī ق, author of *Riyāḍ as-Ṣāliḥīn*? Most of the scholars of Islam were in *Taṣawwuf* and had a shaykh, only very few did not.

Therefore, if someone guides you toward Mecca go with him, because that guidance is coming from Heavens. No one can enter Mecca or Madinah without permission from Heavens. Don't think people are going by themselves, no. These are two sacred places, and the third sacred place is Masjid al-Aqsa, which *Inshā-Allāh* will open up soon. Who will guide you? Millions and millions of people, every moment there are people doing *ṭawāf*. *Allāhu Akbar! Allāhu Akbar, al-ʿizzatu li 'Llāhi wa li Rasūlihi wa li 'l-mu'minīn!*

STORY: "YOUR LOVE IS MY PREPARATION!"

One day, while the Prophet ﷺ was giving his *Jumuʿah khutbah*, a Bedouin stood by the door and said, "*Yā Rasūlullāh*! Tell me, when is the Day of Judgment?" The Prophet ﷺ did not answer as he was giving the *khutbah*. The man asked another time, "*Yā Rasūlullāh*! When is the Day of Judgment?" Still, the Prophet ﷺ did not answer. Then the third time, Jibrīl ﷺ came and said, "*Yā Rasūlullāh*! Allah ﷻ sends His *Salām* and is telling you to answer the Bedouin." The Prophet ﷺ said, "O Bedouin, it is a long and far journey; what have you prepared for it?"

When we travel, we prepare a lot for our families and children. When we go to Hajj, we prepare everything for the trip and arrange everything we leave behind. Do you go without a passport? We cannot go without a passport. Did we get a passport for the Day of Judgment in order to pass through? Everyone is running to the Ministry of Interior to get a passport to travel. Did we think for one day to go to Sayyīdinā Muhammad ﷺ and say, "*Yā Rasūlullāh*, we need a passport to go to the Day of Judgment!"? Did we think that they are going to ask for our ID? Do we have a clearance? Today there is too much security. They will tell you, "Do you have clearance?" The Day of Judgment is not like *dunyā* clearance. They have angels that when you look at them you run away, afraid from Allah ﷻ. They will not let you pass without a clearance. Did we ask ourselves for a clearance? No. Then how are we going to pass?

So that Bedouin didn't know what to answer the Prophet ﷺ, because nothing will benefit you on that day. O Muslims! Open your mouth, open your ears, open your eyes, open your heart! You need that clearance. Someone comes to customs with a badge and a large number of guards; he passes through security, the scanner rings and rings, but no one minds. He keeps going and everyone gives him a salute, saying, "Pass! Pass!" This is because he has a clearance. Can we pass there at that time on the Day of Judgment?

O Muslims, it is not the titles in *dunyā* which make you gain Allah's Love. It is what Allah ﷻ gives you of titles.

وَلِلَّهِ الْعِزَّةُ وَلِرَسُولِهِ وَلِلْمُؤْمِنِينَ

But honor belongs to Allah and His Messenger, and to the Believers.[52]

That comes from Heavens to you, for you to have *ʿizzah*, honor from Allah ﷻ. You pass regardless of security on the Day of Judgment. You move, and no one can stop you!

O Bedouin! We have to tell him from here to 1400 years back, "Thank you for asking that question to the Prophet ﷺ!" He is hearing us, for sure, as their spirits are free in their graves. Allah ﷻ gave them that power, because they loved Allah and His Prophet ﷺ. We are saying to him, "Thank you! You have honored us with that question. If you didn't ask, no one would know the answer to 'Where is the love?'"

So, he asked, "When is Judgment Day, *Yā Rasūlullāh*?" coming with a pure, innocent heart. The Prophet ﷺ looked at the Bedouin and asked, "What did you prepare for that Day?" He said, "Your love is my preparation, *Yā* Muhammad ﷺ! I'm preparing your love, *Yā Rasūlullāh*; I'm building up my heart, myself for your love." That is why love is in the heart. What did the Prophet ﷺ respond? "*Yā Aʿarābī*! That is enough,

---

[52] Sūratu 'l-Munāfiqūn, 63:8.

this is what is needed of you; you don't need more than that!" The Sahabah ◈ were surprised, and Sayyīdinā Abū Bakr ◈ asked the Prophet ﷺ after *Jumu'ah,* saying, "*Yā Rasūlullāh,* we heard something astonishing today." He said, "*Yā* Abū Bakr ◈, I'm astonished also."

O Muslims! Love Allah ﷻ and His Prophet (saw), you will be saved. You have to love the Prophet ﷺ more than you love yourself. As the Prophet ﷺ said in an authentic Hadith, "You have to love me more than you love your parents and your children and everyone else!" Do we have that? No one can say "yes". I cannot say "yes", and you cannot say "yes". Maybe innocent people can say, "Yes, I love Allah ﷻ."

Where is the love? Keep the love of Allah ﷻ, the Prophet ﷺ and all other prophets in your heart--that is where the love is. Allah ﷻ sent the Prophet ﷺ, the Seal of Messengers, to give us the message of love.

Longing for Hajj Amidst Obstacles

Shaykh Muhammad Hisham Kabbani

You have a question to ask yourself: *"Yā Rabbī,* if I cannot be there, am I going to be *maḥrūm,* deprived of this blessing? I would like to go, but I am not able to go. Am I deprived of that?"

Awlīyāullāh say that from wherever you are, you can say *"As-salāmu ʿalayka yā Kaʿbatu 'Llāh! As-salāmu ʿalayka yā Baytu 'Llāh! Allāhu Akbar!"* Do you think you will not get the benefit of that from here? As we said, everything is according to intention and our intention is to be there all the time, to be in the House of Allah ﷻ, in the presence of the Prophet ﷺ and in the presence of Grandshaykh ق and Shaykh Nazim al-Haqqani ق. That intention will be accepted on the condition that we ask for it all the time.

Every day you want to see your children, your wife, your mother, your brother, or any other relatives. Similarly, you have to show a yearning to be in that presence always, and Allah ﷻ is Merciful!

Awlīyāullāh are a focus point for you. They carry and inherit from the reality of *Kaʿabatu 'Llāh,* and when they sit with their followers, they pass all these lights, manifestations, energies, and beautiful blessings to them.

Allah ﷻ describes Paradise as full of jewels, palaces, diamonds, food, etc. for you to understand it is Paradise, but real Paradise is to be in the Divine Presence, and *Awlīyāullāh* are trying to take their followers there with them.

If Man Can Make Metal Fly, Cannot God Make Man Fly?

Shaykh Nazim Adil al-Haqqani

Once I was in Mecca with our Grandshaykh ق making *ṭawāf* around the House of Allah, the Kaʿbah. Grandshaykh ق said to me, "Look up!" When I looked, I saw above the heads of the people another group of worshippers performing their *ṭawāf*; but these people were of a different class: calm, peaceful and graceful. They too were of Mankind, not angels, but they were the ones who had reached the level of seeing every action as issuing from Allah Almighty, therefore they left the level of earthly struggle.

But, meanwhile, back on the ground, amidst the throng, with those who lack such certainty, we were being pushed, shoved and trampled upon. Some groups locked arms and shoved straight through the crowd, full speed ahead, sending all who were unfortunate enough to fall in their path flying through the air, like discarded banana peels. Elbows in my ribs, heels on my toes, but above us, the ones who concur with Allah's Will have no need for earth under their feet.

Now, perhaps, you are thinking that such a thing is impossible, that I am telling a "tall tale", but yet, when you are told that airplanes fly you think nothing of it. If man can make metal fly, cannot God make man fly? They are at peace with their Lord and with everything in creation, therefore, everything carries them.

And so, we have been shown a higher way, the Vision of Unity, and we have been asked to be patient with those events that are not to our liking, remembering their source. This is the best training for our egos. Undergo this training or you will struggle fruitlessly, up to the grave. We are being trained by our Lord to recognize the Unity of Actions, so that we can come to understand the Unity of His Holy Names, which leads us to the knowledge of the Unity of His Holy Attributes; that knowledge will prepare us for that ultimate dive into the Unity Ocean of Allah Almighty's Existence, His Essence. That is the final goal: that raindrop

falls, and it will not emerge again ever, and it is content because it has just gained everything eternally, forever.

Therefore, Allah Almighty addresses Mankind, saying: "O Man! Verily, you are striving towards your Lord, and you will meet Him." He Almighty is teaching us that all our striving on Earth, our running from East to West, here and there, night and day, is, unwittingly, nothing else than our race towards our Lord's endless Unity Ocean, but we cannot understand now. Our souls long for our Lord, therefore we move, and there is nowhere to move save towards the One.

STORY: THE ANT THAT REACHED MECCA WITH A BROKEN LEG

Every person from among Mankind may attain Divine Stations. The Way is not barred to anyone; we are all candidates for the position of "Deputy of God on Earth." The Holy Verse is clear enough: "O Man! Verily you are striving towards your Lord, and you will meet Him."

Therefore, whoever makes a serious attempt to reach, must reach. However, if we consistently take one step forward and two steps back, and make ourselves fit Allah Almighty's description, "They believed, then fell into disbelief, believed again, and once more fell," then we will find ourselves lost.

Steadfastness is the quality that will aid our progress, even if that progress is slow. Be steadfast and you may reach your goal; and even if you don't, your Lord perceives your sincere intention and may convey you towards your goal, just when you have despaired. Our Grandshaykh

ق said that such perseverance in the face of immense odds is most difficult.

Imagine that a person has been told, "There is a treasure waiting for you inside the earth, a fourth of the way to China; you must dig and take it. Here is a broken pick and a spade with a broken handle, now you may start digging." Imagine being ordered to such a task with such tools. You must start! Don't say, "It is impossible; even an oil drill can't reach down that far!" No, you must say, "My Lord has ordered me to proceed, and He has given me these instruments with which to proceed with my task, so I must start digging." Then you dig, and when you collapse from exhaustion, your Lord may deliver that treasure up to you in the blink of an eye.

Perhaps an ant with a broken leg may intend to travel from London to Mecca to perform the rites of pilgrimage. He may intend such a journey and start on his way, but do you think that there is any hope of him arriving?

SHAYKH HISHAM ON TRAIN TO MADINA, ʿUMRAH 2019.

Allah Almighty sends a pilgrim who sets down his handbag; as the ant crawls in to see if there is any food to be found for the way, the pilgrim comes, picks up the bag and gets into the taxi to the airport. When the pilgrim arrives at Jeddah, he boards a bus to Mecca, then a taxi to his hotel. At the hotel he leaves his other bags but takes this valuable one with him to the Holy Mosque to make his *ṭawāf* of the Kaʿbah.

After his *ṭawāf* he sits down to read Qur'an, and the terrified ant slowly emerges, only to find himself in front of the Holy Kaʿbah!

Allah Almighty made a way for that ant because it firmly intended to reach that unattainable station, with its broken leg and he helped it arrive quickly, too.

So don't lose hope! We are like that ant: we are directing our faces towards the Divine Presence and asking to attain to it. He may take us to that state, but we can never make it on our own!

The Blessing of Praying Fajr in Congregation

Shaykh Nour Mohamad Kabbani

SHAYKH HISHAM GAZING AT KA'BAH FROM HIS HOTEL ROOM, 'UMRAH 2018.

If we want to connect and pray with the Prophet ﷺ and all 124,000 saints, to be in a spiritual presence with them, we can do it now! We'll do it tonight and we'll do it tomorrow, and we can do it every night and every day, as Mawlana Shaykh Nazim ق has taught us. He said that when the Prophet ﷺ and Believers, especially those with secrets and lights, go to the Next World, Allah ﷻ clothes them with the attributes of the verse:

بَلْ أَحْيَاء عِندَ رَبِّهِمْ يُرْزَقُونَ

Rather, they are alive, finding their sustenance in the Presence of their Lord. [53]

---

[53] Sūrat Āli 'Imrān, 3:169.

Mawlana Shaykh Nazim ق said that prophets and saints all have an obligation to do the things of this world: perform all the prayers, fasting and worship. When they transition to the Next World, all their obligations stop except for one thing that is required of them. Since all prophets and saints live in the Presence of their Lord, receiving sustenance, they are ordered to pray Fajr behind the Prophet ﷺ who prays in *Bayt al-Maʿmūr*, the Oft-Visited House, which is the Kaʿbah in Heaven. It was raised up at the time of the flood of Noah ﷺ and taken to Heaven. That is where the angels and spiritual beings pray to their Lord, Allah ﷻ. That is the secret of being "alive". The one thing that is not lost from them is Ṣalāt al-Fajr, the pre-dawn prayer. Those who still live in this world are also required to undergo a spiritual journey to *Bayt al-Maʿmūr* and pray together with the prophets and saints behind the Prophet ﷺ, while being instructed to maintain their physical presence in this world with us.

Further, Mawlana Shaykh Nazim ق said that if we pray Fajr prayers in congregation, Allah ﷻ will create an angel who will intercede for us in Heaven behind the Prophet ﷺ, the saints, the shaykh, on the backs of the prophets. So, we are going with them every morning! Anyone who wants to connect spiritually with Mawlana Shaykh Nazim ق, and to connect with Sīdī ʿAbd al-Qādir al-Jilānī ق, Sīdīʿ Abdul-Khāliq al-Ghujdawānī ق, Sīdī ad-Dasūqī ق, Sīdī Āḥmad al-Badawī ق, Sīdī ʿAlī al-Hujwīrī ق, must wake up for morning prayers and go to the mosque to pray Fajr in congregation, even at home. To pray Fajr at the mosque is difficult because no one wants to get up from his bed and drive his car to the mosque, and that's where we lost contact with our *murshid*!

I saw it myself when I was visiting Mawlana Shaykh Nazim ق in Cyprus; I was present in a room when he told two people, confirming that every morning they have to come to visit and mention his name and always try to do the Fajr prayers in congregation in the mosque. He said, "This person connected with me and prayed with me every morning," although that person does not live in Cyprus. That's what we should do: get up, go to the mosque for morning prayers, mention Mawlana's name and you will be connected with him and other shaykhs.

It is our obligation to pray behind the Prophet ﷺ every dawn at *Bayt al-Maʿmūr*. Although we are ordinary Muslims, if we do this, Allah ﷻ will create an angel representing us, praying behind the Prophet ﷺ and our *murshid*, and the reward will be written as charity on our behalf!

When we are in rows in the mosque, you see people who are on your side, and you can shake hands with them and greet them. Similarly, when we are in the rows behind the Prophet ﷺ, we are also connected with every soul there, the saints, the prophets, and the angels. The trick is to get up before dawn and go to the mosque. If you are able to do so, it means, you are connecting with them; spiritually you are there even if you do not feel it.

The second thing Mawlana Shaykh Nazim ق said is that whoever performs the evening prayers at the mosque will be praying behind Abū Bakr aṣ-Ṣiddīq ؓ and all Naqshbandi Saints praying behind him, and Allah ﷻ will create angels from his light that will represent us before Him. The ego does not want to pray in the mosque, especially ʿIshā and Fajr prayers, and that is why the Prophet ﷺ said in a Hadith that these two prayers are most difficult on hypocrites.

Mawlana Shaykh Nazim ق said, "Those who continue to pray the predawn and evening prayers in congregation, will reach *Jihād al-Akbar*, the safety of the hegemony of his ego (*nafs*). You will be putting your ego between two poles, Sayyīdinā Abū Bakr aṣ-Ṣiddīq ؓ and the Prophet ﷺ." If you put a piece of metal between the two poles of a magnet, it cannot escape: the ego is fettered, it has limited movement because now it is between the two poles! That is the secret to free the shackles of the ego, the world, the desires, and the devil.

As taught by Mawlana Shaykh Nazim ق, when we enter the Divine Presence through prayer, we should say, "O my Lord! I have entered the House of Ḥaqq, in the Presence of Ḥaqq, and I've put myself behind the *Imām* who was present at *Ḥadrati 'Llāh*," then our worship will be directly connected with the Almighty in *Ḥadrati 'Llāh*. When we pray behind an *imām* at the mosque, you do not know if it is connected, so Mawlana said this is the best deed we can do, namely Ṣalāt al-Fajr in the mosque, and then everything will be easier for us during the day.

So, the secret to connecting with Mawlana Shaykh Nazim ق is if you can get up from your bed, go to the mosque and pray Ṣalāt al-Fajr; otherwise, you cannot connect. This is an easy, quick way, as they're all praying behind the Prophet ﷺ before dawn.

We ask Allah ﷻ to give us the power to do that! It's very hard on the ego, it's very heavy, but we ask Allah ﷻ to enter us as people who are praying for spiritual guidance behind saints, prophets, the *imāms*, behind the Prophet ﷺ, and for us Naqshbandis to pray behind Sayyīdinā Abū Bakr aṣ-Ṣiddīq ؓ in the evenings. Our Lord, make us able to do so, give us the power, health, wealth, and ability, *yā Rabbī,* and provide love and encouragement to do so, *yā Rabbī*!

bi ḥurmati 'l-Ḥabīb bi ḥurmati 'l-Fātiḥah.

Actions to Attain the Reward of Hajj From Home

Shaykh Muhammad Hisham Kabbani

Fast on the Day of ʿArafah

For those of you who are not going on Hajj, I call your attention to the Day of ʿArafat. On that day, the ninth of Dhul-Hijjah, the *ḥujjāj* go out from Mecca to ʿArafat to stand on that holy valley, making *duʿā* the whole day. For Allah that is a very important day. All the pilgrims who went for Hajj are asking Allah for forgiveness and saying, *"Labbayk Allāhuma labbayk! Labbayka lā sharīka laka Labbayk! Inna 'l-ḥamda wa 'n-niʿamata, laka wa 'l-mulk, lā sharīka lak!"* They are showing unity in one cloth, one dress, kings, presidents, normal people all in one dress keeping the Hadith: "There is no difference between Arab and non-Arab except through righteousness."

Abū Hurayrah ؓ said, as the Prophet ﷺ wants to make us happy, he told his Sahabah ؓ, "You want to be on ʿArafat with me?" and the Prophet's ﷺ message is for everyone, "If you cannot make pilgrimage, then fast the Day of ʿArafah!"

عَنْ أَبِى قَتَادَةَ عَنْ رَسُولِ ﷺ أَنَّهُ سُئِلَ عَنْ صَوْمِ يَوْمِ عَرَفَةَ فَقَالَ " يُكَفِّرُ السَّنَةَ الْمَاضِيَةَ وَالْبَاقِيَةَ "

The Messenger of Allah ﷺ was asked about the observance of fasting on the day of ʿArafah. He said, "It is an expiation for the sins of the preceding year and the current year.[54]

Those staying home asked the Prophet ﷺ about fasting on that day, and he said, "It will waive the sins of two years, the one that passed and the year that is coming." This Hadith shows how much it makes Allah ﷻ happy with those observing the day of ʿArafat and the day of *ʿEid*. The Prophet ﷺ is giving us good tidings: if you cannot go for Hajj, then fast the Day of ʿArafat, Allah will forgive your sins. That is why *al-ḥajju ʿArafat*, "Hajj is ʿArafat."

If you don't stand on ʿArafat, your Hajj is null and void; the most important thing is to stand in that valley as the Prophet ﷺ did, where Allah sends His *Rahmat* over them. Even if you are here and you are fasting on the Day of ʿArafat or celebrating *ʿEid*, you will still receive that *raḥmah*. That is Allah's Generosity, not like us, as we are stingy. Don't be stingy. It is (only) good to be greedy for religion. To ask for more *raḥmah* from Allah ﷻ is good; be greedy and Allah will give you! The Prophet ﷺ is asking for the benefit of the Ummah.

It is so simple, if Allah will give us energy and support to fast that day, the benefit is that all sins you made from before that day have been forgiven and you will be as if newly born. So, O Muslims! Try to fast on that day. If you have an excuse, it is okay, but if you don't have sickness or dizziness, then if you can fast Allah ﷻ will forgive you your mistakes.

You must look to find the days that are most valuable to fast, pray or worship, as you don't know when the Angel of Death will come. As Sayyīdinā ʿAlī ؓ said, "Work as much as you can for *dunyā,* but don't forget you are going to die."

So, if you were unable to go for Hajj and be there with the pilgrims, then fast on the day of ʿArafat and observe the day of Eid! If Eid is on Tuesday,

---

[54] Muslim from Abū Qatādah ؓ.

for example, the one who fasts on Monday is going to have his sins waived for both the past year and the coming year. But we are requesting from the Prophet ﷺ to request from Allah ﷻ a waiver for not only one year, but years before and years after! So, let us make the intention now to fast on that day!

And regarding the fasting of Dhul-Hijjah, Rasūlullāh ﷺ said,

مَا مِنْ أَيَّامٍ أَحَبُّ إِلَى اللهِ أَنْ يُتَعَبَّدَ لَهُ فِيهَا مِنْ عَشْرِ ذِى الْحِجَّةِ، يَعْدِلُ صِيَامُ كُلِّ
يَوْمٍ مِنْهَا بِصِيَامِ سَنَةٍ وَقِيَامُ كُلِّ لَيْلَةٍ مِنْهَا بِقِيَامِ لَيْلَةِ الْقَدْرِ

> *On no days is the worship of Allah ﷻ desired more than in the (first) ten days of Dhul-Hijjah. The fast of each of these days is equal to the fast of a whole year and the worship of each of these nights is equal to the worship of Laylat al-Qadr*[55]

PRAY WITHIN THE FIRST HOUR OF THE *ADHĀN*

Grandshaykh ق said, "Allah ﷻ opened to the heart of *Awlīyāullāh* through the Prophet ﷺ that anyone who prays within the first hour of the prayer, not delaying it, it will be written for him as if he went all the way to Makkatu 'l-Mukarramah and prayed facing the Kaʿbah. It will be considered as if he went to Hajj and came back within that first hour!" That is why there are five daily prayers, so you can be taken to that Presence at every prayer.

SHAYKH HISHAM KABBANI MAKING ṢALĀT, DURING ʿUMRAH 2019.

So, five prayers, five Hajj, with a continuous *tajallī*! If you really want to step into *ṭarīqah* there is a lot of struggle, but Grandshaykh ق gave

---

[55] Tirmidhī, Ibn Mājah and al-Bazzār from Abū Hurayrah ؓ.

us this good tiding that when you pray within the first hour of prayer, Allah ﷻ will open a *tajallī* from His Endless Mercy, more than before (as we are in the Last Days). One of your spirits will be moved there in front of the Kaʿbah, but you cannot see it as you are veiled, and you will get the benefit of one Hajj. That is spiritual knowledge that *Awlīyāullāh* give to their followers.

MAKE *ZIYĀRAH* OF HOLY RELICS ON HOLY DAYS

The Prophet of Allah ﷺ said:

HAJJAH NAZIHA ADIL MAKING *ZIYARAH* TO THE HOLY HAIR OF THE PROPHET.

" يَوْمُ عَرَفَةَ وَيَوْمُ النَّحْرِ وَأَيَّامُ التَّشْرِيقِ عِيدُنَا أَهْلَ الإِسْلاَمِ وَهِيَ أَيَّامُ أَكْلٍ وَشُرْبٍ

The Day of ʿArafah, the Day of Nahr, and the Days of Tashrīq are ʿEid for us, the People of Islam, and they are days of eating and drinking.[56]

The days of ʿArafat and the days of ʿEid are five holy days for *Āhlu 'l-Islām*, the Muslims. On these five days there must be no work and no

[56] Tirmidhī.

school, except for praying, eating, celebrating and being happy. These are days that Allah ﷻ is compensating His servant by eating, being happy and socializing. Don't say, "I want to go to work." Allah's ﷻ work is better! Don't say, "I want to go to school." Allah's school is better! On these five days, Allah ﷻ is saying, "Do in your limits what you like, as long as you keep to the Islamic way."

Allah ﷻ blessed the Ummah with the holy relics of the Prophet ﷺ, the biggest of which is his sacred presence, that he is *Ḥāḍir* and *Nāẓir*, "present" and "seeing." And the greatest relic is going to his house in Madinatu 'l-Munawwarah, praying two *raka'ats*, visiting *Rawḍatu 'sh-Sharīfah*, and going to Mecca, as all of these take away sadness. Many of the Prophet's ﷺ relics have been left for us: his clothes, his turban, his Holy Hair, his teeth, his sword, his *jubbah* and his holy flag. When Īmām Mahdī ؑ comes, he will bring out all these *Amanāt* from Topkapi Palace. There are lots of sacred relics around the world to give happiness to people.

That is why the *Awlīyāullāh* and previous *'ulamā* always open the relics of the Prophet ﷺ with *ṣalāwāt* on special nights, such as on the beginning of Ramadan, the 17th of Ramadan (to commemorate Aṣ-ḥāb Badr), the 27th of Ramadan, 'Eidu 'l-Fiṭr, 'Eidu 'l-Aḍḥā, Mawlid an-Nabī, 'Āshūrā, 14th of *Muharram*, 15th of Sha'bān, as these dates are important. So, try to visit all these relics wherever you find them around the world. Some people go to Mecca and Madinah in these precious days, but if you cannot, Allah ﷻ provided relics all around the world in order that you can be blessed from their *nūr*. These sacred relics cannot be opened whenever we like. Out of respect, they must be opened on these designated holy days. I never saw Shaykh Nazim ق open them except on these important days. *Alḥamdulillāh,* Allah ﷻ provided this place with these sacred relics, but make sure to visit them on precious days. Do not make them like toys, to open and close every day. It must be on perfect days!

STORY: THE PART IS LIKE THE WHOLE

I will give an example of the importance of the Holy Hair of the Prophet ﷺ. This is a cup of water. If I put my finger inside the water and take it out, you will see a drop of water. This drop is part of the water, the whole.

Outside of the water, the drop can be seen with a form, but inside the water, it is gone. So *ziyārah* of the Holy Hair of Prophet ﷺ is like making *zīyārah* to Sayyīdinā Muhammad ﷺ himself, as it is part of him!

I will relate that story in which Sayyīdinā Ibn ʿArabī ق said, "One time my hand saved the boat of Nūḥ 舔, and if not for my hand that boat would have sunk!" The people who heard this were surprised, saying, "Nūḥ 舔 lived 5,000 years ago! How is this possible?" He said, "Yes, I am from the *nasl* of the Prophet ﷺ; I am both *Ḥasanī* and *Ḥusaynī*. It was the Prophet's ﷺ hand that saved the boat of Nūḥ 舔 and I am part of that hand!"

So, any relic will bear witness on the Day of Judgment from the Prophet ﷺ that you visited it and made the Shahadah in front of it. That is why we kiss *Ḥajar al-Aswad*. Why, when you go to Kaʿbah the main focus is how to reach and kiss the Black Stone? First, it is a Stone from Paradise, and who touches Paradise, Hellfire will never touch him. So, when you begin with *"Bismillāh, Allāhu Akbar!"* even from afar, that Stone will reach you. Don't think the Black Stone is waiting for you to reach it within that huge crowd, no. Whether you reach and kiss it or you are not able, that Stone is a live stone and will reach you as if you touched Paradise! And who touches Paradise will never touch Hellfire, as the person who visits the Rawḍatu 'sh-Sharīfah and prays two *rakaʿats* there.

$$ مَا بَيْنَ قَبْرِى ومنبرى رَوْضَةٌ مِنْ رِيَاضِ الْجَنَّةِ $$

The Prophet ﷺ said, "What is between my minbar, pulpit, and my maqām, grave, is a garden from the Gardens of Paradise."[57]

That is Paradise, so anyone who prays there is safe in Paradise. Similarly, any relic of a *Walī*, of our shaykh, will be a mercy and a means to Paradise.

---

[57] Bukhārī and Muslim.

Dhul-Hijjah, the Month of Sacrifice

Shaykh Muhammad Hisham Kabbani

As-salāmu ʿalaykum wa raḥmatuLlāhi wa barakātuh! Kullu ʿāmin wa antum bi khayr. Inshā-Allāh Ḥajj mabrūr wa saʿīan mashkūr wa tijāratun lan tabūr, yā ʿālima mā fi 'ṣ-ṣudūr, yā Rabbī al-ʿizzati wa 'l-ʿaẓamati wa 'l-jabarūt. Ighfir lanā w 'arḥamnā bi jāhi Ḥabībika al-Muṣṭafā wa bi jāhi asrāri kullu man muḥibban laka yā Allah, wa muḥibban li-Ḥabībika al-Muṣṭafā, al-Ḥabīb al-Muṣṭafā, al-Ḥabīb al-Awḥād! Yā Rabbanā, yā Allāh, ash-hadu an Lā ilāha illa 'Llāh wa ash-hadu anna Muḥammadan ʿabduhu wa Rasūluh.

Greetings for the holy days and to the Day of Sacrifice, the day of going against your ego for the love of Allah ﷻ and His Prophet ﷺ, to step on your ego for the sake of love of Allah ﷻ and His Prophet ﷺ.

O Muslims! Dhul-Hijjah, the month of Hajj, is a month of sacrifice. Sacrifice yourself for Allah's ﷻ sake and for Prophet's ﷺ sake by not falling into sin! "Sacrifice" is to give everything in Allah's way. Try as much as possible in this month to fast. Dhul-Hijjah is one of the sacred months in which war is not allowed, killing is not allowed, not even an animal when you are in *iḥrām*. It means, when you are performing Hajj, you have no right to kill even a worm, unless it is something urgent to kill, if it is poisonous, etc.

Dhul-Hijjah is a very precious month, when Allah ﷻ asked Sayyīdinā Ibrāhīm عليه السلام to sacrifice the best of what he had. Sayyīdinā Ibrāhīm عليه السلام didn't have children and that is why he married Sayyidah Hājar, so Allah ﷻ would give him a child. He became old and married her and Allah ﷻ gave him Sayyīdinā Ismaʿīl عليه السلام, but Allah ﷻ wanted to test him.

Although Allah's prophets are *maʿṣūmūn,* innocent, protected from committing sins, still Allah ﷻ tested them. Sayyīdinā Ibrāhīm عليه السلام is one prophet He tested with a big test, not a simple test. Sometimes we have a test coming to us, a difficulty that Allah ﷻ sends. Really, it is a difficulty, and you cannot take it anymore, but compared to what prophets have been tested with, it cannot be described. Imagine someone who doesn't have a child, who gets a child, and Allah ﷻ orders him in a dream, "*Yā* Ibrāhīm, go sacrifice your son for Me. Slaughter him with a knife. Put him on the rock, the altar, take the knife and cut his neck." Who can do that?

Aʿūdhu billāhi min ash-Shayṭāni 'r-rajīm. Bismillāhi 'r-Raḥmāni 'r-Raḥīm.

فَلَمَّا بَلَغَ مَعَهُ السَّعْىَ قَالَ يَا بُنَىَّ إِنِّى أَرَى فِى الْمَنَامِ أَنِّى أَذْبَحُكَ فَانظُرْ مَاذَا تَرَى قَالَ يَا أَبَتِ افْعَلْ مَا تُؤْمَرُ سَتَجِدُنِى إِن شَاء اللَّهُ مِنَ الصَّابِرِينَ فَلَمَّا أَسْلَمَا وَتَلَّهُ لِلْجَبِينِ وَنَادَيْنَاهُ أَنْ يَا إِبْرَاهِيمُ قَدْ صَدَّقْتَ الرُّؤْيَا إِنَّا كَذَلِكَ نَجْزِى الْمُحْسِنِينَ

And when he reached with him (the age of) exertion, he said, "O my son, indeed I have seen in a dream that I (must) sacrifice you, so see what you think." He said, "O my father, do as you are commanded. You will find me, if Allah wills, of the steadfast." And when they had both submitted and he put him down upon his forehead, We called to him, "O Abraham, You have fulfilled the vision." Indeed, We thus reward the doers of good.[58]

He saw in a dream, and that is how prophets usually say it: "We saw in a dream." Look at the humbleness of prophets! They didn't say, "We received it by Jibrīl ﷺ." Today people who have permission to give a *ṣuḥbah* or a *dhikr* will not say, "I saw a dream." They will say, "I saw a vision." Some people are like that; they have the sickness of arrogance.

So, Sayyīdinā Ibrāhīm ﷺ, the father of prophets, was saying, "I saw in a dream that Allah ﷻ is ordering me to slaughter my son Ismaʿīl ﷺ on this month of Dhul-Hijjah." When he took him to the mountain, what did he say? "O my son! We are going to play 'hide and seek'. Do you want to play with me?" That game is old, not something new!

He said, "Yes, my father, I like to play 'hide and seek' with you."

He said, "Okay, let me cover your eyes."

[58] Sūratu 'ṣ-Ṣaffāt, 37:102-105.

He said, "O my father, why are you covering my eyes? For what? What do you want? Don't cover my eyes. I am ready to fulfill the order."

Isma'īl ﷺ knows. He is young, nine years old. He already knew what the order was, for his father to sacrifice his son, the only son that he got at his age of 90 years. He said, "I am ready."

So, the important thing is that he went along to sacrifice his son, who is the most precious person, isn't he? What did his son tell him? "I am ready!"

Our duty now is to learn that Dhul-Hijjah is the month of sacrifice. And what is the best to sacrifice for Allah's sake? It is to stop committing sins, to stop committing forbidden actions. What are these forbiddens? People say, "O, forbiddens is that I must not look at something *ḥarām*." That is correct, but that is not the only thing; the most important thing is to keep your anger down. Not one of us can keep his anger down! Why do people divorce? Because they get angry with each other. What is our duty? It is to sacrifice our ego by putting our anger under our feet. When you get angry say, "*Astaghfirullāh*". That is what Allah ﷻ likes, for us to stop carrying or wearing bad characteristics.

For people to get angry is from Shayṭān. In Dhul-Hijjah, Shayṭān has been chained. If you make a sacrifice to Allah, if you say, "*Yā Rabbī*! I'm not going to do anything bad this month. Help me!" do you think Allah ﷻ will leave you to Shayṭān? But we don't think like that. We never thought about it, that Dhul-Hijjah is the month of sacrifice and Ramadan is the month of fasting. It means, we must fast from everything that is *Ḥarām*. In Dhul-Hijjah we have to sacrifice ourselves, our egos, from all kinds of bad desires, and the trunk of the tree of bad desires is anger.

Can anyone raise his hand and say, "I'm not angry at all in my life?" All of us get angry all the time. If the husband made a mistake and the wife cannot stand it, she wants to fight. If the wife made a mistake, the husband cannot stand it, he wants to fight. No one is patient on the other one and that's why you find a lot of problems today.

So, this is the month of sacrifice. Try to sacrifice for the sake of Allah ﷻ and for the sake of Prophet ﷺ. Try to sacrifice any kind of bad characteristic and throw it away. Say, "*Yā Rabbī*, this month I am not going to be angry." This is the first thing, and some people can recite 100-

1000 times Sūrat al-Ikhlāṣ before they sleep and 100-1000 times " *lā ilāha illa 'Llāh Muḥammadun Rasūlullāh."*

ASK FOR ALLAH'S MERCY ON THE HOLY DAYS!

None of us is *ma'ṣūm*, infallible, except Prophet Muhammad ﷺ. All of us make mistakes, sins; we are not protected except by the *shafa'ah*, intercession, of the Prophet ﷺ. We are asking Allah ﷻ to dress us from the *tajallī*, manifestation of this day, which began on the Hijaz time, which over there is near Fajr, when everyone is rushing toward 'Arafat to stand and be ready there, as Allah ﷻ descends to the First Heaven, granting His Servants who are saying:

لَبَّيْكَ اللَّهُمَّ لَبَّيْكَ، لَبَّيْكَ لاَ شَرِيْكَ لَكَ لَبَّيْكَ، إِنَّ الْحَمْدَ وَالنِّعْمَةَ لَكَ وَالْمُلْكَ لاَشَرِيْكَ لَكَ

> *Labbayk Allāhuma labbayk! Labbayk lā sharīka laka labbayk! Inna 'l-ḥamda wa 'n-ni'amata, laka wa 'l-mulk, lā sharīka lak!*
> *Here I am at Your Service, O Allah! Here I am at Your Service! Here I am Allah at Your Service, and You have no partner! Here I am at Your Service! Yours is (all) praise and favor and dominion! You have no partner!*

He ﷻ is dressing them with the secrets of that *tasbīḥ*, the praises that we just mentioned. *Awlīyāullāh* are gathered there every year; they go there by order, physically and spiritually, some physically and some spiritually, through their spiritual channels, through their hearts, because the heart can reach anywhere, faster than the intelligence, faster than the brain.

The brain has a very high speed of movement, more than the speed of light, which is 300,000 km per second. The speed of the heart to reach anywhere is faster than the speed of light. We hope that Allah ﷻ forgives us for the *barakah* of this day, where three million this year have officially been mentioned, but in reality, it might be five or six million because it is Hajj al-Akbar, when the Day of 'Arafat falls on a Friday.

Why are all these pilgrims, dressed in all white, there? White signifies the purity of the heart, which means, all of them with pure hearts are praising Allah ﷻ and glorifying Him, asking Him to forgive them and to forgive every one of us, *Inshā-Allāh*. We say, "O Allah! The Prophet ﷺ is the real ʿ*abd*, servant, we are only imitational servants. He is the Real One, he is the real *muwwahid*, the Real One who did ʿ*ibādah* and still he is doing ʿ*ibādah*!

We are asking you, *yā Rabbī*, to make us have a share in his prayers, his fasting, his Hajj, his *nawāfil* and all his obligations, with all his supplications and praises of You. Share with us, *yā Rabbī*, *yā* Allah, from all prophets, all *Awlīyāullāh*, and from every person who stood on ʿArafat, observing that day from Sayyīdinā Ādam ﷺ until the Day of Judgment! Share with us, *yā Rabbī*, *yā* Allah, from all prophets, all *Awlīyā*, and from every person who stood on ʿArafat, observing that day from Sayyīdinā Ādam ﷺ until the Day of Judgment! Dress us from their realities, from the *Raḥmah* that You have put on them!

وَرَحْمَتِي وَسِعَتْ كُلَّ شَيْءٍ فَسَأَكْتُبُهَا لِلَّذِينَ يَتَّقُونَ وَيُؤْتُونَ الزَّكَاةَ وَالَّذِينَ هُم بِآيَاتِنَا يُؤْمِنُونَ

My Mercy encompasses everything. That (mercy) I shall ordain for those who do right and practice regular charity and those who believe in Our Signs.[59]

Your Mercy has encompassed everything! Allah ﷻ dresses us with His *Raḥmah*, He will write that for the Believers who have *taqwā* of Allah ﷻ. *Yā Rabbī*, make us from them and accept from us our shortcomings. What can we do? *Yā Rabbī*, turn it into strong prayer, not imitational prayers, but real prayers! And *yā Rabbī*, for one inch, one millimeter, give us millions! His Treasures never end, His Giving never ends, His Mercy never ends, His Greatness never ends! *Yā Rabbī*, dress us with all these Beautiful Names and Attributes that You praised Yourself with! *Yā Rabbanā, yā Allah*, and we are saying:

---

[59] Sūratu 'l-ʿĀrāf, 7:156.

لَبَّيْكَ اللّٰهُمَّ لَبَّيْكَ، لَبَّيْكَ لاَ شَرِيْكَ لَكَ لَبَّيْكَ، إِنَّ الْحَمْدَ وَالنِّعْمَةَ لَكَ وَالْمُلْكَ لاَشَرِيْكَ لَكَ

Labbayk Allāhumma Labbayk! Labbayka lā sharīka laka Labbayk! Inna 'l-ḥamda wa 'n-niʿamata, laka wa 'l-mulk, lā sharīka lak! Here I am at Your Service, O Allah! Here I am at Your Service! Here I am Allah at Your Service, and You have no partner! Here I am at Your Service! Yours is (all) praise and favor and dominion! You have no partner!

Wa ṣall-Allahu ʿalā Sayyīdinā wa Nabīyyīnā Muhammadin wa ʿalā ālihi wa ṣaḥbihi wa sallam. Subḥāna rabbika rabbi 'l-ʿizzati ʿamma yaṣifūn wa salāmun ʿalā mursalīn wa 'l-ḥamdulillāhi rabbi 'l-ʿĀlamīn.

Conditions for an Accepted Hajj

Shaykh Muhammad Hisham Kabbani

JIHĀD AN-NAFS, FIGHTING THE ENEMY WITHIN

Allah ﷻ said in the Holy Qur'an:

وَالَّذِينَ جَاهَدُوا فِينَا لَنَهْدِيَنَّهُمْ سُبُلَنَا وَإِنَّ اللَّهَ لَمَعَ الْمُحْسِنِينَ

And those who strive in Our Way, We will certainly guide them to our Paths for verily, Allah is with those who do right.[60]

Allah ﷻ is saying in this *āyah*, "Those who make jihād for Us, We are going to support them." The Holy Qur'an was revealed in two locations, in Mecca and Madinah; Jibrīl ﷺ brought the first part when the Prophet ﷺ was in Mecca and the second part when he ﷺ was in Madinah. This

[60] Sūratu 'l-'Ankabūt, 29:69.

āyah (about jihād) was revealed in Mecca when there was no permission to fight the enemy who came against them, but only to submit to Allah's Will. This means that "jihād" here does not mean "jihād of war," it means "jihād or struggle of the self." Just as you have to be strong to fight the enemy in war, in the same way you have to be strong fighting the desires within you.

This *āyah* means you have to fight the enemy within you, *jihād an-nafs*, and the *āyah* ordering to fight the physical enemy was revealed in Madinatu 'l-Munawarrah. As it is said, *jihād al-kāfirīn qad shuri'a fī Madinatu 'l-Munawarrah*, "The order to physically fight the unbelievers who fought the Prophet ﷺ was given in Madinah."

رَجَعْنَا مِنَ الْجِهَادِ الْأَصْغَرِ إِلَى الْجِهَادُ الْأَكْبَرُ ، قَالُوا : وَمَا الْجِهَادُ الْأَكْبَرُ ؟

قَال : مُجَاهَدَةُ الْعَبْدِ هَوَاهُ .

The Prophet ﷺ said when they were returning from a battle:

> *"We returned from the smaller jihad to the greater one."* They asked,
> *"What is that, O Messenger of Allah?"* He said, *"The battle of the
> servant against his desires.*[61]

He ﷺ said that the greater jihād is to struggle against yourself, and the Sahabah ؓ were surprised. For them war was the biggest jihad; they were giving their blood for the Prophet ﷺ and for Allah ﷻ, but the Prophet ﷺ said, "No, no, we came from the small jihād to the greater jihād." They said, "What is the greater jihad, *Yā Rasūlullāh?*" He ﷺ said, "*Jihād an-nafs,* the struggle against yourself," because if we don't struggle against ourselves, Shayṭān will grab us.

The Prophet ﷺ said:

الْمُجَاهِدُ مَنْ جَاهَدَ نَفْسَهُ

The mujāhid is one who strives against his own soul.[62]

---

[61] al-Bayhaqī.

[62] Tirmidhī.

"The *mujāhid* is the one who fights himself for Allah's Love." He fights his ego, his bad characters, his bad manners for Allah's Love. That is why, in order to purify the self from the "mud" of the ego we have to know that to struggle against ourselves is an obligation. Just as you pray, fast and make Hajj, you must consider this too as an obligation. Today no one takes into consideration the fight against the ego. That is why people fight with each other, because everyone wants to sit on the chair, they don't want to give the chair to someone else. It is said that *al-mujāhada an-nafs*, the struggle against the ego is *ʿibādah*, worship, because you are trying to follow the order of Allah ﷻ to chase your shayṭān away from you, and you cannot achieve that without *ʿilm*, knowledge.

That is why knowledge of *Sharīʿah* is important, because it will guide you on the highway, but there are too many exits where you see wild animals coming to attack you, and these animals are Shayṭān trying to whisper in your ear. What kind of animals do circuses play with? Lions. How did they make the lion, which is a wild animal and can eat anyone, into a domestic animal? That means there is a way that if you follow, it will make the wild animal within us to be domestic that will no longer harm us, but rather help us.

LEARN ISLAMIC ETIQUETTE FROM *AWLĪYĀULLĀH*

As Shāh Naqshband ق said, "All *ṭarīqahs* are based on *adab*, discipline." *Shuyūkh* are not coming to teach us *fiqh*, *tafsīr* or different Islamic principles, as they consider their *murīds* have already studied what is necessary in Islamic Jurisprudence.

There are two types of shaykhs: the one who teaches *Sharīʿah* and the one who teaches spirituality. Anywhere you go around the world, you will find teachers of *Sharīʿah*, but not everywhere you go will you find teachers of spirituality, *Awlīyāullāh*. They are rare to find, and it is even more rare to have them accept you. So, shaykhs of *Sharīʿah* have huge schools and universities in every country; you can learn from them as long as you like to know about the principles of Islam and what Islam came with. They teach you in detail, even the principles of *tajwīd*, in reciting the Holy Qur'an, where to stop or not stop, where to put a period, a comma, a semi-colon or colon, etc.

A *Walī* is not going to waste his time and your time teaching you *tashkīl* or grammar, because he understands that just as he was with his shaykh, he studied *Sharīʿah* somewhere else and then came to his shaykh to take his guidance on spiritual issues, which we call *ʿIlm al-Ḥaqā'iq*, Knowledge of Realities. Not every shaykh can give that.

Why do we go after *Awlīyāullāh*? Is it to learn how to pray or fast? You know how to pray and fast. You can ask any *ʿalim* and he will teach you. If you go to Hajj and want to know what to do, there are many who can teach that as well, isn't it? You can go to Hajj and pray, fast and do whatever you want to do, and many will teach you, but no one will teach you how to behave, how to handle your discussions and deal kindly with people or how to speak with them. This is what you call "protocol," the Islamic Etiquette, which teaches you how to behave. If people do not understand the meaning of *Maqām al-Iḥsān*, the Station of Moral Excellence, and you want to tell them how to behave, you can explain it as Islamic Etiquette. The Prophet ﷺ taught his Sahabah ؓ how to behave, speak and respect each other and how to be guided to Allah ﷻ and His Prophet ﷺ.

For example, you might be riding a car on the highway, driving a long distance. You keep moving to your destination, but you have to know that you might get a flat tire and then may no longer be able to move. What is that flat tire in the spiritual path? It is when Shayṭān comes and pulls you out from driving normally on the highway. So, on *Sirāṭu 'l-Mustaqīm*, you might advance by your prayers and fasting, but in between Shayṭān pulls you and you might find yourself back to zero, because you are not behaving well. You might be in the car driving with five people to another city and you begin to fight. What will happen? You will find that everyone wants to separate, they don't want to drive together anymore.

The Prophet ﷺ taught the Sahabah ؓ *adab*, moral excellence, and this is very important for everyone. If you have *adab* you will succeed; if you don't have *adab*, you will lose your fasts, prayers, Hajj, *Zakāt* and your *Shahādah*; you are losing everything to your temper! So, what do you go to a shaykh for? To learn how to behave with others. The shaykh makes you fight your ego; he helps put it down.

Awlīyāullāh are those who teach discipline. The Prophet ﷺ said in an authentic Hadith to the Sahabah ؓ, "If you do ninety percent of what I ordered you to do and drop ten percent of that, it is not accepted. However, there will come a time when people do only ten percent of what they have been ordered to do and drop ninety percent of it, but it will be accepted from them!"

Today, if Muslims do ten percent of what Allah ﷻ and His Prophet ﷺ has ordered, they will be saved. So, you now see the extent of the *rahmah*, mercy! There is too much ignorance around because no one is learning other than the five pillars. We know that Islam has five pillars and the station of *Īmān* is based on six pillars, so Islam is different from *Īmān*. Why did the Prophet ﷺ make different categories? Everyone is saying, "I am a Muslim," as to say he is covering all of the levels of faith: Islam, *Īmān* and *Ihsān*. No, they are not! In our mind we think we are Muslim: we do our five prayers, we give *zakāt*, we fast, and we have done Hajj, but in reality, that is the first most basic level that anyone can learn. The highest level is to have real *'aqīdah*.

Muslims are fighting today because *'Aqīdatu 'l-Muslimīn*, the Muslim Belief, has become corrupted. The Prophet ﷺ does not want it corrupted, so he gave it a special level other than the five pillars. He gave the six pillars of *Īmān*, as Allah ﷻ said in Holy Qur'an:

قَالَتِ الْأَعْرَابُ آمَنَّا قُل لَّمْ تُؤْمِنُوا وَلَكِن قُولُوا أَسْلَمْنَا وَلَمَّا يَدْخُلِ
الْإِيمَانُ فِى قُلُوبِكُمْ

The desert Arabs say, "We believe." Say, "You have no faith; but you (only) say, 'We have submitted our wills to Allah,' for not yet has faith entered your hearts." Don't say, "We are mu'min," but say, "We are Muslim," because Īmān did not yet enter the heart.[63]

At that time, you will be raised from the level of Islam to the level of *Īmān*. There is Muslim and there is *mu'min*. The Muslim is the one who wants to enter Paradise, *Inshā-Allāh, Yā Rabb*, by performing his five pillars, but

---

[63] Sūratu 'l-Ḥujurāt, 49:14.

only when he corrects his *ʿaqīdah*. This is very dangerous: if we don't complete it well, it will be a disaster for us. Like for example, if we take *Sharīʿah* as a scale and you stand for prayer, you may wonder, "How much do I have in the bank?" Or you may think, "Ah, this *Īmām* is not correct," or, "How much do I have to entertain myself tonight and where do I have to hide myself so that my wife does not see what I am doing," or this and that. On the normal scale this thinking is accepted, because you cannot stop your mind from receiving such gossip from Shayṭān, as he can go there.

In the other levels, however, in *Īmān* and *Iḥsān*, you are not allowed to do that; slowly you have to try and avoid as much as you can, under the guidance of the shaykh, and that is the role of the shaykh.

Have Good Thoughts in Mecca and Madinah

So, if bad thoughts come to your mind, you will not be questioned about it and it won't be written as a sin, but in Mecca and Madinah, it will be written against you due to the holiness of the place. On the normal scale, around the world it is not written, but in Makkatu 'l-Mukarramah or Madinatu 'l-Munawwarah there is an upgraded scale, like a fine jewelry digital scale that can measure any bad thought that comes to your mind; that scale can detect it.

Only in Mecca and Madinah if you have a bad intention, it is written. Bad thoughts will be written, and good thoughts will be rewarded. Bad thoughts are a sin, as Mecca and Madinah are restricted, highly guarded, pure areas. That is why, the first thing they tell someone going for Hajj is, "Don't get in a fight and don't backbite!" It is as if Shayṭān is telling them to go smoke *narghīla*, smoke cigarettes, and fight with everyone. Shayṭān wants to ruin it for them! If you can control your anger, you can go. If you go, as it is an obligation, make sure you don't have any bad thoughts there, even though it is difficult.

That is why in your countries, other than Mecca and Madinah, if you think of doing something wrong, and you plan it, but did not yet do it, it is not written as something against you, because it has not been materialized. But, if in Mecca and Madinah you think of something wrong, it is written immediately against you, because Kaʿbah is in Mecca and directly above it in the Fourth Heaven there is *Bayt al-Maʿmūr*, where angels are continuously making *ṭawāf*.

CONTROL YOUR ANGER AND DESIRES

Allah ﷻ said in the Holy Qur'an:

فَمَن يَعْمَلْ مِثْقَالَ ذَرَّةٍ خَيْرًا يَرَهُ. وَمَن يَعْمَلْ مِثْقَالَ ذَرَّةٍ شَرًّا يَرَهُ

He who shall have done an atom's weight of good, shall behold it; and he who shall have done an atom's weight of evil, shall behold it.[64]

If anyone shows even one atom's weight of anger for anything from *dunyā* material, he will lose his whole Hajj! It means he is no longer going for Allah ﷻ. Allah ﷻ is saying, "Don't get angry, you are in that ocean. If you lose the whole *dunyā* there, you are coming to Me, you are coming to the ocean. You are not guarding your money there!" So, your money, your luggage or someone made you angry. If you become angry, you lose your whole Hajj and you will be considered from the *musrifūn*, the ones who excessively waste their time and money. It is as if you have wasted what you went for. You had a good intention to go there, but you changed that intention by getting angry about a *dunyā* issue.

You must keep your anger down there. Don't nag or argue, asking, "Why did this happen or didn't happen?" or, "Why I have to do this or that?" There, it is only what Allah ﷻ wants and you will see that you have no will; only Allah's Will is manifest there and you will find whatever He has written for you, so don't argue! Keep your prayers and keep your mouth busy only in *dhikrullāh* and *ṣalāwāt* on the Prophet ﷺ.

The Prophet ﷺ said in a Hadith:

عَن أَبِى هُرَيرَةَ رضي الله عنه قَال سَمَعتُ النَبِى ﷺ يَقُول : مِن مَن حَجَّ لِلَّهِ فَلَمْ يَرْفُثْ وَلَم يَفسُق رَجَع كَيَومَ وَلَدَتُه أمُّه

64 Sūratu 'z-Zalzalah, 99:7-8.

Whoever makes Hajj and does not engage in (lawful) sexual relations and does no wickedness and does not argue, returns as the day his mother bore him.[65]

And as Allah ﷻ said:

الْحَجُّ أَشْهُرٌ مَّعْلُومَاتٌ فَمَن فَرَضَ فِيهِنَّ الْحَجَّ فَلاَ رَفَثَ وَلاَ فُسُوقَ وَلاَ جِدَالَ فِى الْحَجِّ وَمَا تَفْعَلُواْ مِنْ خَيْرٍ يَعْلَمْهُ اللهُ وَتَزَوَّدُواْ فَإِنَّ خَيْرَ الزَّادِ التَّقْوَى وَاتَّقُونِ يَا أُوْلِى الأَلْبَابِ

For Hajj are the months well known. If anyone undertakes that duty therein, let there be no obscenity, nor wickedness, nor wrangling in the Hajj. And whatever good you do, (be sure) Allah knows it. And take a provision (with you) for the journey, but the best of provisions is right conduct. So, fear Me, O you folk that are wise.[66] *So, during Hajj, you cannot have any sexual relations with your wife, and you cannot look at anything that is Ḥarām. If abstaining from that and if you avoid arguing too much, then you will return from Hajj as if you are newly born. It means that Allah ﷻ doesn't like arguments or backbiting or rumors in Hajj and He doesn't allow any sexual relationship, because you are going for worship, and you cannot do that in worship. And the most important principle of Hajj is 'Arafat; if you missed it, you missed the main principle and fundamental of Hajj. That is why 'Arafat is the most important day of Hajj and why the Prophet ﷺ recommended to fast that day.*

ARM YOURSELF WITH *DHIKRULLĀH*

We need an alarm system that if any intruder enters, warns us that our home is not safe.

---

[65] Bukhārī from Abū Hurayrah ؓ.

[66] Sūratu 'l-Baqarah, 2:197.

Allah ﷻ said in the Holy Qur'an:

وَمَن دَخَلَهُۥ كَانَ آمِنًا

And whoever enters it shall be safe.[67]

SHAYKH HISHAM KABBANI AND HIS WIFE HAJJAH NAZIHA, 'UMRAH 2021.

When you go for Hajj and visit the Kaʿbah in Makkatu 'l-Mukarramah, you are safe, as you are entering Allah's House where no one can harm you. Shayṭān cannot enter there and attack you if you enter with the right code. Many people go for Hajj and enter with no code. So, what do they do there? They fight with each other, even though they were warned not to get angry and to be patient when they go for Hajj or else their Hajj is not accepted. So, as you go, you come. You are only torturing yourself!

You have to arm your heart with *dhikrullāh*. Can we say our heart is armed? No one else, no *Walī*, no *Nabī*, except Sayyīdinā Muhammad ﷺ, said, "I won over my Shayṭān, I control him." That is why the *Awlīyāullāh* are trying their best to be armed, which is why you see them in constant worship, in constant *dhikrullāh* and meditation, not like us, wasting our time on different entertainments.

ALL DEEDS SHOULD BE PURELY FOR ALLAH ﷻ

Every *ʿamal* is a pilgrimage, don't let anything disrupt it. This means, any *ʿamal*, good deed you do is like going on Hajj. Why is it Hajj? Because it is done in obedience to Allah ﷻ, so it's as if you are going on a pilgrimage

[67] Sūrat Āli ʿImrān, 3:97.

to the Divine Presence. Any *ʿamal* you do, such as fasting, praying, giving *zakāt* is Hajj. It is a pilgrimage to do something in the way of Allah ﷻ. If in the middle you get upset then that *ʿamal* is canceled, because you have put something in it besides Allah ﷻ. You went only for Allah ﷻ, but when you put a material matter in between, then it is as if you have made *shirk*, and your whole *ʿamal* becomes:

وَقَدِمْنَا إِلَىٰ مَا عَمِلُوا مِنْ عَمَلٍ فَجَعَلْنَاهُ هَبَاءً مَّنثُورًا

And We shall turn to whatever deeds they did (in this life), and We shall make such deeds as floating dust scattered about.[68]

Allah ﷻ is saying, "We know their intentions. We know that they have mixed many things together on that journey. They mixed it up, so that is why We come to that *ʿamal* they did as it is not for Us, because it has been mixed with different issues, many different trades that they made in between. They trade with Shayṭān, which means they did not come for Us. We throw their *ʿamal* in their faces! We do not accept anything that is mixed."

Allah ﷻ does not like that. It has to be something such that when you do it, it is very pure for Allah ﷻ. That should be your intention! If something happens in between, try not to go after that thing, keep on the way of a good *ʿamal*. However, if you go and follow the things that went in between and you get angry and begin to dispute, then you will be responsible and *maḥkūm*, under the control of Shayṭān and his power.

DON'T REJECT ANYONE

Grandshaykh ʿAbdAllāh ق said that if you go for Hajj and a poor man comes to you and extends his hand and you reject him, not giving him anything, your whole Hajj is gone, it is not accepted! It means, if someone comes to you asking for help, saying, "O my brother, help me!" and you throw him out, your Hajj is gone.

Those poor people in Hajj, it is their land, they are living there. The time of Hajj is their crop, like when in the spring you plant something and

---

[68] Sūratu 'l-Furqān, 25:23.

later in the summer you harvest. So, they wait to harvest in Hajj time. You will see thousands of people coming to harvest. Help them in their harvest and Allah ﷻ will help you in your harvest on Judgment Day! Allah ﷻ is checking on Judgment Day, whatever you planted in *dunyā* you will reach in *Ākhirah*. There is a Hajj harvest and a Judgment Day harvest. If you did not put any fertilizer, then you will not find any harvest.

EVEN IF YOU ARE POOR, GIVE CHARITY

The stingy one has no Hajj and no *zīyārah* to the Prophet ﷺ, it is not even considered. It is considered from the meaning of fulfilling the obligation, but it is not accepted from the real meaning of Hajj and *zīyārah*. Even more than this, Grandshaykh ʿAbdAllāh ق said:

البَخِيل لَا زِيَارَةَ لَهُ وَلَاحَج وَلَا صَلَاة مَقبُولَة وَلَا صَدَقَة

> No *Zīyārah* (Visitation of the Prophet), pilgrimage, prayer or charity are accepted from the stingy one!

This goes back to the verse from the Holy Qur'an, where Allah ﷻ says:

> *"We come to what they have done of deeds and throw it in their faces, as if it does not exist!*[69]

Grandshaykh ق said, "The best *ṣiffat*, character, that is accepted by Allah ﷻ is to be *sakhīyy*, generous." Even if you are poor (*al-faqīr*), you must be generous. What is the meaning of "*al-faqīr*" here? We are all "poor" to Allah ﷻ, *al-faqīr billāh.*

In the classical or traditional teachings, when you signed your name at the end of a manuscript, you had to write, "*al-faqīr billāh,* the One Who is Poor Through Allah ﷻ." You can see in all these old manuscripts that people used to write, they didn't write "Dr." at the end. Today everyone signs his name as "Dr." or "Professor" when they write a book. What did they use to write before? *Al-faqīr ilā 'Llāhi taʿālā*, "The Poor One to Allah, so-and-so." That is the *faqīr*! Even if he has money, he is *faqīr* to Allah ﷻ; he has nothing, as his *dunyā* wealth is not considered.

---

[69] Sūratu 'l-Furqān, 25:23.

So, everyone is poor, and as we said, "Even if you are poor, you have to be generous." Generosity is what opens the door for everything. Some people with their generosity Allah ﷻ opened for them something, but because of their ego, they stopped there.

You have to be very careful: when something opens because of your generosity and love, you must not let your ego play a game there. Or else all your generosity is going to be like it didn't exist, as you have blocked it from continuing in the way of Allah ﷻ. What Allah ﷻ is giving you, you are giving to others as a generosity. Even if you are poor now or you gave everything and then became poor, Allah ﷻ opens to you and you open to others by giving to people. Don't close that by saying, "I will not tell you if you don't give me," or, "I will not teach you if you don't give me." No, you cannot do that. Knowledge cannot be stopped. We must not learn the tricks of Shayṭān. You must not take anything in return, as it is for Allah ﷻ. If Allah gives you, you cannot sell Allah's ﷻ Knowledge. Sayyīdinā Muhammad ﷺ didn't take anything for the knowledge he gave. If they gave from their own selves, he took. So, if they give you, take; if not, don't ask, even if you are poor. Then, we will be safe.

LISTEN TO PEOPLE'S ADVICE

Any *ʿamal* you do is like a pilgrimage. When someone comes in between asking for advice, that is like someone coming and raising your level; he is coming to give you even more reward on the Hajj.

This *ṭarīqah* is a pilgrimage; you are following the way of *Awlīyāullāh, zuhhād* and *ittibaʿ an-Nabī* ﷺ. If someone comes to give you advice and you throw him out, it means you are lost. Who sent that person to you? Allah ﷻ sent that person to give you advice. Listen to that advice and check it. If the advice coincides with *Sharīʿah,* then go with it.

People will begin to argue, especially on the Internet. Don't argue with anyone. If it is according to *Sharīʿah,* okay, if not then don't reply or else it will create *fitna,* that is if we want *Ākhirah.* As the Prophet ﷺ said, "The one who doesn't make *fitna* or backbiting in Hajj, he will come back from there like someone newly born."

On the way of Hajj, give, give, give! Accept what people say of advice if it's according to *Sharīʿah,* and don't create problems. Then, you will be able to reach what Allah ﷻ wants you to reach, and it will not be written for you as wasted, but rather as worship. Grandshaykh ق said, "If something takes you on Hajj, or any *'amal,* which we consider to be a pilgrimage, don't let anything disrupt it!"

قُلْ إِنَّمَا أَنَا بَشَرٌ مِّثْلُكُمْ يُوحَى إِلَيَّ أَنَّمَا إِلَهُكُمْ إِلَهٌ وَاحِدٌ فَمَن كَانَ يَرْجُو لِقَاء رَبِّهِ فَلْيَعْمَلْ عَمَلًا صَالِحًا وَلَا يُشْرِكْ بِعِبَادَةِ رَبِّهِ أَحَدًا

Say, "I am but a man like yourselves, (but) the inspiration has come to me that your Allah is one Allah. Whoever expects to meet his Lord, let him work righteousness and in the worship of his Lord admit no one as partner[70]

Anyone who wants to go on pilgrimage to Allah ﷻ, who wants to do any good *'amal,* he must not associate anyone with Allah ﷻ. Don't associate your ego there by rejecting any poor person or rejecting anyone on the way. Grandshaykh ق is teaching us via *adab,* and we know that the eye of his heart was open since he was ten years of age.

[70] Sūratu 'l-Kahf, 18:110.

SACRED SITES SECRETS AND ETIQUETTES

Aʿūdhu billāhi min ash-Shayṭāni 'r-rajīm.
Bismillāhi 'r-Raḥmāni 'r-Raḥīm.
Nawaytu 'l-arbāʿīn,
nawaytu 'l-ʿitikāf,
nawaytu 'l-khalwa,
nawaytu 'l-ʿuzla,
nawaytu 'r-riyāḍa,
nawaytu 's-sulūk,
lillāhi taʿālā fī hādhā 'l-masjid.
I seek refuge in Allah from Satan, the Rejected.
In the Name of Allah, the Merciful,
the Compassionate.
I intend the forty (days of seclusion);
I intend reclusion in the mosque,
I intend withdrawal, I intend isolation,
I intend discipline (of the ego); I intend wayfaring
in God's Path for the sake of God,
in this mosque.

أَطِيعُواْ اللّهَ وَأَطِيعُواْ الرَّسُولَ وَأُوْلِي الأَمْرِ مِنكُمْ

Obey Allah, obey the Prophet,
and obey those in authority among you.
(Sūratu 'n-Nisā', 4:59).

Spiritual Landmarks

Shaykh Muhammad Hisham Kabbani

They say there are seven wonders of the world, but you also find seven wonders in each country. In every country or location, there is a focal point, a landmark wherever you go. There must be a landmark of a *Walī* there! We are only looking at the landmarks of stones or statues or buildings, but there must be a landmark of something different, an inhabitant, like a magnet pulling people and bringing them to that presence.

Shaykh Muhammad Hisham Kabbani and Hajjah Naziha before the Prophet's Mosque, Hajj 2011

There are two places on Earth that came from Paradise: *Ḥajar al-Aswad,* the Black Stone and Rawḍat ash-Sharīfah, the Holy Prophetic Garden. When you enter Paradise, you enter with no sins, as you cannot have any sins in Paradise. That is why people are pushing to touch *Ḥajar al-Aswad,* which is the secret of the Holy Kaʿbah, and to enter Rawḍat ash-Sharīfah, because if they step inside there, they will be stepping into Paradise with no account on Judgment Day. Anyone stepping into the Rawḍah is stepping into Heavens!

Another example is the landmark of visiting your shaykh is not the house, it is the one inside the house. When you go to visit Sulṭān al-Awlīyā, are you visiting the house or himself? If your shaykh doesn't see you, you get upset. You say, "O, my shaykh didn't see me; he didn't even give me five minutes!" Although he is there, you still want to see; you want *kashf*, but there are places that you cannot see, as you are not at that level.

You think when you visit the Prophet's Holy House, his Holy Grave, there is no higher level than that. Of course, there is! *Awlīyāullāh* can feel the presence of the Prophet ﷺ; they can see and meet with the Prophet ﷺ in different shapes and stations according to the level they are in, even from far away!

There are landmarks in Mecca, Madinah, Muzdalifah, Mina, and ʿArafat. Who is on *Jabal Raḥmah*, the Mountain of Mercy in ʿArafat? Who is in *Kaʿbatu 'Llāh*, the House of Allah ﷻ in Mecca? Who is in the house of the Prophet ﷺ in Madinah?

Everyone is running five times a day, directing his face towards the Kaʿbah. Who built the Kaʿbah? They say the first one to build it was Sayyīdinā Ādam ؑ and then Sayyīdinā Ibrāhīm ؑ rebuilt it. What did they build it from? Stones. Are they special stones or normal stones? They built a house, very beautiful and nice. You open the door and there is nothing inside, yet Allah ﷻ wants everyone to direct his face there. Why there, in that desert? There must be a secret there that we cannot understand.

This means that Allah ﷻ has appointed someone, a presence, that inhabits each of these places, someone who is a focal point of gravity.

The *Adab* of Visiting Holy Sites

Shaykh Muhammad Hisham Kabbani

Millions of people go for *ʿUmrah* and Hajj, but what do they do there? Unfortunately, many stay the same: as they come, they will go. There are principles of visiting Makkatu 'l-Mukarramah and Madinatu 'l-Munawwarah. Don't think that the Kaʿbah and the Ḥaram an-Nabawī are empty of *Awlīyāullāh* and spiritual beings. These sacred places must be highly respected. That is why it is always more advisable to make *zīyārah* of the Prophet ﷺ after the performance of *ʿUmrah* or Hajj so that you come to the Prophet ﷺ clean. It is not just by taking a shower and going to the *masjid*, no. There are principles of visiting the Prophet ﷺ and how you need to be clean to visit the House of Allah ﷻ. Cleanliness is to polish the self, to take away the ego. When you take away the ego, you become light; when the ego is there, you are heavy, and gravity pulls you down.

We have been granted the honor to be from the Ummah of the Prophet ﷺ, but how do we approach the Prophet ﷺ? Today, people have no *adab*: they fight outside and then enter the presence of the Prophet ﷺ! We must follow *adab* by following the stars, which means, "Follow your guides, follow the Sahabah," whom the Prophet ﷺ described as guides. Where do the guides take us? To the Prophet ﷺ! Can you go directly to the Prophet ﷺ with your dirtiness? No, that is not *adab*. That is why it is said, "You must first complete your Hajj and then visit the Prophet ﷺ; you must first clean yourself before going to the Prophet ﷺ!"

The Ḥaram al-Makkī, the Sacred Mosque in Mecca, is full of angels and spiritual beings, all around, that descend on the Kaʿbah. If that was not the case, there would be no attraction from the Kaʿbah to people. It is dressed in every moment, and not only with one *khilʿa* every year, but in every moment Allah dresses His House with beautiful dresses that you cannot describe! You can only say that they are beautiful, heavenly dresses that come on the Kaʿbah, and as soon as you enter, those heavenly dresses are dressed on you!

So, what happens then? It cleans you and you become sinless, as if you are newly born, and then you go to Madinah clean, because in Madinah there is an ocean. To visit the Kaʿbah is a cleaning process. Allah ﷻ can clean you, and if He doesn't want to, no one can, not even the Prophet ﷺ. However, Allah ﷻ said to him, "I gave you permission to clean!" and that is his *shafaʿah*, intercession.

So, *adab* with the Prophet ﷺ is to visit Mecca first and then Madinah, which is what the Prophet ﷺ did: first he was in Mecca, then he migrated to Madinah. And *innamā 'l-ʿāmālu bi 'n-niyyāt*, "Every action is according to (its) intention."

SHARĪʿAH REQUIREMENTS FOR MEN AND WOMEN

I raised my hands to obey their command and they brought upon me of mercies that is enough for the entire Ummah, as *Wārith Muḥammadī*, Muhammadan Inheritor, and Madad al-Ḥaqq, along with some other names they granted me. This happened and its end was that Shaykh Nazim ق left me with Shaykh ʿAbdAllāh ق to confirm these stations. Each person has these stations, but he has to struggle. With struggle (*ijtihād*) everything happens, but we are lazy. However, their love for us purifies us from filth and transgressing against the honors of one another.

It is not permissible, as Hajjah Naziha said while we were coming to Madinatu 'l-Munawwarah that we do not eat the flesh of one another, and I especially remind women.

If there is no *maḥram* present (a non-marriageable male relative) then be careful of Shayṭān, men as well as women. It is not permissible according to *Sharīʿah* to sit alone in private with a strange man not from her family (*khalwah*). Thus, if a man sits with a foreign woman by themselves, then in the view of *Awlīyāullāh*, their coming together results in divorce without any return, because this is against *Sharīʿah*.

I am hearing of some men and women who sit privately with one another. I don't know what their position is going to be with Allah ﷻ, with Prophet and Awlīyā. It is not permissible according to *Sharīʿah* as I said, even for five minutes with a shaykh or a foreign man. If her husband is with her, then there is no problem, and vice versa.

We have to follow *Sharīʿah* so we don't fall in this problem. Especially if a man or woman sleeps over in another's house, with no one else present, then in Awlīyā's eyes they are divorced. Thus, we have to repent from all that took place in the past. Let us now repeat the Shahadah three times: *Ash-hadu an lā ilāha illa 'Llāh wa ash-hadu anna Muḥammadu 'r-Rasūlullāh.*

There is absolutely no permission for an unrelated man to sleep in a house of a married woman, for whatever reason. He has to have a maḥram or somebody else, if there was a medical reason, if he or she were sick, then they should take a *maḥram* with them, meaning a man, woman or child who is from the family of the sick person.

And let them not say "I have a shaykh" [as an excuse]. This is against *Sharīʿah*! Allah ﷻ has forbidden such behavior many times in the Qur'an. This is my hand it testifies to this. Every *Walī* enters this ocean, and we are entering with them. For this reason, I'm telling you this so that the Awlīyā are not displeased with what we are doing of what is not correct.

قال رسول الله ﷺ: لَا يَبِيتَنَّ رَجُل عِندَ امرَأة ثيّب، إِلَّا أَنْ يَكُون نَاكِحًا أو ذَا مَحْرَم.

The Prophet ﷺ said, as related by Jābir ؓ that the Prophet ﷺ said: "It is not allowed for an unrelated man or woman to be alone together in a house."[71]

In addition to the Hadith, Shaykh 'AbdAllāh al-Dāghestānī ق said that if a man is secluded with a woman for five minutes, then he is divorced from his wife. This is authentic in the eyes of the *Awlīyā*. Likewise, for the Sahabah and it is the Hadith of the Prophet ﷺ.

This kingdom has a special status because Mecca and Madinah are in it, so let them warn the pilgrims that they should not be alone together except with a *maḥram,* a male relative with whom marriage is prohibited. This is why they said that no woman can perform Hajj except with a *maḥram,* and this is good on their part. This has been the case for the past fifty years. Now they opened everything: this is good from one aspect, but we have to be careful from another aspect.

Inshā-Allāh, this *ṣuḥbah* will be beneficial for those going to Hajj and *'Umrah,* because all of this is from the news of Heavens!

The Prophet ﷺ said to Sayyidah 'Ā'ishā ؓ:

مِن حُوسِب عُذِّب

(O 'Ā'ishā!) Who will be judged will be punished.[72]

He said, "O 'Ā'ishā, whoever is judged will be punished, so ask Allah not to judge you," and she is the wife of the Prophet ﷺ, she does not fall into error. This means that nobody will be saved from punishment if they are judged; even if they are near to the Prophet ﷺ, punishment will take its share. If Sayyidah 'Ā'ishā ؓ was given this advice, then what about us? It is not permissible at all to fall into error!

Thus, repentance is necessary at every time. *Tubnā wa raj'anā ila 'Llāh,* we repent and return to Allah! (3x) This is a *du'ā* in which no two can differ,

---

[71] Muslim from Jābir ؓ.

[72] Bukhārī.

and its power is from the power of prophethood, because it is coming from the Prophet ﷺ.

Whoever is judged will be punished. *Yā Rabbī*, don't punish us! Do not judge us, *yā Allah*! You are the Greatest, You are the Most Powerful, You are the One with All Strength. *Yā Rabbī*! You are the All-Forgiving and All-Gentle, the Intercessor. You, *yā Rabbī*, Your Greatness is not subsumed by any other greatness. And Your Prophet ﷺ is the prophet of the Ummah. We repented on his hands. It is a good fortune that this *ṣuḥbah* comes while you are here, in Madinatu 'l-Munawwarah. This *ṣuḥbah* is accepted by the *Awlīyā*. They are listening to you now and listening to Prophetic Hadiths that have many interpretations and listening in the Ocean of Intimacy. If it was in the Ocean of Punishment, he would have thrown us all there!

Q & A CONCERNING HAJJ PRACTICES

Shaykh Muhammad Hisham Kabbani

Q: While doing *ṭawāf,* is it okay to talk with others or behave casually?

A: It is better not to talk, but rather to be busy with *duʿā* and *ṣalāwāt* on the Prophet ﷺ, and praising Allah ﷻ, or reciting Qur'an if you don't know *duʿā.*[73] If you don't know how to recite Qur'an or *duʿā,* you can make *duʿā* in any language, or you can make *tasbīḥ* of "*Subḥānallāh, alḥamdulillāh, lā ilāha illa 'Llāh, Allāhu Akbar.*" It is recommended not to talk unless it is necessary, like if something happens.

Q: What if I lose my *wuḍū* during *ṭawāf*?

A: If someone loses their *wuḍū,* many *fatwās* state that because it is so crowded, you continue your *ṭawāf,* even if you lose your *wuḍū*. It would be extremely dangerous with perhaps a half-million people in that big circle, all pushing, if many stopped to go make *wuḍū*. So, the majority legal consensus is that you should continue your *ṭawāf* until completed.

Q: If I am separated from my husband during *ṭawāf,* what should I do?

A: If a lady loses her husband in the crowd, she can continue by herself. There are many women making *ṭawāf* and you can join them, no problem.

Q: Are we restricted from using skin care or cosmetic products?

A: Some people are asking whether they can use Vaseline during Hajj (as a moisturizer or sunscreen). It is okay, no problem, as long as it is not perfumed and that you use it out of necessity, not luxury. Those who are very sensitive to the sun can use sunscreen that is unscented, like Vaseline. During Hajj everyone must use unscented soap, like olive oil soap. In Madinah you can find all this before going to Mecca, if you don't want to carry it from here.

Q: What if I (lady) am making *ṭawāf* and *adhān* is called?

---

[73] The Prophet ﷺ said, "Circling around the House is like prayer, except that you speak during it. Whoever speaks during it, let him speak nothing but goodness." (Tirmidhī) Tirmidhī said, "This is practiced by the majority of scholars, that it is recommended for a man not to speak during circumambulation except for a need, to mention Allah, or to spread knowledge."

A: Everyone is side by side in the *ṭawāf* circle, so of course if that happens, stay where you are and pray later, unless you find an easy way to get to the womens' section and pray; otherwise just back up and pray. You may also continue your *ṭawāf* as it is considered a prayer, and after you complete the *ṭawāf* you can make the prayer by yourself. However, sometimes the security will not let you continue *ṭawāf* as the *Īmām* and *jama'ah* are praying, so in that case stop your *ṭawāf*, pray, and continue your *ṭawāf* afterwards. Between the *sunnah* and *farḍ* you can continue doing *ṭawāf*, but at the time of *farḍ* they may stop everyone from doing *ṭawāf*.

Q: What if a lady completes the first *ṭawāf* but later gets her period; what about the remaining *ṭawāfs*?

A: She will wait until she is able to do that. If she is unable because her period did not end, or because she must travel and cannot remain in Mecca waiting for her period to end, current *fatwās* state that since she must leave, two *ṭawāfs* are dropped for her. For example, if she completed *Ṭawāf al-Qudūm*, Ṭawāf of Arrival, then the following are dropped from her religious duty: *Ṭawāf al-Ifādah* (also called *Ṭawāf az-Zīyārah*) and *Ṭawāf* al-Wada', *Ṭawāf* of Departure. If she did *Ṭawāf al-Qudūm*, but she cannot do the last two after *Yawm an-Nahr*, the Day of Sacrifice ('Eid al-Aḍḥā), then she should wait until she is able to do so. However, if her group is traveling and she must leave, the *fatwā* is that it is no problem for her (she gets credit for performing all three *ṭawāfs*) as all actions are by intentions and *ad-darūrāt tubīh al-mahdhūrāt*, "Necessity waives the forbidden (or obligation)."

Q: Some men like to wear a belt over their *iḥrām* (to secure it). As men are discouraged from wearing stitched clothing during the days of Hajj, can they use a stitched belt if an unstitched belt is not available to them?

A: All belts coming from Saudi Arabia in Halal Co are stitched. Mawlana ق said, "Buy what they have at Halal Co and then in Madinah you can buy unstitched belts with buttons"; otherwise, it's okay to use the stitched. The button ones are preferable, but recently *'ulama* gave a *fatwā* that men can wear a stitched belt as it is outside the *iḥrām*. Also, they can use safety pins, or they can tie a rope around their waist; I did that one time. You don't need to have a belt. Also, you can use any kind of elastic, as long as it is not stitched. A stitched belt may be used for necessity, but not for luxury. You can use a belt to secure your money, car keys, etc., or you can keep those items with your wife, if she is with you. Ladies can put what they like.

Q: So as not to be separated, can women hold the upper part of their husband's *iḥrām* while doing *ṭawāf*?

A: Yes, that is no problem. It is also permitted to hold hands so as not to be lost, as long as you are not having desires or crazy thinking.

Q: At Mina, do women cut their hair from the root or the tips?

A: Women cut from the tips of their hair, not from the roots. Hair cut is from the bottom. I searched in Īmām Shafiʿī's *madhhab*, and he said, "from the tips." If they want to cut from the roots, that is preferable, but they will look ugly!

Q: What does one do when a non-*maḥram* (unrelated man) accidentally touches you or you accidentally touch a man during *ṭawāf*?

A: Just continue, as hundreds of men are pushing women and hundreds of women are pushing men. The *tajallī* there removes the desires of worldly life, and you cannot feel that there, like they say the army adds saltpeter in the food (to calm desire). There is a heavenly saltpeter there!

Q: If one breaks *wuḍū* during *ṭawāf* and renews it, does one continue the *ṭawāf* where one left it?

A: Continue from where you stopped or continue from which turn you were in. If you were in the middle of the third turn, then continue at the beginning of the third turn and complete the rest. Someone might have a sickness and constantly lose their *wuḍū*; if they had to go make *wuḍū* and come back and make *ṭawāf* from the beginning, they would never finish! Now everything is permissible, because of the current situation of millions of hajjis making *ṭawāf*. One mistake, one fall and everyone will fall, and:

لاَ يُكَلِّفُ اللهُ نَفْسًا إِلاَّ وُسْعَهَا

Allah does not put a burden on anyone more than he can bear.[74]

---

[74] Sūratu 'l-Baqara, 2:286.

If they can do *ṭawāf* up (on the third floor) that is okay, but the duration is very long; it takes six hours! *Saʿī* (between Ṣafā and Marwa) also has a second floor.

Q: Can we do multiple *ʿUmrah*?

A: If you want that, make your intention before departing from Madinah, "I am doing ʿUmrah Tamattuʿ (not *ʿUmrah maʿ Hajj, ʿUmrah* with Hajj), then do *ʿUmrah*, do *saʿī*, then wear normal clothes for one day, as you only have one day on the seventh; then on the eighth morning put on *iḥrām* because you are in Mecca, you don't need to go out. Then you say, "*Nawaytu 'l-Hajj*," and go for Hajj; that is by itself. That is *ʿUmrah* and *Hajj Tamattuʿ*. That has to be your *nīyyah* from Madinah for *ʿUmrah, ṭawāf* and *saʿī*, and as *qirān* (combined) you say, "*Nawaytu al-ḥajj wa 'l-ʿumrata qirānan* (combined Hajj and *ʿUmrah*). You arrive in Mecca and do *ṭawāf* and *saʿī*, and keep *iḥrām* and go to Mina, ʿArafat, Muzdalifa, then slaughter a lamb, cut your hair and do *Ṭawāf al-Ifadah*, and you are done. You get the same reward as *ʿUmrah* and Hajj. You can make *ʿUmrah* after Hajj, on the days of Mina, by going down to Mecca and to *Miqāt* and take *iḥrām* at the *Masjid* of Sayyidah ʿĀʾishā ☙, which is 60-70 kilometers away. Go there, make your *nīyyah* and come back to Mecca.

Q: Will there be time to visit the Jannat al-Muʿalla, etc.?

A: Yes, if you throw stones at Mina early. It is preferable to throw stones after *zawāl*, after *Ẓuhr*, but there are too many *fatwās* that say you can throw at any time, then go to Mecca and make *ziyārah* of Jannat al-Muʿalla and visit *Jabal an-Nur*, where *waḥīyy* came.

Do not wear pointed turbans (*tajj* under the turban); just wrap something green around a (normal) hat. Be normal.

Q: What is the Correct Manner for Visiting Mecca and Madinah?

A: Keep your anger down, you might always find obstacles because it's a testing place. No bad thoughts, because even the thought there will be written immediately, bad or good. So, in the presence of the Prophet ﷺ make sure you are always in *ṣalāwāt*, praising him; if you are not reading Qurʾan or praying, make sure you are in *ṣalāwāt, awrād* and *dhikr*. Don't waste your time roaming the streets, buying here and there. Everything there is in your country, unless you want Zamzam or something for *barakah*, like dates or beads or something, but people go there and buy gold and this or that, wasting money and time. If you want to buy so as to go back and give some gifts from Madinah or Mecca it's okay, but make sure you're always focusing on *Ḥajar al-Aswad,* the Black Stone or the Happy Stone, especially in Mecca, because the Sulṭān al-Awlīyā is always sitting behind that Stone. So, the reality is that when you are kissing the Black Stone, you are kissing the head of that Sulṭān al-Awlīyā who is sitting there. He is called, *Farḍ al-ʿArsh,* or *Maqām al-Fardānī,* The One Who is Unique, the unique *maqām* is behind that Stone. He is there, his spiritual presence is there with *Ḥajar al-Aswad.*

I heard it from Grandshaykh ʿAbdAllāh ق and Shaykh Nazim ق, when the Prophet ﷺ kissed it, he kissed that Sulṭān! In every time there is a Sulṭān, so he kissed that Sulṭān. That's why when Sayyīdinā ʿUmar ؓ said, "If I didn't see the Prophet kiss you, I would not kiss you, as you are only a stone." And Sayyīdinā ʿAlī ؓ said, "No, he is going to witness for you on the Day of Judgement, *yā* ʿUmar!" So that Sulṭān who is with the Hājar al-Aswad is going to witness for everyone that goes there and kisses and gives their *salāms.* So be careful there and be ready. Prepare yourself not to fight, argue or have anger; be patient, do your prayers and go back to your home.

Q: Will we be able to make *ṭawāf* with you around the Kaʿbah?

A: The message to those who are going to Hajj is, don't say (to me), "I want to be near you and with you." Everyone is free. It is my pleasure and honor to go there by Shaykh Nazim's ق permission and the permission of those who give visas. If you go, you get the *barakah* of those who are going. You can only do *ṭawāf* in small groups and it is impossible to go in one big group as there are two million people making *ṭawāf* and a big group cannot turn (and stay together). So only ten people can do *ṭawāf* together around *Baytu 'Llāh.* It is the same in Madinatu 'l-Munawwarah when visiting *Rawḍat ash-Sharīfah.* Don't put in your mind, "I came because I want to be with you (Shaykh Hisham)." No, you must thank Allah ﷻ that He made you ready to go this year and He brought you, as there is a certain heavenly manifestation for the best of *ḥujjāj* (pilgrims) that we will be part of in that great place! So, we only ask Allah ﷻ to forgive us and grant us to visit His House and His Prophet ﷺ, and that is our only intention. May Allah ﷻ make it true and make it through *bi ḥurmati 'l-Fātiḥah.*

THE NOBLE CITY OF MECCA

"*Every one of the thousands at the airport*
about to leave for Jeddah,
was dressed this way.
You could be a king or a peasant
and no one would know.
Some powerful personages
had on the same thing I had on.
Once thus dressed,
we all had begun intermittently calling out
"Labbayka! (Allahumma) Labbayka!"
Packed in the plane were white, black, brown,
red, and yellow people, blue eyes and blond hair,
and my kinky red hair
—all together, brothers (and sisters)!
All honoring the same God, all in turn giving
equal honor to each other!"

Malik el-Shabazz (Malcolm X)

The Sanctify of Muhammad ﷺ Exceeds the Sanctity of Mecca

Allah ﷻ elevates the greatness of Prophet ﷺ in Sūratu 'l-Balad when He said,

لَآ أُقْسِمُ بِهَٰذَا ٱلْبَلَدِ ۝ وَأَنتَ حِلٌّۢ بِهَٰذَا ٱلْبَلَدِ ۝

What did Allah ﷻ say here at the beginning of Sūratu 'l-Balad – Surah 90? The translation reads: *"I swear by this city."* But, if you speak Arabic you see what is written! What is the literal meaning of *"Lā uqsimu bi hādha 'l-balad"*? "I do not swear by this city." It means, "I do not give an oath by the city."

What is the translation from the Medina version? "I swear by..." But the text is *"Lā uqsimu bi hādha 'l-balad ..."* So the meaning is, "I will not give an oath in that city, since you are there. Rather the priority is to give an oath by you, O Muhammad ﷺ before the city." That is the meaning, under the traditional *tafsīr* of Holy Qur`an. That is the *tafsīr* of Rūhu 'l-Bayān and all other *tafsīrs*. It means, Allah ﷻ placed a condition – that if Prophet ﷺ is in the city, that Allah ﷻ would give the oath by Muhammad ﷺ and not by the city itself. He gave *sharaf*, honor, to Sayyīdinā Muhammad ﷺ by saying *"kayyada 'l-iqsām bil-balad bi qurūnihi 'alayhi 's-salām fīhi hayth qāla lā! Uqsimu bi hādha 'l-balad, wa anta ḥillun bi hādha 'l-balad." "Allah has made conditional giving an oath by the city of Mecca with the presence of* the Prophet ﷺ in the city." If Prophet ﷺ is outside of the city, Allah would not swear by the city. But the translation by Sayyid Muhsin Khan says here, "I swear by the city – And you are free (from sin, to punish the enemies of Islam on the Day of the conquest) in this city, Mecca." The meaning is changed completely.

Thus Allah ﷻ is saying, "If you are in the City, then I make an oath by the City. If you move from the City, I am not giving an oath by it because the honor of the City is by your Presence in it, O Muhammad ﷺ. He put a condition on the oath – swearing by Mecca only if the Prophet ﷺ is in Mecca and if he moves from Mecca, then Allah will not give an oath by that City.

The other scholarly opinion is that the meaning is, "I swear by this City." I'm going to read it differently, then see what is in the translation. *"Lā! Uqsimu bi hādha 'l-balad."* With full stop after *'Lā!'* meaning, "No! I swear by this City… I am confirming that I am swearing by this City." Allah ﷻ is answering the unbelievers, "No!" stating that He cannot swear by this City because that is a city in which fighting is forbidden. No one is allowed to fight in Mecca, especially at the Kaʿbah and in the Ḥaram. There is no way, it is *ḥarām,* forbidden. The only person who was allowed to do what he wanted to do, without any restraint, was the Prophet ﷺ, when he entered victorious, coming back from Medina to Mecca, and Allah said to him, "You can do whatever you like, because the honor, My Honor and Respect, is for you." You are the only one who is allowed to do what you want to do.

And Ibn ʿAbbās ؓ said that *"Lā uqsimu bi hādha 'l-balad"* refers to Mecca, and *"wa anta ḥillun bi hādha 'l-balad,"* means *"Yā* Muhammad ﷺ, you can do whatever you want in Mecca, which I made a sanctified city in which no one has the right to do any fighting whatsoever, but you are the only one who has the right to do whatever you want, according to your judgment, because the honor is for you." So the meaning is, "I keep My oath in this City, and Muhammad may do whatever he wants to do, that City remains holy, because Muhammad ﷺ is holy. Do you understand or not? That city is holy—Mecca. No one can do any fighting in it. So, Allah ﷻ said, "I give permission to Muhammad to fight there—and he is the only one. And if he does do, I am still keeping it Holy, because Prophet ﷺ is permitted to do whatever he likes. Thus, upon the conquest of Mecca, the Muslims killed one person there, who was hanging by the curtains of Kaʿbah, one of the unbelievers, with the Prophet's permission. So even though there was bloodshed in the Kaʿbah, it was only allowed for Prophet ﷺ and no one before him nor anyone after him.

قالَ النبيُّ ﷺ يومَ افْتَتَحَ مَكَّةَ: لا هِجْرَةَ، ولَكِنْ جِهَادٌ ونِيَّةٌ، وإذَا اسْتُنْفِرْتُمْ فَانْفِرُوا، فإنَّ هذا بَلَدٌ حَرَّمَ اللَّهُ يومَ خَلَقَ السَّمَوَاتِ والأرْضَ، وهو حَرَامٌ بحُرْمَةِ اللَّهِ إلى يَومِ القِيَامَةِ، وإنَّه لَمْ يَحِلَّ القِتَالُ فيه لأحَدٍ قَبْلِي، ولَمْ يَحِلَّ لى إلَّا سَاعَةً مِن نَهَارٍ، فَهو حَرَامٌ بحُرْمَةِ اللَّهِ إلى يومِ القِيَامَةِ، لا يُعْضَدُ شَوْكُهُ، ولَا يُنَفَّرُ صَيْدُهُ، ولَا

يَلْتَقِطُ لُقَطَتَهُ إلَّا مَن عرَّفَهَا، ولَا يُخْتَلَى خَلَاهَا. قالَ العَبَّاسُ: يا رَسولَ اللَّهِ، إلَّا الإذْخِرَ، فإنَّه لِقَيْنِهِمْ ولِبُيُوتِهِمْ، قالَ: قالَ: إلَّا الإذْخِرَ.

The Prophet ﷺ said that "Verily Allah made Mecca a sanctified city, forbidden for anyone to fight in it on the Day He created the heavens and the earth, and it remains sanctified by Allah's Sanctity, until Judgment Day. And verily it was never permitted to kill within its precincts to anyone before me and killing was not permitted to me therein except for a single hour of one day, and it is forbidden by Allah's consecration until Judgment Day..."[75]

No one was given to do whatever he wanted in Mecca except Prophet Muhammad ﷺ. No one can even shoot a rabbit. No one can even go hunting in Mecca. But Allah ﷻ allowed His Prophet ﷺ to do whatever he chose, even if it meant to kill someone (by way of retaliation for murder). In this way, Allah is showing the immense respect He gave to His Prophet ﷺ.

ALLAH DESCRIBES THE PROPHET'S Y POWER OF WITNESSING

Allah ﷻ says in Sūratu 'l-Fīl:

أَلَمْ تَرَ كَيْفَ فَعَلَ رَبُّكَ بِأَصْحَٰبِ ٱلْفِيلِ

Alam tara kayfa fa'la Rabbuka bi aṣ-ḥābi 'l-fīl

Have you (O Muhammad ﷺ) not seen how your Lord dealt with the owners of the elephant?[76]

Here Allah ﷻ is addressing Prophet ﷺ in this first verse of the Surah. What do we understand from this? The Prophet ﷺ was born 55 days after the incident of the elephant, but the tone of this text indicates that Allah is saying that the event passed directly before the Prophet's ﷺ witnessing eyes. "Have you not seen?" This is a rhetorical question, the assumption behind it is that of course he did see it, and the purpose is to emphasize

[75] Bukhārī and Muslim.

[76] Sūratu 'l-Fīl, 105:1.

its significance. How could the Prophet ﷺ have seen it when he was born 55 days later? It means the Prophet ﷺ was given to see when he was in the womb of his mother! He was able to see what happened to the Abraha who came to destroy the Kaʿbah.

Allah ﷻ sends us a hint of the knowledge of the Prophet ﷺ by mentioning this event in relation to the Prophet's ﷺ witnessing of it. He is showing Muslims, past and present, that He gave knowledge of that event to His Prophet ﷺ, while no ordinary man could have had knowledge of the event from the womb of his mother.

Our belief, as *Āhl as-Sunnah wa 'l-Jamaʿah* is that Prophet Muhammad ﷺ could see also when he was only a seed in the back of his father ʿAbdAllāh. Even in the time of all his ancestors he could see—from the times of Sayyīdinā Ibrāhīm ﵇, Isma'il ﵇ and even further back—from the time that he was a light in the forehead of Adam ﵇ and even before Adam ﵇ was born he was able to see, because as he ﷺ said,

كُنْت نَبِيًّا وَآدَمُ بَيْنَ الْمَاءِ وَالطِّينِ

"I was a prophet when Adam was between water and clay."[77]

That is enough to establish for every one of today's scholars that the Prophet ﷺ is not just a message deliverer who came, gave his message and left. If he was just here as a delivery person, then how was he able to see from the womb of his mother—the existence of his special sight means that not only the message but also the Messenger ﷺ was a keeper of Divine Light.

IMPORTANCE OF THE EVENT

When they see something strange, people say, "Didn't you see what happened?!" They say this to emphasize the greatness of the event.

By saying *alam tara*, "Have you not seen," Allah ﷻ is indicating the immensity of this incident, that something magnificent happened by asking, "Have you not seen?" At the same time Allah is telling Prophet

---

[77] While this famous wording is not considered a hadith it reflects the meaning of a *ḥasan saḥīḥ gharīb* hadith in Tirmidhī where Abū Hurayrah ؓ asked the Prophet ﷺ when he became a prophet and the Prophet ﷺ replied, "I was a prophet when Adam was between soul and body."

ﷺ, "O Muhammad, did you see how immense this event was?" This is to show also that what happened was beyond the capacity of the mind. There is no way to describe it, it must be seen. That is Allah's Action. It is not like the action of human beings. No one else can do what Allah is referring to when He says, *"Have you not seen, (O Muhammad) how Allah dealt with the Owners of the Elephant?"*

Scholars say that through this story Allah ﷻ wants us to know the greatness of Sayyīdinā Muhammad ﷺ—that he was given power before he was born to see, by *mushāhada*, to witness, from the womb of his mother, what was happening to Abraha. In fact we as *Āhlu 's-Sunnah wa 'l-Jama'ah* believe that Allah ﷻ created this *dunyā*—which does not weigh as much as the wing of a mosquito in the Eyes of Allah—for the sake of the Prophet ﷺ and that in the Kalimat ash-Shahāda, the phrase *Muḥammadun Rasūl Allāh* ﷺ represents the whole creation. *Lā ilāha illa 'Llāh* references the Creator and *Muḥammadun Rasūl Allāh* references the creation. So it may be that Muhammad ﷺ, from the womb of his mother, was directing the birds when they killed Abraha and his people like a commander in chief or the general of an army.

In his *tafsīr* *Rūhu 'l-Bayān*, Shaykh Isma'īl Hakkī says, "This shows you the greatness of Allah's Power and His perfect knowledge and wisdom, and the honor He gave to His house and the honor that He gave to His Prophet ﷺ." He described this event as belongs to *irhāsāt* which are miracles that occur before a prophet is honored by Allah with that miraculous power.

Another example of *irhāsāt* is that before Prophet ﷺ was ordered to deliver the message, he used to have a shade, *ghamāma*, above him to shade him from the sun. Wherever he used to walks, a cloud would move above him – and that's why they call one mosque Masjidi 'l-Ghamāma in Madinatu 'l-Munawwarah. He was able to hear *tasbīḥu 'l-ḥajar* – the stones praising Allah ﷻ. Everywhere he walked in Makkatu 'l-Mukarramah he ﷺ was able to hear the *tasbīḥ* of the mountains, praising Allah ﷻ. So many extraordinary things (*irhās*) happened before the Prophet's ﷺ *bi'tha*—before he was ordered to deliver the message.

THE HOLY KA'BAH

"*I stood in the Presence*
and asked for love and longing.
Those who stand in the Presence
will be dressed with beauty.
I stood in the Presence
and faced the Ka'bah!
Turn toward the Ka'bah
so you can take beauty
and all troubles
and ugliness will leave you!"

Shaykh Nazim Adil al-Haqqani ق

SHAYKH HISHAM STANDING IN THE PRESENCE OF THE HOLY KAʿBAH, HAJJ 2011.

The Kaʿbah, also known as *Baytu 'Llāh*, the House of Allah, is the first house built for humanity to worship Allah ﷻ. It functions as the Qiblah, the direction to which all Muslims pray five times a day. Directly above the Kaʿbah, at its zenith, there is a corresponding place in the Heavens called the *Bayt al-Maʿmūr*, which holds the same status there as the Kaʿbah does here on Earth. Allah ﷻ said:

إِنَّ أَوَّلَ بَيْتٍ وُضِعَ لِلنَّاسِ لَلَّذِي بِبَكَّةَ مُبَارَكًا وَهُدًى لِّلْعَالَمِينَ

فِيهِ آيَاتٌ بَيِّنَاتٌ مَّقَامُ إِبْرَاهِيمَ وَمَن دَخَلَهُ كَانَ آمِنًا وَلِلَّهِ عَلَى النَّاسِ حِجُّ

الْبَيْتِ مَنِ اسْتَطَاعَ إِلَيْهِ سَبِيلاً وَمَن كَفَرَ فَإِنَّ اللهَ غَنِيٌّ عَنِ الْعَالَمِينَ

Most surely the first house appointed for men is the one at Bakkah, blessed and a guidance for the worlds. In it are clear signs, the standing place of Ibrāhīm; and whoever enters it shall be secure; and for the sake of Allah, pilgrimage to the House is incumbent upon men, (upon) everyone who can afford the journey to it, and whoever disbelieves, then surely Allah is Self-sufficient (independent) of the worlds.[78]

[78] Sūrat Āli ʿImrān, 3:96-97.

The Origin of the Kaʿbah

Hajjah Amina Adil

The Lord took from Paradise one red ruby stone and placed it where now the Kaʿbah stands (in Mecca). It was also shaped like the Kaʿbah. There were in it two doors of emerald, one facing East and the other facing West. Inside, were many lamps from the lights of Paradise. The Lord ordered all men to circumambulate this house, just like the heavenly angels circumambulate His Throne. Ādam ﷺ set out to perform this circumambulation. Before he began, the angels brought the Stone which is now known as *Ḥajar al-Aswad* (the Black Stone), only then it was radiant and white, and rays emanated from it that were as bright as the rays of the sun or the moon. Every place reached by these rays falls within the *Mīqāt* of the *Ḥaram* (boundaries within which pilgrims are required to don *iḥrām*—the special garb of pilgrimage). Later, this white Stone turned black, due to the sins of Mankind, as it is found today in the building of the Kaʿbah.

This house was called the *Bayt al-Maʿmūr*, and it remained on Earth until the time of Nūḥ's flood. When the flood was decreed, the Lord had the angels raise the *Bayt al-Maʿmūr* up to the fourth heaven, or perhaps it was the seventh heaven, because on the night of the Miʿrāj the Holy Prophet ﷺ saw the angels circumambulating it in that heaven. It is there today, and the angels make *tawāf* around it. It is exactly the same as the Kaʿbah in Mecca and directly above it. If it should fall it would occupy exactly the same space, but it will not fall or come to Earth again.

When the flood of Nūḥ ﷺ was about to be unleashed, the mountain of Abū Qubays spoke up and said, "O Lord, entrust the Black Stone to me, I will look after it as if it were my own soul." So, the Black Stone was given to Mt. Abū Qubays as a trust, and it was the only part of the *Bayt al-Maʿmūr* left on Earth during the flood. Mt. Abū Qubays is a mountain overlooking the *Ḥaram* of Mecca, and it hid the Stone within itself.

One day Ibrāhīm ﷺ received the Command from his Lord to rebuild the House of the Lord (*Baytu 'Llāh*) in the place where the *Bayt al-Maʿmūr* once had stood on Earth. He and Ismāʿīl ﷺ were to complete the task but they knew not the exact spot where it had stood on. How was Ibrāhīm ﷺ

to find the place in the midst of all the sands of the desert? When the Lord commanded him to erect the Kaʿbah, He sent the angel Jibrīl عليه السلام who pointed to the spot with the tip of his wing, and a cloud hovered above. From the cloud fell a gentle rain, the rain of Mercy as if to cleanse the earth where this holy shrine was to be rebuilt.

When Ibrāhīm عليه السلام wished to begin building the Kaʿbah, Jibrīl عليه السلام was sent to fetch the Stone. The mountain cried and complained to the Lord and was loath to give up its treasure. But Jibrīl عليه السلام took it, and they included it in their building.

They made the mortar with water from the Zamzam well, and they worked until they had roofed the building. Then they sat down to rest awhile and had yet to clean away the rubble left from the work and to sweep the holy precincts, when suddenly there arose a strong wind, like a cyclone, which carried away all the left-over building materials, all the mud, straw, and stone laying about the building site. These bits were blown up into the skies and distributed all over the earth. Wherever any of these pieces landed, a large or small mosque was later built, depending on the size of the debris that fell on it. This is why all the mosques in the world are called *Baytu 'Llāh,* which means, "House of God" after the original *Baytu 'Llāh,* the Kaʿbah.

Ibrāhīm عليه السلام then taught the people there all the rites of the Hajj (the Pilgrimage), as it had been revealed to him. He taught them to perform the *ṭawāf* (circumambulation of the Kaʿbah) seven times, the Sāʿī (running) between the hills of Ṣafā and Marwa, as Hājar had run between these hills in search of water. They stood at ʿArafāt where Ādam عليه السلام had been re-united with Ḥawwā, and they collected stones from the plains of Muzdalifah. Then they went on to Minā and threw the stones at three pillars representing Shayṭān, as Ismāʿīl عليه السلام had actually stoned the Devil in that place. To this very day pilgrims perform these same rites as they were taught by our father Ibrāhīm عليه السلام.

After the Hajj was completed Ibrāhīm عليه السلام returned to his own country, and Ismāʿīl عليه السلام remained at Mecca. Ibrāhīm عليه السلام traveled northwards and looked out over the land from the top of a mountain, towards the lands of Syria and Palestine, and he saw a vision of green and watered fields, palm groves and pleasant gardens, and he prayed to the Lord:

وَإِذْ قَالَ إِبْرَاهِيمُ رَبِّ اجْعَلْ هَـٰذَا بَلَدًا آمِنًا وَارْزُقْ أَهْلَهُ مِنَ الثَّمَرَاتِ مَنْ
آمَنَ مِنْهُم بِاللهِ وَالْيَوْمِ الآخِرِ

And when Ibrāhīm said, "My Lord, make this a land secure, and provide its people with fruits, such of them as believe in Allah and the Last Day.... [79]

Thus Ibrāhīm ﷺ prayed for his progeny to be blessed and to be amply provided for.

وَإِذْ يَرْفَعُ إِبْرَاهِيمُ الْقَوَاعِدَ مِنَ الْبَيْتِ وَإِسْمَاعِيلُ رَبَّنَا تَقَبَّلْ مِنَّا إِنَّكَ
أَنتَ السَّمِيعُ الْعَلِيمُ رَبَّنَا وَاجْعَلْنَا مُسْلِمَيْنِ لَكَ وَمِن ذُرِّيَّتِنَا أُمَّةً مُّسْلِمَةً
لَّكَ وَأَرِنَا مَنَاسِكَنَا وَتُبْ عَلَيْنَآ إِنَّكَ أَنتَ التَّوَّابُ الرَّحِيمُ

And when Ibrāhīm and Ismāʿīl with him, raised up the foundations of the House: "Our Lord, receive this from us; You are the All-hearing, the All-knowing; and, our Lord, make us submissive to You, and of our seed a nation submissive to You; and show us our holy rites, and turn towards us; Surely You are the Accepting of repentance, the Merciful." [80]

A year later Ibrāhīm ﷺ returned with his wife Sārah and Isḥāq ﷺ and together with Hājar and Ismāʿīl ﷺ they all performed the Hajj.

At the Kaʿbah they rested and prayed, and they all prayed for the Nation of Muhammad ﷺ, Ibrāhīm ﷺ prayed for the old among that nation, Ismāʿīl ﷺ interceded for those of middle age. Isḥāq ﷺ prayed for the young, Sārah for the free-born women, and Hājar for the slaves and servants. The Lord accepted all their prayers.

---

[79] Sūratu 'l-Baqara, 2:126.

[80] Sūratu 'l-Baqara, 2:127-128.

The Best Place of Prayer on Earth

Shaykh Muhammad Hisham Kabbani

O Muslims! What is the best place in the whole world to pray? It is where Allah ﷻ said to us, "When you want to pray, face Kaʿbatu'Llāh in Mecca."

قَدْ نَرَى تَقَلُّبَ وَجْهِكَ فِى السَّمَاءِ فَلَنُوَلِّيَنَّكَ قِبْلَةً تَرْضَاهَا فَوَلِّ وَجْهَكَ شَطْرَ الْمَسْجِدِ الْحَرَامِ وَحَيْثُ مَا كُنتُمْ فَوَلُّواْ وُجُوهَكُمْ شَطْرَهُ

We have certainly seen the turning of your face, [O Muhammad], toward the heaven, and We will surely turn you to a qiblah with which you will be pleased. So, turn your face toward al-Masjid al-Ḥarām. And wherever you [Believers] are, turn your faces toward it [in prayer][81]

Allah ﷻ called Kaʿbah "*Baytu 'Llāh,*" The House of Allah. When you pray there, you are praying in His House. And Allah ﷻ gave Hajj as a reward for all humanity when He ordered Sayyīdinā Ādam ﷺ to build a House for Him on Earth, so people know how and where to worship. Then, Sayyīdinā Ibrāhīm ﷺ built it back with his son, Sayyīdinā Ismaʿīl ﷺ. Until today people are going to that Heavenly House, a piece of Paradise that Allah ﷻ sent to Earth. One *ṣalāt* there equals to 100,000 *ṣalāt*. For example, if you pray Fajr there, it is as if you prayed

SHAYKH HISHAM AND HAJJAH NAZIHA BEFORE THE KAʿBAH, ʿUMRAH 2020.

[81] Sūratu 'l-Baqara, 2:144.

100,000 Fajr prayers; if you pray Ẓuhr, it is as if you prayed 100,000 Ẓuhr prayers, and it is the same for the other prayers. That means, Allah ﷻ will write for you 100,000 prayers for every prayer you pray in Mecca and Madinah. So that is why it is important for people to pray in *Ḥaram al-Makkī* and *Ḥaram al-Madanī*, as it will save them from Hellfire and take them to Paradise.

A university or high school student takes an exam at the end of the year and is given a certificate that he was successful and gets a passing grade, and the student cries tears of joy! Similarly, we should also cry tears of joy because of what Allah ﷻ is giving us of rewards, all because of our beloved Sayyīdinā Muhammad ﷺ! These are the rewards for Allah's ﷻ House, and the real house is *Bayt al-Maʿmūr* in the Fourth Paradise.

On the other hand, every *masjid* is a House of Allah ﷻ:

فِى بُيُوتٍ أَذِنَ اللَّهُ أَن تُرْفَعَ وَيُذْكَرَ فِيهَا اسْمُهُ يُسَبِّحُ لَهُ فِيهَا بِالْغُدُوِّ وَالْآصَالِ

(Lit is such a light) in houses that Allah permitted to be raised to honor (and) for the celebration in them of His Name. In them is He glorified in the mornings and in the evenings, (again and again).[82]

By coming to the *masjid*, you are coming to Allah's House. Don't think you are not getting rewards. No matter who speaks, your presence in the *masjid* is what brings the rewards. Allah ﷻ has ordered His Name to be raised up, and today we are coming to a *masjid*, and by His Will, Allah ﷻ made it into a *masjid* in which His Name is raised up and remembered. It means, Allah made this mosque from the Day of Promises to be one to which people will come and remember His Name through *dhikrullāh*.

---

[82] Sūrau 'n-Nūr, 24:36.

Who Inhabits the Holy House?

Shaykh Muhammad Hisham Kabbani

We understand that we run to the Prophet's Mosque in Madinatu 'l-Munawarrah, because Sayyīdinā Muhammad ﷺ is there. What about the Holy Kaʿbah in Makkatu 'l-Mukarramah? There must be someone who is making us run there. We say, "It is the House of Allah ﷻ," and we direct our face toward it, but Allah ﷻ said to the Holy Prophet ﷺ:

مَا وَسِعَنِي أَرْضِي وَلَا سَمَائِي، وَلَكِن وَسِعَنِي قَلْبُ عَبْدِي الْمُؤْمِنِ .

Neither My Heavens nor My Earth contain Me, but the heart of My Believing Servant contains Me.[83]

Isn't the Holy Kaʿbah part of Heavens and Earth? Of course, it is, and Allah ﷻ also said in a Holy Hadith, *qalb al-mu'min bayt ar-Rabb,* "The heart of the Believer is the House of the Lord." You have a House in your heart, but you have to be a Believer in order to see it; you have to be in a race, a struggle against Shayṭān to remove these veils to see.

That *Baytu 'Llāh* in your heart is a duplicate of Kaʿbatu 'Llāh in Mecca! That is to make sure that your home becomes *maẓhar tajallīyāt mina 'l-asmā'i wa 'ṣ-ṣiffāt,* "The Light (or appearance) of the Manifestations of Allah's Beautiful Names and Attributes." When your heart is like that, then it is *āmīna,* safe. So, enter your heart, enter your "inn," say "Allah!" and "*lā ilāha illa 'Llāh!*" and then you are safe.

So, Grandshaykh ʿAbdAllāh ق asked, "What is the landmark of the Kaʿbah?" He said, "There is one, known by *Awlīyāullāh,* whom Allah ﷻ called *'Yamīn Allah ʿalā 'l-arḍ,'* the Right Hand of Allah ﷻ on Earth," meaning, Allah's Power on Earth, as Ibn ʿAbbās ؓ said in a Hadith:

عَن ابْن عَبَّاس رَضِى الله عَنهُ انه قَالَ: الْحجر الْأسود يَمِين الله فِي الأَرْض

يُصَافح بهَا عباده أَو قَالَ خلقه كَمَا يُصَافح النَّاس بَعضهم بَعْضً

[83] Hadith *Qudsī, Al-Iḥyā* of al-Ghazālī.

Indeed, Ḥajar al-Aswad, the Black Stone is Allah's Right Hand on Earth; through it He shakes hands with His servants.[84]

Ḥajar al-Aswad is the *Walī*'s window to Paradise; he is always present, sitting at that corner, and when *Awlīyāullāh* visit, they see him! So, Allah ﷻ dressed him in that dress.

Today, you see the army standing there to move people because it is too crowded. Grandshaykh ق said, "If that *Walī*'s presence was not there, no one would come! His presence is like a magnet attracting millions of people around the world. He looks at the Preserved Tablets and sees whose names are written to come that year, and then sends inspiration to their hearts to perform Hajj. That is his duty."

Don't say, "O, this is too much!" You didn't hear anything yet! This is like the ABCs in kindergarten. When Mahdī ؑ comes, there will be knowledge that has never been heard before.

So, he said, "When someone's name is mentioned on the Preserved Tablets as destined to make Hajj that year, the *Walī* who is present there sends a message to his heart," just as today they send an SMS. If someone in the East is able to send someone in the West a message by hitting a key, a *Walī* cannot do that? Can he not send a message to the heart? As soon as he sends the message, he calls them. He is like a magnet; everything runs to him. He is the governor of Mecca, the hidden, spiritual one!

We are not yet speaking about his *maqām*, station, as we will leave that for later, but at that time Grandshaykh ق added, "I am that one whom the Prophet ﷺ gave that specialty to be present at that spot at *Ḥajar al-Aswad*, and I am dressing that to Shaykh Nazim ق as my successor! Without that presence, no one will go there." What kind of a *maqām* or level Allah ﷻ gave, we will leave alone.

---

[84] Ibn Qutayba in Gharīb al-Ḥadīth.

SHAYKH HISHAM GREETING HĀJAR AL-ASWAD AND THE KAʿBAH, ʿUMRAH 2020.

GREETING THE HOLY KAʿBAH

According to the *sīrah* of the Prophet ﷺ and all other prophets, *Bayt al-Maʿmūr* is the Kaʿbah in the Fourth Heaven, and its reflection on Earth is in Makkatu 'l-Mukarramah.

The Kaʿbah is not mute, it can hear and speak. Grandshaykh ʿAbdAllāh ق said, "If you give *salāms* to the Kaʿbah, it will answer you back, saying, *'Wa ʿalaykum as-salām, yā ʿAbdAllāh.'* If you don't hear that, it means you need to progress in your *ʿibādah*." The way you know your Hajj is accepted is when you give *salām* to the Kaʿbah and it answers back to you. He said, "I went for Hajj ten times and gave *salām* to the Kaʿbah ten times, but only once Kaʿbah returned my *salām*."

When you say, "*As-salāmu ʿalayka, yā Baytu 'Llāh,*" and the Kaʿbah replies, "*Wa ʿalayka 's-salām yā ʿAbdAllāh,*" at that time you will know the true meaning of *ṭarīqah*, shaykhs, guides, Sahabah ﷺ, and you will understand the meaning of the Prophet ﷺ. When *Baytu 'Llāh*, the House of Allah ﷻ, returns your *salām*, that means your name is written in that House; your *salāms* were returned and now you are welcome into that House, you are now at the rank to enter. It is not like those who enter it today in order to clean it. No, they are only seeing four walls.

When you receive that blessing, you will not see four walls, but rather it will be a Paradise, like *Ākhirah*; everything you can imagine in Paradise, you will find there. It is described in the Holy Qur'an, but it cannot be described by words. Only those who receive the *salām* of the Holy Kaʿbah will understand *Maʿrifatu 'Llāh*, Knowledge in Allah ﷻ.

How many of us went for Hajj, but did we hear the *salām* of *Baytu 'Llāh*? All of these people who go, two or three million people, did they hear the *salām*? Grandshaykh ق said, "If you did not hear the *salām*, your Hajj is rejected," not rejected from fulfilling your obligation, as you will be written as one who completed the Fifth Pillar of Islam, but rejected from seeing *Ma'rifatu 'Llāh*, and the one who is blind in this life is blind in the Next Life.

He ق said, "How will you hear the Ka'bah sending *salām* to you when you are deeply inside *ghadab*, anger?" When you are deeply engulfed in anger, in the material life and in the bad whisperings of Shayṭān, how are you going to hear the heavenly voice that Ka'bah brings to you? It is impossible! It is blocked.

Allah ﷻ said in the Holy Qur'an:

فَمَن يَعْمَلْ مِثْقَالَ ذَرَّةٍ خَيْرًا يَرَهُ

Whoever does one atom of goodness will see it.[85]

One atom of good work in the Way of Allah ﷻ is considered pilgrimage and it will open the *salām* of Ka'bah. However, not hearing the *salām* means what we are doing is blended with hidden *shirk*, which is what the Prophet ﷺ feared most for his Ummah. That is what disrupts our journey. Allah ﷻ said, "Whoever does one atom of goodness will see it." Why are we not seeing good? Because we are not able to achieve even one atom of goodness. How do you want to become a *Walī* then? People consider themselves *Awlīyāullāh* or a big shaykh and yet we cannot achieve an atom of good.

Grandshaykh ق said, "The angels are under a big responsibility to make sure you will be rewarded for that atom of goodness," and angels cannot make any mistakes when they are under a responsibility. Yet, we are not seeing or feeling that; when we do an atom, it will open, and we will feel and see. That is who *Awlīyā* are reaching.

So, what is the resolution when we are doing works with hidden *shirk*, polytheism? Allah ﷻ says:

---

[85] Sūratu 'z-Zalzalah, 99:7.

إِلَّا مَن تَابَ وَءَامَنَ وَعَمِلَ عَمَلًا صَٰلِحًا فَأُوْلَٰٓئِكَ يُبَدِّلُ ٱللَّهُ سَيِّـَٔاتِهِمْ حَسَنَٰتٍ

Except for those who repent, believe and do righteous work.
For them Allah will replace their evil deeds with good.[86]

Allah ﷻ will change their evil deeds into rewards! Every atom of good *ʿamal,* deed, has its nearness to the Divine Presence; every good action has engraved in it a divine presence according to that atom of goodness. According to that atom, there is a light, perhaps a very small one, but there must be a divine presence that opens from that *ʿamal*. Slowly, one after another, they increase and that will open to *Awlīyāullāh.*

To Speak with the House of Allah is an Obligation!

So, Grandshaykh, may Allah bless his soul, said, "The first thing we have to do when we go to Kaʿbah to perform Hajj, *ʿUmrah,* or prayer, is to give our *salām* to the Holy Kaʿbah, saying, *"As-salāmu ʿalayka, yā Kaʿabatu 'Llāh! As- salāmu ʿalayka, yā Ḥajar al-Aswad! As-salāmu ʿalayka, yā Baytu 'Llāh!"* As we said before, *Awlīyāullāh* hear a response coming back, saying, *"Wa ʿalayka 's-salām, yā* ʿAbdAllāh!" Where is that *salām* coming from? It is coming from the House of Allah ﷻ and from *Ḥajar al-Aswad.*

Grandshaykh ق said, "Receiving a *salām* from the Holy Kaʿbah is not like receiving a *salām* from you and me. Even if you do not hear it, *Awlīyāullāh* hear, so you must still give it. Whether you hear or not, Kaʿbah will answer you, an answer coming from Heavens, carrying all power of Jannah with it!"

Bayt al-Maʿmūr is the Heavenly Kaʿbah in the Fourth Heaven where the Prophet ﷺ prayed when he went to *Isrā' wa 'l-Miʿrāj,* the Night Journey and Ascension to the Divine Presence on the 27th of Rajab. That *salām* is coming from there! That means, you have already been put in the Fourth Heaven; you have established the first step in Heaven. That is why the Fifth Pillar of Islam, Hajj, is very important, not because you go there to go up and down from Mecca to ʿArafat, but there are secrets that have been carried along all the way. One of these secrets is that Allah ﷻ wants

[86] Sūratu 'l-Furqān, 25:70.

to give those who go for Hajj or *'Umrah* or to pray there to be established in the Fourth Heaven! Allah's Mercy is big and huge. That is why, it is a *fard*, an obligation, to speak with the Holy Ka'bah and say, *"As-salāmu 'alayka, yā Ka'batu 'Llāh!"*

Some people who don't know ask, "Why are you talking to it? It doesn't hear or speak." When Sayyīdinā 'Umar ؓ was kissing the Black Stone, the Happy Stone, he said, "You don't give harm or benefit. If I didn't see the Prophet ﷺ kissing you, I would never kiss you." Today people are dying to kiss the Black Stone. What did Sayyīdinā 'Alī ؓ respond to Sayyīdinā 'Umar ؓ, as reported by Ibn 'Asākir ؓ? He said, "Don't say that, O 'Umar! That Stone is going to witness for you on Judgment Day that you made the *Shahādah* there." And Sayyīdinā 'Umar ؓ said, "Sayyīdinā 'Alī ؓ saved me in two places in my life," and that was one of them. So, knowledge changes in different times and places, and you have to keep looking at *Ḥajar al-Aswad* or to the Ka'bah when praying there.

Allah Protects His Holy House

Shaykh Muhammad Hisham Kabbani

Abraha lived in the time of Najāshī (the Negus). He left Habasha (Abyssinia) and went to Yemen. And in Yemen he heard that in Mecca there is a place that people go for pilgrimage to a house that is called the House of Allah ﷻ where people worship idols. He became very jealous as he was the strongest ruler in the Arab area. He built a huge cathedral in which the ceiling was gold and the floor was gold and he wanted people to make pilgrimage to his place. And yet people were continuing to go to that simple place for pilgrimage. He had built that huge church, and no one was coming there to worship.

He got jealous. He said, "Whose is that small square building? Compared to my temple it is nothing. They go there and don't come to me. I am going to teach them a lesson."

What did he do? He prepared a huge army. What did Allah ﷻ call it in *Sūrat al-Fīl*? He didn't call it anything but *fīl*, elephant. What is the significance of the *fīl*? It is to show something that is huge and well-equipped, something that cannot be conquered, a huge power. That is why Allah ﷻ called it *Sūrat al-Fīl*, to attract our attention.

The problem is we read Holy Qur'an and we don't look into the meanings. How many times do people read the Qur'an, passing through the meanings without understanding? Ask the *huffāẓ*. Where are the *ʿibar*, lessons, to take from it. We aren't taking benefit because we read it like a history book.

Allah ﷻ wanted to show us an *ʿibra*, a lesson, in Sūratu 'l-Fīl.

Abraha said, "Why are those people visiting that 30x30 foot room and not visiting this huge church? I will go and teach them a lesson," and he sent his whole huge army to Mecca.

He sent that whole army with elephants, which he collected from all over the world, *murtazaqa,* mercenaries, buying them with money, sending them to fight. In Īmām as-Suyūṭī's *tafsīr* it is mentioned that they were Indian elephants, the largest in the world, and they were white. Did you ever see white elephants? He brought them to the head of the army. He wanted to show them how well the army is equipped. Who can stand in front of such an army? According to the mind, no one can. So, the people of Mecca came to the grandfather of the Prophet ﷺ and said, "Let us demonstrate."

They said to ʿAbdu 'l-Muṭṭalib, "Are you going to demonstrate or not?" He said, "No."

The grandfather of the Prophet ﷺ said, "No. There is no need. *Inna lil-bayti rabbun yaḥmīh,* "There is for the House a Creator who will protect it."

It means, "That one is on *bāṭil,* and we are on *Ḥaqq*. *Bāṭil* cannot win against *Ḥaqq*. So why are we going to disturb ourselves?"

What happened? Abraha went with that huge army to attack, and he asked the grandfather of the Prophet ﷺ, "Where are your combatants? Don't you intend to fight me?" He said, "For what? I am not responsible except for my camels, cows, and sheep. Give me my camels and cows and sheep that you confiscated. That House is not mine; it belongs to Allah ﷻ. I come here to pray. You want to come? Let me see how clever you are to come against the Owner of the House (*Rabbu 'l-Bayt*)!"

Abraha sent the elephants to the front, but the elephants went onto their knees, not moving. Why? Because those people were believing that the House belongs to Allah ﷻ and that the Creator will take care of their problems, if they truly submit to Allah ﷻ.

Today, Muslims are losing because we are not on the true way of *Ḥaqq,* we are not following the just way. If we were following the right way no one could oppose us.

They said, "This is Allah's ﷻ property, not ours." The elephants went to their knees and would not move. Then, Allah ﷻ sent against them different kinds of birds, as mentioned in the *tafsīr*, filling the horizon. Why did Allah ﷻ say "birds"? Because He ﷻ wanted to show the greatness of the Holy Qur'an. When He sent the Prophet ﷺ as a

Messenger, he ﷺ taught the *Sharīʿah* aspect of Qur'an. He ﷺ did not open to them the scientific aspect of the Holy Qur'an as that was left for the people to discover themselves in the Last Days. Allah ﷻ said:

سَنُرِيهِمْ آيَاتِنَا فِى الآفَاقِ وَفِى أَنفُسِهِمْ حَتَّى يَتَبَيَّنَ لَهُمْ أَنَّهُ الْحَقُّ

We will show them Our Signs in the far horizons."[87]

Sa-nurīhim,"We will show them" is in the future tense. Those who are coming in the future are going to learn about what came in the Holy Qur'an 1400 years ago.

What did He send? Birds. What were they carrying? Three stones each: one in their beaks and two between their claws. According to the traditional commentaries of the Holy Qur'an, such as *Tafsīr ar-Rāzī, ad-Durr al-manthūr, Tafsīr ibn Kathīr, Rūḥ al-maʿanī* and many others, on every stone was written the name of the father, the mother and the person himself for whom that stone was intended to hit. Those stones would not hit anyone but the one whose names were written on them. They were smarter than today's 'smart' bombs. Today they hit each other by mistake but these birds never made a mistake.

From where did those stones come? They came from Hellfire and when they were thrown, they made a red color. The Holy Qur'an was describing these flying stones as showing a red color, and it was said that as these stones were flying, they were also spinning. Today we would describe these as tracer bullets, fired from a high-powered gun.

تَرْمِيهِم بِحِجَارَةٍ مِّن سِجِّيلٍ

فَجَعَلَهُمْ كَعَصْفٍ مَّأْكُولٍ

Striking them with stones of baked clay.

And made them like green crops devoured (by cattle)?[88]

Allah ﷻ caused that army to disintegrate like something that has been eaten. The people were killed but the Kaʿbah was left untouched. It did

[87] Sūrah Fuṣṣilat, 41:53.

[88] Sūratu 'l-Fīl, 105: 4,5.

not kill the people but rather disintegrated completely, like the leaves when they fall and then disappear. Why did this happen? Because ʿAbdu 'l-Muṭṭalib submitted completely to the Will of Allah ﷻ, saying, "I have no power. You can save it, O my Lord! It is Your House."

See how 1400 years ago Allah ﷻ said in the Qur'an, "I am your Lord. Submit to Me and I will protect you." So, say "*Lā ilāha il-Llāh*" and no one can hurt you; Allah ﷻ will protect you.

Story: An Embrace of the Kaʿbah

Shaykh Muhammad Hisham Kabbani

Shaykh Hisham gazing at Kaʿbah, Hajj 2011.

Shaykh Muhammad al-Maʿsum ق, the twenty-sixth shaykh in the Naqshbandi Golden Chain, narrates the following story:

> When I was in Hajj, I saw the Kaʿbah hugging me and kissing me with great compassion and emotion. Then Allah ﷻ unveiled to me in a vision, lights and blessings coming out of myself and increasing and increasing until they filled up all the deserts, then all the mountains, then the oceans. They then filled up all the universes and they entered every atom of these universes. Then all these atoms were drawn back to the love of the Essence of the Kaʿbah. I saw many spiritual beings, among them angels and saints, all of them standing in my presence as if I was their Sulṭān. Then I received a written letter delivered to me by an angel and written on

it was "From the God of Heavens, Universes and all Creation, I am accepting your pilgrimage!"

THE KAʿBAH IS LOOKING AT YOU, SO LOOK AT HER!

Every Jumuʿah is a good Jumuʿah for us. It is not only once a year, but Allah ﷻ gave us one Jumuʿah every week. As every sincere scholar says, "For the Muslim, every prayer is a Jumuʿah," and every prayer for the Muslim is like Hajj, if it is prayed on time, because you are praying toward the Kaʿbah, and the first thing you do on Hajj is make *ṭawāf* and direct your face towards the Kaʿbah. From here in this *minbar* and from any *minbar*, from any *masjid* around the world making Jumuʿah, let him understand that Kaʿbah is looking at him and he is looking at the Kaʿbah! That is a message that sincere, pious scholars and Awlīyā mentioned many years ago. That is why when you pray in Mecca and you are in the Ḥaram, they tell you to look at the Kaʿbah, even when you are praying. Don't look at your place of *sajdah*, but look at Kaʿbah, because the importance is the Kaʿbah, as it is *Baytu 'Llāh,* Allah's House.

So, every time you say, "*Allāhu Akbar!*" and enter prayer, know that you are looking at the Kaʿbah and the Kaʿbah is looking at you. The *faḍīlah,* benefit of looking at Kaʿbah is like the *faḍīlah* of Hajj: whenever you make the *takbīr* to enter prayer, you get the benefit of Hajj.

THE HEARTS OF *AWLĪYĀULLĀH* ARE THE HOUSES OF ALLAH ﷻ

Allah ﷻ said in a Holy Hadith:

مَا وَسِعَنِى أَرضِى وَلَا سَمَائِى وَلَكِن وَسِعَنِى قَلبِ عَبدِى اَلمُؤمِن

Neither My Heavens nor My Earth contain Me, but the heart of My believing servant contains Me.[89]

Just as the Kaʿbah contains the Light of the Manifestations of Allah's Beautiful Names and Attributes, attracting so many worshippers who come to circumambulate it, Allah ﷻ has placed certain people in different countries who are visited by many to receive guidance and blessings, as He said, "Neither My Heavens nor My Earth contains Me, but the heart

---

[89] Hadith *Qudsī, Al-Iḥyā* of Īmām al-Ghazālī.

of My believing Servant contains Me." Who are the Believers, al-Mu'minoon?

قَالَتِ الْأَعْرَابُ آمَنَّا قُل لَّمْ تُؤْمِنُوا وَلَكِن قُولُوا أَسْلَمْنَا وَلَمَّا يَدْخُلِ الْإِيمَانُ فِي قُلُوبِكُمْ

The desert Arabs say, "We believe." Say, "You have no faith; but you (only) say, 'We have submitted our wills to Allah,' for not yet has faith entered your hearts." Don't say, "We are muʿmin," but say, "We are Muslim," because Īmān did not yet enter the heart.[90]

Allah ﷻ is saying, "Do not say that you are a *mu'min*, as faith has not entered your heart." *Īmān* enters the hearts of sincere servants, which is why the number of *Awlīyāullāh* are limited. As the Prophet ﷺ said:

"The heart of the Believer is the House of the Lord."

As Kaʿbah is the House of Allah ﷻ on Earth and *Awlīyāullāh* are the Qiblah for everyone (as we cannot be guided without their guidance), no matter what you do, there is no way to reach your goal without guidance! The Sahabah ❁ needed the guidance of the Prophet ﷺ, which was not only prayers, fasting and donations, as all of these are obligations: *Shahadah*, praying, fasting, reading Qur'an, etc. are all *farḍ*. However, there is something that is not an obligation but is more important together with the Five Pillars of Islam, according to what the Prophet ﷺ said:

إِنَّما بُعِثتُ لِأُتَمِّمَ مَكارِمَ الأَخلاقِ

I have been sent to perfect the best of conduct (your behavior and character).[91]

The Prophet ﷺ insisted, "I have been sent to perfect and complete your character." The character of a person is more important than anything else. Besides your obligations, you must have good character. In guiding

---

[90] Sūratu 'l-Ḥujurāt, 49:14.

[91] Al-Bazzār.

their followers to have good character, *Awlīyāullāh* are inheritors of Prophet ﷺ.

STORY: THE HEARTS OF *AWLĪYĀULLĀH*

After spending a long time in the Blessed City of the Prophet ﷺ, Shaykh Khalid al-Baghdadi ق, the thirty-first shaykh of the Naqshbandi Golden Chain, narrates the following story:

> I was looking for someone of rare piety in order to take some advice when I saw a shaykh on the right-hand side of the Blessed Gravesite, *Rawḍatu 'sh-Sharīfah*. I asked him to give me advice, counsel from a wise scholar to an ignorant person. He advised me not to object when I enter Mecca to matters which might appear to be counter to the *Sharī'ah*, but to keep quiet. I reached Mecca, and keeping in my heart that advice, I went to the Holy Mosque early on the morning of Friday. I sat near the Ka'bah reading *Dalā'il al-Khayrāt*, when I saw a man with a black beard leaning on a pillar and looking at me. It came to my heart that the man was not showing the proper respect to the Ka'bah, but I didn't say anything to him about the matter. He looked at me and scolded me, saying, "O ignorant one, don't you know that the honor of the heart of a Believer is far more than the privilege of the Ka'bah? Why do you criticize me in your

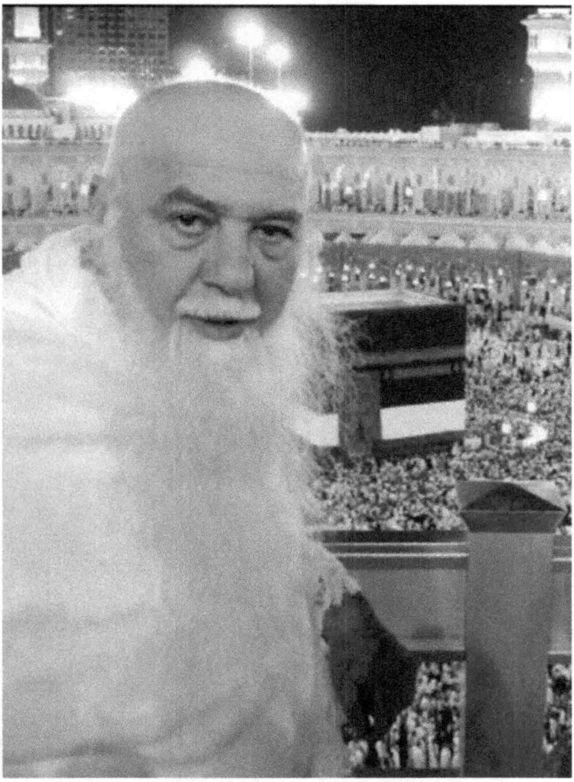

heart for standing with my back to the Kaʿbah and my face to you? Didn't you hear the advice of my shaykh in Madinah who told you not to criticize?" I ran to him and asked his forgiveness, kissing his hands and feet and asking him for his guidance to Allah! He told me, "O my son, your treasures and the keys to your heart are not in these parts, but in India. Your shaykh is there. Go there and he will show you what you have to do." I didn't see anyone better than him in all the Ḥaram!

AERIAL PHOTO OF BELIEVERS FACING THE KAʿBAH DURING PRAYER.

Qiblah: Focal Point of the Circle

Shaykh Muhammad Hisham Kabbani

We are going to mention the importance of *faḍīlat al-ḥalaqah,* the benefits of the circle. Why do they always call it *ḥalaqah,* a circle? Why not rows? Why does it have to be a circle? Because there is a center in the circle; the importance is the center and from the center goes out in radiuses to the circumference of the circle. So, at equal distance it will be reaching everyone, but when you are in rows you are not at the center. There is no center there, they are rows of people.

Allah ﷻ gave us an indication that the *ḥalaqah*, circle, and the center is important. The example is the Kaʿbah, which is in the center; wherever you are praying, if you look at the lines around the Kaʿbah you will see them going in circles. Although when you are standing, you see yourself in a line, but it is not a line, it is a circle. If you look from far, you will see people praying from different sides of the Kaʿbah in circles, and they increase and increase.

Those with a mystic understanding know that the Kaʿbah represents the spiritual pole of this world, around which all creation turns. We can see worshippers moving around it in perfectly arranged concentric circles. This assembly gathers in imitation of the Heavenly Kingdom, for all these circles have one center regardless of their distance from it. At the spiritual level, that center is the Divine Presence. While each worshipper faces the Kaʿbah's walls of stone and mortar, these are not the focus. If we remove the four walls, what do we find? Each person facing someone else! This is a deep and subtle secret that we leave for the reader to ponder.

When the spiritual seeker realizes his station on the circle of the People of the *Qiblah*, he enters what is known as the *dā'irat al-muhibbīn*, Circle of Unconditional Lovers. That is the circle of Muslims at the first level in the way of Allah: the level of love. Such love is not related to any desire, but is a purely platonic, spiritual love between the Believer and his or her Lord. Allah is the center of the circle, and the Believers are each a point on its circumference. Each has his or her own connection to the center. That means, each has his own direction, *Qiblah*, towards the Divine Presence. As that connection becomes apparent to the Believer, that radius becomes like a tunnel into which the seeker begins to step from the circumference of the circle. Upon making his first steps into that tunnel, he begins to discover countless negative characteristics within himself. As he discovers one characteristic after another, he begins to eliminate them, progressing down the tunnel to become a "seeker in the circle of lovers on the spiritual journey," progressing ever nearer to the *Qiblah* at the center.

In the metaphysics of Ibn ʿArabī ق, the renowned mystic scholar, speaks of a spiritual hierarchy in which the emanations from the Divine are received by a single human receptor who is the leader of all these circles of lovers and through him spreads to the rest of humanity, each according to his or her degree or station. This individual represents the Prophet ﷺ in his time as the Perfect Servant of Allah ﷻ. Thus, under one spiritual leader, all are moving constantly closer to the Divine Presence.

In the Sufi understanding, which delves deeply into the mystic knowledge and symbolism of Islam's outward forms, it is said that the Prohibited Mosque represents the heart of the Believer. Thus, the inner direction of prayer is towards the sanctified heart. What is the sanctified heart? At the first level of spirituality, the sanctified heart is the heart that is purified of all wrong thoughts, negativity and dark intent. This level is called 'the Level of the Secret (*Sirr*)'. Once that secret is opened within the sanctified heart, the seeker moves to the heart of the heart, known as 'Secret of the Secret (*Sirr as-sirr*)'. That is the level of purification from any attachment to worldly desires.

Beyond these levels of the heart are 'the Hidden (*Khafā*)' and 'the Innermost (*Akhfā*)' levels, representing further stations of purity, in which the heart becomes ever more removed from attachments, turning away from all that is worldly to focus instead on the spiritual realm of the Hereafter. At the highest level, the heart turns away from even that and begins to focus solely on the Divine Presence.

These are levels of achievement. On the spiritual dimension, the Believer's focus is to reach a perfected level of character, to learn from it and to be enlightened from it. In order to progress beyond our state of ignorance we must strive to learn and educate ourselves. This can only be accomplished by keeping the company of enlightened individuals who have successfully traversed the Path of Allah, to Allah, and who are granted the ability to guide others. As Allah ﷻ says:

يَا أَيُّهَا الَّذِينَ آمَنُواْ اتَّقُواْ اللّهَ وَكُونُواْ مَعَ الصَّادِقِينَ

O you who believe! Fear Allah and be with those who are true (in word and deed).[92]

Allah is aware of every heart. The Holy Qur'an states:

---

[92] Sūratu 't-Tawbah, 9:119.

وَالَّذِينَ جَاهَدُوا فِينَا لَنَهْدِيَنَّهُمْ سُبُلَنَا وَإِنَّ اللَّهَ لَمَعَ الْمُحْسِنِينَ

Those who struggle for Us, We will guide them in the right ways, the ways that are suitable to them.[93]

The polished heart of the sincere and true believer is a receptacle for Allah's Heavenly Lights and Divine Blessings. Such a person is like the sun. When the sun rises, the whole world shines from that source of energy and light, the light of mystical gnosis that makes all things visible. For that reason, the Prophet ﷺ said, "The heart of the (true) Believer is the House of the Lord."

A *Walī* cannot be a *Walī* if he is not inheriting the manifestations of whatever has been manifested on Allah's House, the Kaʿbah; if a *Walī* cannot dress from these manifestations, he cannot take the authority of being a *Walī*, because a *Walī* has to be, *Qiblatuka walīyyuka*, your Qiblah is your *Walī*. I am speaking only about similarity, which means the central focus is your teacher, as when you pray, you are facing the Kaʿbah, your focus is on Allah's House. Also, when sitting in a *dhikr* association the shaykh has to be your focus as he is inheriting the

SUFI DERVISHES STANDING IN A CIRCLE MAKING HADRAH DURING THE OTTOMAN PERIOD (ENGRAVING BY MOURADJEA D'OHSSON).

[93] Sūratu 'l-ʿAnkabūt, 29:69.

Manifestation coming on the Kaʿbah; he is like a focal point for everyone to look at in order to understand and learn from him, and this depends on how much a *Walī* can take. *Awlīyāullāh* say that when you pray here or in any other *masjid*, we must look at the point of *sajdah*, but when you go to Mecca and pray in Masjid al-Ḥarām, the order is to look at Kaʿbah, not at the point of *sajdah*, as that is the House of Allah ﷻ. However, when *Awlīyāullāh* enter their prayers, they are immediately there in front of the Kaʿbah. Not like us, we only see the carpet or floor where we put our head in *sajdah*. That is why, when people are praying you see their eyes going right and left. If your eyes go right or left, your prayers are also going right and left away from you! You must always be looking at the Kaʿbah when you are there, and *Awlīyāullāh* say that looking at the Kaʿbah is better than looking at forty *Awlīyā*, because it is the House of Allah ﷻ, and *Awlīyāullāh* are our central point to which we must focus our gaze.

So, the circle is necessary, and *faḍīlatu 'l-ḥalaqah*, the benefits of an association come from being in a circle; not to be sitting all scattered. People like to sit scattered usually, but if the circle is tightly closed, Shayṭān cannot enter. Did you not notice it: when they do *haḍrah*, Shaykh Nazim ق likes them to stay in a circle? That is the right way, the shaykh will be in the circle and he will send the signals to those in the circle, not in rows as we stand in prayers. So, *dhikrullāh* must always be performed in a circle. Otherwise, we are losing parts of these blessings; evil ones see gaps and enter. Therefore, maintain a tight circle, which becomes a human shield holding the blessings in and not letting them escape.

STANDING IN FRONT OF THE KAʿBAH AT EVERY PRAYER

When you make *sajdah*, make sure your head rests well on the floor as that is the sign of humbleness. Because we are arrogant, Allah ﷻ made us to make *sajdah* to Him, saying, "We are servants and slaves of Allah ﷻ." We have to put three reminders on our forehead: if Allah ﷻ orders something, you have to do it. Allah ﷻ orders you to pray, pay Zakāt, to fast, to make Hajj, to read the *Shahadah*, so you have to do them all.

These five principles of Islam are all embedded in the prayers. When you first enter the prayer, you say, "*Allāhu Akbar*!" facing the *Qiblah*, Kaʿbatu 'Llāh, as if you are on Hajj in *Ḥaram al-Makkī*. If they take away the veils, you will see that indeed you are standing in front of the Kaʿbah! Even if you are in your home, angels will carry you to appear in front of the Kaʿbah, just by you saying, "*Allāhu Akbar*!" That's why you open your hands, as if giving *salāms* to *Ḥajar al-Aswad* and to the Kaʿbah.

However, you will not see it because you are not yet ready, but in reality, they carry you there. You will be in front of the Kaʿbah, which involves *ṭawāf* and all the principles of Hajj. Although you think you are praying at home, you are not, rather, you are there in between the Hands of Allah ﷻ! He is looking to see if you are performing your prayer in a good or bad way. That is why the Prophet ﷺ prohibited to pray like a rooster pecking. You have to be patient and give the *qiyām, sujūd* and *jalsa* their proper time in order for the prayer to be accepted.

ṬAWĀF AROUND THE PROPHET'S ﷺ HEART

Allah ﷻ said in the Holy Qur'an:

وَطَهِّرْ بَيْتِىَ لِلطَّائِفِينَ وَالْقَائِمِينَ وَالرُّكَّعِ السُّجُودِ

Sanctify My House for those who compass it round, or stand up, or bow, or prostrate themselves (therein in prayer).[94]

Allah ﷻ is giving an order to Sayyīdinā Ibrāhīm ﷺ all the way to Sayyīdinā Muhammad ﷺ, to purify His House, saying, *wa ṭahhir*, not only to clean but to purify the status of the House, to make it ready for people to circumambulate it.

Everything is pure, even the mass, which is this physical body that Allah ﷻ created as the house of the soul. The atom is the house, the mass of the electron, and since the mass is pure, the electrons are circumambulating the mass. The electrons will not circumambulate if the mass is not pure, or then everything will be still with no life.

Allah ﷻ made everyone circumambulate around the purified House of Allah ﷻ. The bees circumambulate their queen, birds circumambulate their mother and father, children circumambulate their parents, and Allah ﷻ has made the soul in the body to circumambulate a purified house in the body. That is why Allah ﷻ said "Purify My House" to

---

[94] Sūratu 'l-Ḥajj, 22:26.

Sayyīdinā Ibrāhīm ﷺ and Sayyīdinā Isma'īl ﷺ and all prophets, for the *tāifin*, those who are circumambulating the House and the *'ākifīn*, those who withdrew from *dunyā* or something they like, and everyone likes *dunyā*.

The *'ākifīn* that Allah ﷻ mentions in the Holy Qur'an are those *Awlīyāullāh* who are away, sitting and withdrawing from *dunyā*. The first level of *Awlīyāullāh* are those who are circumambulating in constant motion around the House. Those who are on a lesser level are withdrawing and doing *dhikrullāh*, remembering Allah ﷻ through their hearts, but not circumambulating and standing. The third level are those who are in *ruk'ū* and prostrating in *sujūd*. "*Purify My House*," is meant for those who are in these three categories: those who are circumambulating constantly, who are withdrawn from *dunyā*, sitting, and those who are in *ruk'ū* and *sujūd*.

SHAYKH HISHAM MAKING *ṬAWĀF* AROUND THE KA'BAH, HAJJ 2011.

That message applies to the House of Allah ﷻ. Allah ﷻ made His Angels make *sajdah* to whom? To the Light of Sayyīdinā Muhammad ﷺ that was in the forehead of Sayyīdinā Ādam ﷺ. That is why Īmām Mālik ؓ said to the *amīr* of that time, "Don't turn your face to the Qiblah in Madinah, but turn to the Prophet ﷺ, to the one who took you to Allah's House!" So, turning your face to Prophet ﷺ is the place where *Awlīyāullāh* are circumambulating. The Sahabah ؓ were circumambulating the Prophet ﷺ, as his heart is the House of Allah ﷻ. The revelation of the Message didn't come on the Ka'bah, it came on the heart of the Prophet ﷺ! That heart is what the Prophet ﷺ has given pure for the Ummah to circumambulate.

Awlīyāullāh are inheritors from the Prophet ﷺ, so they have a direction for their *murīds* to run to them, to circumambulate their hearts, as it is the House of Allah ﷻ. As the Prophet ﷺ said, "The heart of the Believer is the House of the Lord." And Allah ﷻ said in the Hadith Qudsī:

> *Neither My Heavens nor My Earth contain Me, but the heart of My Believing Servant contains Me.*[95]

So, your direction is to find one of these purified hearts so you can withdraw from *dunyā* and do *muraqabah* to them and always keep your respect. Then they will take you to the presence of the Prophet ﷺ!

WHY IS *ṬAWĀF* ANTI-CLOCKWISE?

Our Lord is showing us signs to believe in Him, to accept Him and to love Him. Movement is important, which is why all of us are in continuous movement and that movement leads to spirituality. There is nothing in this world that is not moving. How so? Render everything back to its origin. The origin of everything is the Periodic Table. Everything is made from elements and minerals, and they are originally atoms. What do you find in atoms? You find the mass, the electrons, the protons and the neutrons. What are the electrons doing? They are moving anti-clockwise around the mass. There is no way for an atom to exist without an electron moving around the mass. The atom is a combination of mass and energy. Human beings are combination of mass and energy, the soul. If we leave one the other falls down. That is why Allah ﷻ has said, on the tongue of His Prophet ﷺ:

> *My Earth did not contain Me, nor My Heavens, but the heart of My Believing Servant contained Me.*

That is why when you go to Mecca for pilgrimage, *ṭawāf* around the Kaʿbah is anti-clockwise, as the Moon orbits anti-clockwise around the Earth, and the earth orbits anti-clockwise around the Sun. At the Kaʿbah, you are turning around the House of your Lord. If you make your body move in an anti-clockwise way around the House of Allah, which is your

---

[95] Hadith Qudsī, *Al-Iḥyā* of Īmām al-Ghazālī.

heart, then you have established the relationship of the verse, "Those who are remembering their Lord while standing, sitting and lying down, are those who seek His Love and His Mercy!"

الَّذِينَ يَذْكُرُونَ اللهَ قِيَامًا وَقُعُودًا وَعَلَىَ جُنُوبِهِمْ وَيَتَفَكَّرُونَ فِى خَلْقِ السَّمَاوَاتِ وَالأَرْضِ رَبَّنَا مَا خَلَقْتَ هَذا بَاطِلاً سُبْحَانَكَ فَقِنَا عَذَابَ النَّارِ

Those who remember Allah (always, and in prayers) standing, sitting, and lying down on their sides, and think deeply about the Creation of the Heavens and the Earth, (saying),"Our Lord! You have not created (all) this without purpose, glory to You! Give us salvation from the torment of the Fire. [96]

DIRECT YOUR FACE TOWARDS ALLAH ﷻ

Praise be to Allah ﷻ that He guided us to Islam or else we would not have been guided, and we have to praise and glorify the Creator for directing our face towards the Qiblah. The difference between a Believer and an unbeliever is where he directs his face. If you direct your face towards Allah ﷻ and His Obligations, you are a Believer, but if you direct your face to wherever you like, to the other side, then you are an unbeliever.

So, when we direct our faces to Allah ﷻ, then Allah ﷻ will guide us, because that is what He wants from us, to look for His Orders and execute them. It is not only to direct our face towards the Qiblah, but to direct our face towards Allah ﷻ!

The Qiblah is where Allah ﷻ ordered us as Believers to direct our face. Can you perform a prayer without facing the Qiblah? No, it is impossible. If you don't direct your face towards the Qiblah, your obligations are not accepted. So, what is there? "There" is what makes Qiblah important; there must be a secret there.

If you remove the walls of the Kaʿbah, what is inside? Inside there is the real Kaʿbah, *Bayt al-Maʿmūr*, which is in the Fourth Heaven in Paradise.

---

[96] Sūrat Āli-ʿImrān, 3:191.

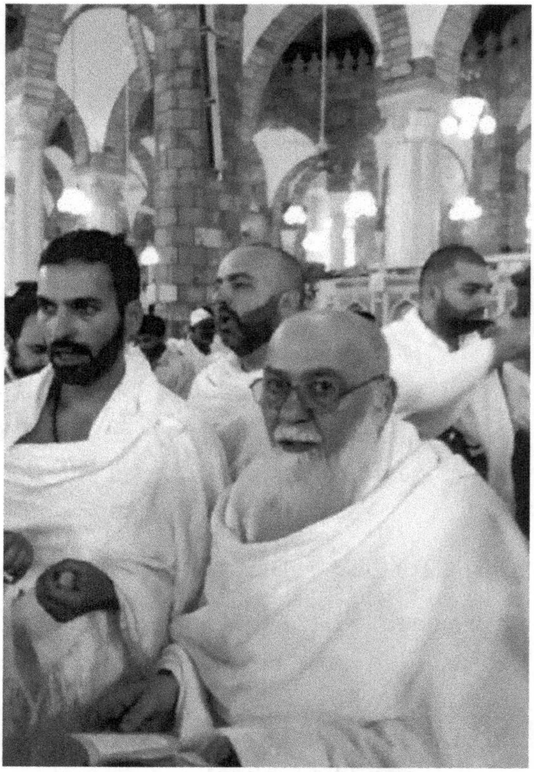

SHAYKH HISHAM INVOKING ALLAH BEFORE THE KAʿBAH, HAJJ 2011.

There, at that time, there is no more time, everything is energy; the inside of Kaʿbah where we are seeing is the *tajallī*, manifestation of Allah ﷻ in every smallest part of time, sending from Heavens different manifestations of His Beautiful Names and Attributes. That is what is also pulling people to Kaʿbatu 'Llāh, to attain that high level of spirituality.

So, the Reality of the *tajallī* Allah ﷻ manifests in every moment on *Bayt al-Maʿmūr*, also reflects on the same place in Mecca, which is Kaʿbatu 'Llāh on Earth. The Prophet ﷺ prayed with all prophets in the Fourth Heaven, where he was directing his face towards *Bayt al-Maʿmūr*. Allah ﷻ is sending the same light from the Kaʿbah in Heavens over the Kaʿbah that He ﷻ ordered Sayyīdinā Ādam ؑ to first build and then Sayyīdinā Ibrāhīm ؑ to renovate it with a Stone from Paradise, *Ḥajar al-Aswad*.

Allah ﷻ is *Arham ar-Rāhimīn*, the Most Merciful, which means, when you say, *"Lā ilāha illa 'Llāh Muḥammadun Rasūlullāh,"* it is enough in that moment to clean you from whatever you are carrying of sins; He is the Most Merciful, all of your sins will be completely erased, as if you are newly born, like the Prophet ﷺ said of anyone who goes for Hajj:

مَنْ حَجَّ لِلَّهِ فَلَمْ يَرْفُثْ وَلَمْ يَفْسُقْ رَجَعَ كَيَوْمِ وَلَدَتْهُ أُمُّهُ

> *Whoever performs Hajj for Allah's Pleasure and does not have sexual relations with his wife, and does not do evil or sins, then he will return (after Hajj free from all sins) as if he were newly born.*[97]

Sins are everywhere, but the Kaʿbah is also everywhere. Allah ﷻ granted you to look at the Kaʿbah five times a day: Fajr, Ẓuhr, ʿAsr, Maghrib, ʿIshā. That means, He is telling us, "You begin your day with sins, and I am beginning that day for you with *maghfirah,* forgiveness. By facing the Qiblah, My House in Makkatu 'l-Mukarramah, I am sending *raḥmah,* mercy, on you and forgiving you. I begin your day with forgiveness, on the contrary you begin your day with sins." That is true for all of us. People think that they are doing a favor to Allah ﷻ by praying. Don't think that you are doing a favor to Allah ﷻ!

Allah ﷻ once asked Bayāzīd al-Bistāmī ق, "O Bayāzīd, how did you come to Me?"

He said, "*Yā Rabbī* I left everything and came to You with *zuhd,* ascetism."

Allah ﷻ asked him, "What have you dropped in your life to become ascetic?"

He said, "I dropped *dunyā,* this world."

He said, "O Bayāzīd! Haven't you heard that *dunyā* has no value to Me more than the wing of a mosquito? That is not real *zuhd,* asceticscm, but real *zuhd* is to leave what I don't like, the forbidden acts, then you can reach My Real *zuhd,* My Eternal Life, My Paradise, the Sidrat al-Muntahā and Jannat al-Mawā."

STORY: THE SCHOLAR WHO COULDN'T TURN HIS FACE TOWARD THE KAʿBAH

Ibn Hājar al-Haythamī records a story in his book <u>*Al-Fatāwa al-Hadīthīyya*</u>:

> Abū Saʿid ʿAbdAllāh ibn Abi ʿAsran, the *Īmām* of the School of Shafiʿi, said, "When I began a search for religious knowledge, I accompanied my friend, Ibn as-Saqā, who was a student in the Nizāmīyya School, and it was our custom to visit the pious. We

[97] Bukhārī from Abū Hurayrah.

heard that there was in Baghdad a man named Yūsuf al-Hamadānī ق [the ninth shaykh of Naqshbandi Golden Chain] who was known as al-Ghawth, and that he was able to appear whenever he liked and was able to disappear whenever he liked. So, I decided to visit him along with Ibn as-Saqā and Shaykh ʿAbd al-Qādir al-Jilānī ق, who was a young man at that time.

Ibn as-Saqā said, "When we visit Shaykh Yūsuf al-Hamadānī, I am going to ask him a question the answer to which he will not know." (....) "We entered his association. He veiled himself from us and we didn't see him until after one hour had passed. He looked at Ibn as-Saqā angrily and said, without having been informed of his name, "O Ibn as-Saqā, how dare you ask me a question when your intention is to confound me? Your question is this and your answer is this!" Then he said to Ibn as-Saqā, "I am seeing the fire of *kufr* (unbelief) burning in your heart." (....)

Ibn as-Saqā was brilliant in his knowledge of the Law of Islam. He preceded all the scholars in his time. He used to debate with the scholars of his time and overcome them, until the Caliph called him to be a member of his court. One day the Caliph sent him as a messenger to the King of Byzantium, who in his turn called all the priests and scholars of Christianity to debate him. Ibn as-Saqā was able to defeat all of them in debate. They were helpless to give answers in his presence. He gave them answers that made them look like mere students in his presence.

His brilliance fascinated the King of Byzantium so that he invited him to his private family gathering. There, Ibn as-Saqā's eyes fell on the daughter of the King. He immediately fell in love with her, and asked her father, the King, for her hand in marriage. She refused except on condition that he accept her religion. He did, leaving Islam and accepting the Christian religion of the princess. After his marriage he became seriously ill. They threw him out of the palace. He became a town beggar, asking everyone for food, yet no one would provide for him. Darkness had come over his face.

One day he saw someone that had known him before. That person relates, "I asked him, 'What happened to you?' He replied, 'There was a temptation that I fell into.'" The man asked him, "Do you remember anything from the Holy Qur'an?" He replied, "I only remember:

رُّبَمَا يَوَدُّ ٱلَّذِينَ كَفَرُواْ لَوْ كَانُواْ مُسْلِمِينَ

Again and again will those who disbelieve wish that they were Muslims.[98]

He was trembling as if he was giving up his last breath. I turned him towards the Kaʿbah (the West), but he kept turning towards the East. Then I turned him back towards Kaʿbah, but he turned himself to the East. I turned him a third time, but he turned himself to the East. Then as his soul was passing from him, he said, "O Allah! That is the result of my disrespect to Your Arch-intercessor, Yūsuf al-Hamadānī!"

PURITY IS ESSENTIAL TO ENTER THE SACRED MOSQUES

If you have any doubts of the Oneness of Allah ﷻ, or anything that is making you to be arrogant or proud against others, or acting bad towards others, or humiliating people, or breaking their hearts, that is *najas*, not pure. People are familiar with the physical *najāsah*; it is when after cleaning yourself you have to go make ablution. There is no shyness in religion, so we may discuss this openly. If you go to the restroom, you have to clean yourself. Sometimes you will see there is no water in the restroom. When water is available, it is advisable to use water, not paper, but if there is no water, use paper. In the old days, people used stones to clean themselves, and when they returned home, they cleaned another time with water. At least clean with rocks, and now you are cleaning with paper. Although there is water readily available now, they still don't put it everywhere. When you clean with water, it gives light to these places and takes sicknesses away from them.

Therefore, we know that there is a physical cleaning process, but there is also a cleaning process for your belief: *Āmantu billāhi wa malā'ikatih*, "We believe in Allah and His Angels," and "We believe in the Pillars of Faith. Incorrect or weak belief is another *najāsah* in you!

---

[98] Sūratu 'l-Ḥijr, 15:2.

The Prophet ﷺ said, "Sicknesses come to clean you." Today we see sicknesses we haven't ever seen before, and as technology advances, Allah ﷻ sends new sicknesses, such as viruses, in order to teach Mankind not to associate with Allah ﷻ. He ﷻ described those sins that cannot be cleaned in the Holy Qur'an:

يَا أَيُّهَا الَّذِينَ آمَنُواْ إِنَّمَا الْمُشْرِكُونَ نَجَسٌ فَلاَ يَقْرَبُواْ الْمَسْجِدَ الْحَرَامَ بَعْدَ عَامِهِمْ

Truly the pagans are unclean, so let them not after this year of theirs approach the Sacred Mosque.[99]

Allah ﷻ is saying, "Don't approach them and don't let them come to Masjid al-Ḥarām or Masjid an-Nabawī! That area is prohibited for them." It means, if we carry any *najāsah*, impurity, in our hearts, how are we going to perform a good prayer? We are directing our faces towards Masjid al-Ḥarām in Mecca, to Kaʿbatu 'Llāh, but how are we directing our faces when we have *najāsah* in us?

So, then what is asked of us? To be peaceful, not to interfere in anything, not to be bossy to people, saying, "Do this, do that!" Bossiness comes from pride and arrogance. When you are arrogant, you think everyone has to listen to you. That is why it is not accepted in Islam to show that you are better than others, which is why Allah ﷻ said:

وَفَوْقَ كُلِّ ذِى عِلْمٍ عَلِيمٌ

Above every knower is a (higher) knower.[100]

The meaning of *ṭahārah*, to be pure, means to be obedient, and prostrating to Allah ﷻ through your heart, your organs and all parts of your body. No one has the right to go beyond the limits of that *ṭahārah*, which means to be obedient: who obeys the Prophet ﷺ obeys Allah ﷻ.

May Allah keep us in His obedience and keep us always under the *shafaʿah*, intercession of His Prophet ﷺ!

---

[99] Sūratu 't-Tawbah, 9:28.

[100] Sūrah Yūsuf, 12:76.

STORY: A SINCERE SERVANT'S SEARCH FOR KHIḌR عليه السلام

There is one story Grandshaykh ʿAbdAllāh ق used to always mention. It is about a person who was very sincere with Allah's Servants. People in the old times were not as rich as they are today. This person used to always stand by the pillar of the Kaʿbah and watch people making *ṭawāf.* These people were poor. There were no roads, maybe just dirt roads, and Jeddah was very small. Now it is connected with Mecca.

So that man always used to pray to Allah, "*Yā Rabbī,* let me see Sayyīdinā Khiḍr عليه السلام so he can give me gold to feed all the poor people in Mecca. *Yā Rabbī,* I am running day and night, give me something! I have heard about Sayyīdinā Khiḍr عليه السلام, but never saw him."

One day as he was making that *duʿā,* someone came and stood next to him and asked, "Why do you want to see Khiḍr عليه السلام?"

He answered, "I want to give to these poor ones. I feel bad for them."

The other person said, "What about you?"

He said, "Forget about me."

Then that person said, "I will give you a sign. If you see a person who can make that mountain move by pointing his finger, you will see Khiḍr."

That man saw the mountain move but did not pay attention because his heart was with all the poor people. He was concerned with how he could help, just like *Awlīyāullāh* are always caring for their students. So Sayyīdinā Khiḍr عليه السلام left and returned one day with a golden turban.

He عليه السلام said, "You are still waiting?"

The man asked, "Who are you and why do you come here every day to waste my time?"

He said, "I will tell you about Khiḍr. If he tells that mountain to move, it will move."

Now that man was awake and said, "You are Khiḍr!"

He said, "Yes I am. Look, I have all this gold to give you, but on one condition: you have to put on my turban, my crown."

The Prophet ﷺ has said, "Turbans are the crowns of Muslims. Whoever doesn't wear it, Allah will put him down, and whoever wears it and dignifies it, Allah will raise him." O Muslims, when you are at home, wear the turban! It is not necessary to have a big one. Just one meter (the length of turban fabric) is enough. Grandshaykh ق used to say, "Keep it in your pocket, because you live in western countries."

As soon as he put on that *tāj* (crown), he looked and all the people around the Kaʿbah disappeared. He did not see their bodies anymore; he only saw their wild characters in the form of wild animals like snakes, tigers, lions, cats, and hyenas. He saw, for example, the characters of people who deal with drugs, money under the table, selling wine and alcohol, and then giving from that money to the *masjid*, etc. Our character is not the body; Allah honored our body, as He said in the Holy Qur'an, *wa laqad karramnā banī Ādam,* "We have honored the Sons of Ādam."

So, to whom was he going to give the money? He found one person between thousands, and today there are millions. He found one and said, "Come, come! I am only seeing bad characters; I can see nobody, but I can see you *māshā-Allah*! Take all of this."

That person said, "O my brother, you want to give me *dunyā*? I have left *dunyā*! Take your money and go away!"

Then above the Kaʿbah, he saw another Kaʿbah (*Bayt al-Maʿmūr*) with men there circumambulating it and their hearts were with Allah. The ones below were in the form of animals. How could he give the "animals" gold and the ones above have no concern for gold?

So, he looked at Khiḍr ﷺ and said, "*Yā* Khiḍr! These are all animals."

He said, "Yes, they came here to be purified, but as they come, they go; they don't clean their bad characters."

So, he said, "Here is your turban back. I am not going to interfere with Allah's Decisions!" And Khiḍr ﷺ took his turban, the animals, the gold, and then disappeared.

إنَّما بُعِثْتُ لِأُتَمِّمَ مَكارِمَ الأَخلاقِ

The Prophet ﷺ said, "I have been sent to perfect the best of conduct (your behavior and character)."[101]

---

[101] Al-Bazzār.

That is the meaning of the Hadith, *innamā buʿithtu li utammima makārim al-akhlāq*, "I have been sent to perfect the best of conduct; I came to build back the perfect character." Grandshaykh ق said that *Anbīyāullāh* (Prophets of Allah) and *Awlīyāullāh* (Friends of Allah) tried their best to change our bad characters to good characters. He asked, "What is important of religion?" He said, "The importance is not to pray too much, but to follow the way of the Prophet, Sayyīdinā Muhammad ﷺ! Follow that way, as it is the shortest way to Allah."

THE BLACK STONE

“ *The kissing of the Black Stone gives*
a (sensation of) pleasure which is
peculiarly agreeable to the mouth,
and as one places his lips against it,
he would fain not withdraw them from its embrace,
by virtue of a special quality reposed in it
and a Divine Favor accorded to it.
What more is required (to prove its sublimity)
than that Allah's Prophet ﷺ said that
it is the Right Hand of God upon His Earth?
May God profit us by our kissing it and touching it,
and bring to it all who yearn for it!
In the unbroken portion of the Black Stone,
near the edge of it, which is to the right as one kisses it,
is a small and glittering white spot,
as if it were a mole on that glorious surface.
You can see the pilgrims, as they make their circuits
of the Kaʿbah, falling one upon the other in the press
to kiss it, and it is seldom that one succeeds in doing so
except after vigorous jostling. ”

Ibn Battuta ق

Ḥajar al-Aswad (The Black Stone) is set in the eastern corner of the Kaʿbah. *Ṭawāf* begins and ends facing this Sacred Stone. Throughout the ages, countless people, including many of the prophets ﷺ the Prophet Muhammad ﷺ himself, the Sahabah ؓ, pious personalities and millions of Muslims who have performed Hajj and *ʿUmrah* have placed their blessed lips on it.

The *Ḥajar al-Aswad* was originally a complete stone but due to various historical incidents now consists of eight pieces of varying sizes affixed to a large stone and encased in a silver frame.

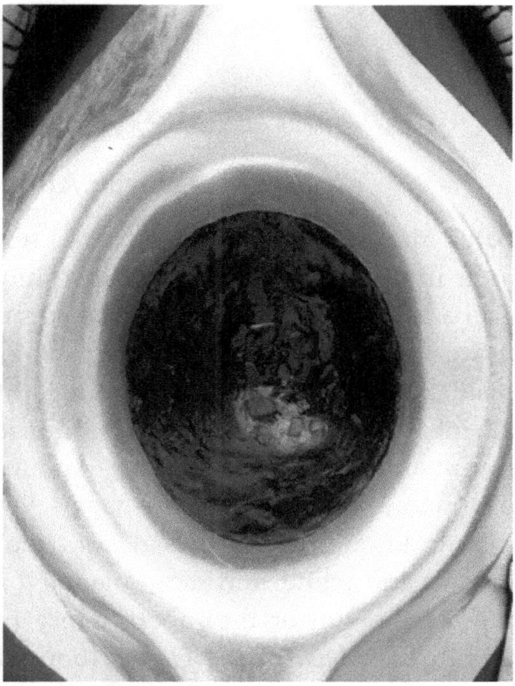

AL-HAJAR AL-ASWAD, THE BLACK STONE.

A Part of Paradise

Hajjah Amina Adil

After Ādam ﷷ was cast out of Paradise and sent down to Earth, the Lord took from Paradise one red ruby stone and placed it where now the Kaʿbah stands (in Mecca). It was also shaped like the Kaʿbah. There were in it two doors of emerald, one facing East and the other facing West. Inside, were many lamps from the lights of Paradise. The Lord ordered all men to circumambulate this house, just like the heavenly angels circumambulate His Throne. Ādam ﷷ set out to perform this circumambulation. Before he began, the angels brought the stone which is now known as *Ḥajar al-Aswad* (the Black Stone), only then it was radiant and white, and rays emanated from it that were as bright as the rays of the sun or the moon. Every place reached by these rays falls within the *Mīqāt* of the *Ḥaram* (boundaries within which pilgrims are required to don *iḥrām*—the special garb of pilgrimage). Later, this white stone turned black, due to the sins of Mankind, as it is found today in the building of the Kaʿbah.

This house was called the *Bayt al-Maʿmūr*, and it remained on Earth until the time of Nūḥ's flood. When the flood was decreed, the Lord had the angels raise the *Bayt al-Maʿmūr* up to the fourth heaven, or perhaps it was the seventh heaven, because on the night of the Miʿrāj the Holy Prophet ﷺ saw the angels circumambulating it in that heaven.

Then the Lord said to Ādam ﷷ, "You must respect your wife Ḥawwā highly, for she is the mother of your children and companion for life." So, the Lord already counseled our father Ādam ﷷ on his relations with women. Ādam ﷷ thanked the Lord and fell down before Him, for he was desirous of meeting Ḥawwā. When he arrived at the Kaʿbah, Ḥawwā had also come from Jeddah to the Kaʿbah but it was said to them, "O Ādam, you must, stand on Ṣafā, and she will stand on Marwa, and until you have completed the rites of Hajj you may not join together." At ʿArafāt, then, they met and recognized each other; hence the place is called "ʿArafat." Together they went to Mina where Ādam, was very happy and delighted to have found his mate; hence this place is called 'Mina' which means wish, desire and the Lord's Mercy and Forgiveness came down at Mina when He granted him satisfaction of his desire.

After they had completed their Hajj, Ādam ﷺ took his wife back with him to India. Every year they returned once to the Kaʿbah and performed Hajj for forty years. Each of Ādam's steps measured a distance of three days' journey. Every place that Ādam's step fell upon became a center of habitation, and cities were built there later by men.

The Prophet ﷺ Resets the Black Stone

Hajjah Amina Adil

When Muhammad ﷺ had reached his thirty-fifth year, the Quraysh wished to dismantle the building of the Kaʿbah and erect a new one on the same spot. Since the time of Ibrāhīm عليه السلام the Kaʿbah had not been rebuilt. It stood between two mountains, and whenever it rained heavily, the water drained into the Kaʿbah and dirtied it. Therefore, the elders of Mecca had decided to rebuild the Holy House in such a way as to make it safe from flood damage, but from fear and awe no one had dared to apply himself to the task. The problem presently arose who was to have the honor of placing the Black Stone (*Ḥajar-al-Aswad*) in its place. The great clans of Quraysh, the Banī Hāshim, the Banī Umayya, the Banī Zuhrā, and the Banī Makhzūm all came together to combine their efforts. They split the task between them, each clan being assigned to one wall. For a long while they hesitated to tear down the venerated ancient structure, but at last one man from among them took it upon himself to breach the wall, and the work began. They had torn the walls down to about a man's height when they hit upon a green stone, which could not be split by any means. This was the stone (foundation) mentioned by Allah in the Holy Verse:

وَإِذْ يَرْفَعُ إِبْرَاهِيمُ الْقَوَاعِدَ مِنَ الْبَيْتِ وَإِسْمَاعِيلُ

"And when Abraham, and Ismaʿīl with him, raised up the foundations of the House..."[102]

---

[102] Sūratu 'l-Baqara, 2:127.

Then they knew they could dig no deeper, so they began to reconstruct the walls upon this foundation, using the original stones. When it came to resetting the Black Stone in its place, all four clans disagreed who should be given the honor of that supreme task. They sat down in the confines of the sanctuary and began to argue about the matter, each man praising the heroic deeds of his forefathers that entitled him to this honor rather than his rivals. Each accused the other of lying, tempers grew heated and soon it would have come to blows.

Finally, they agreed to choose one man to perform the task, and they all agreed that it could be no other than Muhammad al-Amīn ﷺ, no one doubted that he was the right man. Muhammad ﷺ considered their problem, then he took his cloak from his shoulders and spread it upon the ground. He then lifted the Black Stone and set it upon his cloak. Then he called to the men of all four clans to come and each lift a corner of his cloak and to thus carry the Stone to its intended place in the newly built Kaʿbah. In this way each clan would have taken part in the honorable feat and they all could take pride in it. Everyone was highly satisfied with the wisdom of this decision as it saved them the trouble of protracted disputes and, possibly, even tribal warfare, so they happily did as Muhammad ﷺ had suggested. When they had brought the Stone near to the House, the question still arose who was to actually lift it to its place, but now they all agreed that no one was more suitable than Muhammad ﷺ, so he himself placed it there with his blessed hands.

Now all was completed but the roof, which was to be of wood. But in all of Mecca there was no wood and no carpenter to be found. However, it so happened that just at that time a merchant ship had come into Jeddah with a cargo of wood. They bought it from this ship, and they also found a Coptic carpenter who built the roof for them. To this very day the roof that was built at that time is still in its place.

Longing for Our Origin

Shaykh Muhammad Hisham Kabbani

Our souls belong to Paradise, from which the Black Stone came. That is the root of the relationship between the soul and the *Ḥajar al-Aswad*. That relationship makes the soul and stone long for one another, attracting one to the other. Therefore, when you visit the Kaʿbah you are rebuilding your relationship to Paradise.

The Black Stone is a part of Paradise. Anyone seeing it in this *dunyā* will be honored to see it in reality, by Allah's grant, in Paradise. Therefore, as mentioned before, it is also called the *Ḥajar al-Asʿad*, the Happy Stone. Whoever saw the *Ḥajar al-Aswad*, touched the *Ḥajar al-Aswad*, kissed the *Ḥajar al-Aswad*, by day or night, around the clock, will be granted forgiveness by Allah's leave by virtue of the testimony of the Black Stone. Even if through the thronging crowd one was unable to touch the *Ḥajar al-Aswad* but looked at it from far away with love and respect, *Inshā-Allāh* he or she will be granted forgiveness. As Sayyīdinā ʿAlī ﵁ said, that Stone will testify to that person's presence there, and that he or she declared the unity of Allah ﷻ.

قَالَ رَسُولُ الله ﷺ: الْحَجُّ الْمَبْرُورُ لَيْسَ لَهُ جَزَاءٌ إِلَّا الْجَنَّةَ.

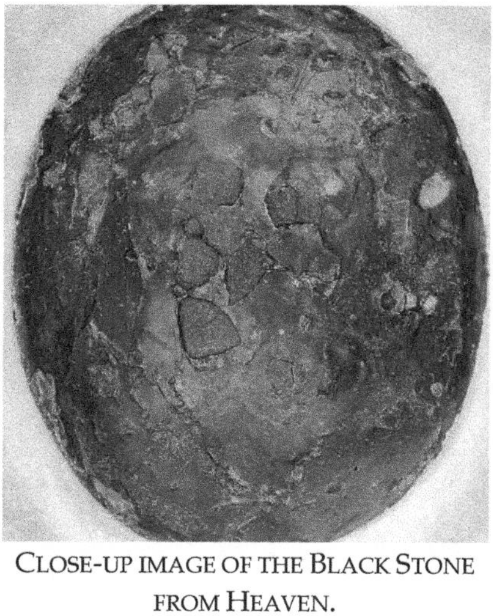

CLOSE-UP IMAGE OF THE BLACK STONE FROM HEAVEN.

Prophet ﷺ said. "There is no reward for an accepted pilgrimage except Paradise." The Prophet ﷺ also said, "Anyone who makes Hajj without obscenity and without wickedness, emerges from it clean of his sins as the day his mother bore him."

No sin! Why? Because *Ḥajar al-Aswad* is a part of Paradise that bears witness on your behalf. It is a witness of your presence there, of your experiencing difficulties and suffering, taking on the great expenses of travel and keeping patience among the millions of pilgrims present. Allah's House bears witness to all the trials you went through to reach it. That little piece from Paradise is witnessing how you took on the difficulties of where to sleep, where to eat, where to obtain water, to make ablution, even where to use the restroom.

The *Ḥajar al-Aswad* is the only thing from the Next Life on Earth. Even if everything on this Earth were destroyed, *Ḥajar al-Aswad* would not be destroyed, because it belongs to the Afterlife and it must return to its origin. That aspect is the essential spiritual secret of *Ḥajar al-Aswad*.

Many hadiths of the Prophet ﷺ mention the *ḥūru 'l-ʿayn*, the blessed maidens of Paradise. If one of them were to unveil even a fingernail to this world, all of this world would swoon from her lovely fragrance, and even the light of the sun would disappear in the light of her beauty. What then of *Ḥajar al-Aswad*, which is a part of Paradise, which Allah ﷻ sent to Mecca and which the Prophet ﷺ picked up with his blessed hands and put in its place in the wall of the Kaʿbah?

> *The Prophet ﷺ said, "The Corner and the Stone are two of the sapphires of Paradise whose light Allah ﷻ has obliterated. If He had not done so, they would have illuminated what lies between East and West."*

Therefore, our spirit longs to reach back to its origin and establish a connection with Paradise in this worldly life before reaching the Afterlife. Like a bridge or a tunnel, the *Ḥajar al-Aswad* is our connection between *dunyā* and *Ākhirah*.

So, during Hajj, with all its particulars and different stages, try to come to the House of Allah ﷻ and spend as much time as possible there, near the *Ḥajar al-Aswad*. Hug it in your heart, with a symbolic intention! Rebuild the relationship with the spirit, which longs for its origin in the verse,

إِنَّا لِلَّهِ وَإِنَّا إِلَيْهِ رَاجِعُونَ

"To Allah we belong and to Him we are returning.[103]

[103] Sūratu 'l-Baqara, 2:156.

When our body dies, we return, longing for our origin. During this life, we are longing for the *Ḥajar al-Aswad*, and it is longing for us. So, when you are blessed to meet it, build that relationship up in your heart.

This good news should make us happy to go there, even every year, if we are able, and even if one day we emigrate to Mecca or Madinah. Everyone wishes to be there, where people are in peace and happiness. It is our fervent hope and prayer that Allah ﷻ makes our home, at least in our hearts, to be in Mecca or Madinah.

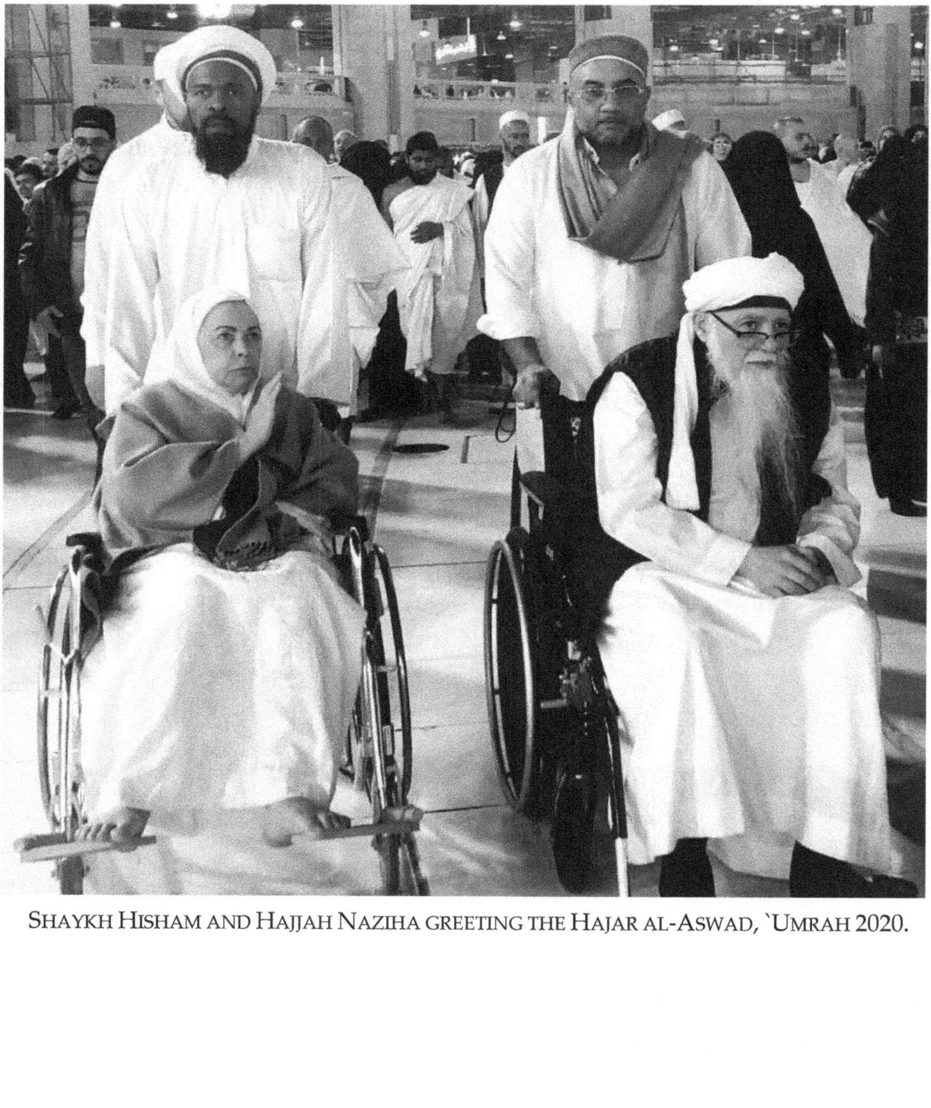

SHAYKH HISHAM AND HAJJAH NAZIHA GREETING THE HAJAR AL-ASWAD, `UMRAH 2020.

The Secret of *Ḥajar al-Aswad*

Shaykh Muhammad Hisham Kabbani

One of two things we like the most in *dunyā* is to touch *Ḥajar al-Aswad*, the Black Stone on the Kaʿbah. Why is it called the Black Stone? Some narrations say that *Ḥajar al-Aswad* was once white, but due to the sins of people making pilgrimage there and touching *Ḥajar al-Aswad*, or saying, "*Bismillāh! Allāhu Akbar*!" while facing it, it turned black, because *Ḥajar al-Aswad* sucks all the sins and keeps you clean.

Ḥajar al-Aswad, the Black Stone, is also called *Ḥajar al-Asʿad*, the Happiest Stone, because it reflects the happiness Allah ﷻ bestows on that Stone immediately onto you! As soon as you see it, or as soon as you direct your face towards it from anywhere around the world, you will be dressed with every happiness that is in it and all your sins will be taken away from you.

So, you see people fighting and pushing each other in order to reach *Hājar al-Asʿad*, because it is a piece from Paradise. When you touch Paradise, do you think Allah ﷻ will burn you? You already touched and landed in Paradise when you went to the Holy Kaʿbah and touched *Ḥajar al-Aswad*. Now there is no longer any way for you to go to Hellfire: all your sins are gone, past, current and future!

Why does everyone begin their *ṭawāf* from *Ḥajar al-Aswad*, raising their hands, saying, "*Bismillāh, Allāhu Akbar*"? Why do you raise your hands? When you want to greet someone in a nice way, what do you do? You raise your hands, give a greeting and go. Raising your hands to that beautiful Stone from Paradise is to give *salām* and ask permission to do *ṭawāf*. If you don't do that, then your *ṭawāf* is not going to be special; it will be like others. Raising your hands is different than putting your hand on your heart. When you put your hand on your heart, it means there is a relation, a respect, but when you raise your hands, you are surrendering and seeking salvation: "O Allah! I am lost. I am coming to You, to Your Presence, surrendering. I am leaving the way of Shayṭān and coming to the Way of *Raḥmān*!" Then, after asking permission, you begin your *ṭawāf*, which will feel different than what you normally do. You now have a different *ṭawāf*, because that Stone is witnessing!

Why did the Prophet ﷺ kiss *Ḥajar al-Aswad*? According to a Hadith, when Sayyīdinā ʿUmar ibn al-Khaṭṭāb ؓ came to kiss the Stone, he said in front of all assembled:

عَنْ عَابِسِ بْنِ رَبِيعَةَ عَنْ عُمَرَ رَضِيَ اللّٰهُ عَنْهُ أَنَّهُ جَاءَ إِلَى الْحَجَرِ الْأَسْوَدِ فَقَبَلَه فَقَالَ إِنِّي أَعْلَمُ أَنَّكَ حَجَرٌ لَا تَضُرُّ وَلَا تَنْفَعُ وَلَوْلَا أَنِّي رَأَيْتُ النَّبِيَّ صَلَّى اللّٰهُ عَلَيْهِ وَسَلَّمَ يُقَبِّلُكَ مَا قَبَّلْتُكَ رَوَى الْحَاكِمُ مِنْ حَدِيثِ أَبِي سَعِيدٍ أَنَّ عُمَرَ لَمَّا قَالَ هَذَا قَالَ لَهُ عَلِيُّ بْنُ أَبِي طَالِبٍ : أَنَّهُ يَضُرُّ وَيَنْفَعُ ، وَذَكَرَ أَنَّ اللّٰهَ لَمَّا أَخَذَ الْمَوَاثِيقَ عَلَى وَلَدِ آدَمَ كَتَبَ ذَلِكَ فِي رَقٍّ ، وَأَلْقَمَه الْحَجَر ، قَال : وَقَدْ سَمِعْتُ رَسُولَ اللّٰهِ صَلَّى اللّٰهُ عَلَيْهِ وَسَلَّمَ يَقُولُ : يُؤْتَى يَوْمَ الْقِيَامَةِ بِالْحَجَرِ الْأَسْوَدِ وَلَه لِسَان ذَلْق يَشْهَدُ لِمَنْ اسْتَلَمَهُ بِالتَّوْحِيد .

> *"No doubt, I know that you are a stone and can neither harm anyone nor benefit anyone. Had I not seen Allah's Messenger kissing you, I would not have kissed you." Sayyīdinā ʿAlī ؓ responded to Sayyīdinā ʿUmar ؓ, "This Stone (Ḥajar al-Aswad) can indeed benefit and harm," and reminded him of where Allah ﷻ says in Holy Qur'an that He created human beings from the progeny of Ādam ؑ and made them witness over themselves and asked them, "Am I not your Creator?" Upon this, all of them confirmed it. Thus, Allah ﷻ wrote this confirmation, and this Stone has a pair of eyes, ears and a tongue and it opened its mouth upon the order of Allah ﷻ, Who put that confirmation in it and ordered to witness it to all those worshippers who confirm their belief in Allah's Oneness.*[104]

So, *Ḥajar al-Aswad* will be a witness for everyone on the Day of Judgment who visited and greeted the House of Allah ﷻ and proclaimed the *Kalimat at-Tawḥīd,* even from a distance. So, if you raise your hand from afar and say, "*Allāhu Akbar, Allāhu Akbar, Allāhu Akbar*!" that is enough for the Black Stone to witness for you that you are a Muslim and a *mu'min* and

---

[104] Al-Ḥākim from Abū Saʿīd al-Khuḍrī.

you are touching Paradise, which means, you will enter Paradise with no account.

So, what do you want better? Say, "*Subḥānallāhi wa bi-ḥamdihi*, Praise be to Allah ﷻ for His Favors," as this is His Favor!

SHAYKH HISHAM, HAJJAH NAZIHA AND GROUP MAKING ṬAWĀF AROUND THE KAʿBAH, ʿUMRAH 2018.

REACHING WITHOUT PUSHING

The Sahabah ؓ used to reach Kaʿbah al-Muazzama easily by just saying, "*Bismillāh, Allāhu Akbar*!" They used to touch *Ḥajar al-Aswad* three times and then begin making *ṭawāf*, and in every *ṭawāf* they used to touch *Ḥajar al-Aswad* and continue.

My first Hajj was in 1967 and it was not as crowded as today, but it was still very crowded at *Ḥajar al-Aswad*. Sometimes with *adab* you could reach the Black Stone, not by pushing, shouting, slapping and hitting, as they do today, but from far away you could say, "*Bismillāh, Allāhu Akbar*!" and then kiss it. Similarly, in Madinatu 'l-Munawwarah, we were able to reach the *Muwājaha ash-Sharīfah* and even touch the grille, not like today as there are too many people. Even in *Rawḍatu 'sh-Sharīfah* we sat and prayed very easily.

So, when you go to Makkatu 'l-Mukarramah to make *ṭawāf* around the Kaʿbah and see that it is crowded, what is the *adab*? What is the *adab* of reaching the Kaʿbah and *Ḥajar al-Aswad*? First, you have to begin *Ṭawāf al-Qudūm*, the *Ṭawāf* of Arrival from Bāb as-Salām, the Gate of Peace (through which the Prophet entered to decide who should lift the Black Stone into its place)._Don't show toughness and roughness by pushing, but from far away say, *"Bismillāh, Allāhu Akbar*!" Like here (in this *majlis*) tonight, if you cannot reach, don't show toughness and roughness by pushing, but greet from far away.

Also, in Madinatu 'l-Munawwarah, you send greetings to the Prophet ﷺ by saying, *"As-Ṣalātu wa 's-salāmu ʿalayka, yā Rasūlullāh,"* like when reciting *qasidas*. When we say, *"Yā Muhammad*!" and *"Yā Allah*!" does it reach or not? Now there are so many people here that it is very difficult to reach everyone, so we raise our hands and there will be a reflection from hand to hand, because Allah ﷻ is Great and the Prophet ﷺ is the first *Nūr* created. It will reach the whole Ummah, his *Nūr* reflecting on each of us. We are not different from any others, we are not claiming anything, but that Light will reach by us saying:

As-Ṣalātu wa 's-salāmu ʿalayka, yā Sayyidi, yā Rasūlullāh!
Aṣ-ṣalātu wa 's-salāmu ʿalayka, yā Ḥabību 'Llāh!
Aṣ-ṣalātu wa 's-salāmu ʿalayka, yā Awwala Khalqillah!
Aṣ-ṣalātu wa 's-salām ʿalayka, yā Khātama Rusulillāh!
Wa 'ṣ-ṣalātu wa 's-salāmu ʿalā Ashrafi 'l-Mursalīn, Sayyīdinā wa Nabīyyīnā Muhammadin wa ʿalā ālihi wa ṣaḥbihi ajmaʿīn. Subḥāna rabbika Rabbi 'l-ʿizzati ʿammā yaṣifūn wa salāmun ʿalā 'l-mursalīn wa 'l-ḥamdulillāhi Rabbi 'l-ʿĀlamīn!

STATION OF IBRĀHĪM عليه السلام

"*The Station of Abraham is*
to hurl oneself into the fire
like Abraham, for God's sake,
thereby transporting oneself
to his station, or near to it,
through effort and struggle
in the way of God.
For he sacrificed himself
for the sake of God,
that is, he no longer had
any concern or fear for his self.
Two cycles of prayer
at Abraham's Station are good,
but the prayer should be such that
the standing part is in this world
and the bowing part in that world!"

Mevlana Jalāluddīn Rūmī ق

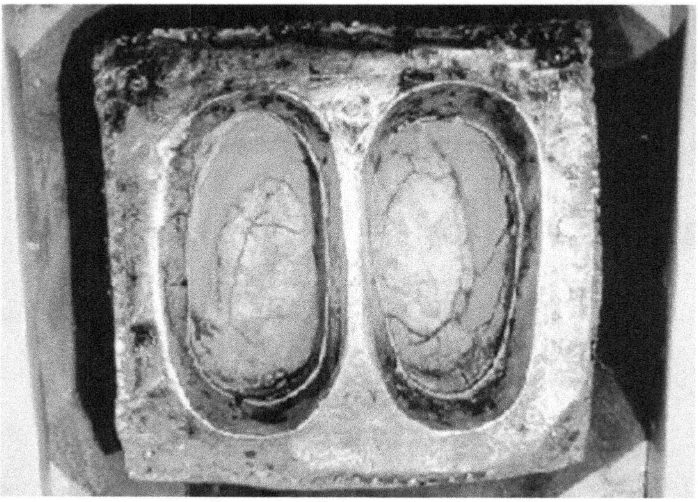

CLOSE UP OF THE FOOTPRINT OF SAYYĪDINĀ IBRĀHĪM ﷺ

Maqām Ibrāhīm refers to the stone on which Ibrāhīm ﷺ stood while he was building the Kaʿbah. When constructing the Kaʿbah, Ibrāhīm ﷺ would stand on the Maqām Ibrāhīm barefooted. Allah ﷻ caused the trace of his footprints to remain on the stone as a reminder to the Believers among his descendants. As Ismaʿīl ﷺ passed stones to his father Ibrāhīm ﷺ, and as Ibrāhīm ﷺ continued laying them in place, the Maqām Ibrāhīm miraculously continued rising higher and higher as the walls rose, like a modern-day elevator. As they were constructing the Kaʿbah, they recited the following verse:

رَبَّنَا تَقَبَّلْ مِنَّآ إِنَّكَ أَنتَ ٱلسَّمِيعُ ٱلْعَلِيمُ

"Our Lord! Accept (this service) from us: for You are the All-Hearing, the All-Knowing."[105]

Ibrāhīm ﷺ constructed the Kaʿbah using rocks from five mountains: Ḥirā, Thubayr, Labnān, Tūr and Jabal al-Khayr. Tūr Sīnā (Mount Sinai) is actually situated in the eastern desert of Egypt.

Juhm bin Hudhayfah ﷺ, a Sahabī who was present when the Quraysh rebuilt the Kaʿbah says that the blessed footprints of the Prophet ﷺ very closely match those of Ibrāhīm ﷺ. The Prophet ﷺ also mentioned, "From all the Children of Ibrāhīm ﷺ it is I who resembles him the most![106]

---

[105] Sūratu 'l-Baqarah, 2:127.

[106] Bukhārī.

Follow His Footsteps and Behold His Beauty

Shaykh Nour Mohamad Kabbani

We know the *āyah* of *tayammum* in the Holy Qur'an. It is that when you have no water, you reach for the dust of the Earth because it is clean. You make *wuḍū* which is *ṭahārah,* purification. Allah ﷻ ordered to purify yourself, and by making *wuḍū,* we are making *ṭahārah,* purifying ourselves. Allah ﷻ says:

فَلَمْ تَجِدُواْ مَاء فَتَيَمَّمُواْ صَعِيدًا طَيِّبًا

(If you) find no water, then seek clean earth and wipe over your faces and your hands [with it].[107]

Our teachers say that "water" here is the water of *tawbah,* repentance and *istighfār,* of asking forgiveness. It means, "If you don't find the conditions of repentance," because we repent, but then we repeat our errors, and this is not how repentance is. Repentance means we have to stop, but we are humans, so we go back to sinning. Allah ﷻ says, "If we don't find the right conditions for *tawbah* and *istighfār,* if we don't find the water of repentance, of asking forgiveness, then reach for pure dust and make *ṭahārah* with that dust. Take your *wuḍū* with that dust and you will be accepted in My Presence!" You will be able to pray in Allah ﷻ's Presence by touching the dust and wiping your face and wiping your arms. You are accepted. Even if you don't find the water.

My teacher, Shaykh Nazim ق, used to say so many times, "I wish I was one of those who were blessed to wipe their faces in the footsteps of an-Nabī ﷺ, the Prophet ﷺ." He also said, "I wish I had wiped my face in the footprint of Sayyīdinā Ḥusayn ؓ!"

The holy ones, where do they step? On dust. Where did Nabī ﷺ walk in Mecca and Madinah? On the sand, on the earth. It is dust! Can we follow the footprints of the Nabī ﷺ? We can do it physically *Inshā-Allāh,* but nowadays you don't find the prints anymore, because it's all concrete and

---

[107] Sūratu 'n-Nisā, 4:43.

HOLY FOOTPRINT OF SAYYĪDINĀ MUHAMMAD ﷺ IN AYYUB SULTAN MOSQUE, ISTANBUL.

whatever they built over it. Spiritually we can follow the footsteps of Nabī ﷺ, and he is saying to us, "Follow me!" to follow in his footsteps.

So, we try to find that dust, that is the *na'l*, Holy Sandal. We are asking for the dust under his *na'l*, sandals, because when the Prophet ﷺ was stepping on earth, his *na'l* was collecting dust, the dust of the earth that is under the *na'l* of Nabī ﷺ!

So, if we don't find water, it is acceptable to take *ṭahārah* to purify ourselves with it and enter into Allah ﷻ's Presence. That means, just by following the Prophet ﷺ we will be accepted into Allah ﷻ's Divine Presence. That is the *na'l* we put on our face. We want that dust, that *tayammum*, to cover our face and our arms.

We ask Allah ﷻ to make us pure, inwardly and outwardly, and to follow the footsteps of the Prophet ﷺ and to behold his beauty. O Allah! Allow him to clean ourselves so our spirit can take over our darkness. We shall enter *Jannah* with him, *Inshā-Allāh*.

The True Meaning of the "Station of Ibrāhīm"

Shaykh Nazim Adil al-Haqqani

In the most distinguished Naqshbandi Order, to be present with the shaykh is so important, daily is excellent. If not, weekly. If not, monthly. If not, even annually must be. It must be!

Hajj, the pilgrimage is ordered once in a life, visiting *Baytu 'Llāh*, the House of Lord Almighty Allah. The one who is representing Allah Almighty as His Khalif, as Allah Almighty's Deputy, is not less than visiting the House of the Lord. Therefore, everyone must look after that point. Allah Almighty is

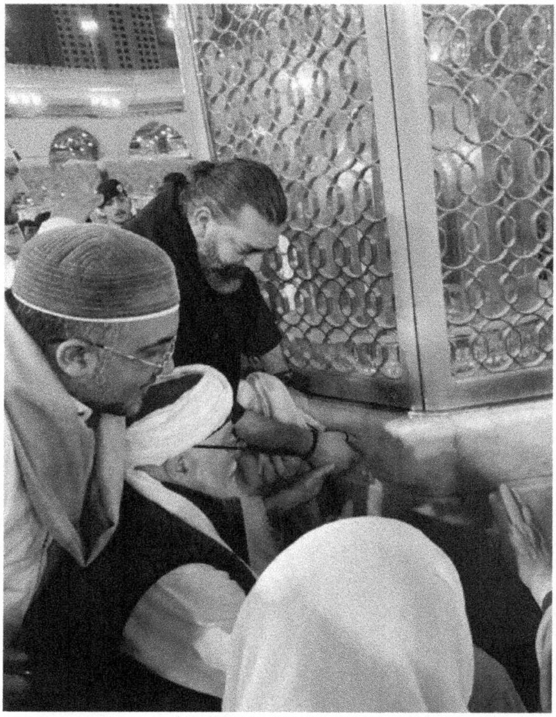

SHAYKH HISHAM AND HAJJAH NAZIHA AT MAQAAM IBRĀHĪM, THE STATION OF ABRAHAM, ʿUMRAH 2020.

inviting people to visit His House, House of the Lord, and He is saying ordering also:

وَاتَّخِذُواْ مِن مَّقَامِ إِبْرَاهِيمَ مُصَلًّى

And take the Station of Abraham as a place of prayer[108]

Allah is ordering to look after Maqām Ibrāhīm, the Station of Ibrāhīm, and to make two *rakaʿats* there. He knows what He means; it is not a place for making two *rakaʿats* and that's it, but the important thing is: who is going to be on the same station as Ibrāhīm, peace be upon him, and to pray with him, even two *rakaʿats*? Allah ﷻ is urging His Servants to look after that person who is on the same station, the same step as Ibrāhīm, peace be upon him.

People are running to Makkatu 'l-Mukarramah to look after (visit) the House of the Lord, but mostly they are going after that building. What is the meaning, if there is nothing in it from that building? Are you going to a castle, to a palace, or to the One who is in it? Are you are asking this? Everyone is looking at that palace, going and coming, but very few people are meeting with the Owner of that palace.

They are lucky people who are reaching to the Owner of that palace. Everyone is coming and looking for the Kaʿbah, looking at that building,

---

[108] Sūratu 'l-Baqarah, 2:125.

but very few people are going in order to meet with the Lord of that House. That is important.

One time, Ḥasan al-Baṣrī ق came to *Baytu 'Llāh*, the House of the Lord, and was looking, but seeing no one there. *Ḥaqīqatu 'l-Ka'bah*, the Reality of the Ka'bah, was not there. The Reality of the Ka'bah is the one appointed by Divinely Order to welcome the Lord's Servants.

When Hasan al-Baṣrī ق came (to Masjid al-Ḥarām), he looked and saw no one there. He asked, "Where is he (the Ka'bah)?" Then *hātif*, an invisible caller, called to him, saying, "Just now (he) left to welcome Rābi'ah al-'Adawiyya, that *Walīyya* (woman saint), who is coming."

Only very few people are meeting with that one who is representing Ḥaqq (Truth) through the Ka'bah. Mostly, people go to look at that building, to make *ṭawāf* and return back. But the real purpose for calling people there, the wisdom or secret of invitation to come is to find that one who is representing the Lord Almighty Allah in Ka'bah! Or else, we are just going and coming. So many camels are going and coming. Don't be like camels! Perhaps camels may understand more than ourselves. Perhaps camels have more feelings about that Divinely Appearances in Ka'bat al-Musharrafah.

Therefore, we must look after someone who is representing the Lord Almighty Allah for our destination, for our health, for our advancing and to be able to reach our destinations in the Divine Presence. So, association with the shaykh is one of the most important pillars of *Ṭarīqat al-'Alīyya*, this most distinguished Sufi Path, as without that there is no *ṭarīqah*. May be a short one (pillar), may be a tall one, but the *barakah* will come the same.

May Allah ﷻ give us from the endless Mercy Oceans, from His Endless Barakah and Blessings.

bi ḥurmati-l Ḥabīb, bi ḥurmati 'l-Fātiḥah.

THE YAMANI CORNER

"*The mount of love of meanings*
has taken away
both my reason and heart.
Ask me where it has taken them.
It has taken them somewhere
beyond which you cannot know.
I have reached under an arch
where there is no moon, nor skies.
I have arrived in such a world
that it is no longer a world.
When the All-Beloved Soul appears
like Canopus from the side of
the Pillar of the Yaman (Rukn Yamānī)
beyond all terms of quality and quantity,
no longer does the moon, nor the sun,
nor the Pole of the Seven Heavens remain.
The Lights of the All-Beloved Soul
overwhelm all of them!"

Mevlana Jalaluddin ar-Rumi ق

This corner of the Kaʿbah is called the Rukn Yamānī because it is situated on the side of the Kaʿbah which faces the land of Yemen. It is on the wall opposite to that of the *Ḥajar al-Aswad.* Because this corner is still standing on the foundation that Ibrāhīm ﷺ built, the narration of ʿAbdAllāh bin ʿAbbās ؓ states that the Prophet ﷺ made *'istilām'* of it, referring to the touching of the corner whether this is done by hand or by kissing. As the Prophet ﷺ touched the Rukn Yamānī by hand, this practice is a Sunnah. It was the practice of the Prophet ﷺ that when he passed between the Rukn Yamānī and the *Ḥajar al-Aswad,* he recited the following *duʿā*: "O Lord, grant us good in this world and good in the Afterlife, and save us from the punishment of the Fire."[109]

AL-RUKN YAMĀNĪ, THE YAMANI CORNER.

The Prophet ﷺ said, "Seventy angels have been put in charge of the Yamani Corner. So, if anyone says, "O Allah! I ask You for pardon and well being in this world and the Next; our Lord, bring us a blessing in this world and the Next, and guard us from the punishment of Hell," they will say, *'Āmīn*!'"

---

[109] Sūratu 'l-Baqara, 2:201.

وَجَاءَ أَنَّ بَيْنَ الْمَقَامِ وَالرُّكْنِ وَزَمْزَم قَبْر تِسْعَةً وَتِسْعِينَ نَبِيًّا وَجَاءَ أَنَّ حَوْلَ الْكَعْبَةِ لِقُبُور ثَلَاثُمِائَةِ نَبِيٍّ وَأَنَّ مَا بَيْنَ الرُّكْنِ الْيَمَانِيِّ إِلَى الرُّكْنِ الْأَسْوَدَ لِقُبُور سَبْعِينَ نَبِيًّا وَكُلُّ نَبِيٍّ مِنْ الْأَنْبِيَاءِ إِذَا كَذَّبَهُ قَوْمه خَرَجَ مِنْ بَيْنِ أَظْهُرِهِمْ وَأَتَى مَكَّة يَعْبُدُ اللَّهَ عَزَّ وَجَلَّ بِهَا حَتَّى يَمُوتَ .

The Prophet of Allah ﷺ said, "Verily around the Kaʿbah are 300 prophets and verily what is between the Yamani Corner to the Black Stone's Corner are the graves of 70 prophets, Allah's blessings upon them all, and every prophet from the prophets when their people disbelieved and rejected them left from among them and came to the Kaʿbah and then worshipped Allah until they died."[110]

In the Last Days of this world, the Yamani Corner will play a pivotal role. In Shari`ah the Mahdī is coming, and he will give *baya`* between the *Ḥajar al-Aswad* and Rukn al-Yamānī, and he is married and has three children, and his father's name is as the Prophet's ﷺ father's name, and his mother's name is like the Prophet's ﷺ mother's name! There are many aḥādīth on Sayyīdinā Mahdī ﵇ and we can quote them one time, but *Awlīyāullāh* have unique experience with signs of Mahdī ﵇.

عَنْ أُمِّ سَلَمَةَ عَنْ النَّبِيِّ صَلَّى اللَّهُ عَلَيْهِ وَسَلَّمَ يَكُونُ اخْتِلَافٌ عِنْدَ مَوْتِ خَلِيفَة فَيَخْرُج رَجُلٌ مِنْ أَهْلِ الْمَدِينَةِ هَارِبًا إِلَى مَكَّةَ فَيَأْتِيَه نَاسٌ مِنْ أَهْلِ مَكَّة فيخرجونه وَهُوَ كَارِهٌ فيبايعونه بَيْنَ الرُّكْنِ وَالْمَقَامِ وَيَبْعَث إِلَيْهِ بَعْثٌ مَنْ الشَّامِ فيخسف بِهِم بِالْبَيْدَاء بَيْنَ مَكَّةَ وَالْمَدِينَةِ فَإِذَا رَأَى النَّاسُ ذَلِكَ أَتَاهُ إِبْدَال الشَّام وعصائب أَهْلِ الْعِرَاقِ فيبايعونه ثُمّ يَنْشَأ رَجُلٌ مِنْ قُرَيْشٍ أَخْوَالِه كَلْب فَيَبْعَث إِلَيْهِم بَعْثًا فيظهرون عَلَيْهِمْ وَذَلِكَ بَعَث كَلْب وَالْخَيْبَة لِمَنْ لَمْ يَشْهَدْ

[110] Risālah Hasan al-Basrī, Al-Sīrat al-Halabīy yā, Sharaf al-Mustafā ﷺ of an-Nisāpūrī.

غَنِيمَة كَلْب فَيُقْسَمُ الْمَالُ وَيُعْمَلُ فِى النَّاسِ بِسُنَّة نَبِيِّهِمْ صَلَّى اللّٰهُ عَلَيْهِ وَسَلَّمَ وَيُلْقِى الْإِسْلَامُ بِجِرَانِهِ إِلَى الْأَرْضِ يَلْبَث سَبْع سِنِينَ ثُمَّ يُتَوَفَّى وَيُصَلِّى عَلَيْهِ الْمُسْلِمُونَ.

Umm Salama ﵂ related that the Prophet ﷺ said:
Strife shall take place after the death of a Caliph. A man of the people of Madina will come forth flying to Mecca. Some of the people of Mecca will come to him, bring him out against his will and swear allegiance to him between the [Yamani] Corner (of the Ka'bah) and the Maqām (Station of Abraham, next to the Ka'bah). An army will then be sent against him from Shām but will be swallowed up in the desert between Mecca and Madina. When the people see that, the Abdāl[111] *(Substitutes) of Shām and the best people of Iraq will come to him and swear allegiance to him between the Corner and the Maqām. Then there will arise a man of the Quraysh whose maternal uncles belong to the tribe of Kalb. He will send an army against them. They (the Mahdī and the Believers) will destroy them and they will be victorious, and he will divide the rewards among the people. He will establish and practice the Sunnah of the Prophet ﷺ among them. Islam will spread all over the earth. He will stay seven years with them. Then he will pass away, and the Muslims will pray [the funeral prayer] over him.*[112]

[111] These are a group of *Awlīyā'* (saints) that the Prophet mentioned in many hadiths.
[112] Sahīh Ibn Hibbān.

HIJR ISMAʿĪL (HATĪM)

“ *It happened one night when I was praying*
in al-Hijr that I heard a voice from between
the Kaʿbah and the curtain saying,
'To Allah and to you, O Jibrīl,
I complain of that which I suffer
from those who circumambulate around me,
(namely) their engrossment in talk,
their babble, and their sport.
If they do not desist,
I will quake until every stone of mine
return to the mountain
from which it was hewn!' ”

Wuhayb Ibn al-Ward al-Makkī ق

View of Hijr Ismā'īl and Mīzāb ar-Rahmah from roof of the Ka'bah.

The Hatīm is the crescent shaped area immediately adjacent to the Ka'bah. Part of it is also known as the Hijr Isma'īl as this was the place where Ibrāhīm ﷺ constructed a shelter for Isma'īl ﷺ and his mother Hājar ﷺ. Some scholars have mentioned that the graves of Isma'īl ﷺ and Hājar ﷺ are beneath the Hijr Isma'īl.

When the Prophet ﷺ was 35 years old, a devastating flood damaged the Ka'bah and it was in danger of collapsing. The Quraysh decided to rebuild the Ka'bah. However, the tribes were unable to collect enough money to rebuild the Ka'bah completely, so a small wall was built showing the boundaries of the original foundation laid by Ibrāhīm ﷺ.

'Ā'ishā ﷺ once said, "When I expressed the wish to perform *ṣalāt* within the Ka'bah, the Prophet ﷺ took me by the hand and led me into the Hijr where he said, "Perform *ṣalāt* here if you wish to enter the Ka'bah, because this is part of the *Baytu 'Llāh*."

There is also a water outlet that channels water from the roof of the Ka'bah down to the Hatīm area known as the *Mīzāb ar-Raḥmah,* The Downspout of Mercy.

HATĪM, THE SHORT WALL ARCH FORMING A SEMI-CIRCLE SEPARATE FROM THE NORTHERN PART OF KA'BAH.

DOWNSPOUT OF MERCY

“*When the pilgrim*
reaches the rainspout (mīzāb),
he says,
‘O Allah, shade me in Your Shade
on a day when there is
no shade but Yours!
O Allah, give me to drink
from the Cup of Muhammad ﷺ,
a wholesome drink
after which I will never thirst!’”

Īmām Abū Hamid al-Ghazālī ق

MIZĀB AR-RAHMAH, THE DOWNSPOUT OF MERCY.

The Mīzāb is the Golden Spout from where rainwater falls from the roof of the Kaʿbah onto the Hijr Ismaʿīl. The Quraysh were the first to construct a roof on the Kaʿbah and therefore the first to attach this downpipe.

Before their construction, there was neither a roof nor a downpipe. It is reported that the Prophet ﷺ supplicated under the Mīzāb. It is commonly referred to as the *Mīzāb ar-Raḥmah,* the Downspout of Mercy.

VIEW OF THE GOLDEN *MĪZĀB* LOOKING UP DIRECTLY FROM HIJR ISMAʿIL.

Sahabah Sought Rain in Mecca

Shaykh Muhammad Hisham Kabbani

There is a place behind Hijr Ismaʿīl (Hatīm), a semicircle where Ismaʿīl ﷺ is buried, which is why they only let you pray there occasionally. Every day the Sahabah ﷺ wished it would rain in Mecca in order to drink the water from the top of the Kaʿbah; that's why they have the *Mīzāb ar-Raḥmah,* the drain for the blessed water when it rains. They touch their chest to the Kaʿbah when it rains and *Mīzāb ar-Raḥmah* channels the rainwater down. When rain fills the roof of the Holy Kaʿbah, it flows through that pipe and the Sahabah ﷺ used to wash under it. The Ottomans made it of gold, but before it was wood and in the time of the Prophet ﷺ people used to sit there and drink its water or make *wuḍū* or whatever they wanted to do. We went there with Shaykh Nazim ق and drank water from *Mīzāb ar-Raḥmah* [see story in the Multazam Wall.]!

THE LOCK & KEY OF THE KAʿBAH

"I was the guard at the door
of my heart for forty years.
I never opened it for anyone except
Allah, Almighty and Exalted,
until my heart did not know anyone except
Allah, Almighty and Exalted!"

Abū Bakr al-Qattani ق

THE LOCK ON THE DOOR OF THE HOLY KAʿBAH.

The Keeper of the Key of the Kaʿbah is known as the Sadin. Guardianship of the Kaʿbah is entrusted to the Banī Shaybah, the Tribe of Shaybah, since an incident from the lifetime of the Prophet ﷺ:

The Prophet ﷺ and the Sahabah ؓ entered Mecca victoriously in the year 630 CE (8 AH). Upon entering the Ḥaram, the Prophet ﷺ went to the Kaʿbah but found it was locked. ʿUthman bin Talha ؓ, who wasn't a Muslim at the time, had locked it and hidden himself away. ʿAlī ؓ was instructed by the Prophet ﷺ to go and find him and retrieve the key. He tracked him down, snatched the key from him and opened the door of the Kaʿbah. The Prophet ﷺ went inside and performed two *rakaʿats* of *ṣalāt*.

ʿAbbās ؓ, the uncle of the Prophet ﷺ then made a request, "You know that our family is in charge of pouring water for the pilgrims who come for Hajj. If you hand the key over to us, we will have two points of honor: one is to pour the water and the other to open and lock the door of the Kaʿbah as and when necessary." Upon this, Allah ﷻ revealed a verse of the Qur'an:

"Allah is commanding you to return the trusts to those whom they belong."[113]

The Prophet ﷺ immediately understood what this meant and instructed ʿAlī ؓ to return it to ʿUthman bin Talha ؓ. ʿAlī ؓ apologized to ʿUthman bin Talha ؓ for the harsh way in which he had taken the key. ʿUthman ؓ was surprised and asked why they had returned the key.

---

[113] Sūratu 'n-Nisā, 4:58.

AN OLD LOCK AND KEY OF THE KAʿBAH PRESERVED IN TOPKAPI PALACE, ISTANBUL, TURKEY.

On being told that a verse of the Qur'an had been revealed regarding him to the Prophet ﷺ about returning this trust, ʿUthmān bin Ṭalha ؓ accepted Islam. The Prophet ﷺ told ʿUthmān bin Ṭalha ؓ, "The key shall remain with you and none but a tyrant shall take it from you."

ʿUthmān bin Ṭalha ؓ descendants are still the custodians of the key to this day and commonly known as the Shaybī people. The wording of the Hadith tells us that the family of ʿUthmān bin Ṭalha ؓ would remain until the Day of Rising and they will always retain the honor of having possession of the key.

Dhikrullāh Is the Key to Allah's ﷻ Holy House

Shaykh Muhammad Hisham Kabbani

Allah ﷻ said in the Holy Qur'an:

وَمَن دَخَلَهُ كَانَ آمِنًا وَلِلَّهِ عَلَى النَّاسِ حِجُّ الْبَيْتِ مَنِ اسْتَطَاعَ إِلَيْهِ سَبِيلاً

Whoever enters the House of Allah is safe, and pilgrimage to the House of Allah is a duty on Mankind (who are able)[114]

[114] Sūrat Āli-ʿImrān, 3:97.

There is an obligation to visit the House of Allah, and as a Believer, like visiting the House of Allah in Makkatu 'l-Mukarramah, you have to visit the "House of the Heart". When you circumambulate the heart, you circumambulate the Light that Allah ﷻ is sending to your heart. Allah ﷻ wants His Servants to visit His House: *man istatāʿa ilayhi sabīla,* those who are able, are in reality those who step on their ego, not those who are happy in *dunyā* doing what they like, who say, "It is enough that we pray." Okay, you have to pray, but you cannot open the door of the House to those lights without stepping on your ego. *Dhikrullāh* is the key to the door of that House with that Light! Whoever entered is in safety, and Allah ﷻ wants you to circumambulate that House, in a kind of movement that expresses your ecstasy, like in *hadrah*: you express your love in a movement, which is similar to circumambulating the House. That is not dancing, but going around the House, and at that time, you go around your own House that Allah ﷻ made ready for you. This moves on to why they said that remembrance is of four types in every level.

STORY: THE HEAVENLY LOVE OF *AWLĪYĀ* KEEPS US SAFE

There once was a *Walī* called Abū Yazīd al-Bistāmī ق. He was deeply in love with Allah ﷻ. Allah ﷻ likes for His Servants to love Him, not to put anyone else in their hearts except for Him. Abū Yazīd al-Bistāmī ق was at that level of love, and all of you are at that level of love or else you would not be here. That indicates the level of love in the heart.

So, he said, "O my Lord! You want to judge us on the Day of Judgment? You judge Yourself, because we are Your shadow." It means, "We are a shadow of what You have created, with no value without You. In reality, You are the One who is being judged through Your Greatness and Mercy and we are all saved." He said, "O my Lord! We are going over a bridge and You have put many bad desires there to make us fall into punishment. Who put them there? If we cross that bridge over to Paradise, we will find You there, because we are shadows," and he went to Mecca, to the House of Allah. The Kaʿbah had a ring through which they put the lock. He held the ring and said, "O my Lord! With the power that You gave to me, I am able to chain all the devils on Earth, to prevent all satanic work, and I can erase all the evils on this Earth, but I need Your permission. Through the Power of Attraction that You gave me, I can drag the whole world into Mecca and turn it to the real religion. Allow me to use that power and I will stop Iblīs from running after Your Servants!"

Don't think saints don't have power; in one instant they can change this whole world, but they have no permission. If there is no permission, no *Walī* and no prophet can do that. The moment he said, "I can erase all satanic power from this world," he heard a Voice. He looked and fainted, as he was not able to hold himself up. Allah ﷻ left him this way for quite some time. Later, when he opened his eyes, he began crawling on his chest toward the door of the Kaʿbah, the House of Allah ﷻ, saying, "*Yā* Ghafoor! O Allah, forgive me, I didn't know that!" It was a surprise for him.

What had happened? When he raised his head, he saw the Mercy that Allah mentions in the Holy Qur'an:

وَرَحْمَتِي وَسِعَتْ كُلَّ شَيْءٍ

My Mercy encompasses everything.[115]

He saw all that Mercy descending on human beings, making them saints without even judging them! Allah ﷻ said, "O Abā Yazīd! My Mercy is as much as My Greatness. Since there is no limit for My Greatness, there is no limit for My Mercy. I created that Mercy for My Servants and am creating it every moment," like an atomic reaction that ends with a huge explosion. "I created human beings, who are never satisfied and are always hungry to do bad things, and I am always happy to bless them and forgive them. I am their Lord. I created them with My Hands. I created that Mercy for them. I don't care for their sins, as that does not affect Me. It only affects them to be far away from Me, and I want them to be near Me!"

So, the importance is how much we move away from negativity and go towards positivity. That love goes more and more to the heart of the listener or goes to the heart of the people who are attracted to Heavenly Love. Be sure you are not attacked by Shayṭān in your heart or else it will ruin everything for you in *dunyā* and in *Ākhirah*.

---

[115] Sūratu 'l-ʿĀrāf, 7:156.

Don't trust Shayṭān and don't mistrust your shaykh, the one whom you have taken as a guide. Shayṭān cannot guide in any *dunyā* matter, just as you and your mind cannot guide you or you will fall. *Alḥamdulillāh* that we have strong *shuyūkh* around us that protect their followers from that, and Allah ﷻ will keep them protected.

THE ROOF OF THE KAʿBAH

“ *Bilāl ﷺ was ordered to climb to the roof*
of the Kaʿbah and call the adhān.
Yet there had been a time not long ago when
he had been forced to lie on a bed of burning hot bricks
for calling out the attestation of Muslim faith.
Even then he had continued to cry out,
'Āḥad, Āḥmad!' thus giving an example
of what religious fervor really means.
Now his voice rose above the rooftops of Mecca,
ringing out with the Muhammadan Adhān.
It sets forth the conditions for the elevation of Man:
to recognize the Eternal Oneness of Allah
and to verify that Muhammad ﷺ is His Prophet.
When he turned to the right,
he remembered the world of the souls,
and he called the blessed souls to prayer.
When he turned to the left,
he called to the multitude of the rebellious
to come to success and to make
their declaration of unity. ”

Hajjah Amina Adil ق

A roof for the Kaʿbah was first installed when the Quraysh rebuilt the Kaʿbah in 605 CE, when the Prophet ﷺ was 35 years old. The Quraysh made the decision to reconstruct the Kaʿbah as it had become eroded over time as a result of regular flooding in Mecca and had sustained severe water damage and in order to deter thieves, they made some changes to the structure of the building. They removed one door, elevated the remaining door off the ground and installed a roof.

CLOSE-UP OF THE KAʿBAH'S ROOF AS IT EXISTS TODAY. ON THE RIGHT IS THE OPENING TO THE ROOF FROM THE STAIRS. THE RECTANGULAR HOLE IS THE DRAINAGE HOLE OF THE *MIZĀB AR-RAḤMAH*. THE METAL ROD SURROUNDING THE ROOF IS USED TO SECURE THE TOP OF THE *KISWAH*.

Sayyīdinā Bilāl's *Adhān* on Top of the Kaʿbah

Shaykh Muhammad Hisham Kabbani

During the time of oppression by the Quraysh, Sayyīdinā Bilāl ﷺ went to the roof of the Kaʿbah to call *adhān* and the Muslims were very happy, saying the *takbīr*. The Prophet ﷺ gave him through his heart a drop of *ʿUlūm al-Awwalīn wa 'l-Ākhirīn*, Knowledges of Before and After, not through *dunyā* knowledge. It's not like today when they go on top of the Kaʿbah, they don't know anything: his heart was open to receive knowledge from Kaʿbatu 'Llāh!

If Sayyīdinā Bilāl ﷺ went to the roof of Kaʿbah and the Sahabah ﷺ said "*Allāhu Akbar*!" what about the Prophet ﷺ going to *Qāba Qawsayni aw Adnā* (the Station of Two Bows' Length or Nearer [to Allah]), when all angels said "*Allāhu Akbar*," welcoming him as he passed by every Paradise?

The Prophet's essence is always pouring out more and more knowledge; no one can reach the complete knowledge of the Prophet ﷺ. You look up and you can see, but you cannot see what the one up can see. If you sit below the roof, you see the roof, but the one on the roof sees much farther!

Grandshaykh, may Allah bless his soul, said, "Allah ﷻ created the essence of the atom of the Prophet's reality from the manifestation of His Beautiful Names and Attributes, especially from the two names, ar-Raḥmān, the Merciful, and ar-Raḥīm, the Compassionate. As Allah ﷻ mentioned in the Holy Qur'an:

$$وَمَا أَرْسَلْنَاكَ إِلَّا رَحْمَةً لِّلْعَالَمِينَ$$

We sent you not, but as a Mercy for all creatures.[116]

That is why the Prophet's reality and his essence came out to know the Ninety-nine Names of Allah ﷻ, because the Ninety-nine Names are like a bouquet of flowers: in the middle you have the most beautiful flower that everyone looks at. These Beautiful Names and Attributes have in between them the two Names, ar-Raḥmān and ar-Raḥīm, and the offshoots of the reality of the Prophet ﷺ are coming out from in between these two Names. That is why the Prophet's name is *ar-Raḥmat al-Muhdāt*, the Gifted Mercy to Humanity.

After Allah ﷻ created the reality of the Prophet ﷺ from the Beautiful Attributes of ar-Raḥmāni 'r-Raḥīm, He decorated him with all kinds of beautiful lights, as every Beautiful Name and Attribute has its own light. When the Prophet ﷺ was looking in *Laylat al-Isrā' wa 'l-Miʿrāj*, he was looking at these lights in the Divine Presence, in the Station of *Qāba Qawsayni aw Adnā*, and he was seeing all these beautiful, differing lights coming from the appearance of these Names!

THE CORRECT TIME FOR PRAYER IN HEAVENS

One time, Grandshaykh ق said that the Prophet ﷺ came to his Sahabah at the time of Ṣalāt azh-Ẓuhr, and Sayyidinā Bilāl ؓ stood up and asked, "*Yā Rasūlullāh!* The time of Ẓuhr has come; do I call the *adhān?*" and the Prophet ﷺ answered, *lā, naʿam*, "No, yes." He said, *lā tuʾadhdhin, tuʾadhdhin*, "Don't call the *adhān*," and then right way, he said, "Call the *adhān*."

---

[116] Sūratu 'l-Anbiyā', 21:107.

Subḥānallāh, what kind of telescope, like the Hubble Telescope, gave the Prophet ﷺ the ability to see the smallest fraction of a second of when to call and when not to call the *adhān*? Then the Sahabah ؇ said, "Yā Rasūlullāh! We saw something we cannot understand. First you said, 'Don't call' and then you said 'call.'" The Prophet ﷺ said, "In that fraction of a second the sun moved from its place fifty thousand years!"

What the Prophet ﷺ said was that in that moment the whole universe had moved! If we want to make a comparison between quantum reality and *Isrā'* reality, we can now make a discussion of that.

Allah ؆ made this whole universe to expand; it is always expanding. These stars and galaxies are always expanding in infinite directions, yet there is no direction there. It moves, and it is completely out of direction though it is moving in the way that Allah ؆ planned, so it has to be up to the point. Also, in Isrā' wa 'l-Mi'rāj, that movement of the Prophet ﷺ expanded to the exalted Station of *Qāba Qawsayni aw Adnā* in one second, and it didn't even need time. It was by *kun fayakūn*, "Be! And it will be." Can Allah ؆ not say, "*Kun fayakūn*" and create the whole universe? Yet He is creating and expanding universes within this universe; those universes are constantly growing and expanding.

In that one second, the solar system moved, as the Prophet ﷺ said to Sayyīdinā Bilāl, "The whole universe moved fifty thousand heavenly years." Similarly, in *Isrā' wa 'l-Mi'rāj*, time expanded for the Prophet ﷺ to reach the Divine Presence, and that Divine Presence expanded also! Allah ؆ is not in the Divine Presence; Allah ؆ is beyond that, beyond distance, beyond space, beyond time. The Divine Presence is the manifestation of Divine Names.

The Divine Manifestation is the expansion of knowledge that the Prophet ﷺ was acquiring in order to perfect him and enable him to reach *Qāba Qawsayni aw Adnā*. That is not yet the Divine Presence; that is only the point when Jibrīl ؇ said, "I cannot continue. You go."

Where was that station *Qāba Qawsayni aw Adnā*? No one knows. *Inshā-Allāh*, that knowledge will be opened in the time of Mahdī ؇, that secret that *Awlīyāullāh* feel shy to ask about. There are secrets in the hearts of *Awlīyāullāh* that would make us melt if they wanted to bring them out.

So, the Prophet ﷺ explained to Sayyīdinā Bilāl, "The moment from when I said 'wait' to the time I said 'call', the sun moved fifty thousand years." That means, in that moment, *Bayt al-Maʿmūr* moved! The reality of the Kaʿbah is the reflection of *Bayt al-Maʿmūr,* the real House of Allah ﷻ located in the Fourth Heaven, where the Prophet ﷺ prayed with all prophets in *Laylat al-Isrā' wa 'l-Miʿrāj,* the holy Night Journey and Ascension.

The *adhān* is not on our time, but it is on the time that the Prophet ﷺ accepted on that Holy Night of Ascension; he established the times, and we pray on the time of *Bayt al-Maʿmūr* in Mecca and Madinah. It is not when we pray Ṣalāt azh-Ẓuhr, the noon prayer, in America, for by then already it was prayed in the Heavens! The right time was what the Prophet ﷺ established. Allah ﷻ accepts our prayer as made at the right time, but in reality, the right time is when the Prophet ﷺ prays.

Who can give you such knowledge if not an inheritor of the secret of Prophet Muhammad ﷺ? You don't know how *Awlīyāullāh* act and what is their knowledge, which is from the heart of Sayyīdinā Muhammad ﷺ. That is why we must not object on how they do things; what they do is according to the Prophet ﷺ, who did not pray except on the right time.

According to a Hadith in Bukhārī and Muslim, it was near the time of Maghrib, and the Prophet ﷺ asked Sayyīdinā ʿAlī ؓ, "Did you pray ʿAsr?"

He said, "*Yā Rasūlullāh,* I did not." So, the Prophet ﷺ stopped the sun for Sayyīdinā ʿAlī ؓ until he finished praying, and then it went to sunset.

The Prophet's ﷺ power is but a drop, and he gives drops to *Awlīyāullāh.* All of them have one drop from that ocean of Prophet's knowledge, and that keeps things moving until the Day of Judgment.

THE ROBE OF THE KAʿBAH

"*There is a robe of honor that descends*
upon the Kaʿbah al-Muʿazzamah,
a garment of honor.
These robes are brought down
from Heaven by the angels.
They descend upon the Ancient House,
the Kaʿbah al-Muʿazzamah:
the Robe of Faith, the Robe of Islam.
Faith is Islam's Robe of Honor!
The Robe of Health, the Robe of Light,
every day they descend
upon the Kaʿbah al-Muʿazzamah."

Shaykh Nazim Adil al-Haqqani ق

AN OLD PHOTO OF THE KAʿBAH WITH ITS BLESSED CURTAINS RAISED.

The *Kiswah* is the cloth that covers the Kaʿbah. It is changed annually on the 9th of Dhul-Hijjah, on the day Hajj pilgrims leave to go to the plain of ʿArafat. The term *Kiswah* means 'robe' and is also known as the '*Ghilāf*'. The cloth is woven from silk and cotton and adorned with verses from the Qur'an. The Prophet Ismaʿīl ﷷ is believed to be the first person who put up a partial covering on the Kaʿbah. According to legend, it was the Yamani King, Abū Qarīb (Tuba) who was the first person to cover the Kaʿbah entirely. He is said to have hung it with red-striped Maʿafir cloth, a special cloth woven in the Taʿizz district of Yemen. After King Abū Qarīb, the Kaʿbah was covered by many people who regarded it as a religious duty. The Prophet ﷺ is known to have witnessed the ceremony for covering the Kaʿbah as a six-year-old child.

Story: The King of Yemen's Gift for the Kaʿbah

Hajjah Amina Adil

SHAYKH HISHAM UNDER THE *KISWAH* OF HOLY KAʿBAH AND HOLDING THE *KISWAH* OF THE BLESSED *MAQĀM* OF RASŪLULLĀH Y IN HIS HANDS.

Abū Ayyūb al-Anṣāri ﷺ was a descendant of the ancient kings of Yemen who were called Tuba in their time. His ancestor was a king, Abū Qarīb, who had lived four hundred years before the time of the Prophet. He was an idol worshipper, but he heard 310from his Christian advisors about the Prophet ﷺ who was to come.

They spoke to him of the description given in the Torah and the Injīl, and of the Divine Guidance he was to bring. The king Abū Qarīb was then impassioned by love for the Prophet ﷺ and began to yearn for him. He asked his wisemen whether he could see this Prophet, and he learned that this could not be, for another four hundred years were to pass before he was to arrive.

They foretold that he was to be born at Mecca where his people would badly mistreat and abuse him, and that he would migrate to Madinah on Divine Command where he was later to die and be laid to rest. This king therefore set out for Mecca with many precious gifts and presented the Kaʿbah with its very first *Kiswah* (covering).

Then he proceeded on to Madinah.

The wisemen in his company made a commitment to stay put in Madinah and stated that if they were fortunate, one day they would meet the Prophet ﷺ. But if they didn't, the dust from the Holy Prophet's ﷺ sandals would land on their graves. This at least, they thought, would bring blessings and be their salvation.

The King, having heard the scholars and counsellors, agreed to build homes for them as well as a large house for our Prophet ﷺ. He left instructions that when the Prophet ﷺ came to Madinah, he should stay in comfort in that house. He also left enough money to provide for the needs of the scholars for a long time.

Along with the house, he voiced his request, in that he wished to offer his services to the Prophet ﷺ to come. He said, "O Prophet of Allah, I have heard of your qualities, and your excellence and power, and I have heard that your nation is to be the best of all nations of the People of the Scriptures, and the most highly honored in the sight of Allah. Without having seen you, I have fallen in love with you. I confirm your prophethood and your mission; I desire to be of your religion and to be accepted as a member of your Nation. However, it is not possible for me to share your blessed lifetime, therefore I wish to dedicate my life to you and hope that my petition may be acceptable to you. I humbly ask that on the Day of Judgment I might find shelter under the Banner of Praise together with those belonging to your nation."

This petition he sealed in several places with seals of amber, wrapped it in layers of silk and placed it within a small box and said, "O my son, I have brought you and your family here from Yemen. Remain here and make your home here and take care of this box for as long as you live. When your end has come, pass it on to your son, and enjoin him to pass it on to his, and he to his, until the honored Arabian Prophet, the Hāshimī, Qurayshī Muhammad ﷺ appears. After he has announced his prophethood, suffered from the injustice of his people and migrated from his home Mecca to this city of Madinah, then the time will come for this box to be handed to him. This is my behest."

Now Abū Ayyūb al-Anṣāri ؓ was the seventh generation since the time of this ancestor. He had kept the box, but everything else he owned had been lost in the course of time, and he had become a poor man. Being totally absorbed with his daily affairs, he had all but forgotten about the box that had been passed down to him.

When the Holy Prophet ﷺ had entered Madinah, people wanted to entice his camel to come to rest before their houses by offering it food and by making noises to attract the animal, but the camel graced none of them with its attentions. In reality, the angel Jibrīl ﵇ had descended and was leading it by its halter.

When they reached the door of the house of Khālid bin Zayd (Abū Ayyūb), the angel forced the camel to kneel, even though there was nothing special about the house. Khālid then spoke to his wife, saying, "The Holy Prophet's camel has knelt down before you, you have attained this bliss!" From happiness both of them began to weep.

With a show of great reverence, he led the Holy Prophet ﷺ into his house. The Holy Prophet moved into the ground floor, saying, "This ground floor is suitable for all those who will come to visit us. Now go and bring us what you have held in safe keeping for us." Khālid thereupon asked, "What have we got in safe-keeping, O Messenger of Allah?" The Holy Prophet ﷺ answered, "Go and bring the piece of paper contained in the box that has come to you from your forefather of the kings of Yemen." Witnessing this manifest miracle of the Holy Prophet ﷺ, Khālid remembered the box that he had inherited, and reciting *ṣalāt wa salām* he went to fetch it. Before the Holy Prophet even looked at the piece of paper, he said, "He wishes to enter my religion and wishes to be of my nation. The Lord Almighty has accepted his ardent wish, and I too accept him into my nation!"

THE ZAMZAM WELL

“*One day I was looking at the Ka'bah.*
It asked me to fulfil the circuits around it,
and Zamzam asked me to drink of its water
out of a desire for friendship with the Believer.
I was able to hear one and the other with my ears.
I was afraid of being veiled by them,
given their immense stature in the Eyes of God,
and of being thus turned away
from my state of Divine Proximity,
which is fitting for this place
according to our knowledge.”

Shaykh Muḥīyiddīn ibn al-ʿArabī ق

AN HISTORIC PHOTO SHOWING THE PULLING OF WATER FROM THE WELL OF ZAMZAM.

The Well of Zamzam is a miraculous spring of Divine Provision gifted to Prophet Ibrāhīm's son, Isma'īl and his mother Hājar when they were left in the desert, thirsty and crying. Zamzam has continued to overflow abundantly for thousands of years to prophets, saints and the Ummah of the Prophet ﷺ. The name of the well comes from the phrase "*zam zam*", meaning "stop flowing", a command repeated by Hājar عليها السلام in her Abyssinian language during her attempt to contain the spring water.

Significance of *Saʿī*

Hajjah Amina Adil

The story is related in Qiṣas al-Anbīyā that Prophet Abraham ﷺ took Lady Hagar (Hājar) and the baby Ishmael ﷺ to the Sacred valley at Bakkah (now Mecca), near the Kaʿbah of Ādam ﷺ, which had been destroyed by the Flood of Nūḥ ﷺ.

Prophet Ibrāhīm ﷺ told Lady Hājar, "Remain here with my child, for thus I have been commanded."

"Upon whom shall I rely?" asked Lady Hājar.

"Upon your Lord," answered Prophet Ibrāhīm ﷺ, who then turned to the right and the left, but seeing no one called upon God:

رَّبَّنَا إِنِّي أَسْكَنتُ مِن ذُرِّيَّتِي بِوَادٍ غَيْرِ ذِي زَرْعٍ عِندَ بَيْتِكَ الْمُحَرَّمِ رَبَّنَا لِيُقِيمُواْ الصَّلاَةَ فَاجْعَلْ أَفْئِدَةً مِّنَ النَّاسِ تَهْوِي إِلَيْهِمْ وَارْزُقْهُم مِّنَ الثَّمَرَاتِ لَعَلَّهُمْ يَشْكُرُونَ

O our Lord! I have made some of my offspring to dwell in a valley without cultivation, by Your Sacred House, in order, O our Lord, that they may establish regular Prayer. So, fill the hearts of some among men with love towards them, and feed them with fruits so that they may give thanks.[117]

When the heat became unbearable, Lady Hājar saw a tree where the Well of Zamzam was destined to be, over which she suspended a robe to shade them from the heat of the sun. As they had finished the water in the jug they had with them and were thirsty, Hājar did not know what to do. First, she ran in the direction of the hillock Ṣafā in search of water, and then towards the hillock Marwa, crying, "Our God, do not destroy us by thirst!"

Then archangel Gabriel ﷺ descended to them bearing tidings of relief, whereupon she went to Ishmael ﷺ, who was scratching the earth with his

---

[117] Sūrah Ibrāhīm, 14:37.

finger; there the well of Zamzam sprang up, and she fell down prostrate in thanks to God. Lady Hājar said, "Zamzam, it is abundant water!" from which the well took its name. Then she gathered stones around the spring lest it the water flow away. Prophet Muhammad ﷺ explained that had she not done that, the water would have flowed across the face of the earth from east to west.

SHAYKH NOUR KABBANI MAKING *DU'A* AFTER *SA'Ī* WITH SHAYKH HISHAM AND HAJJAH NAZIHA, ṢAFĀ AND MARWA, 'UMRAH 2020.

Later a caravan approached from Yemen headed for Syria. When they saw birds hovering above Lady Hājar and the child, they were perplexed and said, "Birds hover only over water and inhabited places." Drawing near, they found Hagar and baby Isma'īl ﷺ beside a well of sweet water. After some discussion, Lady Hājar gave them permission to draw water and they came with their flocks and people and settled there, and eventually Isma'īl ﷺ married a noble woman from their tribe. Lady Hājar died and it is said she was buried by the Ka'bah, in the semi-circular area known as Hijr Isma'īl, where the Prophet Ishmael ﷺ was later buried as well[118] In one narration Lady Hagar, when she was running in search of water between Ṣafā and Marwa, heard a voice and called out, "O you whose voice you have made me to hear! If there is a *ghawth* (help/helper) with you (then help me)!" and an angel appeared at the spot of the spring of Zamzam.[119]

---

118 Al-Kisai, Muhammad ibn 'Abd Allah, *Qisas al-anbiya: Tales of the Prophets*, (Kazi, 1997) p. 152.

119 Bukhārī.

The Prophet's Grandfather Unearths the Treasure of Zamzam

Hajjah Amina Adil

THE OTTOMAN BUILDING HOUSING THE ZAMZAM WELL WAS LOCATED IN THE MIDDLE OF THE MATAF AND CONSISTED OF SEVERAL LEVELS. PILGRIMS WENT UNDERNEATH TO GET WATER.

In a dream it was shown to ʿAbdu 'l-Muṭṭalib that one of the sons of Ismāʿīl ﷺ had hidden two deer-shaped ornaments in the well of Zamzam, made of red gold, as well as one hundred swords from the time of the Prophet-King Sulayman ﷺ, and one hundred suits of mail from the time of the Prophet Dāwūd ﷺ. ʿAbdu 'l-Muṭṭalib was ordered to bring them out of the well in his dream.

When he came before the assembly of the Quraysh and told them what he had seen, they were not pleased and declined to assist him. ʿAbdu 'l-Muṭṭalib at that time had only one son, Harith. He had no way to oppose the ranks of the Quraysh. He went to the Holy House, the Kaʿbah, and prayed fervently to his Lord, Allah Almighty, invoking as intercessor the light of Muhammad ﷺ upon his forehead. He vowed at that time that were he to beget ten sons and live to see them grown, and should they be obedient and willing to dig up the old well of Zamzam despite the Quraysh's opposition; should they, furthermore succeed in this task

VINTAGE PHOTO SHOWING THE LOCATION OF THE ZAMZAM WELL IN THE MATAF AREA. THE ENTRY TO THE WELL AND THIS MARKING WAS REMOVED IN 2003. THE WELL IS LOCATED 21 METERS FROM THE KA'BAH, TOWARDS THE SIDE OF THE MAQĀM IBRĀHĪM.

without losing one drop of holy Zamzam water and unearth the objects he had seen in his dream, then he would sacrifice one of his sons at the threshold of the Kaʿbah, in the Name of the Almighty Lord.

ʿAbdu 'l-Muṭṭalib was a man of eminence among all the tribes of Arabia, and Quraysh could not oppose him unaided. ʿAbdAllāh one night had a dream that instructed him to unearth the precious objects that were hidden in the Zamzam well for such a long time, so ʿAbdu 'l-Muṭṭalib and his ten sons began digging at the site. They eventually found all, as ʿAbdu 'l-Muṭṭalib had been told in his own dream long ago. The swords of steel they melted down and made from them a pair of doors for the Kaʿbah, and the golden deer figures they also melted and fashioned from this a golden ornament to place above those doors. Therefore, the first person to use gold on the doors of the Kaʿbah was ʿAbdu 'l-Muṭṭalib, the Prophet's ﷺ grandfather.

Story: A Waterfall Under the Kaʿbah

Shaykh Muhammad Hisham Kabbani

VIEW OF ZAMZAM WITH PIPES CONNECTINGS THE TURBINES THAT CURRENTLY PUMP ITS WATER TODAY.

In 1980, I used to live in Hijaz, in Mecca. At that time, I was close friends with Prince Majid, the *amir* of Mecca, because of some of the work we used to do in Mecca, he was friendly with us. During that time, there was an order to close down the Zamzam well, because it was considered to be contaminated with the sewage draining from the houses on the hills around. They decided that Zamzam must be getting contaminated, and so it was to be closed.

However, there were some very strong Sunni scholars in Mecca who spoke with the King and asked him to reconsider. They mentioned the importance of Zamzam, in our religion, and its greatness and how the Prophet ﷺ had honored us with it. They mentioned the many hadith about Zamzam, including:

يَقُولَ الرَّسُولُ ﷺ : إِنَّهَا مُبَارَكَةٌ ، إِنَّهَا طَعَامُ طُعْمٍ ، وَشِفَاءُ سُقْمٍ فالشرب مِنْهَا ، والتروش مِنْهَا ، كُلُّ ذَلِكَ مِنْ أَسْبَابِ الشِّفَاء وَالْعَافِيَة ، .

The Prophet ﷺ said, "If you drink Zamzam to quench a thirst, it will do so, and if you drink it to fill the stomach in place of food, it will do so, and if you drink it for a cure from some illness, it will do so."

And:

وَيُرْوِى عَنهُ ﷺ أَنَهُ قَال: مَاءُ زَمْزَمَ لِمَا شُرِبَ لَهُ

the Prophet ﷺ said, "The water of Zamzam is for whatever it is drunk for."[120]

عَنِ ابْنِ عَبَّاسٍ ، أَنَّ رَسُولَ اللَّهِ صَلَّى اللَّهُ عَلَيْهِ وَسَلَّمَ قَالَ : " خَيْرُ مَاءٍ عَلَى وَجْهِ الْأَرْضِ مَاءُ زَمْزَمٍ فِيهِ طَعَامٌ مِنَ الطُّعْمِ ، وَشِفَاءٌ مِنَ السُّقْمِ ،...

The Prophet ﷺ said, "The best of water on the face of the earth is the water of Zamzam for it is a kind of food and a healing from sickness..."[121]

After discussing with these scholars, the King ordered them to check before closing the well.

They dug deep into the Zamzam well. The water was coming through lots of sand that had accumulated over time. As they began to dig the sand out, they found Muslim coins from around the world, jars, and historical relics dropped by pilgrims into the well. The treasure was not only the Zamzam, but it became a *dunyā* treasure as well, full of historical artefacts! If they had not dug it out but closed it instead, then all those relics would have disappeared and all these Islamic historic relics would have been lost.

From the Ka'bah to Zamzam is about 40 feet, so they started to dig there and then the opening began to incline toward the Ka'bah. They went 10

---

[120] Keller, *Reliance of the Traveler*, j11.6 (3), p. 349.

[121] Sahīh Bukhārī, Aṭ-Ṭabarānī in Al-Mu'jam al-Awsat.

meters down, which is like 30 feet, and then they were not able to go down more and found that they must dig in the direction of the Kaʿbah!

More water kept coming so they brought big machinery to pull it out. They then brought two Egyptian divers to go down, who were able to penetrate further and clear more mud until water was filling all the way up to the top of the Zamzam Well. After they had removed all the sand, they were able to see the water gushing from below like a waterfall! It was white and so powerful that they could not keep it down anymore. Therefore, they brought two huge German-made turbines, in order to empty the water gushing up from underneath, to reveal the source of the water. Using these big turbines, they sucked the water out, but after three minutes the water filled back up! So, the divers had only three minutes to film, and they found that the water was coming from directly under *Ḥajar al-Aswad*, the Black Stone. There was a hole, and the water was pouring out from there. They went further and found that Zamzam is also coming from under al-Rukn al-Yamani, the Yamani Corner! So, the King's order came, "Don't close Zamzam water; it is holy water that is coming, and it will never end!"

Subḥānallāh, what began with Sayyīdinā Ismaʿīl ﷺ four-thousand years ago is continuing until today! And that water is coming so strong up until

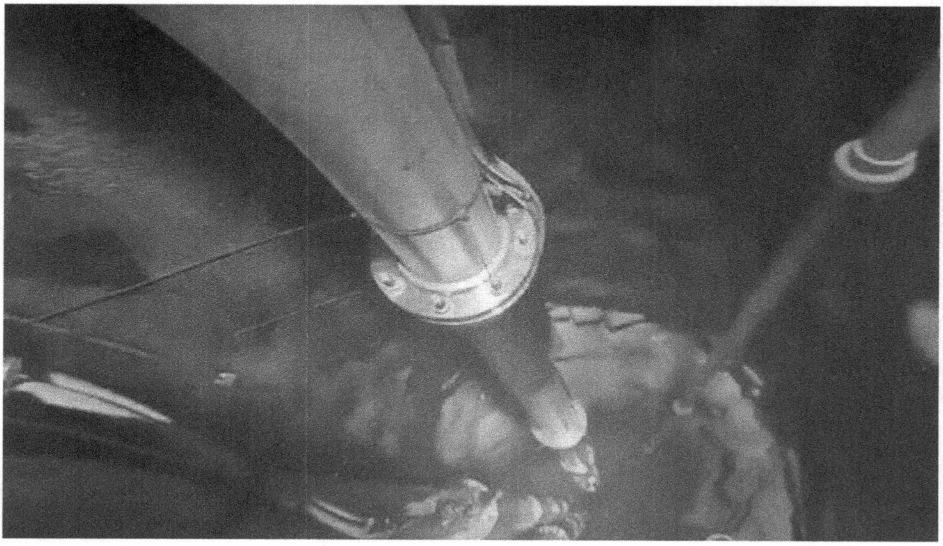

VIEW OF ZAMZAM WITH PIPES CONNECTINGS THE TURBINES THAT CURRENTLY PUMP ITS WATER TODAY.

now, and they are distributing that water around the world. And they say that that water is coming directly from Paradise. We learn a lesson from the water of Zamzam in the middle of the desert. If you dig 1,000 feet, it never runs out; with Allah's Will it increases and never diminishes. If one thousand, one million, one billion, or one trillion people come to drink from it, it will suffice them!

So, when we see that and we understand the greatness of Islam and the greatness of this Message, everything else becomes easy for us, because we see the love that Allah ﷻ gives to us, how much He loves those who believe in Him and in His Prophet, Sayyīdinā Muhammad ﷺ. Therefore, the importance is to develop love more than anything else. That is why, spirituality can do miracles!

Zamzam, the Heavenly Water

Shaykh Muhammad Hisham Kabbani

Two angels washed the heart of the Prophet ﷺ with the water of Zamzam when he was a child, after they had taken it out, then they put it back. The Imām al-Ḥāfiẓ al-'Irāqī said: "The reason why the Prophet's chest was washed with Zamzam water was to make him stronger so that he could see the kingdom of Heaven and Earth, and Paradise and Hell, because one of the special qualities of Zamzam is that it strengthens the heart and calms the soul."

When Allah wanted to bring His Beloved Muhammad ﷺ to visit Himself on the Night Journey and Ascension, first the angels cleansed his heart with Zamzam:

عَنْ مَالِكِ بْنِ صَعْصَعَةَ أَنَّهُ قَالَ : قَالَ النَّبِيُّ ﷺ بَيْنَا أَنَا عِنْدَ الْبَيْتِ بَيْنَ النَّائِمِ وَالْيَقْظَانِ ، وَذَكَرَ يَعْنِى رَجُلًا بَيْنَ الرَّجُلَيْنِ ، فَأُتِيتُ بِطَسْتٍ مِنْ ذَهَبٍ مُلِئَ حِكْمَةً وإيمانًا ، فَشُقَّ مِنَ النَّحْرِ إِلَى مَرَاقِّ الْبَطْنِ ، ثُمَّ غَسَلَ الْبَطْنِ بِمَاءِ زَمْزَمَ ، ثُمَّ مُلِئَ حِكْمَةً وإيمانًا ....

Mālik bin Ṣ'aṣ'a ؆ related that the Prophet ﷺ said, "I was lying in the Hijr (of the Sacred Mosque of Mecca) when someone [the archangel Gabriel ؆] came to me and cut open my chest from throat to belly. He removed my heart and cleaned it with the water of the well of Zamzam before putting it back in its place. Then he brought me a white creature called al-Burāq by whose means I was lifted."[122] *Another narration relates that the two archangels "Gabriel and Mika'il ؆ came to the Prophet ﷺ when he was laying down in al-Hijr [of the Sacred Mosque in Mecca] and carried him to the well of Zamzam. They laid him down on his back and Gabriel ؆ opened his chest from top to bottom, despite which*

---

[122] Bukhārī.

there was no bleeding. He said to Mikā'īl ﷺ, 'Get me water from Zamzam,' which he did. Gabriel ﷺ took the Prophet's ﷺ heart and washed it thrice before putting it back. He filled it with faith and wisdom. Then he closed his chest, and they took him out from the door of the masjid to where the Burāq was waiting."

The Prophet ﷺ prohibited to drink while standing or while laying down. Only Zamzam water may be drunk while standing, because it is a blessed water coming from Heavens, as narrated in a hadith:

عَن اِبن عَبَاس قَال: سَقَيْتُ رَسولَ اللَّهِ صَلَّى اللهُ عليه وسلَّمَ مِن زَمْزَمَ، فَشَرِبَ وَهو قَائِمٌ.

Ibn 'Abbās ﷺ said, "I served water to the Prophet ﷺ from Zamzam and he drank while standing."[123]

Ibn 'Abbās ﷺ said, "Yes, but only with Zamzam." Therefore, you should not drink Zamzam while sitting, rather you should drink it standing to honor Zamzam. It is Sunnah to face the Ka'bah standing while drinking, to breathe three times and say, "*Bismillāh*" each time one drinks and "*alḥamdulillāh*," drinking one's fill of it. Drink with good intentions of benefit because:

عَن جَابِر ﷺ أَن النَبِي ﷺ قَال: مَاءُ زَمْزَمَ لِمَا شُرِبَ لَهُ.

The Prophet ﷺ said, "The water of the well of Zamzam is for whatever intention one wishes, [religious or other-worldly]."[124]

عَن اِبن عَبَاس أَنَ النَبِى ﷺ قَالَ إِنَّهَا مُبَارَكَةٌ، إِنَّهَا طَعَامُ طُعْم ، وَشِفَاء سُقْمٍ

Ibn 'Abbās ﷺ reported that Prophet Muhammad ﷺ said: "The water of Zamzam is blessed. Truly it contains food to satisfy hunger and a cure for illnesses."

---

[123] Bukhārī and Muslim.

[124] Musnad Ahmad, Sunan ibn Mājah.

It is a Sunnah of the Prophet ﷺ to take bottles of Zamzam water home from pilgrimage to share as a blessing (*barakah*) with family and friends and the same *adab* of drinking is observed when drinking it at home.

We see that Zamzam is what purifies the heart, because it is from a heavenly source and Allah has bestowed on it the properties of healing.

When Ibn ʿAbbās ؓ drank water from Zamzam, he said: "O Allah, I ask you for beneficial knowledge, plentiful provision and healing from every disease."

Īmām As-Suyūṭī, one of the greatest *mujtahids* in Islam, said about himself: "When I went on hajj, I drank Zamzam water for several matters. Among them that I reach, in *fiqh*, the level of Shaykh Sirāj al-Dīn al-Bulqīnī and in hadith, that of the Ḥāfiẓ Ibn Hājar."

THE DOOR OF THE KA'BAH

"*The threadbare pilgrim*
may cross snowy mountain passes
and sun-scorched deserts barefoot,
or even on his hands and knees
in order to reach Mecca.
When he finally arrives,
he is struck dumb
by the awesome majesty
of the Holy Ka'bah.
Tears stream down his face
as he clings to its door,
pouring out heart and soul to his Lord,
and the Lord fulfills his heart's
innermost desire in accordance with
the longing that drove him
to suffer freezing wind
and scorching sun."

Shaykh Nazim Adil al-Haqqani ق

THE DOOR OF THE HOLY KAʿBAH.

This is the door of the Kaʿbah on its eastern side. Originally it was at ground level but was raised when the Quraysh rebuilt the Kaʿbah. When the Quraysh renovated the Kaʿbah they raised the eastern side door high above the ground to prevent people entering the Kaʿbah at will. The opening on the opposite side was sealed off.

ʿĀ'ishā ﵂ once asked the Prophet ﷺ what reason the Quraysh had for raising the door above the ground. The Prophet ﷺ replied, "Your people did it so that they could permit into the Kaʿbah only those people whom they approved of and could prevent those whom they pleased. Had your people not been recently removed from ignorance and had I not feared that they would be averse to change, I would have included the Hatīm (Hijr Ismaʿīl) within the Kaʿbah and brought the door level with the ground!"

AERIAL VIEW OF MASJID AL-ḤARĀM, THE HOLY MOSQUE.

Many Doors to Masjid al-Ḥarām, One Door to Kaʿbah

Shaykh Muhammad Hisham Kabbani

Here (in this room), there are so many doors. How many doors are there to enter the Kaʿbah? There are hundreds of doors to enter Ḥaram ash-Sharīf, but only one door to enter the Kaʿbah! *Awlīyāullāh* are like the Kaʿbah, and every *murīd* is a door that someone might enter through. When you have more doors, it is more accessible, whereas if there is only one door it is difficult to enter. To be around or near the Kaʿbah, there are many doors.

Awlīyāullāh are like the Kaʿbah, not in physical shape, but in spiritually. It's like a magnet, but not everyone can reach it; perhaps only ten or twenty can go in, while there are millions going around. Those who enter the presence of the shaykh are very few. They are those who actually enter his oceans, as not everyone can enter!

In *ṭarīqah*, this concept that the shaykh has many doors and anyone can enter is because they want many to come to Kaʿbah, but the outside door is different and the inside door is different, and not many enter through it.

Allah ﷻ says in the Holy Qur'an:

وَأْتُواْ الْبُيُوتَ مِنْ أَبْوَابِهَا

Enter houses through their doors. [125]

You cannot enter through the window, you have to go to Allah through *adab*, through your guide, and from your guide to the Door of the Prophet ﷺ, and from the Prophet ﷺ to the Door of Allah ﷻ! You cannot jump and make imaginary doors, not knowing which door to enter through. How many doors are there in *Ḥaram al-Makkī*? Hundreds, but all are outside the Kaʿbah; there are hundreds of doors for the *masjid*, but only one door to the Kaʿbah. Outside, you can take in millions of people, but you can take maybe one or two dozen people into the Kaʿbah through that one door.

It means, if you want to enter the heart of the shaykh, there is one door that takes you to the Door of Prophet ﷺ, as the Prophet ﷺ said:

أنا مدينة العلم وعلى بابه

I am the City of Knowledge and ʿAlī is its Door (or Gate).[126]

You have to follow the right door to come inside, to enter the city of the Kaʿbah, which is the City of the Prophet ﷺ. Once you enter, there can be twelve, twenty-four, or as many as the shaykh likes there! Allah ﷻ will expand it, but most of the rest will stay outside the Kaʿbah, making *ṭawāf*, and it is okay. Those are the lovers, but when you enter you become like a *murīd*, like Shāh Naqshband ق!

STORY: THE KAʿBAH VISITS ʿABDUL-KHĀLIQ AL-GHUJDAWĀNĪ

Ten years ago, we visited the grave of Khawaja ʿAbdul-Khāliq al-Ghujdawānī ق, his shrine, tomb, and this is what we saw: at the grave there was a door, it was the Kaʿbah's door on that grave! There is security for that door as it was later determined it was Kaʿbah's door.

---

[125] Sūratu 'l-Baqarah, 2:189.

[126] al-Ḥākim, Tirmidhī.

2003: AT THE MAQAM OF ʿABDUL-KHĀLIQ AL- GHUJDAWĀNĪ ق, ELEVENTH SHAYKH OF THE NAQSHBANDI GOLDEN CHAIN. SHAYKH HISHAM KABBANI WITH MUFTI OF BUKHARA STANDING IN FRONT OF THE DOOR OF KAʿBAH, REPORTED TO HAVE COME TO GHUJDAWĀN TO VISIT THIS GRANDSHAYKH.

One year when Sayyīdinā ʿAbdul-Khāliq al-Ghujdawānī ق didn't go for Hajj as there were important issues in Merv, while pilgrims were on Hajj, the Kaʿbah came, and at that moment Sayyīdinā ʿAbdul-Khāliq al-Ghujdawānī ق said in his lecture, "The Kaʿbah is here and I am making *ṭawāf* around Kaʿbah."

The Kaʿbah visited him! That story has been authenticated by many Naqshbandi Shaykhs. And the Kaʿbah visits many *Awlīyāullāh*, and it visited him and left its door to show, "I visited Khawaja ʿAbdul-Khāliq al-Ghujdawānī ق and left my door." When the *ḥujjāj* came back, they confirmed that the door of Kaʿbah was not there and so it was left in Merv.

Some Naqshbandi *murīds* might accept and some might have question marks; regardless, we say may Allah ﷻ guide them and guide us. *Awlīyāullāh* have a lot of miracles and miracles are beyond our minds, such as for Kaʿbah to come and visit.

Yes, we know stories of Shaykh Nazim ق, that he went for Hajj without leaving Lebanon, and this story is very well-known to the Prime Minister of Lebanon [see previous chapters for the story]. So, the Kaʿbah came and visited Khawaja ʿAbdul-Khāliq al-Ghujdawānī ق and left its door!

INSIDE THE KAʿBAH

" *Someone asked me,*
'How can the Man of God
be permitted everything?
If he declares a cherished deviation,
how can we say it is correct,
and how can we know it?'
I answered,
'Everything done by the Man of God is correct,
but may appear as wrongdoing to the ignorant.
It is like someone who is inside the Kaʿbah:
God will accept his prayer
no matter what direction he faces.
In whatever direction he turns,
he always faces God.
But outside the Kaʿbah,
there is only one direction that faces God.
He is an ignorant man, who,
while praying inside the Kaʿbah,
is uncertain about the direction
toward the Source!' "

Sultan Bahauddīn Walad ق

View from the inside of the Holy Kaʿbah. Bāb at-Tawbah on the left.

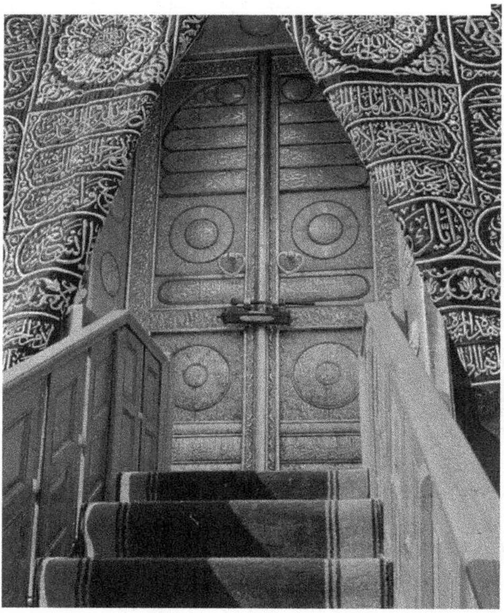

A staircase used for entering the Kaʿbah.

When the Prophet ﷺ arrived in Mecca on the day of victory, he made *ṭawāf* around the Kaʿbah seven times and touched the *Ḥajar al-Aswad* with his staff. He then had the door of the Kaʿbah opened and went inside. Accompanying him were Usama bin Zayd and Bilāl ؓ. He ﷺ closed the door, performed prayer and stayed for some time. Various sculptures and paintings of the pagan gods were held inside the Kaʿbah. The Prophet ﷺ ordered all of them to be destroyed. The Prophet ﷺ also had the chief idol Hubal destroyed as well as all the other idols surrounding the Kaʿbah. A golden door inside the Kaʿbah is known as the Bāb at-Tawbah, the Door of Repentance. It is in the right corner of the entrance into the Kaʿbah. The door opens to an enclosed staircase which leads to the roof of the Kaʿbah.

How to Enter the Kaʿbah

Shaykh Muhammad Hisham Kabbani

RARE HISTORIC PHOTO SHOWING PILGRIMS ENTERING INSIDE THE KAʿBAH.

If you are going to Allah's House, do you think Allah ﷻ will not invite you to enter inside His Home? Think about it. Why does it have a door? They were able to build it with four walls and no door, but Allah ﷻ is showing you that Kaʿbah is a House with a door: "That is My House on Earth, which I am inviting everyone to come and clean themselves for the Day of Judgment when they will appear as they appeared in front of My House in *dunyā*!" Because when you go to Allah's House in *dunyā*, a

SHAYKH HISHAM RECITING THE HOLY QUR'AN IN HIS HOME.

picture (from Heavens) will be taken (as a witness) of you appearing in front of the Kaʿbah.

So, how to enter inside *Baytu 'Llāh*? Anyone who keeps busy with the Holy Qur'an, trying to understand it, memorize it or read it according to his level, automatically he is entering Kaʿbatu 'Llāh, the Home of Allah ﷻ!

Where was the Holy Qur'an revealed? In Kaʿbah, in Mecca. When you put that in your heart, they will transfer you to be in Kaʿbatu 'Llāh; you will be there immediately! Do you think, when you read the Qur'an you are on your chair? Some sit reading on a chair or on the floor, busy reading the Holy Qur'an.

Do you know where you will be at that time? It depends on the level you are in, but the basic level is that you will be at the Kaʿbah, as it was revealed there. Allah ﷻ is The Most Generous One, He is not holding anything; He wants to give and is giving to those who are reciting and reading the Holy Qur'an. Allah ﷻ grants them to be inside the Kaʿbah, where people are killing each other to reach *Ḥajar al-Aswad*, or they put the stairs and you go inside through the door. As soon as you open the Holy Qur'an, you will be there! That is from the blessing of Laylat al-Qadr, the Night of Power!

One time it came to the heart of one of the *murīds* of Sayyīdinā Shāh Naqshband ق to build something to honor and show love to the Holy Qur'an. So, he built an entire room of gold and put the Holy Qur'an in it, to be in a nice place! Now we are putting the Holy Qur'an on floors, on windows, near shoes! Especially if you go to Mecca and Madinah, you will see that they leave the Qur'an on the floor; they do not put it on their laps.

Shaykh Nazim ق was saying that this has been opened from his *munajāt*, supplication, that anyone who only holds the Holy Qur'an or carries it with him in his bag, will be standing at the Door of Kaʿbah! And as soon as you recite one word, one letter from it, like "*Alif. Lām. Mīm,*" you are immediately inside, as that is a code. They say no one knows these codes in the opening chapters of the Holy Qur'an, but they are secrets Allah ﷻ gives to *Awlīyāullāh* to know. So as soon as you say, "*Alif. Lām. Mīm,*" you are inside!

These letters are like lights that will be reflected to you heart. That light that Allah ﷻ gave to us, whoever reads it, or obeys it, or carries it, or respects it, he will be entering Kaʿbatu 'Llāh, the House of Allah ﷻ. Allah gave us a way to do that: He gave us His Secret Word, the Holy Qur'an. He said, "O My Servant, do you want to be in My Home? If you want to be inside the Kaʿbah, then carry My Qur'an in your heart! Then I will give you my Kaʿbah." So, *al-ʿamal bi 'l-Qur'ān,* takes you to the House of Allah ﷻ.

The Qur'an will intercede for anyone who reads it. Every letter will come on the Day of Judgement to ask Allah's Forgiveness on your behalf and will not leave until you are forgiven. That's what Allah ﷻ gave to *Ummat an-Nabī* ﷺ for His Love for His Prophet ﷺ! May Allah ﷻ keep the Holy Qur'an in our hearts, not to forget it, to read it as much as we can, especially during the holy month, in order for Allah ﷻ to be happy with us, *Inshā-Allāh.*

Every Muslim wishes to be in Ḥaram al-Makkī, at the Sacred Mosque, *Baytu 'Llāh,* to be there and observe his prayers there. However, there is a higher-level person who not only wants to pray there, but to enter inside the Kaʿbah and pray two *rakaʿats* there. The one who keeps his prayers, Allah ﷻ will grant him that; He will not prohibit His Servant from praying inside His House!

Many people might not keep their prayers in their lifetime, but they get an opportunity to enter the Kaʿbah and pray two *rakaʿats,* as they might be official people. Allah ﷻ does not look at your image, He looks at the heart: if your aim in your heart is to keep your prayer as much as possible, to keep clean and pure and throw Shayṭān away and put your heart at the Threshold of Allah's Door, be sure that you are not only praying in Kaʿbah in *Ḥaram al-Makkī*, but Allah ﷻ will cause you to pray in *Bayt al-Maʿmūr*, the Reality of the House of Allah in Heavens! Allah ﷻ will give you the *tajallī*, manifestation of the Fourth Paradise, which contains *Bayt al-Maʿmūr*. That is why Allah ﷻ said:

مَا وَسِعَنِى أَرْضِى وَلَا سَمَائِى، وَلَكِن وَسِعَنِى قَلْبُ عَبْدِى الْمُؤْمِن.

Neither My Heavens nor My Earth contain Me, but the heart of My believing servant contains Me.[127]

You cannot "contain" or dare to say your heart "contains" Allah ﷻ, but rather "contains the manifestation of the Light that He will send to your heart". That Light will shine in your heart and give it power in order that you will always be in the Presence of Allah ﷻ.

---

[127] Hadith Qudsī, *Al-Iḥyā* of Īmām al-Ghazālī.

Story: On the Holy Prophet's ﷺ Blessed Shoulders

Shaykh Nazim Adil al-Haqqani

[This story shows us how the prophets, in spite of having attained heavenly stations and being so firmly planted in them that their souls never leave the spiritual world, put themselves on the level of the people in order that they may benefit them.]

When the Holy Prophet ﷺ entered Mecca, he cleaned the Holy house of all the idols, smashing them all to bits. There was one idol that was too tall for a single man to smash, so Sayyīdinā ʿAlī ؓ said, "O Rasūlullāh, please stand on my shoulders so you may reach up to it to break it." The Prophet ﷺ answered, "O ʿAlī, you might not be able to support me, but come, you may stand on my shoulders." It is well known that when Jibrīl ؑ brought the revelation, his body would become so crushingly heavy that it once forced a camel to the ground by its momentous weight and the Prophet ﷺ was concerned in case a revelation came upon him while standing on the shoulders of ʿAlī ؓ.

ʿAlī ؓ said, "I am ashamed to put my foot on your shoulder, may my soul be sacrificed for you." The Prophet ﷺ replied, "Don't worry, I am ordering you, so just step up."

When ʿAlī ؓ climbed on the shoulders of the Prophet ﷺ, he immediately found himself looking at the Throne of Allah, its glory taking him far away from this world. The Prophet ﷺ left him gazing like this for some moments, then he said, "O ʿAlī, have you not broken the idol yet?" With the Prophet's words, ʿAlī returned to the world once more, standing in front of the idol, which he proceeded to break.

This is proof that the Prophet ﷺ was always in the Divine Presence, but with his bodily personality was sitting, moving and speaking with the ordinary people, so that even the simplest Bedouin among them could understand him perfectly well.

Story: A Love Story Inside the Kaʿbah

Shaykh Muhammad Hisham Kabbani

One day in Mecca, Sayyīdinā Abū Bakr ﵁ was not where he normally used to be. Aṣ-ḥāb an-Nabī ﵃ were looking for him because the Prophet ﷺ wanted to meet with him, but no one could find him. The Prophet ﷺ then went to the Kaʿbah, opened the door and found him there praying and crying. The Prophet ﷺ was stunned. Why was Abū Bakr aṣ-Ṣiddīq ﵁ crying? No one had died, no one had a problem, everyone was okay, so what was disturbing him? The Prophet ﷺ kept standing out of respect, he didn't leave him, as he ﷺ was so subtle. *Subḥānallāh,* he had the highest *adab*!

أَدَّبَنِى رَبِّى فَأَحْسَنَ تَأْدِيبِى.

My Lord perfected my good manners and conduct.[128]

Allah ﷻ respected the Prophet ﷺ, who then spread that manifestation of respect, *iḥtirām,* throughout the Ummah for all to have *iḥtirām* towards each other. Souls respect others' souls. When we sit with each other we must have respect. Unfortunately, we still harbor disrespect for others in our hearts, which is not good, we must rid ourselves of that. We must respect everyone, young or old, because we don't know when Allah ﷻ will inspire the young one to say something good and perhaps make you learn *adab.*

Sayyīdinā Abū Yazīd al-Bistāmī ق was once asked, "Why do you respect the young and give them your attention? They are young, they don't understand."

He said, "Because the young have fewer sins than me."

They asked, "Why do you respect the elderly?"

He said, "Because they worshipped more than me."

You must always show respect; that is important! So, the Prophet ﷺ stood without disturbing Sayyīdinā Abū Bakr ﵁, until he calmed down a little.

---

[128] Ibn ʿAsākir.

Then the Prophet ﷺ gently tapped him on his back. Sayyīdinā Abū Bakr ؓ was so happy upon seeing the Beloved Prophet ﷺ that all his tears disappeared! The Prophet ﷺ asked, "What happened, *yā* Abū Bakr? Everyone is looking for you, you didn't show up today. What is going on, why are you crying? Allah ﷻ granted you to be aṣ-Ṣiddīq al-Akbar, the Unique Trusted One, with the highest level of trustworthiness. Whenever I say something, you say, *'Ṣadaqta, yā Rasūlullāh.'* In Miʿrāj, when I felt overwhelmed, I heard your voice in Paradise. Allah ﷻ made you, the most respected, most trusted person, to be my Companion when we migrated from Mecca to Madinah."

Allāhumma salli wa sallim wa bārik ʿalā Sayyīdinā Muhammad wa ʿalā āli Sayyīdinā Muhammad!

Allah ﷻ said in the Holy Qur'an:

إِذْ يَقُولُ لِصَاحِبِهِ لاَ تَحْزَنْ إِنَّ اللهَ مَعَنَا

He ﷺ said to his Companion, "Do not be sad (or afraid), for surely Allah is with us."[129]

Allah ﷻ said in the Holy Qur'an that the Prophet ﷺ called Sayyīdinā Abū Bakr *"aṣ-Ṣāḥib," Ṣāḥibi Rasūlillāh* ﷺ. He was the first among men to believe in the Prophet ﷺ; the first to believe among the youth was Sayyīdinā ʿAlī ؑ and among ladies was Sayyidah Khadījatu 'l-Kubra ؓ.

The Prophet ﷺ said, "Why are you in such a situation?" Sayyīdinā Abū Bakr ؓ said, *"Yā Rasūlullāh*! When I entered Kaʿbah, it came to my heart that how can I respect and deal with everyone when I do not know what Allah ﷻ will do with me on the Day of Judgement? I am looking at myself and thinking, yes, Allah ﷻ made me aṣ-Ṣiddīq and you call me that as well. Allah ﷻ promised me Paradise and will keep me away from Hellfire, but what if Allah ﷻ changes it and says, 'I don't want you to be aṣ-Ṣiddīq anymore'? Can anyone interfere? If Allah ﷻ says, 'I want to send you to Hellfire,' what can I do? Nothing. *Yā Rasūlullāh*, can you do anything for me at that time?"

Of course, the Prophet ﷺ can intercede, but this is to teach us something. What level are *Awlīyāullāh* on compared to this? That is why they don't

[129] Sūratu 't-Tawbah, 9:40.

like to be called *'shuyūkh'* or *'Awlīyā.'* They don't like any titles, because they don't want to be arrogant or proud of themselves. *Awlīyāullāh* are under that load: don't think they are happy all the time; they are crying in their homes! *Allāhumma ṣalli ʿalayka, yā sayyidī, yā Rasūlullāh*!

The Prophet ﷺ said, "*Yā* Abū Bakr! Allah gave you *ʿitqun min an-nār*, freedom from Hellfire. You are from the ten who are granted glad tidings of Paradise with no account." Sayyīdinā Abū Bakr ؓ said, "*Yā Rasūlullāh*! If Allah changes that, what will I do?" The Prophet ﷺ began to cry, then said, "If Allah takes you to Hellfire, I will go with you!" This demonstrates the degree of love they shared. Do we have that? What will we do on that Day? There will be no brother or sister who will take care of you, no uncle or judge, no mother, no one will help you, you will be responsible for yourself. If Allah ﷻ says, "I want to send you to Hellfire," what can you do?

Sayyīdinā Abū Bakr ؓ said, "Give me *baraʿatun min an-nār*, innocence from Hellfire, *yā Rasūlullāh* and I will stop crying, or else I will cry until the Day of Judgement!" The Prophet ﷺ and Sayyīdinā Abū Bakr aṣ-Ṣiddīq ؓ cried for some time, then Allah ﷻ sent Jibrīl ؑ through the power of *kun faya kun, Be! And it is*! Similarly, Allah ﷻ granted *Awlīyāullāh* the power of *Ṭayy az-Zamān wa 'l-Makān*, the Folding of Time and Space: in one moment they can be anywhere on Earth. When the order came, Jibrīl ؑ was immediately there. To cross our galaxy and reach Earth, you need billions or trillions of light years. Sayyīdinā Jibrīl ؑ passed through all that in a moment, penetrating the timeless zone of that blessed, Divine Heaven to Earth. What did he bring with him?

Sayyīdinā Jibrīl ؑ said, "*Yā Rasūlullāh*! Allah ﷻ sends His *Salām* to you and Abū Bakr aṣ-Ṣiddīq ؓ. He is not happy that you are crying and said, "I made you the Seal of Prophets ﷺ, *wa rafaʿna laka dhikrak*, I raised your name with My Name and that is enough for you, and I made him aṣ-Ṣiddīq, which is enough for him. Tell him that Allah's Order does not change. Sayyīdinā Abū Bakr aṣ-Ṣiddīq ؓ will enter Paradise with no account!"

Story: Entering and Washing the Holy Kaʿbah

Shaykh Muhammad Hisham Kabbani

One night I got a call from one of the *murīds* in Mecca that they were washing the Kaʿbah for *barakah*. He promised he would send a video, and *Inshā-Allāh* we will see that, and it will be as if we are there physically. *Alḥamdulillāh,* they cleaned the Kaʿbah and *Inshā-Allāh* Allah ﷻ gives us to participate in that, if we cannot do it physically, we will do it spiritually, to receive the *barakah* of the Prophet ﷺ.

May Allah ﷻ show us the Kaʿbah from outside and inside, more and more. All praise is to Allah the Lord of the Worlds and praise, peace and blessings upon the Most Honored of Messengers and upon his Family and Companions all together. Glad tidings to us and to you for this tremendous honor they told us about and brought to us, the Holy Kaʿbah being washed. As there are many doors of Paradise, this is one of these many doors that the Sahabah used to keep in their places, a part of the Kaʿbah. The *Awlīyā* wanted us to see it, so our brother called us, and *alḥamdulillāh* it was presented with great power.

Inshā-Allāh we go to Hajj and *ʿUmrah* and we can look for a place to demonstrate our love of the Prophet ﷺ. There were some people present at the washing and those people were able to go inside. From far away you may mention the name of the Kaʿbah, saying three times, "*Bismillāh Allāhu Akbar, wa lillāhi 'l-ḥamd*!" *Alḥamdulillāh,* it isn't easy to go inside the Kaʿbah and once inside, it is even more difficult to enter its reality, but because of our friend, who is one of our best *murīds,* who is very near to the king, he arranged that honor for us to see it from inside, and all of you were present there! To see is the best approach to get close to Allah ﷻ and to the door of the Prophet ﷺ. We ask Allah ﷻ to keep sending His Mercy on us through Kaʿbatu 'Llāh.

They say we are going for Hajj or *ʿUmrah,* but what is the secret meaning of that? The meaning is that when you raise your hand and say, "*Bismillāh Allāhu Akbar*!" you are able to reach the reality of the Kaʿbah in front of the Prophet ﷺ, just as the Sahabah ﵃ used to run to the Prophet ﷺ to look at him. So, we ask, "*Yā* Allah, please do not deprive us of Your Mercy and Your Generosity and make the Kaʿbah the light of our eyes."

The many doors of Paradise open as soon as you say, "*Subḥānallāh wa bi-ḥamdihi Subḥān-Allāh al-ʿAẓīm Astaghfirullāh.*"

كَلِمَتَان خَفِيفَتَانِ عَلَى اللِّسَانِ ثقيلتان فِى الْمِيزَان حبيبتان إِلَى الرَّحْمَنِ

سُبْحَانَ اللَّهِ وَ بِحَمْدِهِ سُبْحَانَ اللَّهِ الْعَظِيمِ.

> *There are two words that are very easy to say, yet very heavy on the Scale, most beloved to The Merciful, "Subḥānallāh wa bi-ḥamdihi subḥānallāh al-ʿAẓīm (All glory is due to Allah through His Praise, all glory is due to Allah the Most)."*[130]

If you want to see the Kaʿbah, you can see it. We ask Allah ﷻ to make us enter through one of these doors by which we can see inside the Kaʿbah. Those who send *ṣalāwāt* on the Prophet ﷺ are always in the presence of the Kaʿbah. The Kaʿbah is able to speak and *Awlīyāullāh* can hear it. *Inshā-Allāh* we will one day be able to hear the Kaʿbah speaking, and the Prophet ﷺ is the door for the people to see the Reality of Kaʿbah.

They wrote hundreds and thousands of books about what we mean by the secrets of Kaʿbatu'Llāh, full of nice explanations. I showed some people some of these books. May Allah ﷻ keep us on the love of the Kaʿbah, and *Inshā-Allāh* we shall soon make some books available to be seen about "the Reality of Kaʿbah" and some books "in the Reality of Kaʿbah," and these two are different.

---

[130] Bukhārī and Muslim.

MŪṢĀLLA JIBRĪL

> *When the Prophet ﷺ first met Jibrīl عليه السلام,*
> *from the Heavens there came on Earth*
> *a golden throne.*
> *The angels took Sayyīdinā Muhammad ﷺ*
> *and made him sit on that throne.*
> *Then, Jibrīl touched*
> *the edge of his wing on Earth.*
> *A spring came and Jibrīl made wuḍū,*
> *the Prophet ﷺ watching.*
> *Jibrīl told him to do the same washing,*
> *saying, 'That is for you and your nation.*
> *Whoever does as you are doing,*
> *he will get clean from all sins,*
> *spiritually and physically clean.'*
> *Wuḍū is mentioned in the Holy Qur'an,*
> *but Jibrīl came to show how to make wuḍū.*
> *We are in need to look and to practice!*

Shaykh Nazim Adil al-Haqqani ق

MUṢALLA JIBRĪL, WHERE THE ANGEL JIBRĪL LED THE PROPHET IN PRAYER AFTER THE NIGHT JOURNEY.

CLOSE-UP OF THE EIGHT MARBLE PIECES.

These eight brown marble pieces on the Shadharawan of the Kaʿbah are known as 'Mūṣālla Jibrīl'. They mark the spot where the angel Jibrīl (Gabriel) taught the Prophet how to pray *ṣalāt* following the miraculous Night Journey to Masjid al-Aqsa and to Heavens. The marble is known as 'Mary Stone', one of the rarest types in the world. They were gifted by Caliph Abū Jaʿfar al-Manṣūr.

WHO WAS TEACHING WHO?

It is said that the Prophet and Jibrīl used to study, reading the Holy Qur'an to each other in Ramadan, talking about *ʿIlm al-Awwalīn wa 'l-Ākhirīn*, Knowledge of Before and After. Who was teaching whom? Was it Jibrīl or the Prophet teaching? Allah knows. Look how much Allah has made the relationship strong between Jibrīl and the Prophet, and not every prophet was able to have that relationship.

One time, Jibrīl came down with a revelation and said to the Prophet, "*Kāf*." The Prophet said, "*ʿAlīmtu*, I knew it." It means he knew every knowledge behind the letter *Kāf*. When Jibrīl said "*Ṣād*", the Prophet said, "ʿAlī*mtu*, I knew it!" and each letter in the Holy Qur'an has lots of meanings behind it. When he was speaking about *Kāf*, behind the letter *Kāf* are 24,000 Oceans of Knowledge. When Jibrīl revealed to the Prophet, the Prophet immediately knew all the meanings. That revelation is the Holy Qur'an as well as the Holy Hadith of the Prophet, about whom Allah said:

مَا يَنطِقُ عَنِ الْهَوَى إِنْ هُوَ إِلَّا وَحْيٌ يُوحَى

He does not speak from (his own) desire.
It is no less than inspiration sent down to him.[131]

YOU CANNOT LEARN WITHOUT A TEACHER

The head of every association is:

أَطِيعُواْ اللّهَ وَأَطِيعُواْ الرَّسُولَ وَأُوْلِي الأَمْرِ مِنكُمْ

Obey Allah, obey the Prophet, and obey those in authority among you. [132]

By obeying Allah ﷻ you are obeying the Prophet ﷺ, and by obeying the Prophet ﷺ you are obeying Allah ﷻ. Therefore, always keep your Lord and the Prophet ﷺ in your heart; and when you obey your teacher, it means that you are obeying the Prophet ﷺ.

A HISTORIC PHOTO OF A LADY PRAYING INSIDE THE MUṢALLA JIBRĪL.

A teacher is very important, for without a teacher, no one can progress, and no one can find his way and his path. Therefore, everyone must have a teacher. Even the Prophet ﷺ, and all

[131] Sūratu 'n-Najm, 53:3-4.

[132] Sūratu 'n-Nisā, 4:59.

messengers that Allah ﷻ has sent to this world, had teachers. They had the angel Jibrīl ﷺ who was a teacher for them. That is why we must take a teacher who will show us the way to the Prophet ﷺ and to Allah ﷻ. Don't think that you can arrive anywhere without one; it is impossible. By yourself you can never arrive anywhere because if you lose the way, you will be truly lost. So, use someone who knows the way, who has travelled that way before and is experienced. He will take you by the hand and lead you directly to your goal without going here or there to get lost.

SHAYKH NAZIM ADIL AL-HAQQANI ق ACCOMPANYING HIS TEACHER, GRANDSHAYKH 'ABD ALLAH FA'IZ AD-DAGHESTANI ق BACK TO HIS HOME ON JABAL QĀSIYŪN, MOUNTAIN IN DAMASCUS, SYRIA.

That is why we have a Golden Chain. That chain of teachers and masters related to each other goes back without interruption to the Prophet ﷺ. This is what we need: a direct chain. We don't want a chain that is broken somewhere. A pipe carrying water underground from one village to another has to be completely whole. If there is one hole somewhere, the water will never come. If that chain of saints is broken, you can never arrive to the Prophet ﷺ.

A tree that doesn't have roots doesn't give fruit. A tree that is only slightly rooted in the ground will be thrown down by the first wind. Its grounding is too weak. A teacher must never be "grafted onto," therefore, without one knowing who his teacher is, his grandteacher, his great-grandteacher, and so on, until the origin of your path. That is why true Sufi teachers are the most connected ones and the most powerful masters in this world: they have true connection; they know their origin. If you don't know your origin, you are not connected anywhere, or you don't know where you are connected.

THE MULTAZAM WALL

“*As for the clinging*
to the curtains of the Ka‘bah
and clinging to the Multazam,
let your intention in clinging
be to seek nearness (to God),
(and to show) affection and longing
for the House and for
the Lord of the House.
Also (intend) on obtaining blessing
by touching (the House),
hoping to be fortified against Fire
in every part of your body,
for the sake of the House.”

Īmām Abū Ḥāmid al-Ghazālī ق

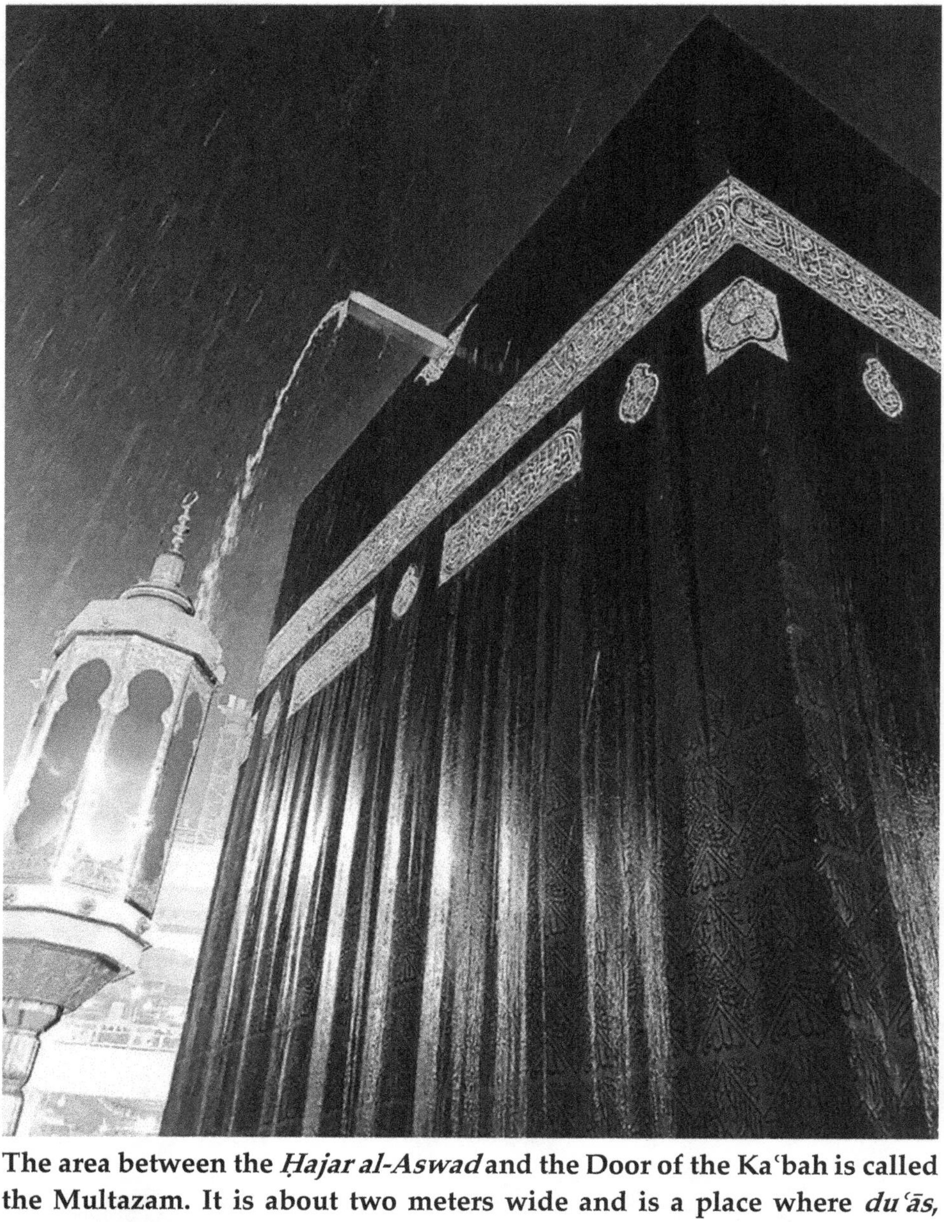

The area between the *Ḥajar al-Aswad* and the Door of the Kaʿbah is called the Multazam. It is about two meters wide and is a place where *duʿās,* supplications, are accepted. It is a sunnah to hold on to the wall of the Kaʿbah in such a manner that a cheek, chest and hands are against the wall. This action is known as *iltizām*. ʿAbdAllāh bin ʿAbbās ﷺ says, "The signs of acceptance for any *duʿā* made between the *Ḥajar al-Aswad* and the door of the Kaʿbah will certainly be seen!"

Jalhama ibn ʿUrfuta ﷺ said, "I came to Mecca during a drought. Some men of Quraysh came to Abū Ṭālib and said, 'O, Abū Ṭālib, the valley is barren, and the families are suffering. Let us go and pray for rain.' Abū Ṭālib came out, and with him was a young boy who looked like the sun after the clouds have cleared. He ﷺ was surrounded by other young children. Abū Ṭālib led him to the Kaʿbah and had him stand with his back against it. There wasn't even a tiny cloud in the sky, but as soon as the young boy rose his hands, clouds started to arrive from every direction and it started raining, then pouring! The valley blossomed and both in Mecca and out in the desert became fertile. About this miracle, Abū Ṭālib wrote the following verses:

To the one of bright complexion,
rain is sent for the sake of his countenance,
He is a refuge for the orphans,
and support for the widows!"[133]

---

[133] Ibn ʿAsākir.

Story: The Immediate Acceptance of a *Walī*'s *Du'ā*

Shaykh Muhammad Hisham Kabbani

Shaykh Nazim, Shaykh Hisham and Shaykh Adnan during Hajj.

In 1968, my brother and I went with Shaykh Nazim ق to Hajj. What do you do when you arrive in Mecca? You go for *Ṭawāf al-Qudūm*, the Circumambulation of Arrival. So, we went for *ṭawāf* around the Ka'bah and after the first, second and third *ṭawāf*, Shaykh Nazim ق stopped at *Bāb al-Multazam*, the Golden Door of the Ka'bah, just passed the *Ḥajar al-Aswad*. We said, "Mawlana, move or they will push us!" but he was not there with us, it was as if he was in a trance.

Do you know how hard it is to stop (in the middle of *ṭawāf*) during Hajj time? You cannot stand there; it's crowded, and they push you, but Mawlana ق was standing in the middle looking at *Bāb al-Multazam* from two meters away, raising his hands making *du'ā*. It's dangerous there and my brother and I were standing with him in his (spiritual) circle while he was making *du'ā*. *Awlīyāullāh* have a circle surrounding them and whoever enters that circle will not be harmed, they will be supported, and we were in that circle of protection. It was as if everything had disappeared, there was no one anymore; I was unable to see anything, only Shaykh Nazim ق making *du'ā*! So, Shaykh Nazim ق raised his hands and said:

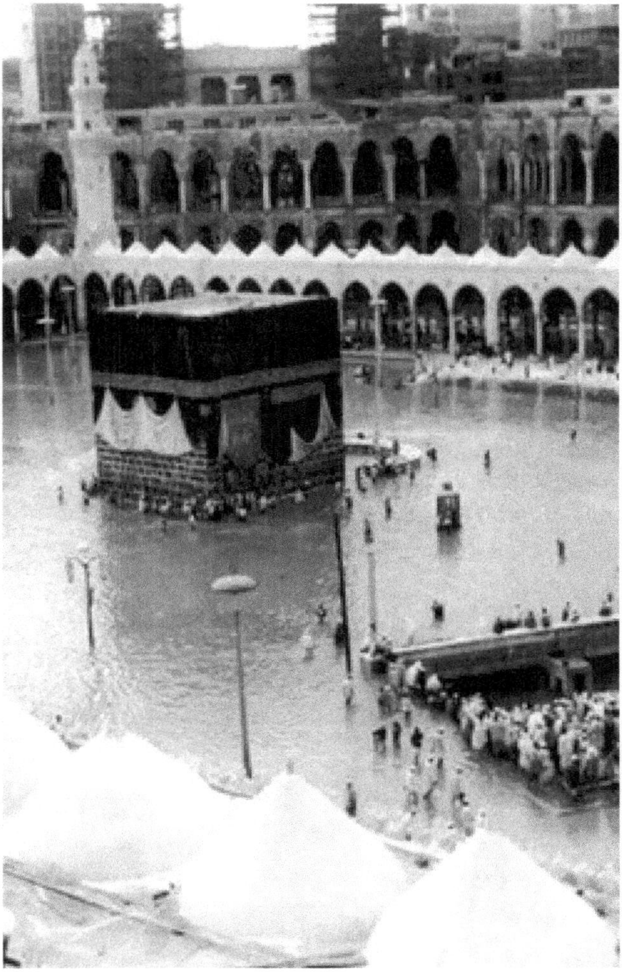

FLOOD IN MASJID AL-ḤARĀM AFTER HEAVY RAIN.

Yā Rabbī! We are coming from far away to Your House that all prophets built for You. *Yā Rabbī*! We are weak servants, full of sins. You brought us from a far place to a hot place with no clouds. We are coming here to be dressed with Raḥmatu 'Llāh. Show us Your *Raḥmah,* Mercy, for the sake of Prophet ﷺ and *Awlīyāullāh. Yā Rabbī*! We are coming all the way here for You and for love of Your Prophet ﷺ, and we will stand under Mizāb ar-Raḥmah (the drain extending from Kaʿbah's roof) begging from You to shower us with Your Rain. I am not moving from here to the fourth *ṭawāf* until You shower us and send rain on all the people doing *ṭawāf* around Kaʿbah! When *Awlīyāullāh* speak, *lahum dālla ʿinda 'Llāh ʿAzza wa jall,* they have like an affinity for your child, whom you love so much, they have affinity towards their Lord and Allah ﷻ likes what they say. So, before he could even complete his *duʿā,* we heard thunder and lightning, and torrential pouring rain showered upon us! In less than five minutes clouds appeared and rain fell so fast until the whole Ḥaram and all of Mecca was flooded, and the water came up to our hips! From our fourth to seventh *ṭawāf* that rainwater began to rise to chest level, and everyone had to run. Traffic was halted, no one could drive. Then Shaykh Nazim ق said, "*Yā Rabbī*! We asked for a little bit of *barakah*. *Alḥamdulillāh,* You showered us with all this Mercy." We could not stay there. We had to go up the stairs to save ourselves from the flood!

How *Awlīyāullāh* can do that is something people cannot understand; if Allah ﷻ gives them that power, they can do it. Allah ﷻ said"

ادْعُونِى أَسْتَجِبْ لَكُمْ

Idʿūnī astajib lakum, "Call on Me, I will answer you."[134]

All that from one *duʿā* of Shaykh Nazim ق that Allah accepted. This is how Mawlana, may Allah bless his soul, behaved throughout his life and this is one of his miracles. You don't see this now. He was one person standing at *Bāb al-Multazam* making *duʿā* at the threshold of the Kaʿbah, asking Allah ﷻ, and Allah ﷻ was showering. That is an example of the immediate acceptance of a *Walī*'s *duʿā*. It means, Allah ﷻ showers any *duʿā* they ask. That is why we come to a *Walī* to ask for *duʿā* as their *duʿā* goes quicker than ours.

We are common people, so we have to keep making *duʿā* in order that Allah ﷻ will check our patience and then He grants us acceptance. Don't forget that the best *duʿā* is through Allah's Beautiful Names and Attributes and through the means of the Prophet ﷺ and *Awlīyāullāh.*

Also, in 2014, on the day of Shaykh Nazim's ق passing, rain was falling in Mecca and Madinah at the time that coincided with Mawlana's soul leaving his body. Later that afternoon, everyone realized that even the sky was weeping for the loss of the world's great saint. It was a mercy, *raḥmah,* from Allah ﷻ that these rains were falling to show how much love Allah ﷻ has for His Saint. We are asking Shaykh Nazim ق from here to make *duʿā* for us (gaze upon us) and to keep us with him in his circle, in the presence of the Prophet ﷺ!

---

[134] Sūratu 'l-Ghāfir, 40:60.

THE HILLS OF ṢAFĀ & MARWA

“*The running between Ṣafā and Marwa*
in the courtyard of the House:
this resembles the movements to and fro
of a slave in the courtyard of a king,
coming and going time after time,
showing his loyalty in service,
hoping for a look of favor,
in the manner of one
who enters the presence of a king
and goes out without knowing
what the king has ordered
with respect to his case,
acceptance or repulsion,
so that he keeps coming back
to the courtyard time after time,
hoping to be forgiven
in the second time if not in the first.”

Īmām Abū Ḥāmid al-Ghazālī ق

Ṣafā and Marwa are two small hills, connected to the larger Abū Qubays and Qaiqan mountains, respectively. Mount Ṣafā is the point from where pilgrims of Hajj and *ʿUmrah* start the *Saʿī* in the Masʿā (the route between the two hills), emulating the actions of Hājar ﷺ, wife of Ibrāhīm ﷺ, who ran back and forth seven times between Ṣafā and Marwa hoping to find water for her son, Ismaʿīl. Her husband, Prophet Ibrāhīm ﷺ had been commanded to leave them there with some water and dates. When Hājar eventually ran out of food and water and could no longer breastfeed Ismaʿīl, Allah ﷻ sent Jibrīl ﷺ to their aid and a spring of water appeared from the ground. The well was named Zamzam and the journey back and forth Ṣafā and Marwa became a ritual during Hajj and *ʿUmrah*. The Hills of Ṣafā and Marwa are described in the Qur'an as being among the Signs of Allah.

MOUNT ṢAFĀ.

إِنَّ الصَّفَا وَالْمَرْوَةَ مِن شَعَائِرِ اللَّهِ فَمَنْ حَجَّ الْبَيْتَ أَوِ اعْتَمَرَ فَلَا جُنَاحَ
عَلَيْهِ أَن يَطَّوَّفَ بِهِمَا وَمَن تَطَوَّعَ خَيْرًا فَإِنَّ اللَّهَ شَاكِرٌ عَلِيمٌ

Indeed, al-Ṣafā and al-Marwa are among the symbols of Allah. So, whoever makes Hajj to the House or performs ʿUmrah, there is no blame upon him for walking between them. And whoever volunteers good - then indeed, Allah is appreciative and Knowing.[135]

[135] Sūratu 'l-Baqarah, 2:158.

Prophet Muhammad's ﷺ Message to the Whole World

Shaykh Nazim Adil al-Haqqani

O People! *As-salāmu ʿalaykum*. Hear and trust what the Prophet ﷺ was saying. Trust what prophets said, then you will be supported by heavenly powers. Yes, the Seal of Prophets, Sayyīdinā Muhammad ﷺ, was coming alone, and he was an orphan. His father passed away when his mother was pregnant with him ﷺ. Then his mom passed away when he was six or seven years old. He was reaching to 40 years of age, then calling people, "O People! Come, come. I am going to say something to you. Come and listen." People were running to hear what he was going to say. He was on Mount Ṣafā in Mecca, calling people, "O People! I have been ordered by the Lord of Heavens to call you to say *'Lā ilāha illa-Llāh Muḥammadun Rasūlullāh.'*"

Some of the Quraysh, powerful ones of his tribe, were so angry. They were asking to rush on him; some of them were trying to run away from him, and they were coming, mixing with each other. They were not knowing what they will say and that one was saying, "O you must say *'Lā ilāha illa-Llāh.'*" There was no one with him, only the Lord of Heavens ordered him to say, "Call and say to them, *'Lā ilāha illa-Llāh!'*" Yes, what happened? He was one and alone, but heavenly support was coming on him. His declaration and his calling to the whole nation was beginning to appear, appearing, appearing, and appearing.

O People! Look and listen and take wisdom and lesson. The Seal of Prophets ﷺ carried every heavy burden from his nation, but his Lord was with him. He never changed his direction to Allah, to Allah, to Allah. When he was saying, "O People! Come and listen to me. We are going to Allah, to Allah, to Allah! Trust me and Allah Almighty will support you." Did Allah ﷻ support that one or not? Yes, supported! People were trusting him, and Allah ﷻ supported them.

MOUNT ʿARAFAT

“ *ʿArafat is noble, and forgiveness comes from*
the Divine Presence to the people as a whole,
only through the dear hearts of Awtād al-Arḍ
(a category of saints). The place is never devoid
of some Substitutes and Stakes, al-Abdāl wa al-Awtād,
or some Pious ones and Masters of Hearts.
And if their resolutions coincide,
and their hearts be directed exclusively to submission
and humility (to God), and their hands raised up
to God Most High, and their necks submitted to Him, and
their eyes lifted up in the direction of Heaven,
and they are all of one mind in seeking forgiveness,
do not think that He will disappoint their expectations
or allow their running (saʿī) to be of no avail or
hold back from them in storage the forgiveness
which encompasses them. It is as though the coincidence of
resolutions and reliance upon the proximity of the Substitutes
and Stakes who have gathered from all corners of the world is
the secret of the Pilgrimage and the (sole) object behind it!
There is no way to elicit the forgiveness of God Most High
like the joining together of resolutions and the cooperation
of hearts in one time and at one place! ”

Īmām Abū Ḥāmid al-Ghazālī ق

PILGRIMS ON MOUNT ʿARAFAT.

Jabal ʿArafat (Arabic: جبل عرفات) is a small, granite mountain in the plain of ʿArafat, about 20km from the Kaʿbah. Standing at ʿArafat is a fundamental requirement of Hajj. Pilgrims travel here from Mina on the second day of Hajj (9th Dhul-Hijjah). The mountain is also known as Jabal al-Raḥmah, meaning "Mountain of Mercy".

The common meaning of the word ʿArafat is 'to know'. After being taken out of Jannah and placed on Earth, it was at Jabal ʿArafat that Prophet Ādam ﷺ and Hawa ﷺ met up again.

ʿArafat (عرفة) is the name of the day, and ʿArafat (عرفات) is the name of the land.

Standing on ʿArafat is an essential part of the Hajj; whoever misses the standing on ʿArafat has missed Hajj, because the Prophet ﷺ said: "Hajj is ʿArafat."[136] The day of ʿArafat has many virtues, as was narrated in many *Aḥādīth*. ʿĀ'ishā ؓ narrated that the Prophet ﷺ said: "There is no day in which Allah sets free more souls from the fire of Hell than on the day of

[136] al-Ḥākim.

'Arafat. And on that day Allah draws near to Earth and by way of exhibiting His Pride remarks to the angels, 'What is the desire of these (servants of Mine)?'"[137]

The Prophet ﷺ said, "The best invocation on the day of 'Arafat, and the best of all the invocations I ever offered or other holy Prophets before me ever offered is: "There is no god but Allah: He is Unique; He has no partner, the whole universe is for Him and for Him is the praise, and He has power over all things."[138]

In another hadith the Prophet ﷺ said: "Apart from the day of the Battle of Badr there is no day on which the Shayṭān is seen to be more humiliated, more rejected, more depressed, and more infuriated than on the day of 'Arafat, and indeed all this is only because of beholding the abundance of descending mercy (on the day) and Allah's forgiveness of the great sins of the servants."[139]

One of the virtues of the day of 'Arafat is that fasting this day expiates for the sins of the past and coming year. It was reported from Abū Qatādah that a man said: "O Messenger of Allah, what do you think of fasting on the day of 'Arafat?" He said: "It expiates for the sins of the previous year and of the coming year"[140]

This fasting is *mustaḥab* (desirable) for those who are not on Hajj. In the case of the one who is on Hajj, it is not Sunnah for him to fast on the Day of 'Arafat, because the Prophet ﷺ did not fast on this day when he was at 'Arafat.

---

[137] Muslim.

[138] Tirmidhī.

[139] *Mishkāt*.

[140] Muslim.

Hajj al-Akbar 1999

14 April 1999 (28 Dhul al-Hijjah 1419)

Shaykh Nazim Adil al-Haqqani

PILGRIMS AT JABAL RAḤMAH (THE MOUNT OF MERCY) FEBRUARY 3, 2015, IN ʿARAFAT. THIS IS THE PLACE WHERE ADAM AND EVE MET AFTER BEING CAST OUT OF PARADISE.

Bismillāhi 'r-Raḥmāni 'r-Raḥīm. It was Hajj al-Akbar this year, the last Hajj al-Akbar of this century and the second millennium. You are lucky people that you have been there. I hope that the next Hajj al-Akbar is going to be in the third millennium, the 21st century according to the Christian calendar. According to the Islamic calendar it is in a Hajj al-Akbar that Mahdī ﷺ is going to be with us.

You were lucky that this year Mahdī ﷺ and his caliphs and ministers, all these grand *Awlīyā*, saints, were present on the Day of ʿArafat, 12,000 *Awlīyā* with Mahdī ﷺ. He did his last prayers when the sun was setting on Friday evening and from Allah Almighty the good tidings came through His Most Respected and Beloved Servant, Sayyīdinā Muhammad ﷺ that all their prayers were accepted. On Friday evening, the beginning of Saturday, when you moved to Mina after sunset, Divine Orders changed to bring Islam up and to put *kufr,* unbelief down. The hegemony of *kufr* is going to melt, to finish, and the Sulṭānate of Shayṭān is going to be destroyed. *Ḥaqq*, the Truth that Allah ﷻ sent, will appear now day by day, and hour by hour it will increase. We hope for new changes day by day. No one is able to keep Islam down now; it is impossible to bring it down. Islam is getting up and *kufr* is going down.

May Allah ﷻ bless you and your Hajj, your charities and visits to holy places. You have also been to Damascus and visited everywhere; Grandshaykh ق accepted you and he gives his *salāms* to all of you. He was happy and proud of you, because you came his way to the Holy Prophet ﷺ, and the Prophet ﷺ was happy with you too, looking to you and blessing you. Now you are on your way home, and there is going to be a new opening for you and around you. Those Divine Lights that were granted to you through Grandshaykh ق from the Holy Prophet ﷺ are going to spread, and people should run from their darkness to your lights.

More than fourteen centuries have passed, and we hope that everything which we were saying, and that you heard about, is going to appear. *Kufr* will be destroyed and disappear, and Islam will grow. The flag of Islam will be raised, and the flag of *kufr* will come down. Who keeps his heart with Allah ﷻ, Allah ﷻ will be with him. If you are not leaving Allah ﷻ, He is not going to leave you! Therefore, as Rasūlullāh ﷺ was saying, "Keep Allah and Allah will keep you."

We are happy and proud of you. You came such a long distance to visit Ḥabību 'Llāh ﷺ and the House of the Lord. You are young people, not easily going to be tired, but it is not an ordinary trip. It is a journey of obedience and worship, and worship is always going to be difficult for our ego. Every time we are carrying difficulties, we are paid more and more by Allah Almighty.

Also, Mahdī ﷺ pointed out our group of Hajjis from western countries. They were Christians before and came to Islam, keeping the Sunnah among those Shayṭānic people... He was saying, "Look, it's Shaykh ʿAbdAllāh's *murīds,* the Naqshbandi followers!" and he was so happy, looking to that group who went there keeping the Sunnah, and giving some spirituality to them that was never given to other people. *Alḥamdulillāh,* they were very happy with you. May Allah bless you! *Alḥamdulillāh,* there is now much more spirituality running through the hearts of people, because they are in need of spirituality more than anything else.

bi ḥurmati 'l-Ḥabīb, bi ḥurmati 'l-sirri Sūratu 'l-Fātiḥah.

Hajj is ʿArafah

MAWLANA SHAYKH MUHAMMAD HISHAM KABBANI

THOUSANDS OF PILGRIMS ON THEIR WAY TO THE PLAIN OF ʿARAFAT.

Why do we all go to the Plain of ʿArafat?

قَالَ النَبِى ﷺ: "اَلحَجُ عَرَفَةُ."

The Prophet ﷺ said, "Hajj is ʿArafat."[141]

This means, if you do not go to ʿArafat, then there is no Hajj. Three or five million people stand there, calling on Allah ﷻ in one voice:

لَبَّيْكَ اللّٰهُمَّ لَبَّيْكَ، لَبَّيْكَ لاَ شَرِيْكَ لَكَ لَبَّيْكَ، إِنَّ الْحَمْدَ وَالنِّعْمَةَ لَكَ وَالْمُلْكَ لاَشَرِيْكَ لَكَ

Labbayk Allāhumma labbayk, labbayka lā sharīka laka labbayk. Inna 'l-ḥamda wa 'n-niʿmata laka wa 'l-mulk lā sharīka lah!

---

141 Īmām Nawawī in his Majmuʿat.

> Here I am at Your service, O Allah, here I am! Here I am at Your service! You have no partner, here I am at Your service. For You alone is All Praise and All Grace, and for You alone is The Sovereignty. You have no partner!

Who is in ʿArafat that brings all these people together? There must be someone to whom the Prophet ﷺ gave authority from Allah ﷻ. You look and see that it is a plain desert. Now they have nice trees and water coming from everywhere and better tents, but in reality, it is a desert. What is there? What are they buying and selling? There, you find everything; it is a huge "mall" that anything you want you will find! It is also like an amazing race, where they want to reach as soon as possible, especially on *Jabal Raḥmah* where the Prophet ﷺ went and gave his famous *Khuṭbat al-Widaʿ*, Farewell Sermon.

What does everyone want to get from there? They say, "We want Allah's forgiveness!" and that is for sure, but Allah ﷻ will forgive us wherever we are. If you ask, "O Allah! Forgive us for the sake of Your Prophet ﷺ," do you think Allah ﷻ will not forgive? But there is something special that Allah ﷻ gave to that plain in ʿArafat. Are we the only ones standing there? Don't you think the Prophet ﷺ is there? There is no Hajj if there is no Prophet ﷺ! If the Prophet ﷺ is not there, there is no Hajj, because the Prophet's presence is important for Allah ﷻ to send His Mercy on us.

O Muslims! Allah ﷻ gave us an important day, the 9th of Dhul-Hijjah without which Hajj cannot be considered accepted, the Day of ʿArafah. That is the day of unity, the day of one voice, the day all Muslims are in the same category. On that day no one better than another, rather all are standing in front of Allah ﷻ, as on Judgment Day. You cannot say this is a king or this is a doctor, no, they are equal before Allah ﷻ, except by their deeds:

لَا فَرْقَ بَيْنَ عَرَبِيٍّ وَلَا أَعْجَمِيٌّ إِلَّا بِالتَّقْوَى

There is no difference between an Arab and a non-Arab, except through righteousness.[142]

---

142 Āḥmad.

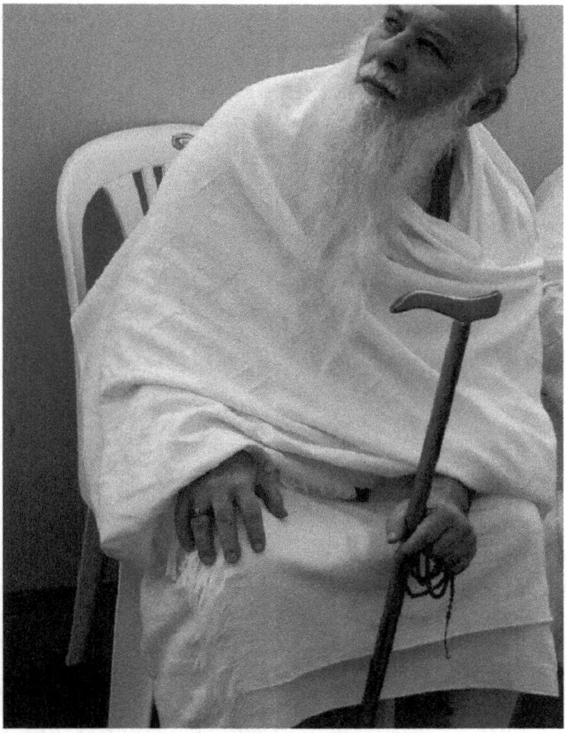

SHAYKH HISHAM IN HIS TENT IN ʿARAFAT, HAJJ 2011.

Because the Prophet ﷺ said, "Hajj is ʿArafat" it might be that you miss some of the principles of Hajj by mistake, as you were ignorant, but Hajj is still accepted as you can make it up by sacrificing a cow, camel, goat, sheep or whatever. However, if you miss ʿArafah, then Hajj is not acceptable. You can make *ṭawāf*, *saʿī*, etc., but it is not considered a valid Hajj without ʿArafah. All of the rituals that you do, such as going to Mina, doing *Ṭawāf al-Qudūm*, *Ṭawāf al-Widāʿ*, etc. are not easy, you have to struggle to do them, and yet Allah ﷻ is saying, "All of that without ʿArafah is nothing!"

What is in ʿArafah? There must be something hidden. Even if you just go to the Valley of ʿArafat, without making any *duʿā* or *ṣalāwāt*, just your presence there will completely purify you as if you were a newly born baby. There, Allah ﷻ comes to the First Heaven, looks at His Servants and forgives them all, as the rest of *Ummat an-Nabī* ﷺ cannot be left without the Shower of Mercy of the Merciful One, which Sayyīdinā Muhammad ﷺ distributes.

In a Hadith it is mentioned that the Prophet ﷺ stood on the night of ʿArafah, asking for *Raḥmatu 'Llāh*, for Allah ﷻ to forgive the whole Ummah, and Allah ﷻ said, "I forgive them all, except the one who is an oppressor. I am going to take the rights of the oppressed!" And, from his mercy, the Prophet ﷺ was sad.

رَسُولَ اللَّهِ صَلَّى اللَّهُ عَلَيْهِ وَسَلَّمَ دَعَا عَشِيَّةَ يَوْمِ عَرَفَةَ لأُمَّتِهِ بِالْمَغْفِرَةِ وَالرَّحْمَةِ ، فَأَكْثَرَ الدُّعَاءَ ، فَأَوْحَى اللَّهُ إِلَيْهِ : إِنِّى قَدْ فَعَلْتُ ، إِلا ظُلْمَ بَعْضِهِمْ لِبَعْضٍ ، وَأَمَّا ذُنُوبُهُمْ فِيمَا بَيْنِى وَبَيْنَهُمْ فَقَدْ غَفَرْتُهَا ، فَقَالَ : يَا رَبِّ إِنَّكَ قَادِرٌ عَلَى أَنْ تُثِيبَ هَذَا الْمَظْلُومَ خَيْرًا مِنْ مَظْلَمَتِهِ ، وَتَغْفِرَ لِهَذَا الظَّالِمِ ، فَلَمْ يُجِبْهُ تِلْكَ الْعَشِيَّةَ فَلَمَّا كَانَ غَدَاةَ الْمُزْدَلِفَةِ أَعَادَ الدُّعَاءَ ، فَأَجَابَهُ اللَّهُ تَعَالَى : إِنِّى قَدْ غَفَرْتُ لَهُمْ " ، قَالَ : فَتَبَسَّمَ رَسُولُ اللَّهِ صَلَّى اللَّهُ عَلَيْهِ وَسَلَّمَ ، فَقَالَ لَهُ بَعْضُ أَصْحَابِهِ : يَا رَسُولَ اللَّهِ ، تَبَسَّمْتَ فِى سَاعَةٍ لَمْ تَكُنْ تَتَبَسَّمُ فِيهَا ، قَالَ : " تَبَسَّمْتُ مِنْ عَدُوِّ اللَّهِ إِبْلِيسَ ، إِنَّهُ لَمَّا عَلِمَ أَنَّ اللَّهَ تَعَالَى قَدِ اسْتَجَابَ لِى فِى أُمَّتِى أَهْوَى يَدْعُو بِالْوَيْلِ وَالثُّبُورِ ، وَيَحْثُو عَلَى رَأْسِهِ التُّرَابَ

The Messenger of Allah ﷺ supplicated for forgiveness and mercy for his Ummah on the night before ʿArafah. Then Allah ﷻ revealed to him, "I have forgiven them except their oppression of each other. As for their sins between Me and them, I have forgiven them." He said, "O my Lord, truly You are able to reward the oppressed one more than what he suffered of oppression and to forgive the oppressor." He ﷻ did not respond that night. The following day at Muzdalifah, the Prophet ﷺ repeated the supplication and Allah ﷻ responded to him, "I have forgiven them," He granted them both and forgave the ẓālim, oppressor and the maẓlūm, the oppressed one, is also free. The Messenger of Allah ﷺ laughed and some of his companions ﷺ asked him, "O Messenger of Allah, you are laughing at a time you did not used to laugh?" He said, "I am laughing at the enemy of Allah, Iblīs. When he heard that Allah has forgiven the ẓālim and maẓlūm, he fell down wailing and started throwing dirt on his head.[143]

---

[143] Ibn Mājah, Āḥmad, Bayhaqī.

Are we from the Ummah or not? We are under the *tajallī* that Allah ﷻ has forgiven all the Ummah on the night of ʿArafah. This means, Iblīs is running away, and Allah is forgiving us for the love of Sayyīdinā Muhammad ﷺ; Allah ﷻ is sending His Love, in spite of the noise of Iblīs. So, we have to make *ṣalāwāt*, and that is why it is important to fast on that day.

So, Hajj is to stand on that valley. If you went there forty years ago, there was a wide sandy valley, nothing on it. They would have to carry water and food with them in order to survive in that valley. What is there? Jabal Raḥmah, the Mountain of Mercy, where Allah ﷻ manifested mercy to the Prophet ﷺ. The Prophet ﷺ wanted to take his Sahabah ؓ to that place to taste the difficulty, because when you suffer in *dunyā*, you receive reward in the Next Life. Allah ﷻ wants to test Muslims in their patience. You go to that valley and stand, and all Muslims in one voice are saying, *labbayk Allāhumma labbayk, labbayka lā sharīka laka labbay*k, "Here I am (at Your service), O Allah! There is no partner for You; You are the Creator, we are here at Your service." Allah ﷻ likes His Servants to declare His Oneness and to say, "*Ash-hadu an lā ilāha illa 'Llāh, wa ash-hadu anna Muhammadan ʿabduhu wa rasūluh*"; He ﷻ doesn't like *shirk*, to associate anyone as a partner with Him.

Some might ask where the name ʿArafat came from. It comes from the word 'to know' and that comes from the story of Sayyīdinā Ibrāhīm ؑ and Ismaʿīl ؑ and the place where Allah ﷻ informed Sayyīdinā Ibrāhīm ؑ to slaughter Sayyīdinā Ismaʿīl ؑ. It is called ʿArafat because ʿArafat is from ʿArafah, meaning that Allah ﷻ introduced or made something clear. What did He make clear? He made it clear to Ibrāhīm ؑ to sacrifice his son and that is one of the reasons that Allah ﷻ makes us clean by ʿArafah. Allah ﷻ gave us a lot of opportunities to be cleaned, one of them is ʿArafah.

It is said, "Allah ﷻ honored four prophets on the Day of ʿArafat: He honored Ādam ؑ with forgiveness on that day for eating from the forbidden tree; He honored Sayyīdinā Mūsā ؑ to speak with Him without an intermediary; He honored Sayyīdinā Muhammad ﷺ with Hajj and the perfection of religion; and He honored Sayyīdinā Ibrāhīm ؑ with replacing the sacrifice of his son Sayyīdinā Ismaʿīl ؑ with a lamb. May Allah ﷻ forgive us and bless us.

The Prophet's ﷺ Care for His Ummah Is Beyond Our Grasp

Shaykh Muhammad Hisham Kabbani

Alḥamdulillāh Who made us from the nation of Sayyīdinā Muhammad ﷺ and enlightened us with the Light of His Beloved and the Light of Holy Qur'an and He made us to follow His Beloved Prophet ﷺ and said in Holy Qur'an:

قُلْ إِن كُنتُمْ تُحِبُّونَ اللّهَ فَاتَّبِعُونِي يُحْبِبْكُمُ اللّهُ وَيَغْفِرْ لَكُمْ ذُنُوبَكُمْ وَاللّهُ غَفُورٌ رَّحِيمٌ

Say (O Muhammad), "If you (really) love Allah, then follow me! Allah will love you and forgive your sins, and Allah is Oft-Forgiving, Most Merciful. [144]

The Prophet ﷺ brought us Islam, the Message of Allah, where He said:

إِنَّ الدِّينَ عِندَ اللّهِ الإِسْلاَمُ

The religion in Allah's view is Islam (submission to His Will).[145]

As related, on the night before ʿArafah, on Prophet's Farewell Hajj, the Prophet ﷺ was sad and made *duʿā, "Yā Rabbī,* forgive my Ummah." He awaited the answer, which came, "*Yā* Muhammad! I forgave them all, except *aẓ-ẓālim*, the oppressor."

Who is not an oppressor? We are even oppressors to ourselves: Allah assigned us *ʿibādah*, worship, and we are not doing it, although it is the energy, the fuel for the soul, just as food is fuel for the body. If we don't worship correctly, we are oppressors to our *nafs*, our soul, the *rūḥ*. That comes by the order of Allah ﷻ *al-arwāḥu junūdān mujannada*. When we

[144] Sūrat Āli-ʿImrān, 3:31.

[145] Sūrat Āli-ʿImrān, 3:19.

were souls in the Presence of Allah ﷻ on the Day of Promises, Allah ﷻ asked:

أَلَسْتُ بِرَبِّكُمْ قَالُوا بَلَىٰ

"Am I not your Lord?" They said, "Yes!"[146]

That soul needs nourishment, which is worship. You will be given according to how much you worship. Like the body needs food, the soul needs worship. So, Prophet ﷺ said, "*Yā Rabbī*, forgive my Ummah!" Allah ﷻ said, "I forgive them all but the oppressors." We are all oppressors to ourselves. When we sin, we oppress our *ʿamal*, we do what we are prohibited and we will be asked about it, as Allah ﷻ said:

ا أَيُّهَا الَّذِينَ آمَنُوا اجْتَنِبُوا كَثِيرًا مِّنَ الظَّنِّ إِنَّ بَعْضَ الظَّنِّ إِثْمٌ وَلَا
تَجَسَّسُوا وَلَا يَغْتَب بَّعْضُكُم بَعْضًا أَيُحِبُّ أَحَدُكُمْ أَن يَأْكُلَ لَحْمَ أَخِيهِ
مَيْتًا فَكَرِهْتُمُوهُ وَاتَّقُوا اللَّهَ إِنَّ اللَّهَ تَوَّابٌ رَّحِيمٌ

O you who believe! Avoid suspicion as much (as possible) for suspicion in some cases is a sin, and spy not on each other, nor speak ill of each other behind their backs. Would any of you like to eat the flesh of his dead brother? No, you would abhor it![147]

We are even eating our own flesh by following Shayṭān! So, the Prophet ﷺ was sad that Allah was forgiving everyone except the *ẓālim*, and how many *ẓulām* are there? The people on high chairs, controlling everything in the world, are not the only *ẓulām*: we are also *ẓulām* to ourselves, our neighbors, our brothers and sisters, to our countries and even to our governments. We are meddling in everything. Leave that and spend time in worship! Don't interfere, do your work and business, then worship and sleep nicely. When you run after *dunyā* it runs away from you, but when you run towards *Ākhirah*, *dunyā* runs after you.

The Prophet ﷺ was sad, because he wanted to save the *ẓālim*. His love for his Nation is not like our love for our children or our parents.

---

[146] Sūratu 'l-ʿĀrāf, 7:172.

[147] Sūratu 'l-Ḥujurāt, 49:12.

لَقَدْ جَاءَكُمْ رَسُولٌ مِّنْ أَنفُسِكُمْ عَزِيزٌ عَلَيْهِ مَا عَنِتُّمْ حَرِيصٌ عَلَيْكُم بِالْمُؤْمِنِينَ رَؤُوفٌ رَّحِيمٌ

There has certainly come to you a Messenger from among yourselves. Grievous to him is what you suffer; [he is] concerned over you and to the Believers is kind and merciful.[148]

He said, "*Yā Rabbī,* Your Treasures are vast so give the *ẓālim* something, give him *maghfirah* from Your Treasures as You gave *raḥmah* and *maghfirah* to all the sincere ones and forgave everyone. Give the *ẓālim* from Your *Maghfirah* and Your *Jannah.*" There was no answer. Jibrīl ﷺ did not come and the Prophet ﷺ was sad, because the first time he asked for forgiveness for everyone the answer had come, "I forgive everyone but the *ẓālim*."

The night before ʿArafat, not on the day, where there are too many *duʿās,* the Prophet ﷺ asked for His Ummah. That is what the Prophet ﷺ wants: he wants for his Ummah! If you are from his Ummah, you are safe! Say, "*Lā ilāha illa 'Llāh,*" and enter Paradise, but of course we say, "*Lā ilāha illa 'Llāh Muḥammadun Rasūlullāh.*" Look how easy it is, yet we are not saying it. You must not do your obligations to reach Paradise, but Allah ﷻ wants us to say, "*Lā ilāha illa 'Llāh,*" to acknowledge that "there is no creator except Allah." They say (it translates as) "there is no god but Allah" but it is, "there is no creator but Allah."

So, he called for his Ummah, "*Yā Rabbī!*" And whatever Allah ﷻ opened to his heart, Prophet ﷺ asked and Allah answered to His Prophet ﷺ, "I forgave them, all of them except one, the one who has this particular bad character. The rest I am forgiving them for you, *yā* Muhammad!"

شَفَاعَتِى لأَهْلِ الْكَبَائِرِ مِنْ أُمَّتِى

My intercession is for the people in my Ummah who committed the major sins.[149]

---

[148] Sūratu 't-Tawbah, 9:128.

[149] Tirmidhī.

Allah ﷻ gives *shafaʿah,* intercession to the Prophet ﷺ on Judgment Day, *dunyā* and *Ākhirah,* to intercede by Allah's Order and no one can say it is *shirk,* because Allah ﷻ gave it to him! So, He said, "I accept all of them except the oppressor. Whatever I forgive, it is up to Me for the sins people make, but for the oppressor, there are also the oppressed and it is up to them. How do I forgive him when the oppressed will say, 'Yā *Rabb*! What is this? We want our rights.' So first I take the right of the oppressed from the oppressor." And the Prophet ﷺ answered, "You are The Merciful and Generous One; if You want, You can give the oppressed from Your Paradises as You are The Generous One; you can give whatever You like. What can the oppressor give him? If he was able to give him in *dunyā,* he would. *Wa ghafarta li 'ẓ-ẓālim,* and You can also forgive the oppressor! Give the oppressed from Paradise and forgive the oppressor." And Allah ﷻ didn't answer him.

That *duʿā* was on the night of ʿArafat. No answer came and they were in ʿArafat. After that, they go to Muzdalifah, where they spend the night there, and after Fajr they go to Mina.

So, the next day after Fajr, Sayyīdinā Abū Bakr ؓ and Sayyīdinā ʿUmar ؓ saw Prophet ﷺ smiling, his teeth were shining, and a beautiful breath came from his mouth. They were so happy to see him laughing and they asked, "*Yā Rasūlullāh,* what happened? Yesterday you were sad and this morning you are not only happy but laughing in a loud voice!"

The Prophet ﷺ said, "I am laughing and laughing because I saw Iblīs and when he heard that Allah ﷻ has forgiven and granted the *ẓālim* to go to Paradise by my *duʿā,* he became so upset and threw dirt on himself and his army! I am laughing at Iblīs, the Cursed One, because he is running

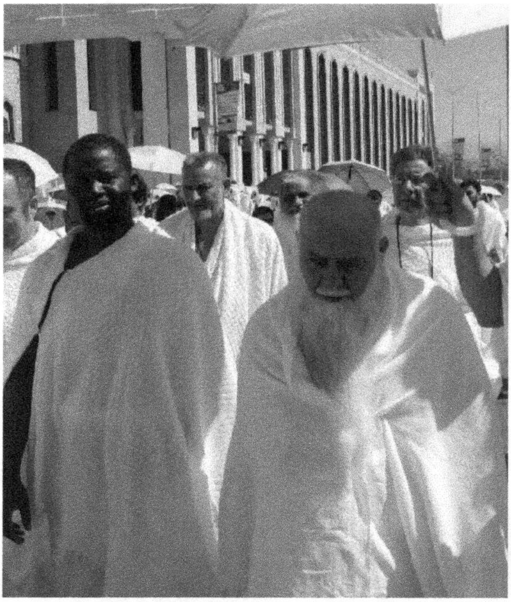

SHAYKH HISHAM AND MURIDS AT ʿARAFAT, HAJJ 2011.

after my Ummah, but Allah ﷻ forgave them and instead put their *sayyiʿat*, sins, on him!" After that event, the Prophet ﷺ was so happy on the day of ʿArafah.

The Prophet ﷺ is caring for us, but what are we caring for? What are we giving in return? He is giving us everything! At least we should show him love. If you love someone, what do you do? You mention his name and follow him, then he will guide you. That is why *shuyūkh* are important in our lives. The Sahabah ؓ were companions of the Prophet ﷺ and after them the *Imāms* came and learned from *Tābiʿīn* or *Tābi at-Tābiʿīn*, and they went on to form the *madhāhib*, the schools of thought.

It is for us to follow guides who show us the way to *Maḥabbat an-Nabī* ﷺ, Love of the Prophet ﷺ. Allah ﷻ showed the whole Ummah the way when He said, "If you really love Allah, then follow the way of Muhammad ﷺ."

قُلْ إِن كُنتُمْ تُحِبُّونَ اللهَ فَاتَّبِعُونِى يُحْبِبْكُمُ اللهُ وَيَغْفِرْ لَكُمْ ذُنُوبَكُمْ وَاللهُ غَفُورٌ رَّحِيمٌ

Say (O Muhammad), "If you (really) love Allah, then follow me! Allah will love you and forgive your sins, and Allah is Oft-Forgiving, Most Merciful."[150]

If your son is with you, you come here and leave at night, would you leave your son on the street and tell him, "Go find your way!" or would

[150] Sūrat Āli-ʿImrān, 3:31.

you take him by his hand? *Shuyūkh* take us with them through their knowledge and *Sharīʿah* they learned and guide us to the love of Prophet ﷺ, as Allah ﷻ said, "If you follow Muhammad ﷺ, Allah will love you." When Allah loves you, it is *nūrun ʿalā nūr,* light upon light. The whole Message is, "To be loved by Allah, you have to follow Muhammad ﷺ." Then you will be loved by Prophet ﷺ, and he will take you to the Door of Allah ﷻ for *maghfirah,* Allah's Forgiveness. May Allah ﷻ forgive us!

So, see how important ʿArafat is, how much *mashaʿari 'l-ḥajj,* and how all this, ʿArafat, Muzdalifah and Mina and Mecca, are important in the life of Muslims. For that *duʿā* of Prophet ﷺ in ʿArafat and Muzdalifah, Allah ﷻ has forgiven everyone from *Ummat an-Nabī* ﷺ! He forgave the oppressor and admitted the oppressed into Paradise.

STORY: THE PRESENCE OF RĀBIʿAH AL-ADAWĪYYA ON JABAL ʿARAFAT

What did Rābiʿah al-ʿAdawīyya ؓ say to show her *adab* and love to her Lord? She said, "*Yā Rabbī*! I love You with no limits, there is nothing in my life but Your Love. If You put me in Paradise, *shukran yā Rabb,* and if you put me in Hellfire, *shukran yā Rabb*; that is my love, even I would not feel in Hellfire due to my love of You."

Grandshaykh ق once told the story of Rābiʿah al-ʿAdawīyya ؓ, who was on Hajj with millions of pilgrims going to ʿArafat, and due to her monthly cycle, she could not pray. She cried about that, while today they all go with the monthly cycle or not; who is checking? She heard a voice from Heavens, "*Yā Rābiʿah*! This year was not going to be a blessed year for those on ʿArafat, but because you are there, I am giving a heavenly manifestation because of your presence!"

It was not due to being near her that they got the blessings, but it was due to them being there (with her). That is a *barakah* place and the most important thing is whether or not there is a heavenly invitation for us to be present there.

SEEKING A HEAVENLY MANIFESTATION

Millions of pilgrims are on the plain of ʿArafat at the same time, and the heavenly manifestation reaches them equally, it doesn't differentiate.

You are present in that place, and you get the *barakah*, whether you are a sinner or a *Walī*. The Prophet ﷺ said, "Whoever goes for Hajj and stands on ʿArafat without any mistake or fighting to be this or that, surrendering to Allah ﷻ and His Prophet ﷺ, will return to his home with no sin on him, like a newborn baby."

You can be at any place in ʿArafat, in the center or at the perimeter, and it is the same, as if you are in the center with those who manifest themselves spiritually. You are not seeking a person, but rather a heavenly manifestation!

SHAYKH HISHAM, HAJJAH NAZIHA AND GROUP LISTENING TO QASĪDAHS IN PRAISE OF THE PROPHET Y IN ʿARAFAT, HAJJ 2011.

Millions of people send *salāms* on the Prophet ﷺ at every moment, and he replies to all of them one by one, and not by holding hands! This is not a circus; when we speak of heavenly areas or heavenly time, it is not necessary to be physically near a person to be with him, like your guide. It is impossible for a hundred people, for example, to physically be with someone all at the same time. So, we are not after people; we are after heavenly manifestations! It is enough to be in that heavenly area, because at that time you will receive the same manifestation everyone is receiving from Allah ﷻ and His Prophet ﷺ.

Appearance of Īmām Mahdī ﷷ on ʿArafah

Friday, 4 November 2011 (9 Dhul Hijjah 1432)

Shaykh Nazim Adil al-Haqqani

SHAYKH NAZIM GIVING *SUHBAH*, LEFKE, CYPRUS.

I didn't even know if I was alive or not; it was a *ḥāl,* spiritual state, and they wanted to take us there to ʿArafah. After the *waqfa* was completed there, I saw my *ḥāl* was opened! During that time [Friday after Fajr up to 11:00 a.m. Lefke time] I slept very comfortably. The night before, I was very pressurized; they pressurized me.

Here they brought me a doctor, but there was no need, it was only annoyance! The doctor came and left, but I didn't even realize it; when he came, what he did, I did not realize it at all. Why did this doctor come, for what reason? Then I fell asleep.

I prayed Fajr prayer. After that, I renewed *wuḍū* and went to bed at 6:30 a.m. A spiritual state (*ḥāl*) came upon me. They took me and I didn't even realize it as I was half awake. I woke up well about 11:00 a.m.; I woke up comfortably, thanks to Allah ﷻ. It was the exact time of *waqfa* there [11:00 a.m. Lefke time]. They told me that we have two-and-a-half-hour difference with Hijaz and *waqfa* service is at noon. They must have taken me, for sure, then when I returned it was 11:00 a.m. [in Lefke].

Such an astonishing *ḥāl* has happened this year! Therefore, I have understood that the Ṣāḥib, Sayyīdinā Mahdīi ﷺ has declared his *ẓuhūr*, appearance there, but his appearance has not opened yet to the public. He ﷺ took over the power now, it is in his hands. The actions will start on Muharram. Allah ﷻ knows; the actions will start, to clean, to arrange. We seek refuge in Allah ﷻ from the events that will happen. May Allah ﷻ make the Nation of Muhammad ﷺ to reach safety and security, and send on them Ṣāḥib al-Waqt, the Master.

SHAYKH HISHAM IN 'ARAFAH, FRIDAY, 4 NOVEMBER 2011.

The common people could not tolerate the *tajallī* of yesterday; no one could tolerate it! A strong *tajallī* took place and there was not a single man from the common people there. Mahdī ﷺ will appear in 'Arafah, but not among the common people, because his *jazbah* (attraction) is strong and all of them will lose their minds; they will go mad! Therefore, the spiritual masters carried the strong *tajallī* of that day (yesterday), and the next day (today) the people can recite, "*Labbayk Allāhumma, Labbayk*!" They recite, and let them recite, and may Allah accept it from us as well, as from the common people.

This year *Awlīyāullāh* were looking for Īmām Mahdī ﷺ who is carrying and bringing heavenly support to human beings, and especially to Muslims, to restore their damaged hearts. His *khulafā* and 99 deputies were with him. They were asking Allah ﷻ to authorize them to clean what has been done by oppressors.

The matter is in the hand of Prophet ﷺ. The Prophet ﷺ takes from the Divine Presence and delivers. Now it is in the hand of Prophet ﷺ, who is waiting for the appropriate time to give authority and permission for that one who Prophet ﷺ described in many *aḥadīth*:

لَوْ لَمْ يَبْقَ مِنَ الدَّهْرِ إِلاَّ يَوْمٌ لَبَعَثَ اللَّهُ رَجُلاً مِنْ أَهْلِ بَيْتِي يَمْلأُهَا عَدْلاً كَمَا مُلِئَتْ جَوْرًا "

> *The Prophet ﷺ said, "If only one day of this time (world) remained, Allah would raise up a man from my family who would fill this earth with justice as it has been filled with oppression.*[151]

That key has not yet been delivered. It is going to be delivered soon in order that what Allah ﷻ likes to happen is going to happen on Earth. That's why *Awlīyāullāh* are not saying next year, but they are saying it might be tomorrow. What we are waiting for tomorrow, if it didn't happen today, then it is going to happen tomorrow. If it didn't happen tomorrow, it is going to happen after tomorrow. If not this month, then next month. If not this year, then next year; but it is going to happen!

For Allah ﷻ, time is not so important. Sayyīdinā Mūsā ﷺ was asking Allah ﷻ to destroy for him the tyrant, Firʿawn. He was a tyrant giving a lot of troubles and difficulties to Banī Isrā'īl and killing them. Sayyīdinā Mūsā ﷺ asked, "*Yā Rabbī*! Destroy for me that tyrant." And Allah ﷻ said to him, *alaysa 'ṣ-ṣubḥu bi qarīb*, "Yā Mūsā, don't worry! Fajr is so near." It means, he was asking at night and Allah ﷻ said, "Wait! Fajr is coming quickly." That Fajr took forty years! And in Holy Qur'an it is saying, "It is very

---

[151] Sunan Abī Dāwūd.

soon, only night comes, goes, and then morning comes." That was forty years.

Awlīyāullāh are waiting and anyone who can recite on this day of ʿArafat 1000 times Sūrat al-Ikhlāṣ and 1000 times " *Lā ilāha illa 'Llāh Muḥammadun Rasūlullāh,"* it will be written as if he had sacrificed for Allah's sake, and there will be thrown away from his heart all bad manners.

Lā ilāha illa 'Llāh Muḥammadun Rasūlullāh, ʿalayhā nahyā wa ʿalayhā namūt wa ʿalayhā nalqā 'Llāh. Ash-hadu an Lā ilāha illa 'Llāh wa ash-hadu anna Muḥammadu 'r-Rasūlullāh. ʿAfwaka wa riḍāk, yā Allah.

STANDING AT MOUNT ʿARAFAT, HAJJ AL-AKBAR 2011.

MASJID NAMIRAH

On the Day of ʿArafah,
the Prophet ﷺ stayed in Namirah
until the sun had passed its zenith
(the beginning of Ẓuhr), then he rode,
then he stopped at the bottom of Wadi ʿUranah
(a valley between Namirah and ʿArafat),
where he prayed Ẓuhr and ʿAsr,
shortening them to two rakʿahs
and joining them together at the time of Ẓuhr,
with one adhān and two iqāmahs.
Then he rode on until
he came to the place of standing
and stood there.
He said, 'I am standing here,
but all of ʿArafah is the place of standing.'
Then he remained standing,
facing the Qiblah,
raising his hands, remembering Allah ﷻ
and calling upon Him,
until the sun had set completely.
Then he went on to Muzdalifah.

Jābir bin ʿAbd Allāh ؓ

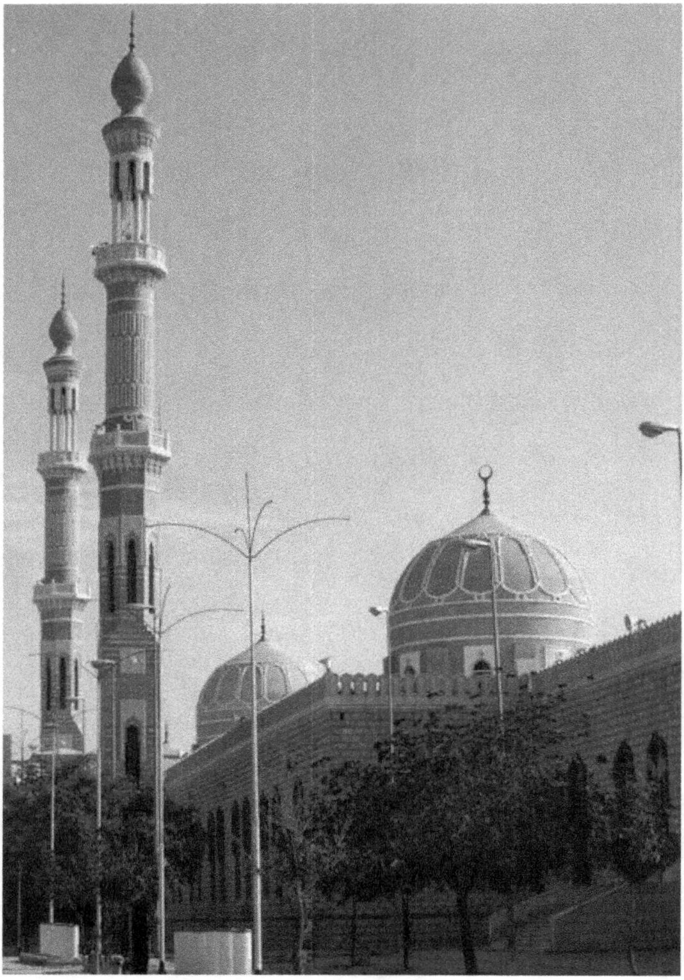

MASJID NAMIRAH, 'URANAH.

This Masjid is located in Wādī 'Uranah (just outside the boundaries of 'Arafat) and marks the site where the Prophet ﷺ camped on his Farewell Hajj on the 9th of Dhul-Hijjah 10 AH. It is here that he delivered his famous farewell sermon, while seated on his camel. Over 100,000 Sahabah ؓ accompanied him on this pilgrimage. The masjid was built in the second century of Islam.

The Prophet ﷺ delivered the sermon of the Farewell Pilgrimage at Masjid Namirah. The Hajj Khutbah is delivered from this mosque and pilgrims pray Ẓuhr and 'Asr prayers there.

It's very difficult to reach on 'Arafat, not everyone can reach the mosque, but on other days it is empty; the courtyard is open, but the inner hall is closed.

VIP Hajj al-Akbar

Friday, 4 November 2011 (9 Dhul-Hijjah 1432)

Shaykh Muhammad Hisham Kabbani

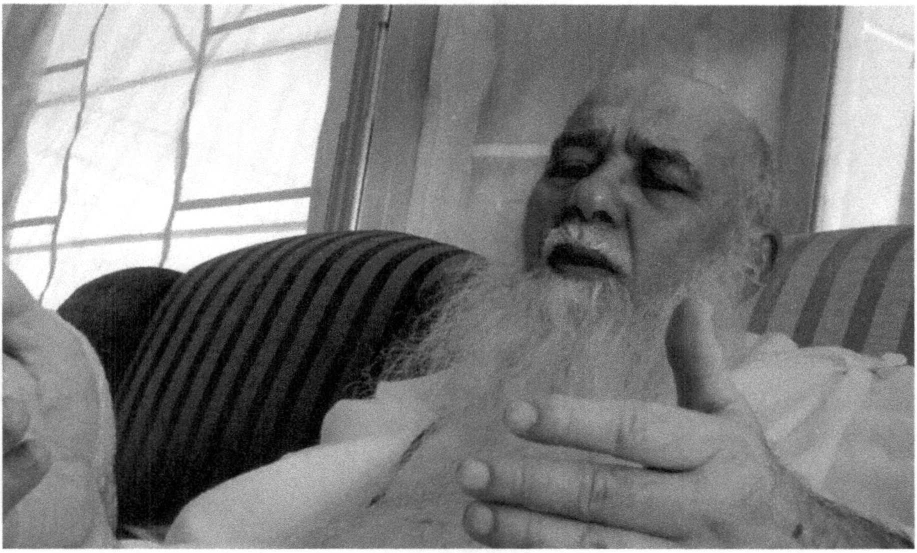

SHAYKH HISHAM KABBANI MAKING *DU'A* AFTER *DHIKR* IN 'ARAFAT, HAJJ AL-AKBAR 2011.

Bismillāhi 'r-Raḥmāni 'r-Raḥīm. Allāhumma salli 'alā Sayyīdinā Muhammadan Nabī al-ummi wa 'alā ālihi wa ṣaḥbihi wa sallam. Nawaytu 'l-arba'īn, nawaytu 'l-'itikāf, nawaytu 'l-khalwah, nawaytu 'l-'uzlah, nawaytu 'r-rīyāḍa, nawaytu 's-sulūk, lillāhi ta'ala al-'Azhīm fī hadha 'l-masjid. Atī'ūllaha wa atī'ū 'r-Rasūla wa ūli 'l-amri minkum. Dastūr, madad yā Sulṭān al-Awlīyā, Shaykh Muhammad Nazim al-Haqqani. Dastūr, madad yā Sulṭān al-Awlīyā, Shaykh 'Abd Allāh al-Fā'iz ad-Dāghestānī.

This year Hajj has its own taste that was never opened before, which contains the taste and benefit of every Hajj from the time of the Prophet ﷺ up to today, given to all those who stood on 'Arafat. Last year they accumulated all of them except this one, and this year they got the benefit of all the years including last year, and also this is a "VIP year" for the people who did Hajj! Allah is Allah. When He gives, don't ask how or why. He gave! When He gives, He gives. When He doesn't want to give, it doesn't mean He is not happy with that servant, but rather there is

another wisdom related to that servant. Some people might have more in *dunyā* and less in *Ākhirah* and some have a lot in *Ākhirah* and less in *dunyā.* A poor person might have a high station in Heaven: Allah decides who gets what. That is why the Prophet ﷺ said, *Allāhumma lā takilnī ilā nafsī ṭarfata ʿaynun wa lā aqalla min dhālik,* "O my Lord! Don't leave me to myself for the blink of an eye."

Alḥamdulillāh, we came for Hajj this year, as Mawlana Shaykh Nazim, may Allah bless him, said this year is Hajj al-Akbar, but due to certain reasons *Awlīyāullāh* made it Saturday. *Awlīyāullāh* were there on that day, and who was there felt that presence, and they are from the Rijālullāh, described by Allah ﷻ in the Holy Qur'an:

رِجَالٌ صَدَقُوا مَا عَاهَدُوا اللَّهَ عَلَيْهِ فَمِنْهُم مَّن قَضَى نَحْبَهُ وَمِنْهُم مَّن
يَنتَظِرُ وَمَا بَدَّلُوا تَبْدِيلاً

Men that kept their covenant with Allah ﷻ and some passed, and some are waiting.[152]

That is why they insisted to come this year, and we arrived here. Around twenty years ago, I saw a dream in which Shaykh Nazim ق and Grandshaykh ق were telling me, "You will go to lead the prayer for all Muslims in Masjid Namirah!" This was in the year 2002. I said to myself, "What is the meaning of that dream to go and lead the prayer with Muslims in Masjid Namirah?" *Awlīyāullāh* see far away. They showed me that vision, and two days ago [in 2011] I spoke with Shaykh Nazim ق from Madinatu 'l-Munawwarah, and he said, "Go this year!" Awlīyāullāh have pushed those who are responsible to see the moon, to

[152] Sūratu 'l-Aḥzāb, 33:23.

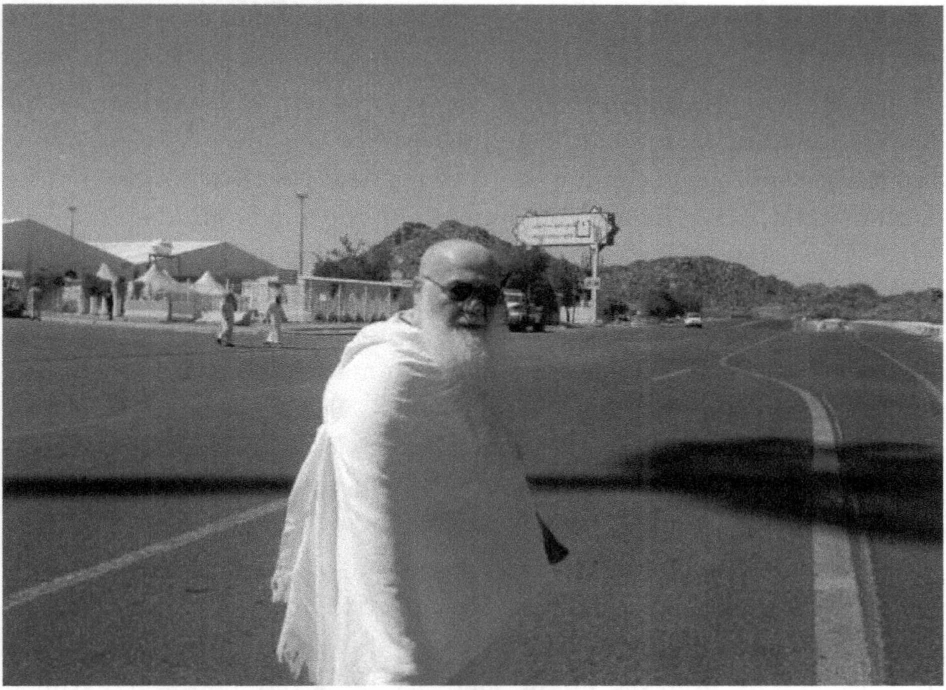

SHAYKH HISHAM GOING TO JUMUʿAH, HAJJ AL-AKBAR 2011.

move the Day of ʿArafat from Friday to Saturday, one day after the original day.

Both Arabic calendars shows that ʿArafat was supposed to be on Friday this year, but they moved it to Saturday, because *Awlīyāullāh* don't like crowded areas; they want areas in which there are a few people in order that they can do their own *duʿās* and petitions to Allah ﷻ to forgive *Ummat an-Nabī* ﷺ.

Tomorrow there will be millions of people here, you cannot even go there; you might have to go after Fajr to find a place to pray Ẓuhr and ʿAsr combined, but there are speakers, so people can also pray in their rooms. But *alḥamdulillāh* Allah ﷻ has honored us to have it today, which is a Jumuʿah, so you can understand. Mawlana said, "This year is Hajj al-Akbar." He said it a long time ago, but on the telephone, two days ago, he insisted that this year is Hajj ul-Akbar, telling me, "You have to go to ʿArafat on Friday, because the *Awlīyāullāh* are meeting there. Therefore, you must all go, as you will receive the same *tajallī* that those *Awlīyā* are receiving."

That's why at the beginning of the year when we decided, as the inspiration came to my heart to go this year for Hajj, they didn't say why, but it was coming and coming and coming. And people who are working with me said, "O! Why are you doing this? The whole Middle East is on fire!" Also, Mawlana ق gave many *ṣuḥbahs,* saying that there will be too many problems and that people should stay at home, but we kept continuing in proceeding toward Hajj, because a strong instruction to do it was coming. The people who work with me said, "Let's get insurance for everyone so if something happens, we will get our money back." I kept insisting that we have to go and *alḥamdulillāh* we came. I explained that the presence is what is important; you can be on your own, but because you are present, you will receive these *tajjalīyāt,* manifestions.

So, I spoke with Mawlana ق on the phone, and he said, "Go to ʿArafat, as your presence is important there." How to go to ʿArafat (one day before)? It's not that easy; you need a special permit in order to go there, unless you walk, but to walk might take six or seven hours! We called everywhere and finally someone helped us with it. All of your presence was important there, because all of you took *bayaʿ* with Shaykh Nazim ق, which means you will be lucky; those who came today are lucky, because they received that manifestation that was descending on *Awlīyāullāh* when they were on that ʿArafat; their meeting was on Jabal Raḥmah.

I was thinking, if we come to ʿArafat, we would stay at the border. Here is the border, but *Subḥān-Allāh,* the one who was with us to show us the tent, lost his way and he didn't know where the tents were. Then the drivers got upset and they said, "We decided to go to Masjid Namirah!" So, when he said, "We will go to the tent," and the others said, "We cannot go to the tent!" I said, "Go to Masjid Namirah! Even if you find the tent, continue to Masjid Namirah," because that dream, that vision, came back to me. So, we prayed *Ẓuhr* and *ʿAṣr* at Masjid Namirah and thus performed the spiritual Hajj.

In Hajj al-Akbar, it will be as if you have performed seven Hajj, not with normal people but with *Awlīyāullāh,* who were on Jabal Raḥmah, the Mount of Mercy. There were 124,000 *Walī* present asking Allah ﷻ for the Ummah, for the best of the Ummah. So, we did that, then we said, "Let's go to Jabal Raḥmah," which we did. Then we performed one *dhikr* and made the *duʿā* of ʿArafat. These were all counted like 100,000 *dhikr,* 100,000 *duʿā,* 100,000 visits to Jabal ʿArafat.

You must thank Allah ﷻ day and night and not let yourself come against you to bring you down and depress you and make you not feeling well. If *Awlīyāullāh* open by Allah's permission and Prophet's permission to show you what you have received today from the *barakah* of going to ʿArafat, you will spend all your life in a corner worshipping, thanking Allah, and you will say, "It is still not enough thanks and worship!"

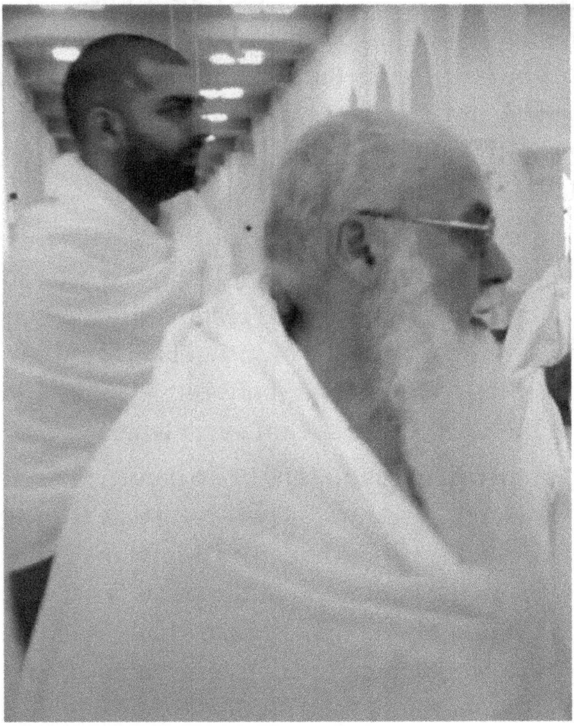

SHAYKH HISHAM ENTERING MASJID NAMIRAH TO PRAY ẒUHR AND ʿASR COMBINED, FRIDAY, 4 NOVEMBER 2011, HAJJ AL-AKBAR.

That Hajj is a special Hajj; it is the limit between *Ḥaqq* and *bāṭil. Bāṭil* is going and *Ḥaqq* is coming. Your presence is going to be like stars between the Ummah. Those who were present today, on that mountain, on ʿArafat, are going to be like stars in dark nights for the Ummah; they can see them from far away. Allah ﷻ is granting us and to all of you.

Shaykh Nazim ق said, "Go even for five minutes!" When he said, "even for five minutes," I understood there was permission and a means to reach there, so we tried to work on it and *alḥamdulillāh* we were able to go through that.

There, every one of you was presented by a spiritual heavenly angel in the presence of *Awlīyāullāh*. It is rare to have Hajj al-Akbar, as it comes once every seven years. Now you got the *barakah* of Hajj al-Akbar and it will be as if you were born today and enter Paradise with a new account. *Al-ḥajju 'l-mabrūr, jazāuhu 'l-jannah,* the reward of Hajj that it is *mabrūr,* accepted and blessed, is Jannah.

This Hajj, this Friday, if you said "Saturday" you might not get that *barakah,* but because we went Friday, we will get the spiritual *barakah* of it, and on Saturday we will also get the physical *barakah* of it. You hit two birds with one stone, so don't be angry, don't be like a fish struggling in the water.

Allah ﷻ loved this group, so He facilitated for this group to be here. That is from Allah's Mercy, it doesn't always happen, it's rare. I know you have paid, but you bought Jannah with this small amount of money. Be happy! Dance and enjoy yourself, entertain yourself after Hajj, everywhere, entertain yourself by praying, by making *dhikr,* by praying, by fasting, by making *qaṣīdah,* any kind of ways with which Allah and His Prophet ﷺ are happy. May Allah ﷻ forgive us.

I cannot explain the dream more for certain reasons, but *Inshā-Allāh* we can explain it later. I never expected that I would pray in Masjid Namirah, because it's too crowded; it's impossible to reach it during Hajj time, but Mawlana ق said two days ago, "It will be written Hajj al-Akbar, go and make *duʿā* there, even if it's at the border between ʿArafah and Mina." *Subḥān-Allāh,* but with their *barakah,* we went everywhere!

Something like this never comes in dreams; you cannot do it even in your dreams. In two hours to go all this way in ʿArafat? There is no way during Hajj time, and to get the benefit of Hajj al-Akbar! And Mawlana ق has been saying, by Allah's Mercy, from the beginning of the year, "This year is Hajj al-Akbar, Hajj al-Akbar, Hajj al-Akbar!" *Subḥān-Allāh,* Allah ﷻ facilitated for us to go there. *Alḥamdulillāh* may Allah forgive us all and bless us all.

Bi ḥurmati l-Ḥabīb, al-Fātiḥah.

STORY: YOU DON'T KNOW WHEN AND HOW YOU WILL BE TESTED

After we finished recitations at Jabal ar-Raḥmah, the Mount of Mercy, one person came out of the blue and whispered in my ear, "*Yā* Shaykh! I am stuck with my wife here and I have a problem with the airline; they are asking to change our tickets. They want two-thousand riyals, and I don't have one penny. Finally, they dropped it to 420 riyals. Whatever you can give to help us, Allah ﷻ will reward and compensate you."

Why did he choose me, why not someone else? That was not an ordinary person; he was sent as a test. It was right after ʿArafat and you have to go out, then they test you to see what you are going to do. That is why he said, "Whatever you want to give, give." They want to see if you give the whole amount or a little bit. I understood they were sending that *Walī,* who is responsible in ʿArafat for all *ḥujjāj,* to check on us. Immediately, without question, I put my hand and gave him 500 riyals. He kissed my hand and disappeared. Someone tried to pull him away from me and I said, "Stop!"

You don't know who you are going to face. That is why Grandshaykh ق always kept small money in his pocket. You don't know what they will ask, and they might come in a form you don't like. Don't say, "That one will use it in a bad way;" rather give for Allah's sake as all forms of charity have a unique taste.

The Prophet Muhammad's ﷺ Farewell Sermon

MIḤRĀB OF MASJID NAMIRAH.

Every year the pilgrims go to Jabal ar-Raḥmah, Mount of Mercy, in ʿArafat, where all *Awlīyāullāh* cast their visions and their sights on that mountain. On that Jabal ar-Raḥmah, the Prophet ﷺ stood and gave his last speech known as the *Khutbat al-Widaʿ*, Farewell Sermon, delivered on the 9th day of Dhul-Hjjah, 623 AD, in the ʿUranah Valley of Mount ʿArafat in Mecca:

[After praising and thanking Allah, the Prophet ﷺ began with the words:]

O People! Lend me an attentive ear, for I know not whether after this year I shall ever be amongst you again. Therefore, listen carefully to what I am saying and take these words to those who could not be present here today.

O People! Just as you regard this month, this day, this city as sacred, so regard the life and property of every Muslim a sacred trust. Return the goods entrusted to you to their rightful owners. Hurt no one so that no one may hurt you. Remember that you will indeed meet your Lord, and that he will indeed reckon your deeds.

Allah ﷻ has forbidden you to take usury, therefore all interest obligation shall henceforth be waived. Your capital is yours to keep. You will neither inflict nor suffer any inequality. Allah ﷻ has judged that there shall be no interest and that all interest due to ʿAbbās Ibn ʿAbdul-Muṭṭalib be waived.

Every right arising out of homicide in pre-Islamic days is henceforth waived and the first such right that I waive is that arising from the murder of Rābiʿah ibn al-Hārithah.

O Men! The unbelievers indulge in tampering with the calendar in order to make permissible that which Allah ﷻ forbade, and to prohibit what Allah ﷻ has made permissible. With Allah, the months are twelve in number. Four of them are holy, they are successive, and one occurs singly between the months of Jumāda and Shaʿbān.

Beware of Satan, for the safety of your religion. He has lost all hope that he will be able to lead you astray in big things, so beware of following him in small things.

O People! It is true that you have certain rights with regard to your women, but they also have rights over you. Remember that you have taken them as your wives only under Allah's trust and with His permission. If they abide by your right, then to them belongs the right to be fed and clothed in kindness. Do treat your women well and be kind to them for they are your partners and committed helpers. And it is your right that they do not make friends with any one of whom you do not approve, as well never to be unchaste.

O People! Listen to me in earnest, worship Allah ﷻ, say your five daily prayers, fast during month of Ramadan, and give your wealth in *Zakāt*. Perform Hajj if you can afford it.

All Mankind is from Ādam and Eve, an Arab has no superiority over a non-Arab nor a non-Arab has any superiority over an Arab; also, a white has no superiority over a black nor a black has any superiority over a white except by piety and good action. Learn that every Muslim is a brother to every Muslim and that the Muslims constitute one brotherhood. Nothing shall be legitimate to a Muslim which belongs to a fellow Muslim unless it was given freely and willingly.

Do not therefore do injustice to yourselves. Remember one day you will meet Allah ﷻ and answer your deeds. So beware, do not astray from the path of righteousness after I am gone.

O People! No Prophet or apostle will come after me and no new faith will be born. Reason well, therefore, O People, and understand words that I convey to you. I leave behind me two things: the Qur'an and my Sunnah, and if you follow these, you will never go astray.

All those who listen to me shall pass on my words to others and those to others again; and may the last ones understand my words better than those who listen to me directly. O Allah ﷻ, be my witness, that I have conveyed Your Message to Your people!

[As part of this sermon, the Prophet ﷺ recited to them a revelation from Allah ﷻ, which he had just received: *This day I have perfected your religion for you, completed My Favor upon you, and have chosen for you Islam as your religion.*[153] Towards the end of his sermon, the Prophet ﷺ asked, "O People, have I faithfully delivered unto you my message?" And the words "*Allāhumma na'm,* O Allah, yes!" arose from thousands of pilgrims and rolled like thunder throughout the valley. The Prophet ﷺ raised his forefinger and said, "O Allah! Bear witness that I have conveyed Your Message to Your Servants!"]

---

[153] Sūratu 'l-Mā'ida, 5:3.

MASJID AS-SAKHRAH

" *We know the day and the place in which*
that was revealed to the Prophet ﷺ;
it was when he was standing on ʿArafat,
on a Friday! "

ʿUmar Ibn al-Khaṭṭāb ؓ

HISTORIC PHOTO OF MASJID AS-SAKHRAH.

Masjid as-Sakhrah was a small mosque on the right slope of Mount ʿArafat. This mosque no longer exists but was in use well into the twentieth century. It marked the spot where the Prophet ﷺ after leading the Ẓuhr and ʿAsr prayers faced towards the Qiblah and engaged in *duʿā* until sunset. It was at this spot where the Prophet ﷺ received the revelation:

الْيَوْمَ أَكْمَلْتُ لَكُمْ دِينَكُمْ وَأَتْمَمْتُ عَلَيْكُمْ نِعْمَتِى وَرَضِيتُ لَكُمُ الإِسْلاَمَ دِينًا

"Today I have perfected your religion for you and completed My Favor upon you, and I have chosen Islam as your religion."[154]

[154] Sūratu 'l-Mā'ida, 5:3.

VINTAGE PHOTO OF MASJID AS-SAKHRAH AT THE BASE OF MOUNT ʿARAFAT.

رجلًا مِنَ الْيَهُودِ قَالَ لِعُمَرَ: "يَا أَمِيرَ الْمُؤْمِنِينَ آيَةٌ فِى كِتَابِكُمْ تَقْرَؤُونَهَا لَوْ

عَلَيْنَا مَعْشَرَ الْيَهُودِ نَزَلَتْ لَاتَّخَذْنَا ذَلِكَ الْيَوْمِ عِيدًا!" قَالَ: "أَيَّةُ آيَةٍ؟"

قَالَ: " ﴿ . . . الْيَوْمَ أَكْمَلْتُ لَكُمْ دِينَكُمْ وَأَتْمَمْتُ عَلَيْكُمْ نِعْمَتِى وَرَضِيتُ لَكُمُ

الْإِسْلَامَ دِينًا ﴾ " . قَالَ عُمَرُ: "قَدْ عَرَفْنَا ذَلِكَ الْيَوْمِ وَالْمَكَانُ الَّذِى نَزَلَتْ فِيهِ

عَلَى النَّبِيِّ ﷺ وهو قَائِمٌ بِعَرَفَةَ ، يَوْمَ جُمُعَةٍ" .

A man from among the Jews came to ʿUmar ❧ and said: "O Amīru 'l-
Mu'minīn, there is a verse in your Book which, if it had been revealed to
us Jews, we would have taken that day as a festival." ʿUmar ❧ asked,
"Which verse?" to which the Jew replied:

الْيَوْمَ أَكْمَلْتُ لَكُمْ دِينَكُمْ وَأَتْمَمْتُ عَلَيْكُمْ نِعْمَتِى وَرَضِيتُ لَكُمُ

الْإِسْلَامَ دِينًا

"This day, I have perfected your religion for you, completed My Favor upon you, and have chosen for you Islam as your religion."[155]

Umar ﵁ said: "We know the day and the place in which that was revealed to the Prophet ﷺ; it was when he was standing on ʿArafat, on a Friday." This masjid no longer exists.

[155] Sūratu 'l-Ma'idah, 5:3.

Story: The Revelation that Made Abū Bakr ⍥ Cry!

Shaykh Muhammad Hisham Kabbani

The last year that the Prophet ﷺ made Hajj was the last year of his life. After he conquered Mecca with no bloodshed, Allah ﷻ revealed the *āyah*:

$$\text{الْيَوْمَ أَكْمَلْتُ لَكُمْ دِينَكُمْ وَأَتْمَمْتُ عَلَيْكُمْ نِعْمَتِى وَرَضِيتُ لَكُمُ الإِسْلاَمَ}$$

$$\text{دِينًا}$$

This day I have perfected your religion for you, completed My Favor upon you, and have chosen for you Islam as your religion.[156]

With that *āyah*, Allah ﷻ completed Islam and made it a perfect moon, no more and no less. Therefore, don't accept anyone that comes and tells you we have to renovate or reform Islam, or westernize or 'Americanize' Islam! Islam is a complete religion and accepted by Allah ﷻ.

Upon this revelation, the Sahabah ⍥ were very happy. If we were Sahabah ⍥, would we not be happy? We learn from them; they are our teachers, and we hope to be with them in Paradise. They were all happy except for one Ṣaḥābī ⍥, who was crying. They were wondering why he is crying, as they were thinking, "*Mashā-Allah*, we entered Mecca and we entered Ka'bah and destroyed the idols and went to 'Arafat for *manāsik al-Ḥajj*." They came to him, and it was Sayyīdina Abū Bakr aṣ-Ṣiddīq ⍥, and asked him, "Why are you crying?" He said, *mā b'ad al-kamāl illa an-nuqṣān*, "After perfection, there is nothing but decrease." Sayyīdina Abū Bakr ⍥ cried, because he knew that after the full moon, there is no further perfection, so he knew the Prophet ﷺ is leaving *dunyā*. After that *āyah* came, he understood the deeper meaning, that Jibrīl ⍥ will stop coming and the Message is now complete. He said, "We are going to see sadness in our lives. I feel that the Prophet ﷺ is not going to be among us."

After exactly 80 days, the Prophet ﷺ left *dunyā*, because finished, perfection came. He delivered the perfection and now the responsibility of the Ummah is to carry the Message until the Day of Judgment. That

---

[156] Sūratu 'l-Ma'ida, 5:3.

hadith came for the importance of fasting on that day, as the Prophet ﷺ wants to make us happy. Abū Hurayrah ؓ said, the Prophet ﷺ told his Sahabah ؓ, and the Prophet's ﷺ message is for everyone: "You want to be on ʿArafat with me? Then fast the Day of ʿArafah!" It was the last Hajj and the last *ʿUmrah* for the Prophet ﷺ.

MUZDALIFAH

"*On the way to Muzdalifah,*
the pilgrim should raise his voice chanting the talbīyah.
When he reaches al-Muzdalifah, he must perform the major ablution, because al-Muzdalifah is a part of the Ḥaram; therefore, let him enter it clean. If he is able to enter on foot, it is better and more respectful of the Ḥaram.
He should say, 'O God, this is Muzdalifah where many different languages have been gathered together asking of You lofty requests. Let me be among those who prayed and You accepted their prayers and those who relied upon You and You sufficed them.'
When the night reaches its middle-point,
the pilgrim prepares for departure.
Let him take with him some pebbles from al-Muzdalifah for it has smooth pebbles. Let him take seventy pebbles, the quantity required. There is no harm in having more on hand, for he may lose some of them. Let the pebbles be light so they can be kept between the knuckles and let him say the morning prayer (while it is still) dusk."

Īmām Abū Ḥāmid al-Ghazālī ق

PILGRIMS ARRIVE IN MUZDALIFAH AFTER MAGHRIB.

Muzdalifah is located southeast of Mina, on the way between Mina and ʿArafat. On the 9th Dhul-Hijjah (second day of Hajj), pilgrims arrive here after sunset from ʿArafat and spend the night here. During Hajj, it is *wājib* to perform Maghrib and ʿIshā together here at ʿIshā time. Staying at Muzdalifah is also *wājib* and its time begins from *ṣubḥ ṣādiq* and ends at sunrise. If one spent even a little portion of their time here, he/she will be absolved of this obligation. However, it is best to remain until just before sunrise. Pebbles for stoning the Jamarāt are collected here, it is best to collect small ones. During the Farewell Hajj, the Prophet ﷺ performed the Maghrib and ʿIshā prayers together here. He stayed at the spot where the present Masjid Masharu 'l-Ḥarām currently is (towards the Qiblah side). From there, the Prophet ﷺ said, "Although I am staying here, you may stay anywhere throughout Muzdalifah."[157]

---

[157] Saḥīḥ Muslim.

Riot Against Shayṭān

Shaykh Muhammad Hisham Kabbani

SHAYKH HISHAM KABBANI AND MURĪDS MAKE DU'A AT MUZDALIFA AFTER COLLECTING PEBBLES FOR STONING THE PILLARS WHICH REPRESENT SATAN, HAJJ 2011.

After you finish at 'Arafat, making *tasbīḥ*, praising Allah ﷻ all day long, you go to Muzdalifah, where everyone is busy collecting stones. What is the symbol of that? This whole universe is praising Allah ﷻ and reciting *tasbīḥ*, as Allah ﷻ said in the Holy Qur'an:

وَإِن مِّن شَيْءٍ إِلاَّ يُسَبِّحُ بِحَمْدَهِ

And there is not a thing but celebrates His Praise.[158]

So, everything in the universe and in Heavens is making *tasbīḥ*, but we cannot hear them. The Prophet ﷺ, however, heard the *tasbīḥ* and recitation of stones and mountains, whenever he passed by them.

When the Prophet ﷺ held stones in his blessed hands, Sayyīdinā Abū Bakr aṣ-Ṣiddīq ؓ and Sayyīdinā 'Umar ؓ heard the *tasbīḥ* of those stones.

---

[158] Sūratu 'l-'Isrā, 17:44.

Imagine! Allah ﷻ gave the Prophet ﷺ the ability to hear the *tasbīḥ* of angels and everything in this universe to show His Love to Sayyīdinā Muhammad ﷺ!

So, what are these stones for? To take to Mina the next day and throw them at the biggest Shayṭān, saying, "*Raghman li 'sh-shayṭān wa riḍan li 'r-Raḥmān,* for Allah to be happy with us and for Shayṭān to be down!" And the smaller the stones you collect, the more *barakah,* so don't pick the large stones! Unfortunately, some people even take their shoes and throw them, which will be rendered by the angels on their face!

So, Allah ﷻ likes it when you come back after making *tasbīḥ* in ʿArafat and Muzdalifah and throw stones at Shayṭān, saying, "*Allāhu Akbar!*" That is a symbol, to show that, "*Yā Rabbī,* I don't want that Shayṭān to be in me!"

Today they are rioting everywhere in the streets, they are not even sleeping, they are not even eating, their mouths are always open saying something. And Allah ﷻ ordered us to remember Him:

وَالذَّاكِرِينَ اللَّهَ كَثِيرًا وَالذَّاكِرَاتِ

Men who remember God unceasingly and women who remember God unceasingly.[159]

To open your mouth for Allah ﷻ to say, "*Allah! Lā ilāha illa 'Llāh!*"

O Muslims! Say, "Allah!" and let them do whatever they like: let them play, who cares for them? Say, "*Lā ilāha illa 'Llāh, Lā ilāha illa 'Llāh, Lā ilāha illa 'Llāh!*" Keep your mouth open with that. Is it not better for this crowd of four million to say, "*Lā ilāha illa 'Llāh,*" instead of carrying a Communist or Socialist or violent extremist banner? It's okay to carry banners but carry one for your own self.

Today I write a banner against my radical Shayṭān, tomorrow I will write a banner against my violent Shayṭān, tomorrow I will write a banner saying, "Leave me alone!" And what you have to say is not, "Go away," to Shayṭān, but you need to say, "*Allah! Lā ilāha illa 'Llāh Muhammadan Rasūlullāh, yā Rabbī, yā Allah!*"

---

[159] Sūratu 'l-Aḥzāb, 33:35.

What do you do when you go to ʿArafat? Do you just sit there, or do you open your mouth? In ʿArafat you say, "*Labbayk Allāhumma labbayk,* Here I am, O Allah, Here I am. *Lā ilāha illa 'Llāh,* there is no god but Allah." You are saying, "O Allah, I am here to answer what You want from me, *Labbayk Allāhumma labbayk!* I am making *tawḥīd, labbayk Allāhumma labbayk, Lā ilāha illa 'Llāh Muhammadan Rasūlullāh, inna 'l-ḥamda wa 'n-niʿamata laka wa 'l-mulk lā sharīka lak,* everything to You!

What are they doing in these demonstrations? I am not saying don't demonstrate, as they are doing throughout the sub-continent, the Middle East and North Africa, what must you do? Riot against your Shayṭān and say, "*Lā ilāha illa 'Llāh, Lā ilāha illa 'Llāh Lā ilāha illa 'Llāh!*" What do you have to do in ʿArafat? Do you have to keep your mouth closed or do you have to say, *Labbayk Allāhumma labbayk inna 'l-ḥamda wa 'n-niʿamata laka wa 'l-mulk lā sharīka lak.* You are praising Allah ﷻ.

Allah ﷻ wants us to riot against Shayṭān by praising Him. After you finish ʿArafat, praising Allah all day, you go to Muzdalifah, where everyone is busy collecting stones. What is that a symbol of? What are the stones for? To go the next day, morning or noon, to throw seven stones at the biggest Shayṭān, saying, "*Allāhu Akbar, riḍan li 'r-Raḥmān!*" to make Allah happy with you. *Raghman li 'sh-Shayṭān, riḍan li 'r-Raḥmān!* Throw them one by one, not all in one go. Allah ﷻ likes if after making *dhikr* you come back saying, "*Allāhu Akbar!*" and throw stones at Shayṭān. That is a symbol: you are saying, "*Yā Rabbī,* I don't want that Shayṭān to be in me!"

Is that only for ʿArafat and Mina? Can't you do that in your daily life? ʿArafat, Muzdalifah, Mina and Kaʿbah are all in you, five times daily. When you say "*Allāhu Akbar,*" and pray, to where do you direct yourself? The most significant events of Hajj are two things: one is to visit the Kaʿbah, and the other is to be on the Mountain of ʿArafat. You praise Him and then circumambulate His House. When you say "*Allāhu Akbar*!" where are you going? Are you not going to His House spiritually? When you say "*Allāhu Akbar,*" you must say it in a way that you are sure you are going to Kaʿbah. You reflect and think that Kaʿbah is in front of you when you are praying.

Hajj is ʿArafat, and then you go and throw stones at Shayṭān. That *ṣalāt* is throwing stones in Shayṭān's face and is also remembering your Lord. Allah ﷻ gave us to perform a symbolic Hajj five times daily. It is like fasting, you cannot eat or drink. Also, it is like giving charity, you are giving to Allah from your own time that He gave to you. And you are witnessing *tawḥīd*, as at the end of the prayer you say, *Ash-hadu an lā ilāha illa 'Llāh, wa ash-hadu anna Muḥammadan ʿabduhu wa Ḥabībuhu wa Rasūluh,* "I bear witness there is no god but Allah and Muhammad ﷺ is His Servant and Beloved Prophet ﷺ" In both *sunnah* and *farḍ* prayers you have to say the Shahadah at the end.

O Muslims! Let us take Shayṭān away from our hearts. Let us take *ʿibra*, a lesson, from what is going on around the world. We want to get rid of the tyrants in the Muslim world, but remember you have to get rid of the tyrant inside you, the biggest tyrant!

MASJID MASHʿAR AL-ḤARĀM

“*The pilgrim will then start walking*
until the time when he reaches
al-Mashʿar al-Ḥarām,
which is the end of al-Muzdalifah.
Then let him stop and pray
until just before sunrise, saying,
"O God, by the right of
al-Mashʿar al-Ḥarām
and the Sacred House
and the Sacred Month
and the Corner
and the Place (of Abraham),
convey to Muhammad's ﷺ spirit
our greetings and peace
and let us enter the House of Peace (Paradise),
O Possessor of Majesty and Generosity!”

Īmām Abū Ḥāmid al-Ghazālī ق

MASJID MASHʿAR AL-HARAM IN MUZDALIFAH.

Masjid Mashʿar al-Ḥarām, is a mosque in Muzdalifah which is situated where the Prophet ﷺ made *duʿā* (supplication) during his Farewell Pilgrimage. It is located midway between Masjid al-Khayf in Mina and Masjid an-Namirah in Arafat. Mashʿar al-Ḥarām means the 'Sacred Monument' and is mentioned in the Qur'an:

فَإِذَا أَفَضْتُم مِّنْ عَرَفَاتٍ فَاذْكُرُواْ اللّهَ عِندَ الْمَشْعَرِ الْحَرَامِ وَاذْكُرُوهُ كَمَا هَدَاكُمْ وَإِن كُنتُم مِّن قَبْلِهِ لَمِنَ الضَّآلِّينَ

Then when you pour down from ʿArafat, celebrate the praises of Allah at the Sacred Monument, and celebrate His praises as He has directed you, even though, before this, you went astray."[160]

The Mashar al-Ḥarām is regarded as a part of Muzdalifah but not all of it. Jābir ﷺ reported that the Prophet ﷺ stayed in Muzdalifah overnight. He then performed Fajr *ṣalāt,* mounted his she-camel until he came to

[160] Sūratu 'l-Baqarah, 2:198.

Mashʿar al-Ḥarām. After dismounting and facing the Qiblah, the Prophet ﷺ made *duʿā*, proclaiming the Greatness and Oneness of Allah. The *masjid* can accommodate more than 12,000 worshippers.

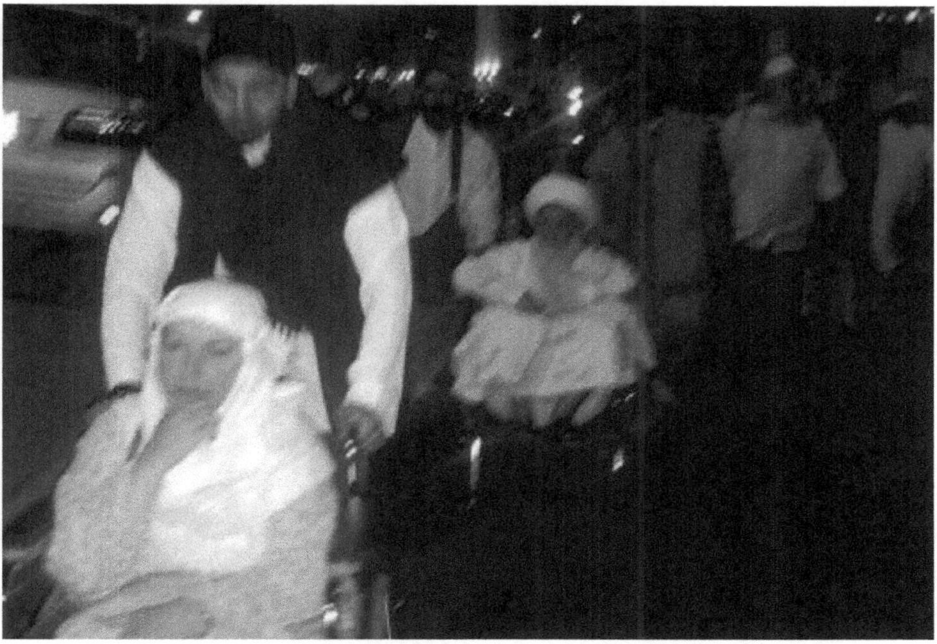

SHAYKH HISHAM, HAJJAH NAZIHA AND *MURĪDS* MOVING TOWARD MINA, HAJJ 2011.

MASJID AL-KHAYF

"*Let him (the pilgrim)*
not fail to attend obligatory prayers
with the Īmām at the Mosque of Khayf,
for its merit is great!
Then, when he proceeds from Mina,
it is better for him to stay at al-Muhassab
(a place) at Mina to perform
the ʿAsr, Maghrib, and ʿIshā prayers,
then have a short nap,
for this is a custom that is reported
by a group of Companions,
may God be gracious to them."

Īmām Abū Ḥāmid al-Ghazālī ق

MASJID AL-KHAYF IN MINA.

Masjid al-Khayf is located at the foot of a mountain in the south of Mina, close to the smallest Jamarāt. It was at this spot that the Prophet ﷺ and numerous other prophets before him performed *salah*. It is also known as the 'Mosque of the Prophets'. According to a Hadith of Ibn ʿAbbās ؓ, the Prophet ﷺ said, "Seventy prophets prayed in Masjid al-Khayf!"[161]

This is a place where the pilgrim makes a firm resolution that from this day forward all they will do will be for the sake of Allah ﷻ and to acquire benefit in *Ākhirah*. This was the emphasis of the Prophet ﷺ at this very place.

ʿAbd Allāh bin ʿAbbās ؓ narrates that it was in Masjid al-Khayf that the Prophet ﷺ addressed them. After praising Allah ﷻ he said, "Allah will set right the affairs of the person whose prime concern is *Ākhirah*. Allah will also grant him self-sufficiency and the world will humble itself before him. As for the person whose prime concern is this world, Allah will scatter his affairs, place poverty in front of him and all he will get of this world will be what has been predestined for him."[162]

---

[161] *Majmaʿu 'z-Zawāʾid*.

[162] Ṭabarānī.

Yazīd bin Aswad ؓ says that when he performed Hajj with the Prophet ﷺ it was at the Masjid Khayf that he performed the Fajr *salah* with the Prophet ﷺ.

ʿAbdur-Raḥmān bin Muʿadh ؓ reports that when the Prophet ﷺ delivered a sermon in Mina, he instructed the Muhājirīn to set up camp in front of the Masjid al-Khayf and the Anṣār to set up camp behind it. The rest of the Muslims were to camp behind them.[163]

HISTORIC PHOTO OF MASJID AL-KHAYF.

[163] Abū Dawūd.

MINA

“*There is a flat plain,*
where the pilgrim caravan
encamps on return from Mina.
In the vicinity of this place,
about a mile out of Mecca, is a mosque,
in line with which there is a stone
placed upon the road, like a platform,
and surmounted by another stone.
There was once some engraving
upon the latter,
but its lines have been effaced.
It is said that the Prophet,
God bless and give him peace,
sat in this place to rest himself
on coming back from his ʿUmrah,
so, people seek to gain a blessing by kissing it,
and lean up against it
(so their bodies may gain
the blessing of contact with it).”

Ibn Baṭṭūṭa ق

VIEW OF THE PLAIN OF MINA WITH JAMARĀT.

Mina is a valley six kilometers east of the Masjid al-Ḥarām in Mecca. It's where Hajj pilgrims sleep overnight on the 8th, 11th, 12th (and some even on the 13th) of Dhul-Hijjah. The valley of Mina contains the Jamarāt, the three stone pillars which are pelted by pilgrims as part of the rituals of Hajj. Around three million pilgrims stay here during Hajj. There is a cave in Mina where Sūrat al-Mursalāt was revealed, it is known as the Cave of Mursalāt. Mina is referenced in the Qur'an:

وَاذْكُرُواْ اللّهَ فِى أَيَّامٍ مَّعْدُودَاتٍ فَمَن تَعَجَّلَ فِى يَوْمَيْنِ فَلاَ إِثْمَ عَلَيْهِ وَمَن تَأَخَّرَ فَلا إِثْمَ عَلَيْهِ لِمَنِ اتَّقَى وَاتَّقُواْ اللّهَ وَاعْلَمُوا أَنَّكُمْ إِلَيْهِ تُحْشَرُونَ

And remember Allah during (specific) numbered days. Then whoever hastens (his departure) in two days, there is no sin upon him; and whoever delays (until the third), there is no sin upon him, for him who fears Allah. Fear Allah and know that unto Him you will be gathered.[164]

Mina is derived from the word with the root letters *ma-na-yā* which means 'to be put to the test' or 'to undergo' or 'to find'. It is connected to the word '*manna*' and '*tamanna*' which means 'to awaken a desire' or 'to hope for'. Another reason it is called Mina is because it is connected to the test that

[164] Sūratu 'l-Baqarah, 2:203.

Prophet Ibrāhīm ﷺ had to undergo when he was ordered to slaughter his son. When his resolve was proven, he sacrificed a ram in place of his son. The name implies the 'place where he was tested' and the 'place where he succeeded'. The word Mina can also mean 'to flow' because here the blood of sacrificial animals flows during the festival day of ʿEid al-Aḍḥā. During the Farewell Pilgrimage (*Ḥajjat al-Wadaʿ*) the Muslims had brought with them 100 camels to be sacrificed. On the 10th of Dhul-Hijjah the Prophet ﷺ stoned the Jamarāt and went back to his camp in Mina where he sacrificed 63 of the camels. ʿAlī ؓ slaughtered the remaining 37 camels and the Prophet ﷺ instructed that a part of each camel be cooked and served to him and his Companions ؓ.

Chain Your Devil and Stone It

Shaykh Muhammad Hisham Kabbani

What is the landmark in Mina? There must be a landmark. It is the *Jamarāt,* the place where Allah ﷻ chained Iblīs and his devils with him on the three pillars; it is where the pilgrims throw the stones that they collected in Muzdalifah at Shayṭān. The smaller the stones you throw it is better, and we have to throw them one by one, not all in one go, because its symbol alone will come on Shayṭān and his army like the size of Earth and break their faces, killing them after Allah ﷻ brings them back to life again and again.

Allah ﷻ ordered us to stone *ar-rajīm,* the Accursed One. Every *hajji* who says, "*Astaghfirullāh,*" that *istighfār* is like a stone falling on the head of shayṭān. By order of Prophet Muhammad ﷺ, Sayyīdinā ʿAlī ؓ fought *ash-shayṭāni 'r-rajīm,* and Allah ﷻ also made the stoning of shayṭān to symbolize the stoning of all the bad characters that were taken from him. When you say, "*Aʿūdhu billāhi min ash-shayṭāni 'r-rajīm,* I seek refuge in Allah from shayṭān to be stoned," immediately angels stone him on your behalf, making him run away from you!

Story: How the Prophet ﷺ Honored Women

Shaykh Muhammad Hisham Kabbani

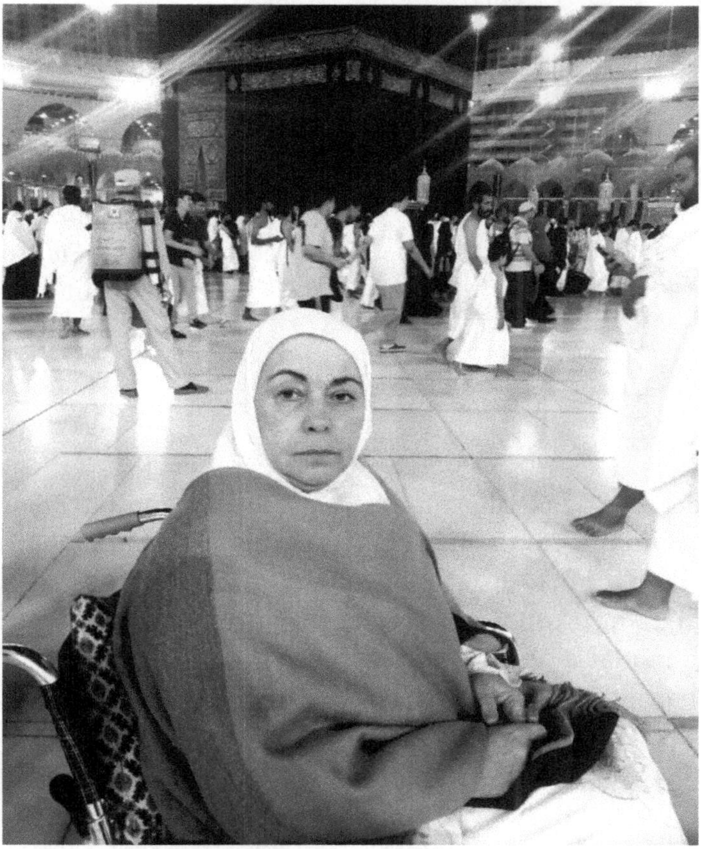

HAJJAH NAZIHA, 'UMRAH 2020.

The Prophet ﷺ is the teacher for the whole Ummah. A man from among the Companions ؓ of the Prophet ﷺ said, *"Yā Rasūlullāh*! You said religion is advice, so please advise me." Do you want to be a Muslim, a Believer? Then accept advice. The entire religion is based on advice from men to men, men to women, women to men; everyone receives their share, and don't think women have no role in Islam! I will give you an example to show how much women in Islam have been honored.

SHAYKH HISHAM & HAJJAH NAZIHA ARRIVING IN MINA AT FAJR.

Grandshaykh ق has mentioned this story, which is also in the *aḥādīth*, but we are not reciting the Hadith today. One time, Prophet ﷺ and his Companions ﷺ came from ʿArafat going towards Muzdalifah and then to Mina on the first day of ʿ*Eid*, when you have to cut or shave your hair by Allah's Order:

مُحَلِّقِينَ رُءُوسَكُمْ وَمُقَصِّرِينَ

...shaving their heads and cutting (their hair).[165]

So, Prophet ﷺ told his Sahabah ﷺ to shave their heads, but no one shaved. Prophet ﷺ did not cut or shave his head, but asked his Sahabah ﷺ to do so, and they didn't do it (they delayed it). The Prophet ﷺ went inside his tent and he was sad, as the Sahabah ﷺ did not follow his order. You cannot disobey Allah ﷻ and His Prophet ﷺ or you might face a difficulty in your life from Allah. When Prophet ﷺ entered the tent, his wife, Umm Salama ﷺ, said, "*Yā Rasūlullāh*! Why are you sad?"

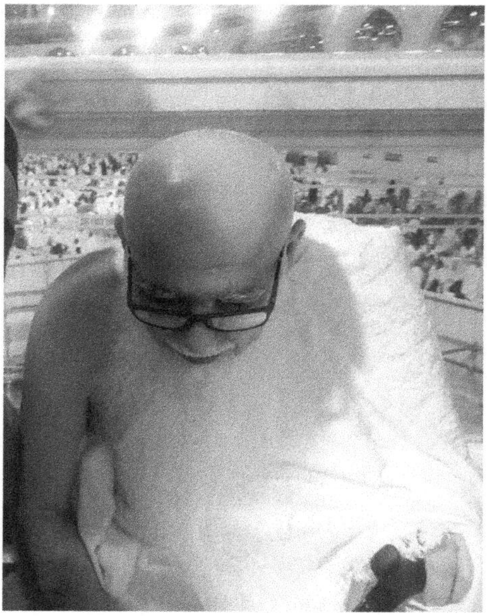

He said, "I asked the Sahabah ﷺ to shave and they didn't shave." She looked at him and said, "*Yā Rasūlullāh*, can I give an advice?"

[165] Sūratu 'l-Fatḥ, 48:27.

This is his wife, a lady giving advice to the Prophet ﷺ. He said, "Of course," because he wants to show how much Allah ﷻ gave women mind and intelligence. She said, "*Yā Rasūlullāh*! First you shave and then they will shave after you." He listened to her advice, and immediately as the Prophet ﷺ shaved, everyone else shaved.

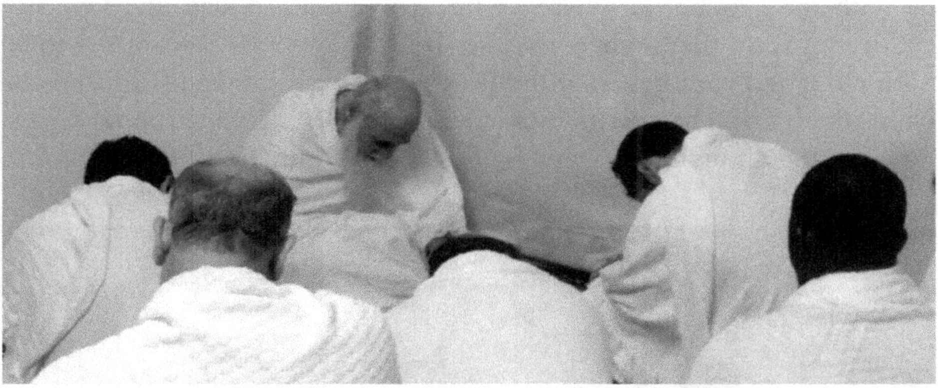

ṢALĀT AL-FAJR IN A TENT IN MINA WITH SHAYKH HISHAM KABBANI, HAJJ 2011.

You see how Allah ﷻ gave inspiration to women to consult and give advice. Even the Prophet ﷺ consulted his wife! So, it was an advice from his wife to him, as Prophet ﷺ said, "Religion is advice."

We are arrogant to say, "Will we take advice from our wife?" Advice can be taken even from a child! You see what the child is doing, and you learn the nature of children and you begin giving advice to other parents.

So, the Prophet ﷺ said it in a general way, "Religion consists of human behaviors and one of the human behaviors is to be just with Allah ﷻ with the Prophet ﷺ, with the community, with yourself, with your spouse, with your children, with your politicians and members of the parliament, and in what you say."

However, today justice is lost, and we need to bring it back to our hearts. That means, you must not get angry, or you will not be just as you might do something against justice.

To show the respect of women he has in his heart, the Prophet ﷺ said, "Allah made me to love three things from this *dunyā* so much," and one of them is women:

حُبِّبَ إِلَىَّ مِنَ الدُّنْيَا النِّسَاءُ وَالطِّيبُ وَجُعِلَ قُرَّةُ عَيْنِى فِى الصَّلَاةِ

In this world, women and perfume have been made dear to me, and my comfort has been provided in prayer.[166]

If the Prophet ﷺ loves someone, then that someone or something must be with the Prophet ﷺ wherever he is, in Paradise also. If I love my children, I want them wherever I go. If I love my wife, I want her to be with me wherever I go. So, if the Prophet ﷺ loves someone, it means he wants that person to be with him wherever he goes. If the Prophet ﷺ says he loves the Ummah, it means he wants the Ummah to be with him in Paradise.

[166] an-Nisā'ī.

THE JAMARĀT

“*O Traveler on the Way to Truth!*
Stoning the devil is indeed
a significant act of devotion,
just as fasting expresses a state of godliness,
prayer means to engage in a dialogue
with the Almighty Lord,
and Hajj is a visit to the House of God.
The person performing Hajj
announces his intention to renounce
the claims of his lower soul (nafs)
by stoning Shaytan at Mina,
thus, signaling that henceforth
he will struggle against the ego,
which holds him in its grip.”

Hajjah Amina Adil ق

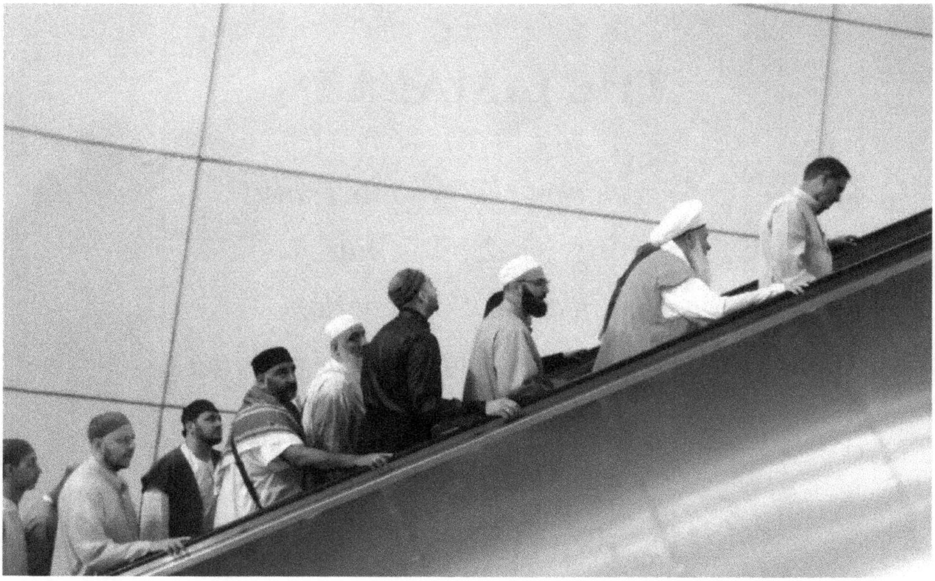

SHAYKH HISHAM LEADS THE MURĪDS TO THE FIRST JAMARAH, HAJJ 2011.

The Jamarāt are three stone walls, formerly pillars, which are pelted as a compulsory ritual of Hajj in emulation of the actions of the Prophet Ibrāhīm ﷺ. They represent the three locations where Ibrāhīm ﷺ pelted the Shayṭān (Satan) with stones when he tried to dissuade him from sacrificing his son Isma'īl ﷺ. The pillars are called Jamrat al-Ulā, Jamrat al-Wusṭā and Jamrat al-Kubrā.

SHAYKH HISHAM AND GROUP GOING TO PELT THE *JAMARĀT*, HAJJ 2011.

Become Shooting Stars Against Shayṭān!

Shaykh Muhammad Hisham Kabbani

Aʿūdhu billāhi min ash-Shayṭāni 'r-rajīm. Bismillāhi 'r-Raḥmāni 'r-Raḥīm. I met a physicist who works in the space field, who said she "weighs the stars." I asked her how does she weigh stars, with a scale? She said, "By their light," as every star emits light. Then I mentioned to her that some stars are smaller, but they emit more light. She said, "Yes, that is true, and some of the bigger stars emit less light." Our conversation ended there, because it wasn't a place to give a *ṣuḥbah*.

In reality, Allah ﷻ created the stars to represent human beings. Everyone has a star that corresponds to them, and you cannot find two human beings with the same star. Allah ﷻ honored every human being with a unique star with his own reality, as we know from the verse:

وَلَقَدْ كَرَّمْنَا بَنِي آدَمَ

We have honored the Children of Ādam.[167]

"We have honored the human being," can have an infinite number of interpretations, and human beings have no capacity to really understand the honor given to them because Allah ﷻ gives according to His Greatness that cannot be measured or described, so no matter what you understand, the real meaning is higher. A created person cannot understand the Creator, because whatever you understand is within limits. So according to the interpretations that Shaykh Nazim ق is sending us, Allah ﷻ honored everyone with a specific star that emits light, and this corresponds to the *āyah*:

وَلَقَدْ زَيَّنَّا السَّمَاءَ الدُّنْيَا بِمَصَابِيحَ وَجَعَلْنَاهَا رُجُومًا لِّلشَّيَاطِينِ
وَأَعْتَدْنَا لَهُمْ عَذَابَ السَّعِيرِ

And we have (from old) adorned the lowest Heaven with lamps, and We have made such (lamps) ﷺ missiles to drive away the evil ones and have prepared for them the penalty of the blazing Fire.[168]

Allah ﷻ said, "We have decorated the first level of this universe, *as-samā' ad-dunyā*," He didn't say, *"jannat ad-dunyā"* or, *"jannat al-Ākhirah,"* but He said, *"samā',"* which means there are levels in the universe. Scientists have found levels and they now understand this a little. He said, *as-samā' ad-dunyā*, "the nearest level to *dunyā*," and Allah ﷻ decorated it with stars. *Wa jaʿalnāhā rujūman li 'sh-shayāṭīn*, "We made it for stoning (pelting) the *shayāṭīn*." Allah ﷻ made these stars for pelting.

Who did Allah ﷻ make to pelt *shayāṭīn* with stones? The people who go to Hajj! This means that Allah ordered the people who went on Hajj to be shooting stars against Shayṭān, for the universe and for humanity. Every stone you throw, and you throw seven stones on Hajj, is an indication that you are a star whose light decorates the first level of the sky, *samā'*

---

[167] Sūratu 'l-Isrā', 17:70.

[168] Sūratu 'l-Mulk, 67:5.

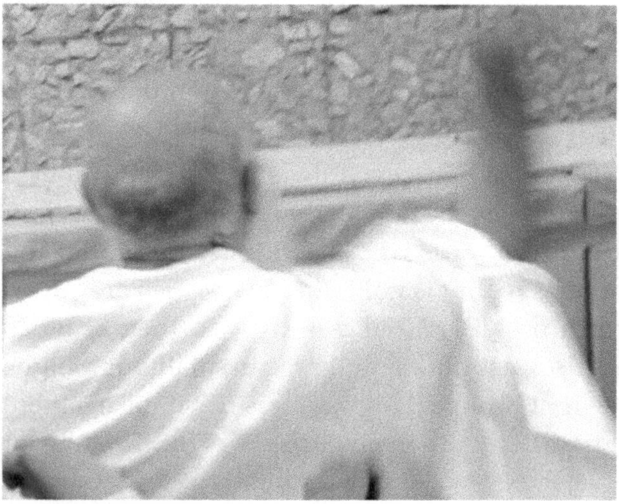

SHAYKH HISHAM PELTING THE *JAMARĀT*, HAJJ 2011.

ad-dunyā. That is Allah's ﷻ honor for you and everyone, so if you want to reach that honor, go on Hajj at least once in your lifetime and it will open the reality that makes your star a shooting star on devils!

That is an honor that Allah ﷻ gave to Muslims, not just to anyone. And on top of that, the one who makes Hajj doesn't shoot devils with that star, but its light is like a red bullet moving in the skies. Īmām as-Suyūṭī ؓ said in his *tafsīr* of Sūrat al-Fīl that each of the birds carried three stones, one in his beak and two in his claws, and when they threw their pebbles, they traveled at a high speed that made them like red, spinning stones shooting from a volcano. I have explained before that these stones look like red-hot bullets that appear as lights when they are shot at night. So, whoever goes on Hajj and shoots their pebbles on the big Shayṭān, Iblīs, that honor is given to them by Allah ﷻ. He made them like stars in *samā' ad-dunyā*, with their lights shooting and spinning; you can see them moving until they hit, then they disappear and are finished. Allah ﷻ granted every human being a star. Some of them are faint, not active. Muslims' stars are active and stars of *mu'minīn* are not only active, but shooting, and the light of the stars of *muḥsinīn* are able to reach the Divine Presence! So, a shaykh will not look at the *murīd*, but rather will look at his star to see what his level is, his purpose of being created in life, what he will do, the kind of life he will live; it is all written there.

Every day, all the *Awlīyāullāh* pray Ṣalāt an-Najāt and make *sajdah*. Grandshaykh ʿAbdAllāh, may Allah bless his soul, said, "All the *murīds* written to follow me, those who know it and those who don't know (because they are known through visions or dreams, not physically) in

Ṣalāt an-Najāt they pass by me one by one, and I see them and I ask Allah to forgive them, then every day I pass them to the Prophet ﷺ clean." Ṣalāt an-Najāt is like that, but the power of the *Walī* depends on the strength of his star, the light of which can't be described!

If a physicist weighs the star by its light, even if a small star, it can be a very strong star which will make it a heavyweight. What is the heaviest, most valuable weight on Earth? That is why Sayyīdinā Muḥyīddīn Ibn 'Arabī ؓ said that the Prophet's reality is gold, the *Awlīyāullāh* are silver, and the rest are iron, worth nothing. Gold is heavy, so their realities cannot be weighed. It surprises astronomers that it is small but weighs so much, which means the light is huge. How can this be? It means there is something in their weight different than any other weight. So, in front of them, during Ṣalāt an-Najāt, every 24 hours, millions of *murīds* in the world pass. How much *barakah* and power he must have to name them one by one, and not by their *dunyā* name, which isn't considered, but to call them by their spiritual name!

Everyone has seven names, and why seven? One name is for *dunyā*, and the name appearing in Ṣalāt an-Najāt (which is like DNA, showing everything related to that person in his life), then it goes to the first level of his spiritual name and the six levels of Heavens. Then they raise him to the level of the second, third, fourth and so on for each spiritual level and every level carries a different characteristic for that person. Everyone has seven names, but each has a unique spiritual name, without repetition. Imagine how many spiritual names a *Walī* must know! In *dunyā* it is okay to have the same name, but the

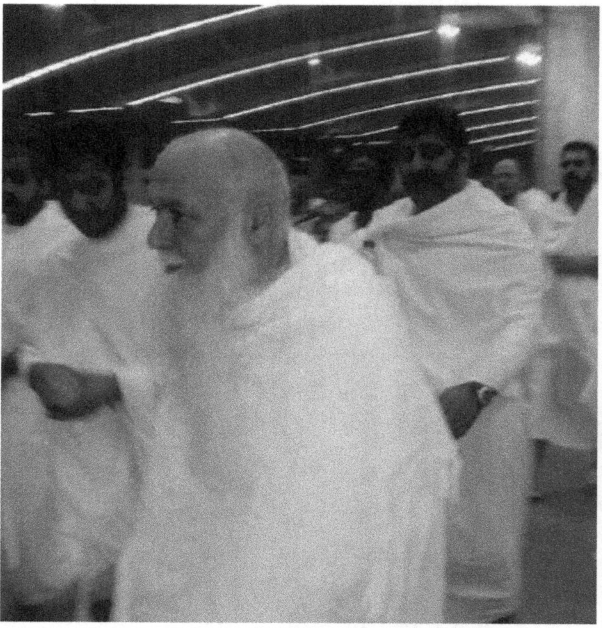
AFTER COMPLETING JAMARAT KUBRA, HAJJ 2011.

spiritual name has to be different. A *Walī* has to know everything about that person in that level in Paradise. *Subḥānallāh, alḥamdulillāh, lā ilāha illa 'Llāh, Allāhu Akbar wa lā ḥawla wa lā quwwata illa billāhi 'l-'Alīyyi 'l-'Aẓīm!*

May Allah ﷻ forgive us and bless this meeting and every meeting around the world (held for the sake of Allah), and may Allah make you not in hundreds but in millions, and bless you and all of us together in front of Shaykh Nazim al-Haqqani ق and Grandshaykh 'AbdAllāh ad-Dāghestānī ق in the presence of Prophet ﷺ.

Wa min Allāhi 't-tawfiq, bi ḥurmati 'l-Ḥabīb, bi ḥurmati 'l-Fātiḥah.

‘EID AL-AḌḤĀ

“

And the camels and cattle
We have appointed for you
as among the symbols (i.e., rites) of Allah;
for you therein is good.
So mention the name of Allah upon them
when lined up (for sacrifice);
and when they are (lifeless) on their sides,
then eat from them and feed the needy
(who does not seek aid) and the beggar.
Thus have We subjected them to you
that you may be grateful.
It is not their meat, nor their blood,
that reaches Allah,
It is their piety that reaches Allah! ”

Holy Qur'an, Sūratu ’l-Ḥajj, 22:36-37

The Sacrifice: Whose Love Do You Have in Your Heart?

Shaykh Muhammad Hisham Kabbani

'Eid of al-Aḍḥā is to honor the day that Allah ﷻ ordered Sayyīdinā Ibrāhīm ؑ to slaughter and to give as a sacrifice his son to Allah ﷻ. That important day that Ibrāhīm ؑ was being tested was the day of 'Arafat, one day before 'Eid. When Allah ﷻ wanted to see if Ibrāhīm ؑ would listen and obey or not.

In *Tafsīr an-Nisābūrī* it is said that Hājar, the wife of Sayyīdinā Ibrāhīm ؑ, was not happy after Sayyīdinā Ibrāhīm ؑ married her. She was feeling that there was a problem with his first wife Sara, so she decided to leave. As she was leaving, she heard a message saying to her, "Where are you going? You are going to have a child. You are going to have too many offspring that are coming from you. Stay where you are, don't run away!" She stayed and Allah ﷻ made her pregnant with Sayyīdinā Isma'īl ؑ.

After the boy grew up, Sayyīdinā Ibrāhīm ؑ was taking care of that child and used to love him so much. One day, in a certain moment, Allah ﷻ ordered Jibrīl ؑ, "Go, yā Jibrīl and tell Ibrāhīm to slaughter his son for Me!" And Jibrīl ؑ said, "Yā Rabbī, I made a good relationship with Ibrāhīm. You were sending me with revelation to him. I will follow Your Order, but if there is a way, he can get that news without me giving it to him directly, that would be great."

Allah is the Merciful One, so He sent that *ru'yā*, dream, to Ibrāhīm ؑ.

فَلَمَّا بَلَغَ مَعَهُ السَّعْىَ قَالَ يَا بُنَىَّ إِنِّى أَرَى فِى الْمَنَامِ أَنِّى أَذْبَحُكَ فَانظُرْ مَاذَا تَرَى قَالَ يَا أَبَتِ افْعَلْ مَا تُؤْمَرُ سَتَجِدُنِى إِن شَاءَ اللَّهُ مِنَ الصَّابِرِينَ

Then, when (the son) reached (the age of) (serious) work with him, he said: "O my son! I see in a dream that I offer you in sacrifice: Now see what is your view!" (The son) said: "O my father! Do as you have been commanded: you will find me, if Allah so wills, one practicing patience and constancy!"[169]

The first time Sayyīdinā Ibrāhīm ﷺ saw the dream, he sacrificed 100 sheep for the sake of his son. That is why sincere people today, when they have a serious sickness like cancer, go and sacrifice 100 sheep and many times we observe that the patient was cured due to the sacrifice.

After that, he had the dream another time; he had thought that Allah ﷻ would accept the slaughter of 100 sheep, but he saw the dream again and then a third time. Then he told his wife to put oil on the head of his son, and he would take him. His wife asked, "Where are you taking him?" He said, "I have been ordered by Allah ﷻ to sacrifice my son." She looked at her son and looked at Sayyīdinā Ibrāhīm ﷺ and said, "If Allah ordered you to do that, you do it." And then he took his son up to the mountain and told him, "We are going out to play." He placed him on a big stone and covered his eyes.

Sayyīdinā Ismaʿīl ﷺ asked, "O my father, why are you covering my eyes?"

Ibrāhīm ﷺ replied, "Because we are playing." His heart was crying for the love of his son! He could not bear to see his son looking at him while he cuts his throat.

Sayyīdinā Ismaʿīl ﷺ said, "O my father, why are you wasting my time? Do what you have been ordered. I am not afraid. If Allah ﷻ wants me to be a sacrifice, let it be. O my father, be patient in difficulty, in problems. Don't lose your temper. I am okay, take me and slaughter me, but first take off the shirt that is on me and take it to my mother before it gets blood on it. Take it to my mother so she will remember me with that shirt and tell my mother that I left my son to the One who is better than everyone. I left my son to Allah ﷻ!"

Sayyīdinā Ibrāhīm ﷺ said, "O Allah, be merciful with me!" They say Sayyīdinā Ismaʿīl ﷺ was seven or nine years old and the angels fell into crying and the Doors of Heavens opened.

---

[169] Sūratu 'ṣ-Ṣaffāt, 37:102.

As soon as that happened, he took the knife and put it on Ismaʿīl's ﷺ neck, and in some narrations, they say that he smelled some meat barbecuing. He said, "O my father, what happened? I am smelling barbecue!"

He said, "O my son, this is the smell of my heart." That was the heart of Sayyīdinā Ibrāhīm ﷺ burning!

He said, "*Yā abatā,* O my father! Follow Allah's orders. Don't think that I don't know. I am ready, cut my throat! There is no need to close my eyes. I am happy with what Allah ﷻ wants, cut my throat!"

Sayyīdinā Ibrāhīm ﷺ put the knife to his son's throat and was crying out of love for his son, his flesh smelling like barbecue meat. He put the knife to his throat and recited, "*Bismillāh, Allāhu Akbar*!" and started cutting!

Look how Allah ﷻ is giving us a good life and we are complaining. Then Allah ﷻ ordered Jibrīl ﷺ to go quickly, saying, "If you don't stop it, I will take you away from My Presence!" and Jibrīl ordered the knife to stop. In the *tafsīr* of an-Nasafi, Ibrāhīm ﷺ felt he didn't fulfill the order of Allah ﷻ, so he took the knife and threw it as to him it had become a useless knife. Allah ﷻ hid from him that He had ordered Jibrīl to prevent the knife from cutting.

His son's throat was not cut, but the heart of Sayyīdinā Ibrāhīm ﷺ was cut. So, he placed the knife on his son's throat a second time but still, the knife would not cut. He tried a third time and still it would not cut.

Then he said, "O knife! Why are you not cutting?"

The knife said, "O Ibrāhīm! I am obeying Allah's Order not to cut and I obeyed from the first time, but you did not! You waited to see the vision three times before you obeyed! If you are angry with me, why are you not angry with the fire of Nimrod that they threw you in and it did not burn you?"

He said, "Because Allah ﷻ ordered the fire not to burn me."

And the knife said, "And Allah ﷻ ordered me not to cut your son's neck. Jibrīl ﷺ ordered me 70 times not to cut! I was cutting and I was ordered not to cut."

So why did Allah ﷻ order Ibrāhīm ﷺ to sacrifice Ismaʿīl ﷺ in the first place? Because Allah ﷻ does not like anyone of His servants to love anyone more than Him or share their love with Him. Allah *lā sharīka lahū*, you cannot put your children inside your heart together with Allah ﷻ. You have to choose: your children or Allah ﷻ? Do you want your children? Look at the story of Sayyīdinā Isma'īl ﷺ. Allah ﷻ wants you to put only Himself in your heart:

مَا وَسِعَنِى أَرْضِى وَلَا سَمَائِى، وَلَكِن وَسِعَنِى قَلْبُ عَبْدِى الْمُؤْمِن .

Neither My Heavens nor My Earth contain Me, but the heart of My Believing Servant contains Me.[170]

When we put Allah's Love and Prophet's ﷺ love in our heart, then we will be able to fly, but when we share our love of *dunyā* in our heart with love to Allah ﷻ, we cannot fly.

A *qasīdah* was recited in which the last verse read, *qata'tu kabadī,* "I have cut my liver into very small pieces to make it a rope in order for me to reach the love of Muhammad ﷺ!" These are the ones we need to follow: Allah's Pious and Sincere Servants.

Then Allah ﷻ ordered Ibrāhīm ﷺ to slaughter a ram for the safety of Sayyīdinā Isma'īl ﷺ, who then said to his father, "Let me ask this question of you. Are you more generous, or am I?" Ibrāhīm ﷺ said, "I gave you; I gave my son!" Sayyīdinā Isma'īl carries the light of Sayyīdinā Muhammad, so how is he going to die? It was a test for Sayyīdinā Ibrāhīm ﷺ. It was a test for us. Are we going to sacrifice for the sake of the Prophet or not? Are we going to follow his Sunnah or not? Are we going to obey or not?

So Sayyīdinā Isma'īl ﷺ said, "No, I am better. You were generous to give me, but I gave my own soul! I am the one who was losing (his life); you were not giving your own soul, but you were giving me." Sayyīdinā Isma'īl ﷺ gave himself for the sake of the whole Ummah, and he was carrying the secret of Sayyīdinā Muhammad ﷺ.

So 'Eid al-Aḍḥā is about sacrifice, which means not to spend on yourself, but what you can save from spending on yourself. Whatever you save, give to the poor, give them food, give them shelter, give them a home, anything. Remember on this day that there are poor people there, everywhere, who need your help. May Allah ﷻ enable us to help each

---

[170] Hadith *Qudsī*.

other and to be with those who help, and those whom their *du'ā* are never rejected, which is Sayyīdinā Muhammad ﷺ! And let us try to fast on 'Arafah and ask Allah, "O our Lord! Forgive our sins for the sake of Sayyīdinā Muhammad ﷺ, for the sake of Sayyīdinā Ibrāhīm عليه السلام, for the sake of Sayyīdinā Isma'īl عليه السلام and for the sake of those standing on 'Arafah. Share their pilgrimage with us and write for us from those who went on this pilgrimage and on every pilgrimage, including the Prophet's pilgrimage!

Khutbah of ʿEidu ʾl-Aḍḥā

Shaykh Muhammad Hisham Kabbani

Allāhu Akbar, Allāhu Akbar, Allāhu Akbar, lā ilāha illa ʾLlāh!

Allāhu Akbar, Allāhu Akbar wa lillāhi ʾl-ḥamd.

Tūbā lakum, maʿshara ʾl-muʿminīn!

O Muslims, Believers, good tidings! Good tidings for those who left their families, their countries and they left everything behind to say, "*Allāhu Akbar, Allāhu Akbar, Allāhu Akbar, lā ilāha illa ʾLlāh! Labbayk Allāhumma labbayk! Labbayka lā sharīka laka labbayk. Inna ʾl-ḥamda wa ʾn-niʿmata laka wa ʾl-mulk, lā sharīka lak!*"

SHAYKH HISHAM AND FAMILY MAKING *DUʿA* AFTER *ṬAWĀF AL-IFĀDAH*, HAJJ 2011.

They left everything, calling on Allah ﷻ, "*Yā Rabbī!* O Allah, we are coming to You!" and they went for Hajj and *Zīyārata ʾn-Nabī* ﷺ; they left their work and went for Hajj or *ʿUmrah*. If they were not able to go for Hajj or *ʿUmrah*, they left their work and came to the *masājid*, especially the young ones whom they have school; they left their school to come for Hajj, for *ʿUmrah* and *Zīyārah*, but in a *masjid*. Will Allah ﷻ write for them that day, or not? They left and they came. They didn't say, "We have to study, or we will get a zero or failing marks," but they said, "Let us come to the *masjid* to pray Ṣalāt al-ʿEid."

The Prophet ﷺ said, "The best days in the whole year are these ten days of Dhul-Hijjah. They are even better from the days that we go and do jihad in the Way of Allah ﷻ."

مَا الْعَمَلُ فِى أَيَّامِ الْعَشْرِ أَفْضَلَ مِنَ الْعَمَلِ فِى هَذِهِ ". قَالُوا وَلاَ الْجِهَادُ قَالَ " وَلاَ الْجِهَادُ، إِلاَّ رَجُلٌ خَرَجَ يُخَاطِرُ بِنَفْسِهِ وَمَالِهِ فَلَمْ يَرْجِعْ بِشَىْءٍ".

"No good deeds done on other days are superior to those done on these (first ten days of Dhul-Hijjah)." Then some companions of the Prophet ﷺ said, "Not even jihad?" He replied, "Not even jihad, except that of a man who does it by putting himself and his property in danger (for Allah's sake) and does not return with any of those things.[171]

To do jihad is in many ways: to study, as education is a jihad, keeping peace is a jihad, learning is a jihad, helping people is a jihad. So, they asked, "*Yā Rasūlullāh* ﷺ! They are better than jihad in the Way of Allah ﷻ?"

He ﷺ said, "Yes! They are considered more rewarded than jihad in the Way of Allah ﷻ!" He continued, "There is no one day in the year that is better than the Day of ʿArafah."

Allah ﷻ descends to the First Heaven on the Day of ʿArafah, sending down His Blessings on all those who are standing in the field of ʿArafat, calling on Allah ﷻ, "*Labbayk Allāhumma labbayk! Labbayka lā sharīka laka labbayk. Inna 'l-ḥamda wa 'n-niʿamata laka wa 'l-mulk, lā sharīka lak!*"

As narrated by Jābir ؓ, the Prophet ﷺ said:

مَا مِنْ يَوْمٍ عِنْدَ اللَّهِ عَزَّ وَجَلَّ أَفْضَلُ مِنْ يَوْمِ عَرَفَةَ يَنْزِلُ فِيهِ رَبَّنَا إِلَى السَّمَاءِ فَيُبَاهِى أَهْلِ الْأَرْضِ وَأَهْلِ السَّمَاءِ وَيَقُولُ لِمَلَائِكَتِهِ: أُنْظُرُوا هَؤُلَاءِ عِبَادِى جَاءُونِى مِنْ كُلِّ فَجٍّ عَمِيقٍ يَرْجُونَ رَحْمَتِى وَلَمْ يَرَوْا عَذَابِى.

And there is no day better in the sight of Allah than the Day of ʿArafah. On this day, Allah descends to the nearest Heaven, and He is proud of

[171] Bukhārī.

His Servants on the Earth and says to those in Heaven, "Look at My Servants. They have come from far and near, with hair disheveled and faces covered with dust to seek My Mercy even though they have not seen My Chastisement."[172]

Allah ﷻ descends to the First Heaven and He makes sure, telling the angels, "Look how much My Servants are worshipping Me! They are better than anyone. I will give them what an eye never saw, what an ear never heard and what a mind never thought about. They came from everywhere, they came for Me, they left their countries, they left everywhere, and they came calling on Me as they only want My Mercy. Even they don't look at My Punishment! They are asking, *"Raḥmah yā Rabbi, arḥamnā yā Allah!"*

And will Allah ﷻ not forgive them? He will forgive them! Those who are in Hajj, who went to ʿArafat, those who are in Muzdalifah today and then went to Mina and some went to Kaʿbah in Masjid al-Ḥarām in order to finish their duties of Hajj, all these people left their duties and went for that. And here in the West, they left everything and came to pray the ʿEid prayer in *jamaʿah*. May Allah ﷻ bless us as He is blessing them with whatever He is blessing them!

May Allah ﷻ bless us with His Mercy for the sake of His Beloved One, Sayyīdinā Muhammad ﷺ! Allah ﷻ said, *"Yarjūn raḥmatī,* they ask for My Mercy, *wa lam yaraw ʿadhābī,* and they never saw My Punishment."

مَا مِنْ يَوْمٍ أَكْثَرَ مِنْ أَنَّ يُعْتِقَ اللهُ فِيهِ عبدًا مِنْ النَّارِ مَنْ يَوْمِ عرفة.

Sayyidah ʿĀ'ishā ﵂ related that the Prophet ﷺ said, "There is no day on which Allah sets free more slaves from Hell than He does on the Day of ʿArafah."[173]

Yawm al-ʿArafah is the day that Allah ﷻ frees people from Hellfire, and on that day, there is no way to count how many people are given freedom from Hellfire! May Allah ﷻ give us that and dress us with that.

---

[172] Al-Bazzār and Ibn Ḥibbān.

[173] Muslim.

سُئِلَ رَسُولُ اللَّهِ صَلَّى اللَّهُ عَلَيْهِ وسلم: عَنْ صَوْمِ يَوْمِ عَرَفَةَ؟ قال: " يُكَفِر السَّنَةِ الْمَاضِيَةِ والبَاقِيَة ".

The Messenger of Allah ﷺ was asked about the observance of fasting on the Day of 'Arafat. He said, "It is an expiation for the sins of the preceding year and the current year.[174]

And the Prophet ﷺ said that anyone fasting the Day of 'Arafat, Allah ﷻ will waive his sins of the year before and the year after.

يَوْمِ عَرَفَةَ، وَيَوْمَ النَّحْرِ وَأَيَّامِ التَّشْرِيقِ عِيدُنَا أَهْلَ الْإِسْلَامِ، وَهِيَ أَيَّامُ أَكْلٍ وَشُرْبٍ وذِكْرِ اللَّهِ.

The Day of 'Arafah, the days of 'Eid, and the days of tashrīq are holy days for Āhl al-Islām; these are the days of eating, drinking and remembering Allah. [175]

Prophet ﷺ said, "The Day of 'Arafah, *yawm an-nahr* (the first day of '*eid*), *wa ayyām at-tashrīq* (the three days after the first day) are our holy days." For the People of Islam, these are our holy days and how are you going to spend it? Not coming and spending them in the *masjid*? He ﷺ said, "These are days of eating, drinking and remembering Allah." How many days? The Day of 'Arafah and four days of 'Eid, so five days, are the days of eating and drinking. So, don't say, "Come and give *ṣuḥbah* and *dhikr*!" Eat and drink, don't leave any food (uneaten) today! Anything you like is not a waste; you eat and you drink and thank Allah ﷻ.

May Allah ﷻ forgive and bless us. May Allah ﷻ support us on this beautiful day, the day of rewards, *barakah* and mercy, the day of people coming together and in a nice sitting, a Circle of Remembrance. This is a Circle of Remembrance and everyone around the world observing 'Eid is in a Circle of Remembrance to which Allah ﷻ will give endless blessings that no one knows, for everyone who is observing 'Eid al-Aḍḥā, who fasted the Day of 'Arafat and is then enjoying eating and drinking

---

[174] Muslim from Abū Qatadah.

[175] Bukhārī and Muslim.

in these four days. Anything you eat or drink will be written for you as *Ḥasanāt* in these four days and, as Prophet ﷺ said, up to 700 times Allah will multiply them!

Inshā-Allāh every one of you coming are in good health and well dressed.

Now we are going to make *zīyārah* for the many Holy Hairs of the Prophet ﷺ which were passed to us.

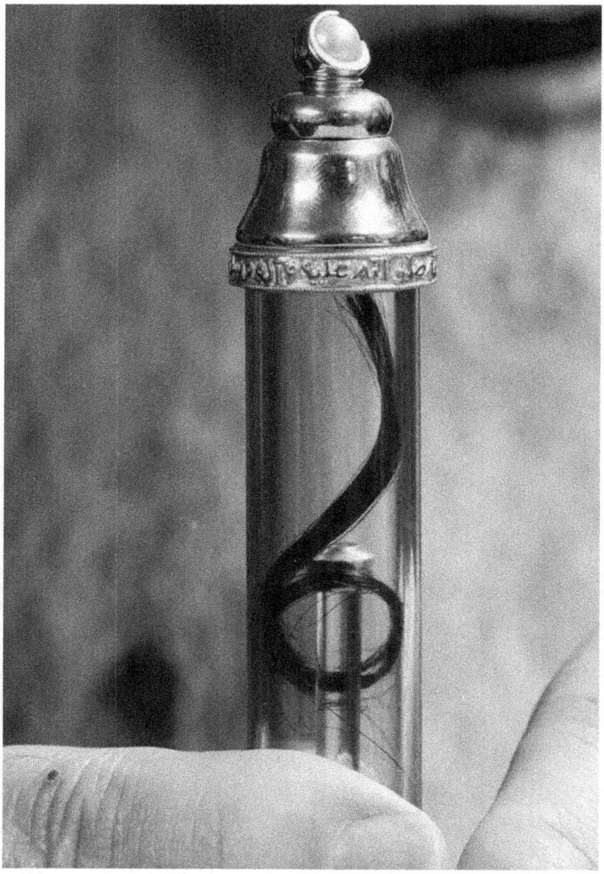

A LOCK OF THE HOLY HAIR OF THE PROPHET ﷺ KEPT BY SHAYKH HISHAM KABBANI.

BIRTHPLACE OF THE PROPHET ﷺ

“

When the Best of Mankind ﷺ was born,
O what marvels did his mother Amina see!
The Beloved's mother spoke:
"I saw a strange light; the sun was like its moth.
It flashed up from my house
and filled the world with light up to the sky.
Heavens opened, vanquishing the dark.
I saw three angels with three flags:
One was in the East, one in the West,
and one stood upright on the Ka`bah's roof!
Rows of angels descended from Heavens
and circumambulated my house.
Then came the Houris group on group!
The light from their faces made my house so bright.
An angel laid out a cover in mid-air, called 'brocade'.
When I witnessed these events,
I became bewildered and confused.
Suddenly the walls were split apart
and three Houris entered my room.
Of these charming three,
one was Asiyah of moonlike face,
one was Lady Mary without doubt,
and the third was a Houri, O so beautiful!
These moonfaced three drew gently near,
greeting me with kindness here.
Then they sat around me and gave good tidings
of the birth of Muhammad ﷺ!

”

Sulayman Chalabi ق

The Prophet ﷺ was born in a house not far from the Kaʿbah, the Prophet ﷺ said, "I am a result of the supplication of my father Ibrāhīm ﷺ and the glad tidings brought by ʿIsa ﷺ. And my mother, when she bore me, saw that a light shone out from her, which lit up the palaces in Syria."[176]

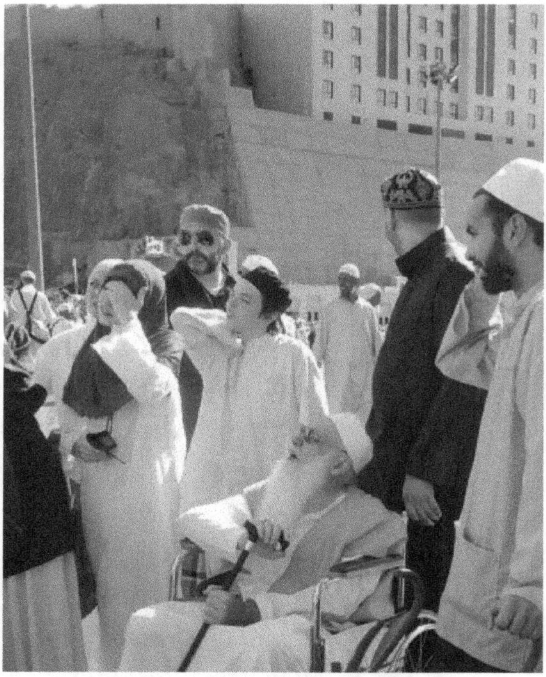

SHAYKH HISHAM AND FAMILY VISITING THE BIRTHPLACE OF THE PROPHET ﷺ, HAJJ AL-AKBAR 2011.

Monday is a blessed day, since Ibn ʿAbbās ؓ said, "The Prophet ﷺ was born on a Monday, commissioned with prophethood on a Monday, passed away on a Monday, left as a migrant from Mecca to Madinah on a Monday, arrived in Madinah on a Monday and raised the Black Stone on a Monday."

When the Prophet ﷺ migrated to Madinah, the house was confiscated by Aqil bin Abū Ṭālib, a cousin of the Prophet ﷺ and not Muslim at the time. Sometime after the Prophet's ﷺ death, the house was bought by Muhammad bin Yūsuf al-Thaqafī (brother of the tyrant Hajjāj bin Yūsuf).

[176] al-Ḥākim.

The house was then bought by al-Khayzurān, the mother of the Abbasid Caliph, Hārūn ar-Rashīd. She converted the house into a mosque. The site was maintained as a mosque into the twentieth century.

In 1953 the mayor of Mecca, established a small library on the foundations of the home.

1910 DRAWING OF THE HOLY BIRTHPLACE AFTER IT WAS CONVERTED INTO A MOSQUE [COURTESY ISLAMIC LANDMARKS].

THE PROPHET'S ﷺ BIRTHPLACE THAT WAS TURNED INTO A LIBRARY.

A Commentary on the Chapter of the Blessed Birth in *Mawlid ad-Dayba'i*

Shaykh Muhammad Hisham Kabbani

Mawlid ad-Dayba'i
مولد الديبعي
Shaykh 'Abd ar-Rahman ad-Dayba'i
Compiled by
Shaykh Muhammad Hisham Kabbani
INSTITUTE FOR SPIRITUAL AND CULTURAL ADVANCEMENT

MAWLID AD-DAYBA'I BOOK COMPILED BY SHAYKH HISHAM KABBANI, 2008.

Shaykh Abdur-Raḥmān ad-Dayba'i writes in his renowned _Mawlid_:

أَحْضِرُوْا قُلُوْبَكُمْ يَا مَعْشَرَ ذَوِى الأَلْبَابِ * حَتَّىْ أَجْلُوا لَكُمْ عَرَائِسَ مَعَانِى أَجَلِّ

الأَحْبَابْ * الْمَخْصُوْصِ بِأَشْرَفِ الأَلْقَابْ * الرَّاقِى إِلَى حَضْرَةِ الْمَلِكِ الْوَهَّابْ *

حَتَّى نَظَرَ إِلَى جَمَالِهِ بِلا سِتْرٍ وَلاْ حِجَابْ

_Be present with your hearts, O possessors of deep understanding, whilst I
present to you the qualities of the Most Beloved, who received the most
honored titles, the Ascender to the Divine Presence of the Owner, the
Granter of all requests, until he looked to His Beauty without obstruction
or veil._

فَلَمَّا آنَ أَوَانُ ظُهُورِ شَمْسِ الرِّسَالَةِ فِى سَمَاءِ الْجَلالَةِ * خَرَجَ مَرسُوْمُ الْجَلِيْلِ

لِنَقِيبِ الْمَمْلَكَةِ جِبْرِيلْ يَا جِبْرِيلُ نَادِ فِى سَائِرِ الْمَخْلُوقَاتِ * مِنْ أَهْلِ الأَرْضِ

وَالْسَمَاوَاتِ * بِالْتَّهَانِى وَالْبِشَارَاتْ

_When the time arrived for the dawn of the sun of prophethood in the sky
of majesty, it was directed by Allah to Gabriel, the chief of the kingdom,
"O Gabriel, announce the good news to all creations, from among the
dwellers of the Earth and the Heavens with My congratulations and good
tidings."_

When Allah ﷻ created Creation, He first created that Light ﷺ in Makkatu
'l-Mukarramah; He ﷻ ordered Jibrīl ◌ to put the _Nūr_ (Light) that was
under Allah's Gaze in Ka'bah al-Musharrafah. That is the reason why
when we go to Makkatu 'l-Mukarramah, we make _ṭawāf_ around where
they built the Ka'bah.

After that _Nūr_ was under Allah's Gaze for 2,000 years, and some _aḥādīth_
say 70,000 years, Allah ﷻ took that _Nūr_ out and the entire universe shone,
with no more _ẓulmah_, darkness. That is why when you look into the skies,
you see that it is dark above the atmosphere, there is no light; that is
where Allah ﷻ didn't gaze. Whatever Allah ﷻ gazed upon at that time
illuminated the whole universe!

So, that is where (the Light of) Sayyīdinā Muhammad ﷺ was placed while he was still in the womb of his mother (he had not been born yet). And on that night (the night of his birth), he (his Light) didn't leave the House of Allah ﷻ in Makkatu 'l-Mukarramah, where every prophet stood in a line.

Then, Allah ﷻ gazed upon the Prophet ﷺ with the power of Bahru 'l-Qudrah, the Ocean of Power, the *Nūr* Allah ﷻ gave to Prophet ﷺ, and no one was able to see it.

هُ نُورُ السَّمَاوَاتِ وَالْأَرْضِ مَثَلُ نُورِهِ كَمِشْكَاةٍ فِيهَا مِصْبَاحٌ الْمِصْبَاحُ فِي زُجَاجَةٍ الزُّجَاجَةُ كَأَنَّهَا كَوْكَبٌ دُرِّيٌّ يُوقَدُ مِن شَجَرَةٍ مُّبَارَكَةٍ زَيْتُونِةٍ لَّا شَرْقِيَّةٍ وَلَا غَرْبِيَّةٍ يَكَادُ زَيْتُهَا يُضِيءُ وَلَوْ لَمْ تَمْسَسْهُ نَارٌ نُّورٌ عَلَى نُورٍ يَهْدِي اللَّهُ لِنُورِهِ مَن يَشَاءُ وَيَضْرِبُ اللَّهُ الْأَمْثَالَ لِلنَّاسِ وَاللَّهُ بِكُلِّ شَيْءٍ عَلِيمٌ

Allah is the Light of the Heavens and Earth. The parable of His Light is as if there were a niche and within it a lamp: the lamp is in a glass, the glass like a Brilliant Star lit from a blessed tree, an olive tree that is neither of the East nor of the West, the oil of which is so bright that it would certainly give light of itself. Light upon Light! Allah guides whom He will to His Light. Allah sets forth Parables for men and Allah knows all things.[177]

He put the Light of the Prophet ﷺ in that *misbāḥ*, Lamp. From that time, the existence of the Prophet ﷺ was put in that Lamp where he became the *Nūr*, and from him Creation was created. Allah ﷻ made him understand Creation and how it moves from time to time.

Shaykh ad-Dayba'i continues:

[177] Sūrat an-Nūr, 24:35.

فَإِنَّ النُّورَ الْمَصُونَ وَالْسِرَّ الْمَكْنُونَ الَذِى أَوْجَدْتُهُ قَبْلَ وُجودِ الأَشْيَاءِ * وَإِبْدَاعِ الأَرْضِ وَالْسَمَاءْ * أَنْقُلُهُ إِلَى بَطْنِ أُمِّهِ مَسْرُورًا

"For the chosen light and the secret (of existence), which I created before the existence of all things and before the creation of the Heavens and Earth, on this night I move him to the womb of his mother happy!"

Allah ﷻ said about the Light, *al-Maṣūn*, "As I have created the Light and the secret of that Light, I send it to the Prophet ﷺ, who sends it everywhere; wherever his Light ﷺ touches, becomes a human being.

He ﷺ filled the Earth with that *Nūr* and I am responsible for him." It means, Allah ﷻ is responsible for anyone who touched that holy place (Kaʿbat al-Musharrafah), and in reality, they will be touching Heavens! That is why we go to Mecca: to touch the *Nūr* of the Kaʿbah, because it contains the Prophet's Power and his *Nūr*!

أَمْلأُ بِهِ الْكَوْنَ نُوْرًا * وَأَكْفُلُهُ يَتِيْمًا وَأُطَهِّرُهُ وَأَهْلَ بَيْتِهِ تَطْهِيْرًا *

I fill this world with his Light, support him in his orphanhood, and I purify him and his House with the utmost purification.

He said, "I filled the Earth and the whole universe with his Light, and I protect him, and I will clean him and his Family." Who is his Family? Sayyīdinā al-Ḥasan ؑ, Sayyīdinā al-Ḥusayn ؑ, Sayyidah Fāṭimatu 'z-Zahrā ؑ, and Sayyīdinā ʿAlī ؑ are the Family of the Prophet ﷺ. They have honor, and Āhlu 's-Sunnah wa 'l-Jamaʿah have honored them more than any other creatures on Earth: whatever respect they give to them, our respect is higher and higher and higher! Āhlu 's-Sunnah wa 'l-Jamaʿah are connected with Allah's *Nūr*, so they never go down, they always go up! So, be happy!

فَاهْتَزَّ الْعَرْشُ طَرَبًا وَاسْتِبْشَارًا وَازْدَادَ الْكُرْسِيُّ هَيْبَةً وَوَقَارًا وَامْتَلأَتِ السَّمَاوَاتُ أَنْوَارًا * وَضَجَّتِ الْمَلآئِكَةُ تَهْلِيلاً وَتَمْجِيْدًا وَاسْتِغْفَارًا *

So, the Throne shook with happiness and delight. And the Footstool increased in magnificence and greatness. The sky was filled with brilliant

light, and the voices of the angels vibrating with the recitation of God's Oneness, praising Him and seeking His Forgiveness.

All Heavens are filled with the *Nūr* that now reaches everyone in our *jamaʿah,* because they are celebrating the Prophet's birthday according to the reality of the Mawlid, not like others with no goal, who only read it quickly and leave. There is no "read and go," but *Nūr*, and *ẓulmah* will go and it will be replaced with Nūr an-Nabī ﷺ, Light of the Prophet ﷺ.

سُبْحَانَ الله وَالْحَمْدُ لِلّهْ وَلاَ إِلَهَ إِلاَّ الله وَالله أَكْبَرْ

Subḥāna 'Llāh wa 'l-ḥamdulillāh wa Lā ilāha illa 'Llāhu wa 'Llāhu akbar (4x)

وَلَمْ تَزَلْ أُمُّهُ تَرَى أَنْوَاعًا مِنْ فَخْرِهِ وَفَضْلِهِ إِلَى نِهَايَةِ تَمَامِ حَمْلِهْ فَلَمَّا اشْتَدَّ بِهَا الطَّلْقُ بِإِذْنِ رَبِّ الْخَلْقِ * وَضَعَتِ الْحَبِيْبَ صَلَّى اللهُ عَلَيْهِ وَسَلَّمَ سَاجِدًا شَاكِرًا حَامِدًا كَأَنَّهُ الْبَدْرُ فِيْ تَمَامِهْ (محل القيام)

So, his mother continued to experience a variety of (signs of his) eminence and honor until the completion of her pregnancy. When the labor pains strengthened, with the permission of Allah (the Creator of All Creations), his mother gave birth to the Beloved Prophet ﷺ in prostration thanking and praising Allah as if he were the full moon in its splendor!

It was explained to us, when the Prophet ﷺ was born in *dunyā*, and of course he was present before in that House of Light: Allah ﷻ put His Light in a House of Light, *Allāhu nūru 's-samāwāti wa 'l-arḍ*, like the Kaʿbah. The Kaʿbah now is the House of Allah, is it not? If you make *sajdah* there, you cannot say, "O, you are making *shirk*." No, it's Allah's House, so you do your prayer there, and from any side you make *sajdah*, it's accepted.

Allah ﷻ gave Sayyīdinā Muhammad ﷺ in Heavens, as we have said before, in that unknown presence where the Prophet was created from Allah's Light, Allah ﷻ made for him a House of Light from His Light, from Allah's Light. He put the Prophet ﷺ in that House and was under the Gaze, the Observation of the Manifestation of Allah's Beautiful Names and Attributes. That is where he was raised up and trained, and that's the meaning of the Hadith, *adabanī Rabbī fa-aḥsana tā'dībī,* "Allah ﷻ taught me and gave me the best manners." It's that kind of preparation with which Allah ﷻ has prepared His Prophet ﷺ. So, here we can now understand when Sayyīdinā Muhammad ﷺ was born, as soon as he came out, he went into *sajdah*, saying, "*Ummatī, ummatī*! My nation, my nation!"

Story: The Birth of the Holy Prophet ﷺ in Mecca[178]

Hajjah Amina Adil

When the term was fulfilled and the moment of delivery approached, the Holy House, the Kaʿbah at Mecca, all at once was seen to split in two.

The Quraysh were appalled by this event, and everybody searched for an explanation. The Banī Hāshim said, "This is on account of ʿAbdAllāh, the son of ʿAbdu 'l-Muṭṭalib's ﷺ death that this happened" while the Banī Zuhair said, "This Holy House split asunder because the father of Amina ﷺ, Wahb ibn ʿAbdu Manāf died, and he was one of the bravest men of Quraysh."

While they were thus engaged in finding explanations for this inexplicable happening, they heard a voice coming from inside the Kaʿbah that said, "O Men of Quraysh! This Holy House has not come apart on account of the death of any, but rather because the time of birth has drawn nigh for the Light of this World, the Glory of the World to come, the Shining Lamp of Paradise, Muhammad bin ʿAbdAllāh ﷺ to emerge from his mother's womb. He is to be a great prophet; he will cleanse this Holy House of the abominations and idols that are polluting my precincts, and he will make me pure and pristine once more with the light of true faith; I will become Qiblah of all his nation and the annual pilgrimage will be held on my grounds. Know that it is an honor of his long-desired advent that this edifice has cracked and split."

The night that Muhammad ﷺ was born, Allah Almighty, Exalted be He, commanded angels to open all gates of Heaven and of Paradise; on that day the sun shone with more brilliance, and greater was its light than on other days, and the whole world was gladdened.

The Prophet's ﷺ blessed mother, Amina ﷺ, relates:

> At the time I was ready to give birth, there was no one with me, neither man nor woman attended me (for everyone, including ʿAbdu 'l-Muṭṭalib ﷺ, had gone to make *ṭawāf* of the Kaʿbah). I was all alone in the house. Suddenly there was a terrifying noise and I

---

[178] Excerpted from *Muhammad ﷺ the Messenger of Islam.*

felt great fear. Then a white bird alighted upon my breast and my fear left me, I became calm, and no trace of pain or anxiety remained. Next, I was handed a cup of white sherbet, and when I drank of it, my heart filled with peace, joy and light. After this, I beheld a number of tall women approaching me, tall and slender as cypress trees, and of astounding beauty. I took them to be the daughters of ʿAbdu Manāf. They came and sat around me in a circle, and I was mostly surprised and wondered how they had come to know of my condition and who had informed them. While I was yet pondering this question in my heart, one of the ladies spoke and said, "I am Hawa, the wife of Prophet Ādam ﷷ," and another one of them said, "I am Sarah, wife of Prophet Ibrāhīm ﷷ." Yet another said, "I am Asīyā, the wife of Firʿawn of Egypt." And another said, "I am Maryam, the daughter of ʿImrān, the mother of ʿIsa ﷷ." The others introduced as the Ḥourīs of Paradise, all of whom had come to usher the Holy Prophet ﷺ into his earthly life and to welcome him with due veneration.

All the while the noises I had been hearing became stronger and louder and more fearful. Suddenly I perceived a white curtain being drawn from the skies down to Earth, so that I was veiled from the eyes of the Jinn. Then, there was a flock of birds with beaks of green emerald and ruby red wings. These birds flew down and fluttered about me so closely that I could feel the beating of the wings upon my skin. They flew around and around me as if in *ṭawāf*. The Lord Almighty then removed the veil from my eyes so that I beheld the whole world from east to west. Three flags I saw them bring down from Heaven: one they planted in the east, one in the west and one right atop of the Kaʿbah. In the Heavens, that were open to my eyes, I beheld men bearing bejeweled vessels of gold, and they assisted at the birth of the blessed child, and I suffered neither pain nor trouble. And when I looked again, I saw that the child was born circumcised, and that his umbilical cord was cut, and he as wrapped in a piece of white silk. He touched the ground with his blessed head, lifted the forefinger of his right hand, and made humble supplication to Allah Almighty. I bent down to hear what he was saying, and these were the words I heard:

Ash-hadu an lā ilāha illa 'Llāh wa innī Rasūlullāh! Allāhu Akbar kabīran, wa 'l-ḥamdu lillāhi kathīran, wa subḥānallāhi bukratan wa aṣīlan. Allāhumma, ummatī, ummatī!

I testify that there is *no* god but Allah and that I am the Messenger of Allah. I declare Allah's Greatness with Greatness, and All Praise is due to Allah in Abundance and May Allah be Glorified all mornings and nights. O Allah, (*take* care of) my community, my community!

Amina ﵂, the mother of the Holy Prophet ﷺ recounts:

I then beheld a white cloud in the sky moving towards me, and from it came as if the sounds of horses. This cloud descended and enveloped the little child Muhammad ﷺ and carried him away out of *my* sight. I heard a voice calling: "We are taking Muhammed ﷺ, to show him the whole world. We shall encircle it and dive into the depths of the oceans, so that all that lives in and under the earth may know of the advent of the noble being and shall have seen his face and learnt of his arrival. Hereafter the world shall be filled with the light of faith. Of unbelief and rebellion against the Lord Almighty nothing will remain. I heard the voices speak to me."

After a brief moment, that cloud alighted anew, and I saw my son Muhammad ﷺ again, wrapped now in a piece of green silk, dripping with milk. His face was radiant as the moon on her fourteenth night, and he exuded a fragrance sweeter than that of yellow musk. I then beheld three persons standing aside; one of them held in his hand a jug of silver, another held a bowl of green emerald, and the third held a piece of folded white silk. The later unfolded this bit of silk and took from its folds a ring so bright it dazzled the eyes of the beholder.

They first took the baby Muhammad ﷺ and washed him seven times from the silver jug; then the next person took a ring from the folds of silk cloth and impressed its bezel in a place between the baby's shoulders. After *that* he wrapped it up again in the bit of silk. He then took the baby Muhammad ﷺ from me and held him under his wing for a whole hour, all the while whispering many secrets into his ears. At last, he kissed him upon both his eyes and said, "*Ṭūbā laka, yā* Muhammad ﷺ, blissful tidings to you, O Muhammad

> ﷺ, in all Allah's creation, you are the most awesome and venerable of all that serve Him Almighty. Triumph has been given to your companions and your nation. It is you who holds the keys to the castle of bliss."

It is related by Ibn ʿAbbās ﷺ:

> The night the Holy Prophet ﷺ was born, all idols in the Kaʿbah fell from their places and broke into pieces. At *that* time a voice was heard calling out from the Unseen and it said, "Woe and perdition on Quraysh, for the glorious and trusted Prophet ﷺ has come in truth, embellished with adornments from the loftiest gardens of Paradise. Laat and Uzza and all other idols are now finished and done for, Iblīs himself is imprisoned."

The Kaʿbah itself was inwardly hung with golden lamps from Paradise, and all creatures of the Heavens and the Earth, the youths and the maidens of Paradise, all created beings other than Mankind rejoiced and gave each other the glad tidings, "O Muhammad ﷺ!" they wished, "may Allah make you happy and always pleased, for there is no creature born with greater honor than you, and none that is more excellent. Never have the angels celebrated any birth of any created being as they now celebrate your birth into this world!" Between Heaven and Earth, there were raised pillars of support, and all were made of precious stone and not one of them was alike unto another.

Story: The Sinner Who Reached Sainthood for Honoring the Prophet ﷺ

Shaykh Muhammad Hisham Kabbani

SHAH BAHA'UDDIN NAQSHBAND ق, SEVENTEETH MASTER OF THE NAQSHBANDI GOLDEN CHAIN.

Grandshaykh ق told us of something that happened one Monday night on the 12th of Rabiʿ al-Awwal, coinciding with the night that the Prophet ﷺ was born, as many narrations say. Monday night is also the night about which the Prophet ﷺ said in a famous Hadith that Allah ﷻ will release Abū Lahab from Hellfire every Monday because he released his slave Thuwayba ﵂ out of happiness when she informed him of the birth of Sayyīdinā Muhammad ﷺ. Allah ﷻ releases him every Monday from Hellfire even though he became the biggest enemy of the Prophet ﷺ in Mecca.

You are going to see miracles in this story. You must believe in the unseen or else there is no need for being in *ṭarīqah*, better to go home and sleep!

Grandshaykh ق said that on that same night, coinciding with Monday night, Shāh Naqshband ق was sitting in his room. And on that night, the highest level of Awlīyā are always there in the presence of the Prophet ﷺ, they will never disconnect. That is why they ordered all of us, all of you to make *sajdah* after Ṣalāt an-Najaat, which will take you under the ʿArsh, Throne of Allah ﷻ, to the presence of Prophet ﷺ and to the Presence of Allah ﷻ.

So, Shāh Naqshband ق was in this heavenly feeling in *sajdah* after Ṣalāt an-Najāt when he suddenly received *al-Hāṭif ar-Rabbānī,* the Heavenly Call, telling him, "On this precious night of Mine that I created My Beloved One, Sayyīdinā Muhammad, I want you to find the biggest and worst sinner of this time. I want you to guide that person, so I will forgive him."

The high caliber *Awlīyāullāh* can look at the whole of humanity without being disturbed, one overlapping the other. As your TV box can receive thousands of channels all at the same time, why are we amazed that a *Walī* could see thousands at one time? Now these digital boxes have very sharp wavelengths; the *Awlīyā* have even sharper, perfect, precise wavelengths. They can see everyone as everyone has a different, acute wavelength. They see with their box, which is their heart.

Shāh Naqshband ق threw all his *baṣīra*, insight, from East to West and found one who was written from the people of Hellfire, the one who was the worst of that time. At that moment, the person said to herself, "Like everyone celebrating the Prophet's birthday, tonight I will not work," and that had never happened before. She said, "I am tired of my work, I want to celebrate that event!" and then she lit a candle, as that is a tradition to show love to the Prophet ﷺ, to put a lamp in a dark place so people can see. If there was no candle, they used honey wax to give light to a dark area.

Shāh Naqshband ق looked and saw the deed of that lady and decided to go to her. With the power of "*Bismillāhi 'r-Raḥmāni 'r-Raḥīm*," he was at her door by folding space and time. Don't say this is too much. Today they use airplanes to shorten distances. By *Bismillāhi 'r-Raḥmāni 'r-Raḥīm*, you also can have these powers and miracles, but we don't use it with its power. We are saying it by tongue, but not feeling it in the heart. *Awlīyāullāh* want to make sure you are feeling it in your heart, so they keep uploading the secret and *barakah* of *Bismillāhi 'r-Raḥmāni 'r-Raḥīm* until one day you will be able to use it, as they already prepared you for that. Don't underestimate the power of Naqshbandi Golden Chain shaykhs. As Sulṭān of the Time, there must be a Sulṭān al-Awlīyā in every *ṭarīqah* and we believe our shaykh is Sulṭān al-Awlīyā of all *Awlīyā* of all *ṭarīqas*. He can fill you with the power of *Bismillāhi 'r-Raḥmāni 'r-Raḥīm*,

When you recite *Bismillāhi 'r-Raḥmāni 'r-Raḥīm* 100 times every day, that will raise you higher and higher in levels and make it easy for your shaykh to uplift you. Then one day he will give you your keys and you will find yourself already inside. As when children play PlayStation, it will open more and more doors, and it never ends, and all that game is put on a very small chip. Can a *Walī* not do that, put on a very small chip and fill you up with all kinds of games of *Ākhirah*? They are games, you have to be able to move around all kinds of difficulties and obstacles that come to you in the way of religion.

So, he looked and found her the worst, but lighting a candle which he saw as a good excuse to go and help her, he went there and knocked on her door. She said, "O, today I declared I am not working, who is that?" She went to the door and opened it and found Shāh Naqshband ق, the famous scholar; he is one of the top *Awlīyāullāh* in *Sharīʿah*. We always like to break *Sharīʿah*, but they never break *Sharīʿah*.

She said, "O you!" she didn't know him, "what are you coming here to do with your turban and big beard?" Shāh Naqshband ق has a huge beard, and it goes all the way to the ground, it is never cut. Looking at him from his back you can see his beard coming very wide from the sides, like two hands width. I saw him one time with this huge beard, as Grandshaykh ق described it.

She said, "O, you are a shaykh coming here to do what?" She was a lady that meets with men. She said, "You cannot come here, it is not your way! What is this? Has *dunyā* changed?"

He said, "Don't argue with me! You have a business, and I am a customer. You cannot reject me or else my people will come and throw you out. I have to go inside."

She was worried, so she said, "Do you have the money for that?"

He said, "I don't only have money, but I have more than that!" And he showed her a bag of golden coins. He went inside with two followers to be witnesses, so as not to break the *Sharīʿah* [i.e., to be alone with a non-*maḥram* lady].

She said, "Okay, I am ready. What do you want?"

He said, "No, it is not what you are thinking. I am not here for that. Now you must do what I say! We are not coming here for what you think."

She said, "Okay, where is the money?" She was the richest woman in her time.

He gave her the golden coins and then said, "Take my turban and my *jubbah*, put them on and go to the end of the room." The lady began to move from there to the end of the sitting room and then he said, "*Yā Rabbī*! I am seeking forgiveness for that lady. I am asking for her forgiveness as she is obeying me. I am authority here and that is based on the verse, 'Obey Allah, obey the Prophet and obey those in authority.' She is listening to what I am telling her, and she is regretting what she has done, so for the sake of the Prophet ﷺ, forgive her!" As he said these words, mercy was descending and reaching her. When she reached the end of the room, Shāh Naqshband ق said, "Now come towards me; leave *dunyā* and come towards *Ākhirah*." Then he said, "*Yā Rabbī*! That lady is asking forgiveness and she is repenting, completely asking You to send Your Mercy on her."

As soon as she arrived back to Shāh Naqshband ق, she fainted from Allah ﷻ forgiving all her sins and within seconds, he delivered her Trust! *Awlīyāullāh* can reach their *murīds* immediately, whether they're sinners or not, they can reach them and bring them back to normal by uploading into their hearts.

Some people are quickly granted to be *Awlīyā*. This lady became a worshipper sitting in her room, never going out again, and some ladies dedicated themselves to serve her. She dedicated all her wealth to Shāh Naqshband ق which was used to buy so many properties. Today they are still using those properties.

Why did that happen? Because Allah ﷻ wanted to forgive the biggest sinner on the night of Mawlid an-Nabī. The worst sinner was that lady, who attracted *ināyatullāh*, Allah's Care, because she said, "I don't want to work (sin) that night," and she lit a candle for the sake of Mawlid an-Nabī ﷺ, for the sake of the birth of Rasūlullāh ﷺ.

So, to do Mawlid an-Nabī, even every day, you will be rewarded with endless unimageable rewards. That is the importance of Mawlid an-Nabī ﷺ, that someone can come to a Mawlid only at the end, to eat or receive food from it, and then have all his sins taken away by Allah ﷻ! You will receive the manifestation of the *tajallī* of forgiveness due to the *tajallī* on that Mawlid.

JABAL AN-NŪR

“*This mountain, Jabal an-Nūr,*
the Mount of Light and Jabal Uḥud,
are talking mountains.
When Allah ﷻ wanted to stop Earth
from shaking,
He sent two mountains on Earth,
and it immediately stopped shaking,
until today.
And when we take something
from these mountains,
they will shake!”

Shaykh Muhammad Hisham Kabbani ق

JABAL AN-NŪR, WHERE THE PROPHET MUHAMMAD ﷺ RECEIVED THE FIRST REVELATION.

Jabal an-Nūr, the Mountain of Light, is a mountain which lies about two miles from the Kaʿbah. Near the top is a small cave known as Ghāri Ḥirā, the Cave of Ḥirā. It was here that the Prophet Muhammad ﷺ received the first revelations of the Holy Qur'an during the month of Ramadan in 610 CE.

Prior to the revelation, he would often retreat to the cave to find peace, solitude and an opportunity to reflect and meditate. The mountain is also known as Jabal Ḥirā and Jabal al-Islam, the Mountain of Islam.

The First Revelation in the Cave of Ḥirā

Hajjah Amina Adil

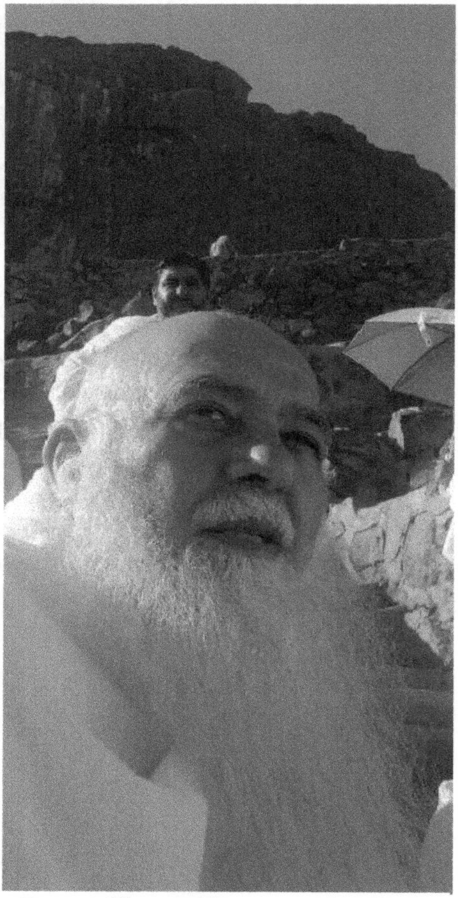

Shaykh Hisham Kabbani at Jabal an-Nūr, Hajj 2011.

The Prophet ﷺ was known throughout his tribe as aṣ-Ṣādiq al-Amīn, the Truthful and Trustworthy One. When he was 35 years of age, the Quraysh Tribe was renovating the House of Allah, the Kaʿbah. They disputed among themselves as to who should put the sacred Black Stone in its place. They finally came to an agreement that the most trustworthy person should replace it, and that person was the Prophet ﷺ.

At that time inspirations and revelations were coming to the Prophet's ﷺ heart. He was always in a state of spiritual vision and insight, but he was not authorized to speak about it. He preferred to be alone and used a cave in a mountain called al-Ḥirā for contemplation and meditation. He sought seclusion as the means to reach the Divine Presence of Allah Almighty and Exalted.

He avoided all kinds of attachment, even with his family. He was always in meditation and contemplation, afloat on the Ocean of the *Dhikr* of the Heart. He disconnected himself completely from everything, until there appeared to him the Light of Allah Almighty and Exalted, which graced him with the condition of complete intimacy and happiness. That intimacy allowed the mirror of revelation to increase in purity and brightness, until he attained the highest state of perfection, where he observed the dawning of a new creation. The primordial signs of beauty shone forth to spread and decorate the universe. Trees, stones, earth, the stars, the sun, the moon, the clouds, wind, rain, and animals would greet him in perfect Arabic speech and say, "*As-salāmu ʿalayka yā* Rasūlullāh, Peace be upon You, O Prophet of Allah!"

At forty years of age, when standing on the Mountain of Ḥirā, there

THE CAVE OF HIRA.

appeared on the horizon a figure he did not recognize, who said to him, "O Muhammad, I am Jibrīl, and You are the Prophet of Allah whom He has sent to this Nation." Then he handed him a piece of silk which was decorated with jewels. He put it in his hand and told him, "Read!" He asked, "What am I to read?" He hugged the Prophet ﷺ and told him, "Read!" He again said, "What shall I read?"

He hugged him again and said:

اقْرَأْ بِاسْمِ رَبِّكَ الَّذِى خَلَقَا قْرَأْ بِاسْمِ رَبِّكَ الَّذِى خَلَقَ ٱقرَأْ وَرَبُّكَ

ٱلأَكْرَمُ ٱلَّذِى عَلَّمَ بِٱلقَلَمِ عَلَّمَ ٱلإِنسَـٰنَ مَا لَم يَعلَم

Read in the Name of your Lord, Who created, created Man out of a sperm-cell. Read! And your Lord is The Most Bountiful, The One Who taught Man by the Pen, taught Man what we did not know.[179]

Then he ordered him to climb down the mountain to the plains below; he placed him on a large white stone and gave him two green robes. Then Jibrīl ﷺ hit the earth with his feet. Immediately a spring poured forth and the angel made ablutions in it and ordered him to do the same. Then Jibrīl ﷺ took a handful of water and threw it on the face of the Prophet ﷺ. Sufi saints say that the water he threw was a sign that the Prophet ﷺ was granted authority to spread to human beings the Knowledge of the Secrets of Allah's Divine Presence, either by physical means or by spiritual means. Then he observed two cycles of prayer (*raka'ats*) and told the Prophet ﷺ, "This is the way to worship," and he disappeared.

The Prophet ﷺ returned to Mecca and told his wife, Sayyidah Khadījah ﷺ all that had occurred. She believed him and she was the first Muslim. Then she went with the Prophet ﷺ to Waraqah bin Nawfal, her cousin, who was considered a person knowledgeable in spirituality. The Prophet ﷺ told him what happened. He believed him and he was the first man to believe in the Prophet ﷺ. He said, "This is the Holy Spirit who descended on Moses ﷺ." He said, "Would that I be alive when your people expel you from Mecca!" The Prophet ﷺ asked, "Are my people going to put me out of Mecca?" He said, "Yes, that is what is written." Then Abū Bakr ﷺ became a Believer, and he was followed by 'Alī ﷺ. In public the Prophet ﷺ gave guidance needed for daily life, and in private he would give the special advice needed for attaining the state of *Iḥsān* (perfect good character). That is why Abū Hurayrah ﷺ said in an authentic hadith mentioned in Bukhārī, "The Prophet ﷺ has poured into my heart two kinds of knowledge: one I have spread to people and the other, if I were to share it, they would cut my throat."

The knowledge Abū Hurayrah ﷺ referred to is the hidden, secret knowledge that the Prophet ﷺ gave to his Companions. He did not authorize them to spread that knowledge because it is the secret

[179] Sūratu 'l-'Alaq, 96:1-5.

knowledge of the heart. From these secrets all Masters of the Naqshbandi Golden Chain and all other Sufi Orders receive their knowledge. This knowledge was transmitted only from heart to heart, either through Abū Bakr aṣ-Ṣiddīq ﵁ or through ʿAlī ﵁.

For three years, as the Muslims increased in number, they used Dāru 'l-Arqam as a mosque in which to teach, to worship and to hide. Then the Prophet ﷺ was ordered to proclaim the religion openly. Allah ﷻ sent a Sūrah of the Qur'an challenging anyone to write anything like it. Poets, leaders and famous people tried until they openly accepted the self-evident fact that it was not possible!

Shaykh Hisham Kabbani descending Jabal an-Nūr, Hajj al-Akbar, 2011.

Seek Refuge in the Prophetic Heart!

Shaykh Muhammad Hisham Kabbani

When the Prophet ﷺ was in a state of meditation in the Cave of Ḥirā, Sayyīdinā Jibrīl came down to him ﷺ with the Lord's Revelation. According to some interpretations, the Prophet ﷺ was trembling from fear of Sayyīdinā Jibrīl, and that's why he said, *daththirūnī* "Cover me!" to his wife, Sayyidah Khadījah.

How can we say that he was afraid of Jibrīl, given that this angel was with him during his birth and in other events in his life? What is the actual meaning of "*daththirūnī*"? Allah ﷻ said in the Holy Qur'an:

يَا أَيُّهَا الْمُدَّثِّرُ قُمْ فَأَنذِرْ وَرَبَّكَ فَكَبِّرْ

O you, wrapped up (in the mantle)! Arise and deliver your warning, and your Lord magnify![180]

What is the real meaning of "*al-Mudaththir* (to be covered up by something)"? When the Prophet ﷺ was asked by Jibrīl to read, even though from our point of view he was illiterate, the Prophet ﷺ said, "Cover me!" In reality, it meant, "Cover me with what Allah ﷻ has adorned me!" The Prophet ﷺ asked Jibrīl, "What do you wish for me to read?" And Jibrīl answered, "With *Bismillāhi 'r-Raḥmāni 'r-Raḥīm,* read from all the secret knowledge about all existing creations; read with these secrets!" Trembling, the Prophet ﷺ said, "O Angels! Cover me with all the realities, knowledge, and secrets manifested to me since the Day of Promises."

The Prophet ﷺ also once said, "People of *dathr* (giving), have taken the reward." So, another meaning for "*daththirūnī*" other than "cover me" is "bestow on me".

Allah ﷻ is saying, *Yā ayyuha 'l-muddaththir,* "O the rich one, to whom Allah ﷻ granted knowledge not previously open to anyone, get up and warn!" It does not mean "warn distant persons," but rather it means,

[180] Sūratu 'l-Mudaththir, 74:1-3.

"Notify the close ones about the esoteric knowledge that has not yet been opened to anyone."

This verse of Sūrat al-Fatḥ, is a witness to the verse of Sūrat al-Mudaththir we mentioned.

إِنَّا فَتَحْنَا لَكَ فَتْحًا مُّبِينًا

Verily, We have granted you a manifest victory (opening).[181]

It means, "We have opened to you a Revelation!"

The Prophet ﷺ said, "On every letter of *'lā ilāha illa 'Llāh,'* Allah creates an angel who makes the same remembrance on his behalf until the Day of Judgment."[182]

Allah ﷻ is saying, "We have opened to you a Revelation that is impossible to absorb. Inform people about it so that I forgive them through you, as you are carrying their burdens." So, without feeling it, we are all beseeching the Prophet ﷺ to carry our sins and intercede for us. This is why Allah is saying, "O Muhammad ﷺ! I have manifested on you this opening, to enable you to carry this responsibility."

إِنَّا فَتَحْنَا لَكَ فَتْحًا مُّبِينًا لِيَغْفِرَ لَكَ اللَّهُ مَا تَقَدَّمَ مِن ذَنبِكَ وَمَا تَأَخَّرَ
وَيُتِمَّ نِعْمَتَهُ عَلَيْكَ وَيَهْدِيَكَ صِرَاطًا مُّسْتَقِيمًا

Verily, We have granted you a distinct opening, so as to absolve you from all previous and future sins that you will intercede on behalf of your Ummah.[183]

In general, if you commit a sin, you come in the presence of the Prophet ﷺ asking him to intercede for your forgiveness. And Allah ﷻ is saying, "O Muhammad ﷺ! When you have opened to them from the inner and outer secrets, they realized their darkness and oppressive natures, so they came to you, asking for your forgiveness."

---

[181] Sūratu 'l-Fatḥ, 48:1.

[182] Sha'rānī.

[183] Sūratu 'l-Fatḥ, 48:1-2.

Sayyidah Rābīʿah al-ʿAdawīyya ق used to say to her Lord, "O my Lord! I am not serving You for the sake of Your reward, nor in fear of Your punishment, but because You deserve being loved and served!"

Whatever knowledge *Awlīyāullāh* have attained is nothing compared to what was granted to the Prophet ﷺ of *ʿUlūm al-Āwwalīn wa 'l-Ākhirīn,* the Knowledge of Before and After.

What we can do is resort to the Cave, where Allah ﷻ will spread His Mercy upon you. "Mercy" is Prophet Muhammad ﷺ, and "The Cave" is the heart of Prophet ﷺ! Therefore, those who seek refuge must go to the Prophetic Heart.

Similarly, in Sūrat YāSīn, Allah ﷻ is saying:

وَآيَةٌ لَّهُمْ أَنَّا حَمَلْنَا ذُرِّيَّتَهُمْ فِى الْفُلْكِ الْمَشْحُونِ

And a sign to them is that We carry them and their descendants in a loaded ship.[184]

The "loaded ship" is the prophetic heart carrying all the Believers. It is related in the book *Tabaqāt,* regarding *lā ilāha illa 'Llāh,* that Allah ﷻ takes the worst servants for His Judgment and puts in front of them 99 books or records of all their sins. He commands angels to weigh those records against one utterance of *lā ilāha illa 'Llāh,* which turns out to be heavier in the Scale than all their sins, and thus they are taken to Paradise! If one remembrance is able to weigh that much, then is it not worthy for us to remember Allah ﷻ at least one-hundred times a day?

---

[184] Sūrat YāSīn, 36:41.

DĀRU 'L-ARQAM

> " *When ʿUmar accepted Islam,*
> *Angel Jibrīl came down and said,*
> *'O Muhammad!*
> *Undoubtedly, the inhabitants of Heaven*
> *have celebrated ʿUmar's conversion!'* "

ʿAbd Allāh ibn ʿAbbās ❧

SITE OF DAARU 'L-ARQAM, BETWEEN ṢAFĀ AND MARWA.

Dāru 'l-Arqam, the House of Arqam ﷺ, was located at the foot of Mount Ṣafā. It was here in the initial period of Islam that the Prophet ﷺ secretly preached Islam.

For some time after the Prophet ﷺ proclaimed his prophethood, the Muslims gathered here to perform *ṣalāt* and to learn about Islam without fear of torture or persecution. As it was a short walk away from the Kaʿbah and its bustling crowds, the pagans who lived nearby did not take notice of the many people who used to gather here. It effectively became the first Madrasa, Islamic school, in Islam.

Many people embraced Islam at Dāru 'l-Arqam including ʿAmmār bin Yāsir ﷺ and Suhayb bin Sinān ﷺ who embraced Islam together. Hamza ﷺ also embraced Islam here, followed a few days later by ʿUmar ﷺ. When ʿUmar wanted to take his Shahadah, he asked al-Khabbāb ﷺ, "O Khabbāb! Where will Muhammad ﷺ now be, that I may go to him and enter Islam?" Khabbāb ﷺ told him that he was at the House of Arqam near the Ṣafā Gate with many of his companions. It was after his conversion to Islam that the Muslims started performing *ṣalāt* in the open and Islam was propagated in public.

Story: The Conversion of Sayyīdinā 'Umar ☙

Shaykh Muhammad Hisham Kabbani

Sayyīdinā 'Umar ibn al-Khaṭṭāb ☙ was aggressive against Islam before he became Muslim. He fought anyone who said, "I converted to Islam." He could not accept that, but he didn't know the Prophet ﷺ had made a *du'ā*, "O Allah! Give me one of the two 'Umars!" and Allah ﷻ gave him Sayyīdinā 'Umar Ibn al-Khaṭṭāb ☙.

How did he become Muslim? They told him, "Your sister has accepted Islam." He was so upset that he went to her immediately, and everyone in Mecca feared him, so no one could say anything to deter him, or he would have beat them. He had a very strong personality.

So, he went to his sister's home where she, her husband, and Khabbāb, the one teaching them Qur'an, were reading the Holy Qur'an. Immediately, his sister hid the skin or tree bark on which verses of the Holy Qur'an were written.

Sayyīdinā 'Umar ☙ asked her, "What am I hearing? Did you become Muslim?"

She said, "Yes, I became Muslim."

He hit her with such force that it knocked her to the ground, and he said, "Show me that paper!" While everyone was afraid of him, she said to his face, "No! You are dirty and you cannot touch it! First go take *ghusl*, a shower!"

Those words hit him hard because she showed she was not afraid of him. "Now I am a Muslim, and I am not afraid of non-Muslims; I stand up for Muslims!" That amazed him, and he wondered what had changed her. So, he went and took a shower.

Allāhu Akbar! See how much he brought his ego down. When someone is arrogant in his opinion, it is impossible to advise him because his ego is there. He cannot accept to lower himself, but with the great power that Allah ﷻ gave him, when she said, "You are dirty," he realized something is going on here, so he took a shower with good intention to read that paper, and then Allah ﷻ poured *Īmān* into his heart. He said, "Give it to me now." She showed him the paper, which he read and said, "Take me to the Prophet ﷺ!" Then he became a Muslim in the presence of the Prophet ﷺ.

So (in reference to what Allah said in the previous *āyah*), Sayyīdinā 'Umar ibn al-Khaṭṭāb ؓ heard that his sister had become Muslim and went to see with his own eyes, which means first comes hearing then comes seeing. So, the first level of *Īmān* is to hear, and the highest level of *Īmān* is *iḥsān*, to see. Why didn't Allah ﷻ begin the *āyah* by first saying "seeing" and then "hearing," but instead He said, *inna s'-sam'a wa 'l-baṣara, "Verily! The hearing and the seeing,"* starting with the lower level? You might hear and not accept, but if you see, you are the first to accept as then there is no way to deny, as Allah ﷻ showed you the truth. That is why a judge needs a witness, someone who has seen what took place; he will not conclude a court case by taking a decision based only on what was heard, so when there are no actual witnesses, they throw out the case.

JABAL ABŪ QUBAYS

"*The moon traverses*
the constellations of the zodiac
in a single night,
so why do you deny the Miʿrāj?
That wondrous, unique Pearl (the Prophet)
is like a hundred moons,
for when he made one gesture,
the moon was split in two.
And the marvel that he displayed
in splitting the moon (on Mt. Abū Qubays)
was in keeping with the
weakness of the creatures' perception.
The work and business of
the prophets and messengers
is beyond the spheres and the stars.
Transcend the spheres and their revolution!
Then you will see that work and business."

Mevlana Jalāluddīn Rūmī ق

Jabal Abū Qubays is a mountain adjacent to Masjid al-Ḥarām. It is believed that it was from the top of this mountain that the Prophet ﷺ pointed to the moon and split it into half. The mountain was known as "al-Amīn (The Trustworthy or The Safekeeper)". This name arose from the tradition that this mountain safeguarded the *Ḥajar al-Aswad,* the Black Stone, when the flood in the time of Prophet Nūḥ ﷺ rushed through Mecca, destroying it along with the Kaʿbah.

Jabal Abū Qubays, believed by some to have been the first mountain on Earth created by Allah ﷻ, is narrated in several records as having been the final resting place of the *Ḥajar al-Aswad* during this catastrophic event. According to aṭ-Ṭabarī, Prophet Ādam ﷺ died at the foot of Jabal Abū Qubays and was subsequently buried there. A royal palace currently exists on top of the mountain.

Story: A Mountain's Deep Love for the Kaʿbah

Hajjah Amina Adil

Sayyīdinā Ibrāhīm عليه السلام was ordered to rebuild the Kaʿbah, which had been hidden in the earth after the flood of Nūḥ عليه السلام. At the time of the flood, Mount Abū Qubays, a mountain outside of Mecca, asked Allah ﷻ, "Let me hide your *amānāt*, trusts!" So, Allah ﷻ placed the Black Stone safely inside the mountain. Then Allah ﷻ put a little hill over the spot on which the Kaʿbah had stood to mark it. Ibrāhīm عليه السلام asked his Lord, "Where and how should I build it?" Jibrīl عليه السلام came and removed the hill with his wing. Then a cloud appeared and shaded the area of the sanctuary so that its boundaries were made clear. Then Mount Abū Qubays asked Allah ﷻ that the Kaʿbah be built from its stones. This Ibrāhīm عليه السلام and Ismaʿīl عليه السلام did and mixed the mortar with Zamzam water.

The order came from Allah ﷻ. Jibrīl عليه السلام was the architect. Ibrāhīm عليه السلام was the mason and Ismaʿīl عليه السلام was the laborer. Ibrāhīm عليه السلام built the walls as high as he could reach. Then he took one large stone to stand on so that he could build higher. As the building grew, the stone increased in height, and it moved around the Kaʿbah on its own with Ibrāhīm عليه السلام standing on top of it. After the Kaʿbah was completed, this stone stayed nearby and became what we now know as Maqām Ibrāhīm عليه السلام. Then Hājar عليه السلام, Sara عليه السلام, Ismaʿīl عليه السلام and Isḥāq عليه السلام came to make *ṭawāf*. Sayyīdinā Ibrāhīm عليه السلام was tired and he sat down. He was exhausted but he wanted to clean the area before making *ṭawāf*. Just then a big wind blew through and carried all the debris and dust and dirt away. Those small bits of rock were distributed by the wind all over the world. Wherever a stone fell a mosque was or will be built until the end of time!

The Kaʿbah is called *Baytu 'Llāh*, the House of God, because all people are welcome there. Sayyīdinā Ibrāhīm عليه السلام made *duʿā* that out of his love for the community of the coming Prophet Muhammad ﷺ, he could make *shafaʿah*, intercession, for all the old people who would journey to the House. Sayyīdinā Ismaʿīl عليه السلام asked for *shafaʿah* for all the middle-aged people. Sayyīdinā Isḥāq عليه السلام asked for *shafaʿah* for all the young people. Sayyidah Sara عليه السلام asked for *shafaʿah* for all the women, and Sayyidah Hājar عليه السلام for all the slaves and servants, both men and woman. Then Ibrāhīm عليه السلام

put up his hand and said, "We love the community of the Prophet Muhammad ﷺ and the pilgrims who will come will love him. They will only pray for their Prophet ﷺ, and they will forget all about us." Allah ﷻ answered that He would make it obligatory in the five prayers to remember Ibrāhīm ﷺ and his family. Ibrāhīm ﷺ was very satisfied with this promise.

After making Hajj, Ibrāhīm ﷺ left Hājar ﷺ and Isma'īl ﷺ and returned to the mountains on the border of Arabia and Palestine. One side of the mountains is green and one side brown and dry. There he prayed, "O my Lord, I left some of my family in a distant desert valley (Mecca), so You make people come to them." And today whatever you might want you will be able to find in Mecca! Then, Allah ﷻ ordered Ibrāhīm ﷺ to call the people to come for Hajj, pilgrimage. Sayyīdinā Ibrāhīm ﷺ asked, "But my Lord, who will hear me?" Allah ﷻ ordered him, "Call and they will hear." So, Ibrāhīm ﷺ raised his voice and began calling the people. When he finished, he started to hear voices from far away like the buzzing of bees. "*Labbayk Allāhumma Labbayk*!" cried the voices. "O Allah!" Ibrāhīm ﷺ cried, "All those people are coming! How will I host them?" Sayyīdinā Jibrīl ﷺ came down with a glass of water. He told Ibrāhīm ﷺ to throw this water into the wind. The wind took the drops of water all over the world. Wherever they landed they became salt. On the mountains they became rock salt. On the sea they became sea salt. Whoever uses this salt is enjoying the hospitality of Sayyīdinā Ibrāhīm ﷺ until the end of time.

The souls who answered "*Labbayk*!" once will make Hajj one time. The souls who answered twice will make Hajj two times and so on. The first Ka'bah was actually the *Bayt al-Ma'mūr* which, at the time of the flood, was raised to the Fourth Heaven. It is there today, and the angels make *ṭawāf* around it. It is exactly the same as the Ka'bah in Mecca and directly above it. If it should fall, it would occupy exactly the same space, but it will not fall or come to this Earth again.

Story: The Moon Enters the Heart of Its Beloved ﷺ

Shaykh Nazim Adil al-Haqqani

The Holy Prophet ﷺ tells us, one full moon night the unbelievers of the Quraysh, the idol worshippers from among the Quraysh, said, "If you can split the moon into two parts, we will believe you." He said, "O my Lord, this is what they are asking!" And the Archangel came saying, "You may do this, you may do this, you may do even more than this, O Ḥabīb, if you request it. Just point with your *shahadah* finger, it is enough." And he pointed like this, and the moon became two halves, one on this side of the mountain (Mount Abū Qubays) and the other on that side of the mountain! That is what those who were looking only with this physical view saw – that the moon split into two, one part on this side, the right side, and the other part on the left side, and then coming together again, complete.

However, those who saw the whole truth saw that the two pieces of the moon moved to the Prophet ﷺ, one came through his right hand, one came through his left hand, then they entered here (indicates the heart) as a full moon and made *sajdah*! That is real, that is reality! What the Quraysh asked for, what the idol worshippers asked for, they saw, but the Sahabah saw another vision!

No doubt, before the greatness of Rasūlullāh ﷺ, the moon did this. Rasūlullāh's ﷺ greatness may carry the whole universe. And that Divine Power, Heavenly Power, must run through all prophets. If it were not so they would not have attracted anyone, and that the Last Prophet, with the Last Message, was the most powerful, there is no doubt. And Heavenly Power runs from Rasūlullāh ﷺ to his Companions.

THE HOUSE OF UMM HĀNĪ ﵂

“*That night (in my dream)*
I saw the Prophet ﷺ hugging me and
I saw myself disappearing in him.
As soon as I disappeared in him,
I saw myself ascending
from the Dome of the Rock, the Baytu 'l-Maqdis,
from which the Prophet ﷺ ascended
in the Night Journey.
I saw myself astride the same Burāq
which carried the Prophet ﷺ
and I saw myself carried up in a true vision,
to the Station of Two Bow-lengths,
where I could see the Prophet ﷺ but not myself.
I felt myself to be a part
of the entirety of the Prophet ﷺ.
Through that Ascension,
I received the Realities that the Prophet ﷺ poured
into my heart from what he had received
on the Night of Ascension.”

Shaykh ʿAbd Allāh al-Fā'iz ad-Dāghestānī ق

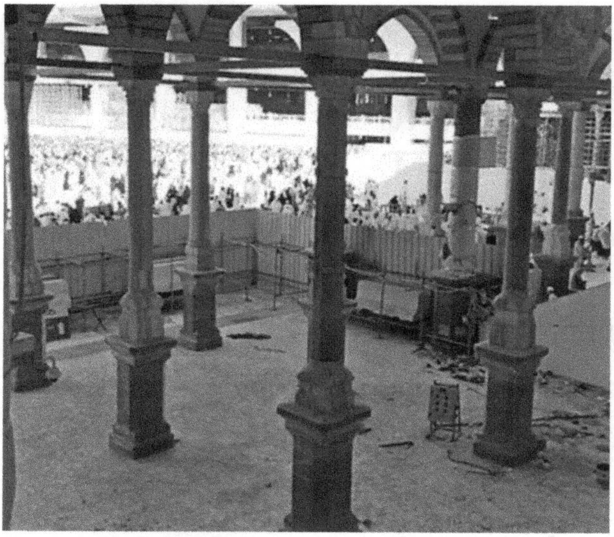

The site is believed to be in the current Masjid al-Ḥarām, on the side of the Abdul Aziz Gate. Umm Hānī ﵂ was the cousin of the Prophet ﷺ and the daughter of Abū Ṭālib ﵁. Her real name was Fakhitah. She grew up with the Prophet ﷺ, accepted Islam and migrated to Madinah with the Muslims.

It was from her house that the Prophet ﷺ was taken on the Night Journey by Jibrīl ﵇. This area, on the side of Bāb Abdul Aziz in the Masjid al-Ḥarām, is believed to have been the location of the house of Umm Hānī ﵂.

SHAYKH HISHAM AND GROUP IN FRONT OF KING ABDUL AZIZ GATE NEAR HOUSE OF UMM HĀNĪ, ʿUMRAH 2020.

From House of Umm Hānī ﷺ to the Divine Presence

Hajjah Amina Adil

When the Prophet Muhammed ﷺ had reached his fortieth year, he was sent with mercy for the whole world and the Prophet and Messenger to all people. He began to preach his message and invite people to faith. It was in the twelfth year of his calling, on the twenty-sixth day of the month of Rajab that the Prophet ﷺ went to *Baytu 'Llāh*, the Kaʿbah, and sat by himself in front of one of the pillars. There he engaged in remembrance and meditation of the Lord Almighty. Just then, Abū Jahl came in to meet with his helpers and henchmen. He saw the Prophet ﷺ sitting there all on his own, engaged in the worship of his Lord. Seeing him thus, he thought to himself, "I will play a prank," and going up close to him, he bent down and asked him, "O Muhammed ﷺ! Are you a prophet?" The Prophet ﷺ answered him directly, saying, "Yes, I am a prophet." Abū Jahl went on to say, "How can you be a prophet whilst you sit here all alone? Where is your following, where are your helpers? Had there been any necessity for a new prophet, the call to prophethood certainly would have come to me. Look at my following, look at the number of my retainers!" And, striking an arrogant pose, he turned around and left.

After Abū Jahl had gone, another one of his parties came by with his group of followers. He, too, approached the Holy Prophet ﷺ sitting there on his own, with the intention of doing something hurtful to the Prophet ﷺ. He spoke as Abū Jahl had spoken, and then he turned and left. In this way, no less than seven of the notables of Quraysh came by with their accomplices and they all spoke the same words as Abū Jahl, as if they had previously devised a plan. As a result, the Holy Prophet ﷺ became very dejected, and his spirits fell. He thought to himself, "It is now twelve years that I am calling them to Islam and to the belief in the Unity of Allah Almighty. However, far from accepting the Truth, they don't even understand the concept of the Messenger. A prophet has no need of a following of servants and retainers. All that is needful to a prophet is

Divine Revelation and the order to make known His Divine Command." Thus, the Holy Prophet ﷺ grew sad.

That night was the twenty-seventh night of the month of Rajab, a Monday night. He proceeded to the house of Umm Hani who was the daughter of Abū Ṭālib, the sister of Sayyīdinā Ali. She lived in her father's house, which was situated between Ṣafā and Marwa. The Prophet ﷺ arrived at her house, and finding him downcast and dispirited, she asked him for the reason of this. The Prophet ﷺ explained to her what had happened and why he felt as he did. Now, Umm Hani was an intelligent and resourceful woman. She comforted the Holy Prophet ﷺ and said, "These men undoubtedly know that as a Prophet of Allah bringing the message of Truth you are not in need of servants and accomplices. But as they are a stubborn, envious and ill-tempered lot, they spoke these words with the sole purpose of insulting you and wounding your spirit." These words served to comfort the Prophet ﷺ somewhat, but he still remained distraught. It is reported that soon after praying the night prayer, Ṣalātu 'l-ʿIshā, he fell asleep in Umm Hānī's house in a saddened state of mind.

Then the Lord of all Created Beings who had created Rasūlullāh ﷺ before anything else, destining him to be a Messenger of many miracles and gifts of mercy to all the people in the world and endowing him with perfection and the ability to awaken love in the hearts of men; the Lord Almighty whose Glory reaches from end to boundless end, other than whom there is no God, in His aspect of Majesty and Might addressed Himself to the angel Jibrīl, saying, "My Beloved whom I have chosen from amongst all My Creation, the Best of them all, lies sleeping in the house of Umm Hani, aggrieved by the hurtful words of the unbelievers. Let your piety and obedience be an invitation to My Beloved. Go, adorn your dazzling wings with the gems of Paradise and enjoy the dignity of being at his service. Go and tell Mikā'īl to leave off the weighing out of provisions this night, tell Isrāfīl to abandon his trumpet for one hour, and tell Azrā'īl for this one night to refrain from taking any souls. Tell the angels of the lights and luminaries to festoon the Heavens with lamps; tell Riḍwān to embellish the gardens of Paradise and admonish the angels to keep the gate to the pits of Hell firmly fastened and the demons of Hell not to move from their places. Tell the Ḥourīs to bedeck themselves and to set about scattering precious gems, preparing all the Paradise mansions. Say to the Throne-bearing angels: 'Wrap the sphere of the skies in its blessed robes and equip yourselves each with seventy thousand angels.' You, Jibrīl, repair to Paradise and there select a Burāq steed, then descend to the face of the Earth. All the punishment in the graves shall be lifted for the duration of this night. Go to My Beloved who fell asleep of sad and dejected mind in Umm Hānī's house and be his companion. Awaken him gently and explain to him that this night he is to be shown his great destiny and the Station of Nearness (*qurb*), that excels all other stations of elevation and honor. Invite him to come along with you."

Story: Who Was Carrying the Burāq?

From Muḥyīdīn Ibn al-ʿArabī's ق *Futūhāt al-Makkiyyah*

Shaykh Muhammad Hisham Kabbani

PAINTING OF MUḤĪYIDDĪN IBN AL-ʿARABĪ ق.

I will tell you a story from Shaykh Muḥīyiddīn ibn al-ʿArabī ق, one of the greatest scholars in Islam and one of the big *Awlīyāullāh*. His *wilāyah* spread East and West and his books, *Futūhāt al-Makiyyah,* are taught in every generation.

In the chapter describing the love of the Prophet ﷺ, and we hope to have even one percent of that love, Shaykh Muḥīyiddīn ibn al-ʿArabī ق said, "When Allah's Will was to bring the Prophet ﷺ to *Qāba Qawsayni aw Adnā*, Allah ﷻ was able to say at any moment '*Kun fayakūn*! O My Prophet, be here!' and he would have been there immediately!" but why did Allah ﷻ take him from Mecca to Masjid al-Aqsa, and on a Burāq, an angel from Paradise?

Allah ﷻ ordered Sayyīdinā Jibrīl عليه السلام to look for a Burāq to honor the Prophet ﷺ. Jibrīl عليه السلام said, "I went inside and as I was looking, I wondered which one to take; I thought there would be only one." Allah ﷻ was also showing Sayyīdinā Jibrīl عليه السلام his helplessness in front of Allah ﷻ, as He even shows His Angels miracles to tell them, "O, you are only servants, you are My Servants!"

So, as Jibrīl عليه السلام began looking for one Burāq, he immediately saw oceans of Burāqs! He thought, "How to choose one? There are infinite numbers of Burāqs here!" He was looking for which one to pick when he saw one of them continuously crying. He approached him and said, "*Yā* Burāq, why are you crying?"

The Burāq replied, "*Yā* Jibrīl, leave me alone. When Allah ﷻ created us, Allah mentioned that one of us will be the one on whose back the Beloved ﷺ will be riding. So, I have been crying from that time as I do not want to lose that chance. My *tasbīḥ* has been written as '*Muhammad Rasūlullāh*!' and I was created to fulfill that position."

Where is our love and where is their love? Every teardrop that the Burāq shed was a pearl from which Allah ﷻ will make a palace for all of *Ummat an-Nabī* ﷺ.

Sayyīdinā Muḥīyyidīn ibn ʿArabī ق continues in his book: Jibrīl ﷺ said, "You are the one! Come with me," and in one moment they were at the door of the Prophet ﷺ [Umm Hānī's house].

Jibrīl ﷺ said, "*Yā Rasūlullāh*! Allah is inviting you; Allah is inviting His Beloved Prophet ﷺ!"

What an honor and greatness for *Ummat an-Nabī* ﷺ! Therefore, we must be happy! You must be happy to say:

Allāhumma ṣalli ʿalā Sayyīdinā Muhammadin wa ʿalā ālihi ṭib al-qulūbi wa dawā'ihā wa ʿafiyyati 'l-abdāni wa shifā'ihā.

O Allah, send prayers and peace upon our Master Muhammad, the medicine of hearts and their treatment, the soundness of bodies and their cure.

The love of Prophet ﷺ is the cure of all our ailments!

As the Prophet ﷺ was ascending, the Burāq felt like he was falling, so the Prophet ﷺ held him. Who is holding who now? The Burāq is carrying the Prophet ﷺ or the Prophet ﷺ is carrying the Burāq? And that is still in Isrā', not yet Mʿirāj.

Since the Prophet ﷺ was the one holding the Burāq from Mecca to Masjid al-Aqsa, couldn't he have gone directly to *Qāba Qawsayni aw Adnā,* the Station of Two Bows' Length or Nearer (to Allah)? But he went to the First Heaven. Why? Doesn't Jibrīl ﷺ know that Allah ﷻ invited him? Why did he take him to the First Heaven, Second Heaven, Third Heaven and to all the rest? To salute him and for all the angels to know *qīmat an-Nabi* ﷺ, the value of the Prophet ﷺ.

Heavens were decorated; each Heaven had a different procession of angels. At the entrance of each Heaven, they were asked, "*Man at-ṭāriq*, who is knocking?" This is how we learned it when we were young.

"It is Jibrīl."

"Who is with you?

"Sayyīdinā Muhammad ﷺ."

"Has he been invited?"

"Yes."

"You may enter!" That is how it is in the *sīrah*. "Of course, he has been invited. So, enter!"

There, the honor that he received no one knows, and he went up to the Second, Third, Fourth, Fifth, Sixth, and Seventh Heavens. No one knows how much more he went, as Allah ﷻ cannot be limited in Heavens. He created Heavens, so He cannot be in something He created. He is Greater, *Allāhu Akbar*, there are no limits! Although, He will be seen in Paradise, but who knows what will be seen! We don't want to go there now.

So, the Prophet ﷺ was raised until he reached a station that Jibrīl ﷺ could not continue. Allah ﷻ invited the Prophet ﷺ until he reached *Qāba Qawsayni*, "Two Bows' Length," *aw Adnā*, "and less," meaning, nearer and nearer. How much nearer? If it is Two Bows' Length, then you are already so near. Then what is "nearer"? It means the Prophet ﷺ disappeared! Allah ﷻ sent His *Ṣiffat an-Nūr*, this is secret of the Name, *an-Nūr*. Allah ﷻ dressed the Prophet ﷺ, and he became *Nūr*, Light, and *Nūr* can go anywhere; you cannot block the Light. This is to show *'Aẓamat an-Nabī* ﷺ. With all this that Allah ﷻ gave to the Prophet ﷺ of greatness, what did he say? It is in the Holy Qur'an:

قُل لَّآ أَسْأَلُكُمْ عَلَيْهِ أَجْرًا إِلَّا الْمَوَدَّةَ فِى الْقُرْبَى

Say (O Muhammad), "I do not ask you for a reward except the love of my Family."[185]

He ﷻ said, "Say to them, 'I don't ask anything of you, except for one thing: to love and take care of my Family!'" That is what will save us.

---

[185] Sūrat ash-Shu'ara.

يَا أَيُّهَا النَّاسُ إِنِّى قَدْ تَرَكْتُ فِيكُمْ مَا إِنْ أَخَذْتُمْ بِهِ لَنْ تَضِلُّوا كِتَابَ اللهِ وَعِتْرَتِى أَهْلَ بَيْتِى

O people! Indeed, I have left among you that which, if you hold fast to it, you shall not go astray: the Book of Allah and my Family, the People of my House.[186]

He made them near each other, the Holy Qur'an and His Family! *Allāhu Akbar! Allāhu Akbar, ʿala kulli man tagha wa tajabbar, Allāhu Akbar* on every tyrant and on everyone who creates problems!

Love of the Prophet ﷺ is your safety and ticket to Paradise! Don't drop from your life to recite at least 500 times *ṣalawāt* on the Prophet ﷺ. If you cannot, at least 100 times, and if you cannot, at least ten times. Allah ﷻ loves His Prophet ﷺ, and says that if you pray on him one time, He will pray on you ten times. Ten what? What is the meaning of *ṣalawāt*? What kind of rewards, *ajar*, are in these *ṣalawāt*? What kind of Paradises do these *ṣalawāt* carry?

O Muslims! O Believers! Keep love of the Prophet ﷺ in your heart, and you will be saved. It is easy, as Allah ﷻ says in a Holy Hadith:

أَنَا جَلِيْسُ مَنْ ذَكَرَنِى

I sit with him who remembers Me.[187]

Allah ﷻ is saying, "I am sitting and am the Companion of the one who mentions Me." '*Jalees*' here means 'with.' So, "I am with that one who remembers Me with My Mercy and *Rahmah*."

They say, "Don't do excessive *ṣalawāt* on the Prophet ﷺ; it is *shirk*." Then, why does Allah ﷻ make "excessive" *ṣalawāt* on the Prophet ﷺ by ordering the angels to make *ṣalawāt* on him ﷺ? Give me an answer! Allah ﷻ ordered all His Angels to make *ṣalawāt*, so is that excessive *ṣalawāt*? Show me one order in the Holy Qur'an that says, "don't do *ṣalawāt* on the Prophet ﷺ" or "do only a little bit."

---

[186] Tirmidhī , narrated by Jābir bin ʿAbd Allāh,.

[187] Āḥmad, Bayhaqī.

So, since the Prophet ﷺ was given that title, anyone who does *ṣalawāt* on him will enter Paradise. Allah ﷻ will give him back that reward. May Allah ﷻ bless us and forgive us.

Wa min Allāhi 't-tawfīq bi ḥurmati 'l-Fātiḥah.

MASJID AL-HUDAYBĪYYAH

“*Certainly, was Allah pleased*
with the Believers
when they pledged allegiance
to you, (O Muḥammad),
under the tree,
and He knew what was
in their hearts,
so, He sent down tranquility
upon them
and rewarded them
with an imminent conquest.”

Holy Qur'an, Sūrat al-Fatḥ, 48:18

THE OLD HUDAYBIYYAH MOSQUE WITH NEW MOSQUE IN THE BACKGROUND.

Masjid al-Hudaybīyyah marks the area where the Prophet ﷺ and the Quraysh signed a peace treaty, "The Treaty of Hudaybīyyah". There exists a historic mosque and a new one next to it. Hudaybīyyah also functions as a *miqāt* for pilgrims to enter into the state of *iḥrām*.

After six years of living in Madinah, the Prophet ﷺ had a dream that he entered Mecca and did *ṭawāf* around the Kaʿbah. The Companions were delighted when he told them about it as they all revered Mecca and yearned to do *ṭawāf* around the Kaʿbah. Recognizing the dream as a sign, the Prophet ﷺ left Madinah for Mecca on Monday, 1st of Dhul-Qaʿdah, 6 AH, with the intention of performing *ʿUmrah* in peace. Accompanying him were 1400-1500 Muslims dressed as pilgrims for *ʿUmrah* and animals they had brought for sacrifice.

The Prophet's ﷺ scout came back with the news that the Quraysh were determined to prevent the Muslims from entering Mecca. Taking a detour to avoid the Quraysh, the Muslims continued to travel until they reached Hudaybīyyah, about 40km west of the Kaʿbah. They pitched camp there.

The Prophet ﷺ sent ʿUthmān ؓ to the Quraysh to convince them that they had only come to perform *ʿUmrah* and to invite them to Islam. He was

also instructed to visit the believing men and women still in Mecca to tell them that Allah ﷻ will make His religion victorious in Mecca and the time was close when they would no longer be required to conceal their faith.

ʿUthmān ؓ was in Mecca longer than the Muslims had expected and the rumor spread that he had been killed. The Prophet ﷺ called for a pledge of allegiance. He sat beneath an acacia tree and the Muslims promised that they would fight with him to the last man. Placing one hand on the other, the Prophet ﷺ said, "This is the pledge on behalf of ʿUthmān! ʿUthmān ؓ shortly turned up. The Believers were spared from going into battle, but they had proved their sincerity with their pledge. Allah ﷻ revealed a verse referring to this pledge in Sūrah al-Fatḥ,

لَقَدْ رَضِيَ اللَّهُ عَنِ الْمُؤْمِنِينَ إِذْ يُبَايِعُونَكَ تَحْتَ الشَّجَرَةِ فَعَلِمَ مَا فِي

قُلُوبِهِمْ فَأَنزَلَ السَّكِينَةَ عَلَيْهِمْ وَأَثَابَهُمْ فَتْحًا قَرِيبًا

"Allah was pleased with the Believers when they swore allegiance unto you beneath the tree."[188]

From that day, the pledge under the tree came to be called Bayaʿ al-Riḍwān, the pledge of those who had earned Allah's pleasure. When the Muslims saw the terms of the truce and what it meant to the Messenger of Allah, they were very distressed.

When the Prophet ﷺ had finished drawing up the treaty, he sacrificed a camel and then shaved his head. This was a difficult time for the Muslims because all their hopes had been dashed. They had left Madinah with the firm intention of entering Mecca and doing *ʿUmrah.* Now they felt beaten and crushed. However, when they saw the Messenger of Allah had made the sacrifice and shaved his head, they rushed to follow his example.

The remains of the old stone mosque are still present. The new mosque is known as Masjid Shumaysī and has modern facilities to enable pilgrims to get into the state of *Iḥrām* for performing *ʿUmrah.*

[188] Sūratu 'l-Fatḥ, 48:18.

The Importance of Bayaʿ in *Sharīʿah* and *Ḥaqīqah*

Shaykh Muhammad Hisham Kabbani

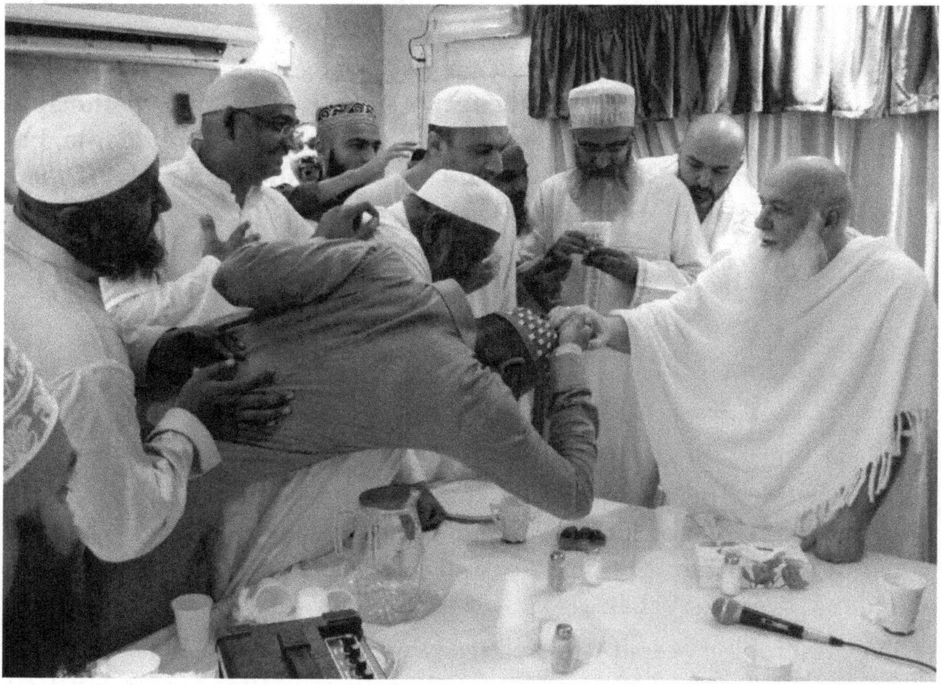

When you find your *murshid* and you know he is a good guide who will take you in the right direction, you have to promise him that you will walk with him in that journey without *takhalī ʿan*, deserting him. You cannot leave him as he gives you his confidence and you give him your attachment, but then in the middle of the way you get tired, and then you walk away. You cannot! When you give your promise to him that you will be with him, it means you have to follow the good manners because *shuyūkh* don't like the bad manners, they like the good manners. There are a lot of obstacles on that way, but you asked for it. Like a promise, *ʿahad*, a covenant, or we call it *bayaʿ*, *tuʿahid ʿalā ʿs-sarāʾi wa ʾd-darāʾi*, you take an oath, a promise to the shaykh that you will follow for good and through difficulty, so you don't take back your promise as it is finished, you are committed. That is why Allah ﷻ said in Holy Qur'an:

إِنَّ الَّذِينَ يُبَايِعُونَكَ إِنَّمَا يُبَايِعُونَ اللَّهَ يَدُ اللَّهِ فَوْقَ أَيْدِيهِمْ فَمَن نَّكَثَ فَإِنَّمَا

يَنكُثُ عَلَى نَفْسِهِ وَمَنْ أَوْفَى بِمَا عَاهَدَ عَلَيْهُ اللَّهَ فَسَيُؤْتِيهِ أَجْرًا عَظِيمًا

Verily, those who swear allegiance to you (Muhammad) swear
allegiance only to Allah. The Hand of Allah is above their
hands, so whoever breaks his oath does so only to his soul's
injury, while whoever keeps his covenant with Allah, on him
will He bestow immense reward.[189]

A group of ten Sahabah ◈ came to the Prophet ﷺ under a tree in
Hudaybīyyah and said, "*Yā Rasūlullāh!* We want to take *bayaʿ* from you."
Allah ﷻ said to Prophet ﷺ, "(Say) Yes, I will give you, but you have to
know that your *bayaʿ* is not for me, your *bayaʿ* is for Allah," and that is
the *āyah.* "You are a *khalīfah* for Allah on Earth: you take from them their
promise, but that will be for Allah." That is pure *tawḥīd,* no shirk.

"Allah's Hand is above their hands." When you put your hand under the
Hand of Allah, and that is not literal, but Allah's Hand is above your
hand, how can you dare to pull your hand out? When you give *bayaʿ* the
matter is finished! We gave *bayaʿ* to Grandshaykh ʿAbdAllāh ق and we
gave *bayaʿ* to Shaykh Nazim ق and we give *bayaʿ* to anyone for certain
reasons, and Allah ﷻ is saying in the Holy Qurʾan, "Those who gave you
bayaʿ, yā Rasūlullāh, that *bayaʿ* is for Me and My Hand is over their
hands!" *faman nakatha fa innamā yankuthu ʿalā nafsihi,* "Anyone who drops
it will be in a problem,"*fa man awfā bimā ʿahada ʿalayhu 'Llāha fasayū'tīhi
ajran ʿaẓīma* "and who will fulfill his promise," because the Prophet ﷺ said,
"A Believer keeps his promise."[190] If a Believer makes a promise, he
fulfills it, so "if they promise you you have to fulfill it, they cannot pull
their hands away," "Who fulfills their promise, I will give them from Me
a reward that is so great that no one can imagine!"

That is why *bayaʿ* is so important, because it takes you to the Shore of
Safety, where Allah will reward in *Ākhirah* with the greatest reward that
no one can imagine. Extend your hand as the Sahabah ◈ extended their
hands to Prophet ﷺ! Since the *bayaʿ* is for Allah, the Prophet ﷺ is taking

---

[189] Sūratu 'l-Fatḥ, 48:10.

[190] Abū Dawūd.

it and giving to Allah ﷻ, Allah has warned anyone not to drop it where, He said in Holy Qur'an:

وَأَوْفُواْ بِعَهْدِ اللهِ إِذَا عَاهَدتُّمْ وَلاَ تَنقُضُواْ الأَيْمَانَ بَعْدَ تَوْكِيدِهَا وَقَدْ
جَعَلْتُمُ اللَّه عَلَيْكُمْ كَفِيلاً إِنَّ اللّهَ يَعْلَمُ مَا تَفْعَلُونَ

*Fulfill the Covenant of Allah when you have entered into it,
and break not your oaths after you have confirmed them;
indeed, you have made Allah your surety; for Allah knows all
that you do.*[191]

"Fulfill your promise to Allah ﷻ and don't decline it after you have said 'yes' and after you admitted it." Allah was *kafīl*, sponsoring you when you put your hand with the Prophet ﷺ, then Allah put His Hand over everyone's hand, so don't drop your promise to Allah ﷻ! That is why in the Holy Qur'an many verses have been mentioned on *bayaʿ* and from the Sunnah, the Prophet ﷺ gave *bayaʿ* in groups, in private, in different categories, for men, for women, for children and for those who are not yet mature.

So, *bayaʿ* is a principle of Islam that you have to follow; it has importance in *Sharīʿah* and *Ḥaqīqah*, *Taṣawwuf*, because Sahabah ؓ made *bayaʿ* to the Prophet ﷺ and they promised they will follow, *lā ilāha illa 'Llāh*, not to commit shirk, not to steal, not to commit adultery and not to spread bad rumors. May Allah ﷻ pull us out from all these sins and clean our hearts and fill our hearts with *tawḥīd* and love to Allah ﷻ, love to Prophet ﷺ and love to our *shuyūkh*!

Wa min Allāhi 't-tawfīq, bi ḥurmati 'l-Ḥabīb, bi ḥurmati 'l-Fātiḥah.

---

[191] Sūrat an-Nahl, 16:91.

BANĪ SHAYBAH GATE

"We entered the illustrious Holy House,
wherein 'he who enters is secure'
by the Gate of the Banī Shaybah
and saw before our eyes
the illustrious Kaʿbah,
God increase it in veneration,
like a bride who is displayed
upon the bridal chair of majesty
and walks with proud step
in the mantles of beauty,
surrounded by the companies
which had come to pay
homage to the God of Mercy,
and being conducted to
the Garden of Eternal Bliss!"

Ibn Baṭṭūṭa ق

HISTORIC PHOTOS SHOWING BANĪ SHAYBAH GATE, MAQAM IBRĀHĪM AND THE KAʿBAH.

The Banī Shaybah Gate was a freestanding arch that was one of the main entry points to get into the area of the Kaʿbah in the time of the Prophet ﷺ. Usually called "Bābu 's-Salām, (the Gate of Peace)," the name "Gate of the Banu Shaybah" was given to an arcade adjacent to the Well of Zamzam. It was removed in the 1960s to provide more space in the *maṭāf* area, no markings were left to show its position. During the time of the Prophet ﷺ, there were seven known entrances into the area of the Kaʿbah. The Banī Shaybah Gate was the most prominent. The gate belonged to the Banī Shaybah clan, the custodians of the keys to the Kaʿbah. The Banī Shaybah Gate was the Kaʿbah's main northern gate, and the one used by visitors coming from the north.

When the Quraysh rebuilt the Kaʿbah, a conflict arose on the issue of who would have the honor of placing the *Ḥajar al-Aswad* back in its place. Abū Umayya Ibn al-Mughīra, one of their elders, asked Quraysh to agree on the judgement of the first person to come through the Banī Shaybah Gate and they all agreed on this suggestion. The first to come through this gate was the Prophet ﷺ!

Replacing the Black Stone

Shaykh Muhammad Hisham Kabbani

The Prophet ﷺ doesn't say anything from his desire, but it is *waḥīy*, Divine Revelation. When asked about one of the Signs of the Last Days, he said, *innahā nubūwwah wa raḥmah*, "The first of it is a prophecy and a mercy," so with the appearance of the Prophet ﷺ is the end of *dunyā*, it begins with him. The Sign of the Last Days is the coming of the Prophet ﷺ; it wasn't Sayyīdinā Mūsā ؏, Sayyīdinā ʿIsa ؏, Sayyīdinā Nūḥ ؏, Sayyīdinā Ibrāhīm ؏ or Sayyīdinā Ādam ؏, no. The splitting of the moon took place with the Prophet ﷺ, as Allah ﷻ mentioned in the Holy Qur'an:

$$ اقْتَرَبَتِ السَّاعَةُ وَانشَقَّ الْقَمَرُ $$

The Hour (of Judgment) approached and the moon split.[192]

The Day of Judgement is so near now, which is why he said, *innahā nubūwwah wa raḥmah*, meaning, with the Prophet's ﷺ appearance there is mercy, because he is *Raḥmatan li 'l-ʿĀlamīn*, Mercy for all the Worlds; it is not after 40 years, but his appearance is *raḥmah*, so from his birth he has been known as *Raḥmatan li 'l-ʿĀlamīn*. That's why he was known as al-Āmīn, The Trustworthy One.

When the tribes were rebuilding the Kaʿbah and brought the Black Stone to be restored there, the 41 tribes began to fight as to who will be the one to put the Black Stone in its place. They began to argue, not like today when the one with a machine gun takes the lead and they threaten you with death, not with words! Your word is enough, you don't need to kill. So, they argued and finally agreed to accept the decision of the first person to enter from outside the Kaʿbah (through the Gate of Banī Shaybah).

When they saw the Prophet ﷺ coming, although he had not yet declared his message, they were very happy, and they said, "We trust him, he is al-Amīn, the Trustworthy One!" Even the unbelievers trusted him!

---

[192] Sūratu 'l-Qamar, 54:1.

The Prophet ﷺ told them to put the Black Stone in a blanket or sheet and asked each tribe to hold a corner of it, and then he placed the Stone back in its place with his own hands. That made everyone happy, so that is *nubūwwah* and *raḥmah,* and *raḥmah* here means "peace". The Prophet ﷺ brought peace between the tribes; he brought them together and built them with a new education, *Sharīʿah,* which until today is the main education people like to study.

GATE OF VICTORY

"*The special attribute of the Prophet ﷺ*
was to conquer the hearts of people.
When hearts are conquered, they come to surrender.
The Prophet ﷺ worked for thirteen years
to establish Īmān, faith.
Once Īmān was established,
he was able to conquer the hearts of people
because the center of Īmān is the heart!
This is how the Companions of the Prophet ﷺ
surrendered to Allah Almighty
and were able to reach to the level
of the Messenger of God ﷺ.
This was the way by which they reached to
the Light of Faith, Nūr al-Īmān.
Then this method reached out to the Far East
and Far West and to all places!
There is no way of conquering hearts except by
the methodology of dhikr and
by the way of Sufi Orders."

Shaykh Nazim Adil al-Haqqani ق

VIEW OF THE KAʿBAH FROM BĀB AL-FATḤ.

This gateway to the Kaʿbah is known as Bāb al-Fatḥ, Gate of Victory. It was from here that the Prophet ﷺ entered during the conquest of Mecca on Friday, 20 Ramadan, 8 AH. When the army of Muslims came towards Mecca, they first halted at Dhu Tuwa. When his camel, Qaswa, came to a halt, the Prophet ﷺ bowed his head until his beard almost touched the saddle, in gratitude to Allah ﷻ.

The Prophet ﷺ then drew up his troops to enter Mecca. The sheer surprise of the attack stunned the Quraysh and very little resistance was put up against the Muslims. A red leather tent was pitched for the Prophet ﷺ in which he made *wuḍū* and performed eight *rakaʿats* of *nafl ṣalāt*, after which he rested for an hour or more. Some of those who had ridden with him that morning were already in line outside the tent, and they made an escort for him as he went to the Ḥaram, talking to Abū Bakr ؓ, who was at his side. The Prophet ﷺ went to the Kaʿbah and performed *ṭawāf*. Around the Kaʿbah were three hundred and sixty idols. With a stick he was carrying, he pushed them over, saying:

وَقُلْ جَآءَ ٱلْحَقُّ وَزَهَقَ ٱلْبَـٰطِلُ إِنَّ ٱلْبَـٰطِلَ كَانَ زَهُوقًا

"Truth has come, and falsehood has departed. Indeed, is falsehood (by nature) ever bound to depart."[193]

After performing the circle, the Prophet ﷺ dismounted from his camel and prayed at the Maqām Ibrāhīm, then drank from the Well of Zamzam. He then asked for the keys to the Kaʿbah and went inside for a while. By the time he came out the Quraysh had filled the Ḥaram, waiting anxiously to see what he would do next.

LOCATION OF BĀBU 'L-FATḤ IN MASJID AL-ḤARĀM.

The Prophet ﷺ stood at the door of the Kaʿbah, holding its frame and spoke at length to his former persecutors humbled before him, explaining several laws of Islam and abolishing all pagan practices. Then he asked them, *"Men of the Quraysh! What do you think I will do to you?"* They said, *"We hope for the best. You are a noble brother and the son of a noble brother!"* The Prophet ﷺ replied, *"I say to you what Yūsuf said to his brothers, 'No reproach shall be on you this day.' Go on your way, you are free!"*

The Prophet ﷺ ordered Bilāl ؓ to climb up on the roof of the Kaʿbah and give the *adhān*. It is narrated that the Prophet ﷺ himself offered his shoulder for Bilāl ؓ to climb from. It was the first time the leaders of the Quraysh had heard the word of Allah ﷻ rising up; the valley of Mecca reverberated with the sound.

Many eminent members of Quraysh, former bitter enemies, came into the fold of Islam on this day.

[193] Sūratu 'l-Isrā, 17:81.

Enter the Gate of Victory by Imitating the Victorious Ones!

Shaykh Muhammad Hisham Kabbani

The Sunnah of the Prophet ﷺ must be highly observed and, therefore, we must know what he did, or else how will we follow the *Ṣirāṭ al-Mustaqīm*, the Straight Path?

Allah ﷻ said:

يس وَالْقُرْآنِ الْحَكِيمِ إِنَّكَ لَمِنَ الْمُرْسَلِينَ عَلَى صِرَاطٍ مُّسْتَقِيمٍ

YāSīn. By the wise Qur'an, Lo! You are sent on a Straight Path.[194]

"He is My *Ṣirāṭ al-Mustaqīm*! The Prophet ﷺ is on *Ṣirāṭ al-Mustaqīm*." If we want to find the Way, *Ṣirāṭ al-Mustaqīm*, we have to know the Sunnah of the Prophet ﷺ! How did he dress, what did he wear on his head? He had an *imāma*, and it is said that when he conquered Mecca, he had a black turban. What else did he have? How did he walk, how did he put on his shoes, what did he do before he ate, how did he make *wuḍū*, how did he act with people? All these are Sunnah, which most of us are unaware of. *Alḥamdulillāh*, we follow the Qur'an as much as we understand and we follow the Sunnah, but we have to learn more about the Sunnah of the Prophet ﷺ.

It is said, one time when Sayyīdinā ʿAbd Allāh Ibn ʿUmar ؓ entered Mecca on his camel, he made a circle. The people did not understand why. When they asked him, he said, "On this spot, the Prophet ﷺ made a circle with his camel and to follow the Sunnah and preference of the Prophet ﷺ, we went around in a circle." So, they followed the Prophet ﷺ to the extreme, to the last point because they wanted to be with him in everything he did.

Inshā-Allāh we can be like that. We can't be like him as he is the Prophet ﷺ, but we can try to imitate and follow the Companions ؓ and the Holy

---

[194] Sūrah YāSīn, 36:1-4.

Family of the Prophet ﷺ and find out what he did and then try to do it, because then we will know we are on *Ṣirāṭ al-Mustaqīm*.

THE SUNNAH IN RESPONDING TO ABUSE

O Muslims! Islam is very delicate. Islam is not only praying the five prayers, fasting, paying charity or doing Hajj. These are all obligations; it is a must to fulfil them, but besides them is the taste! You have to show good manners and good character to people, especially to those who harm you.

Who has been harmed the most? Is it not the Prophet ﷺ? Yet how did he enter Mecca? He entered while forgiving everyone. One of the Sahabah ؓ said, "Today is the day of revenge!" He was carrying the flag, and the Prophet ﷺ took it from him and said, "Today is the day of friendship and making peace with the enemy," and they all reconciled.

What do you think Sayyīdinā Muhammad ﷺ said when he entered Mecca victorious?

اذْهَبُوا فَأَنْتُمُ الطُّلَقَاء.

Go (as you please) for you are freed![195]

"I am freeing you all although you abused me, tortured me, abused my family and my Sahabah and you killed us, I am forgiving everyone." That is Islam, it is not to take revenge. That is how to come to Allah ﷻ, not by revenge, but to come to His Mercy. He said, "Who comes to Me walking, I will come to him running."

قَالَ اللهُ عَزَّ وَجَلَّ أَنَا عِنْدَ ظَنِّ عَبْدِي بِي وَأَنَا مَعَهُ حَيْثُ يَذْكُرُنِي وَاللهِ لَلَّهُ أَفْرَحُ بِتَوْبَةِ عَبْدِهِ مِنْ أَحَدِكُمْ يَجِدُ ضَالَّتَهُ بِالْفَلَاةِ وَمَنْ تَقَرَّبَ إِلَيَّ شِبْرًا تَقَرَّبْتُ إِلَيْهِ ذِرَاعًا وَمَنْ تَقَرَّبَ إِلَيَّ ذِرَاعًا تَقَرَّبْتُ إِلَيْهِ بَاعًا وَإِذَا أَقْبَلَ إِلَيَّ يَمْشِي أَقْبَلْتُ إِلَيْهِ أُهَرْوِلُ

---

[195] Sīrah of Ibn Hisham, Tārīkh of Ṭabarī.

Allah the Exalted says: I am as My servant expects Me and I am with him as he remembers Me. If he remembers Me in himself, then I will remember him in Myself. If he mentions Me in a gathering, then I will mention him in a greater gathering. When he draws near to me by the span of his hand, I draw near him by the length of a cubit. When he draws near me by the length of a cubit, I draw near him by the length of a fathom. When he comes to me walking, I will come to him running.[196]

So, you try to make the Ummah feel welcomed by forgiving them like the Prophet ﷺ forgave all of the people of Mecca. What did he do for Abū Sufyān, the worst enemy? He freed him!

Awlīyāullāh ask Allah ﷻ to free us from Hellfire and that is what we need to ask. Do you ask for Paradise? *Rabbanā ātinā fi 'd-dunyā ḥasanatan wa fi 'l-Ākhirati ḥasanah,* "We ask for good in *dunyā* and good in *Ākhirah.*" In *dunyā,* good is to be given to work for *Ākhirah* and in *Ākhirah* good is to be in the highest level of Paradise to see Allah ﷻ, as Allah ﷻ promised, "They will see Me in Paradise." May Allah ﷻ make us from them, that we can reach that level; that is not something in our hands.

---

[196] Saḥīḥ Bukhārī.

THE HOUSE OF LADY KHADĪJAH ﵂

“*It is only fitting for these places*
that were filled with revelation,
visited by Jibrīl and Mikaʿīl,
and by the angels
and the Spirit (ar-Rūḥ),
the earth of which holds
the body of
the Leader of Mankind,
and from which spread
the religion of Allah
and the example
of His Messenger,
the first land to touch
the skin of the Chosen One,
that their courtyards be honored,
and their fragrances be inhaled,
and that their buildings
and walls be kissed!”

Al-Qāḍī ʿIyād ق

THE SITE OF THE HOUSE OF SAYYIDAH KHADIJAH ﷺ DURING THE EXCAVATIONS

The House of Sayyidah Khadijah ﷺ is no longer visible; it was situated just outside the Marwa exit of Masjid al-Ḥarām. The house is reported to have had five key areas. The first area was the guest area or the reception room. The second area was the children's quarters and where Sayyidah Fāṭima ﷺ was born. The third area was the prayer room where the Prophet ﷺ prayed and the fourth area is the blessed room of Sayyidah Khadījah ﷺ, the Prophet's trusted advisor and loyal companion, known by the title 'Mother of the Believers'. The fifth area constituted the hallways and the circulation space. It was in this house that the Prophet ﷺ lived from the time of their marriage until he migrated to Madinah. They were married for 25 years until her death. Most of their children were born in this house, including Sayyidah Fāṭima ﷺ. They lived there with extended family: Barakah ﷺ, a loyal servant; Zayd ibn Hāritha ﷺ, an adopted son of the Prophet ﷺ; and Sayyīdinā ʿAlī ﷺ, the Prophet's ﷺ young cousin.

In this house, Sayyidah Khadījah ﷺ became the first person to accept Islam. It was here too that Zaid bin Hāritha ﷺ joined the religion, as did ʿAlī bin Abī Ṭālib ﷺ, who grew up in the house. The Prophet ﷺ received

CLOSEUP OF THE PROPHET'S PRAYER NICHE AS ONE ENTERS THE ROOM OF THE DOME OF REVELATION.

many revelations here, and the spot where Jibrīl ﷺ used to bring the revelations became known as the Dome of Revelation. At-Ṭabarī once said, "The House of Khadījah is the best place in Mecca after the Sacred Mosque!" So, any prayer made on this site is believed to get accepted, *Inshā-Allāh.*

It was in this house that the Prophet ﷺ spent some of his most difficult years whilst living in Mecca under the persecution of the Quraysh, and it was here from where he started his momentous Hijrah, leaving Sayyīdinā ʿAlī ﷺ in his blessed bed.

In the 1980s when the mosque was extended, construction workers excavated the site, photographed it, covered it with pure sand and then built over it (meaning that it is still preserved underground). It is now within the prayer area at the Marwa Gate.

THE CURRENT SITE OF THE HOUSE OF SAYYIDAH KHADĪJAH NEAR THE MARWA GATE, DESIGNATED BY A DIFFERENT TEXTURE IN THE MARBLE FLOORING.

Story: Sayyīdinā ʿAlī ☙ in the Prophet's ﷺ Blessed Bed

Shaykh Muhammad Hisham Kabbani

The Prophet ﷺ said "I am the City of Knowledge and ʿAlī is its door." And he ﷺ said in another place, "Whatever Allah put in my heart I put in the heart of Abū Bakr aṣ-Ṣiddīq."

What was the wisdom of migration from Mecca to Madinah? Why was the Prophet ﷺ not able to stay in Mecca and do what he did in Mecca? It was very simple, but he wanted to execute Allah ﷻ's plan.

The Quraysh enemies knew about that decision to go to Madinah and wanted to kill the Prophet ﷺ. Can anyone kill the Prophet ﷺ? No, but they conspired to kill him. And Iblīs was whispering conspiracy to the tribes, so that all the leaders of the tribe would come together and hit the Prophet ﷺ at one time, with one hit.

Who stayed in the bed of the Prophet ﷺ? Sayyīdinā ʿAlī ☙. Why did he stay in his bed? Was the Prophet ﷺ not able to recite from Sūrah Yāsīn and throw sand on them so they could not see anything and pass out? He could have stayed in the bed and thrown sand on them, and they would not have seen him, but he put Sayyīdinā ʿAlī ☙ in his bed. Sayyīdinā ʿAlī ☙ didn't say "no." He gave himself to the Prophet ﷺ; he sacrificed himself to the Prophet ﷺ. He sacrificed himself to the Ummah. He said, "Let me die for you, *yā Sayyīdī, yā Rasūlullāh!* You go." The Prophet ﷺ tested him: is he going to give his life for me or not, and ʿAlī ☙ said, "*Fidāka abī wa ummī*, I sacrifice my father and mother for you, my beloved Prophet." He stayed in that bed, the same bed that was still warm when the Prophet ﷺ went for Isrā' and Miʿrāj, the Night Journey when Allah ﷻ shortened time and distance, brought him to His Presence, and then sent him back.

When a king has a kingdom, who can sit on the chair of the king? Only the king. Sometimes not even the queen can do that. When the king is alive, who sits on the throne? The king. Sometimes if he has a child, the son of the king sits there, they don't say anything. When the king goes away, who sits on the chair? It is the son. What does that mean? It means,

"You will inherit the kingdom and you will become a king." It means, when Sayyīdinā 'Alī ☙ gave up his life for the Prophet ﷺ, the Prophet ﷺ put him in his bed which symbolizes the City of Knowledge. That is why the Prophet ﷺ said, "I am the City of Knowledge and 'Alī is its door." That bed belonged to the City of Knowledge in which Allah ﷻ put the knowledge of *Awwalīn*, the First, and *Ākhirīn*, the Last. Otherwise, the Prophet ﷺ would have gone to Madinah without putting Sayyīdinā 'Alī ☙ in that bed, but he wanted him to inherit that knowledge, which is flowing until today and people are taking wisdom from it. He dressed him from that knowledge, and that is one of the importance of Hijrah.

THE HOUSE OF ABŪ BAKR ﷺ

> *Never was anything revealed to me*
> *that I did not pour*
> *into the heart of Abū Bakr!*

Prophet Muhammad ﷺ

The Hijrah to Madinah commenced from Sayyīdinā Abū Bakr's house. A large hotel (Mecca Towers) has been built on the site of Sayyīdinā Abū Bakr's ؓ house. There is a mosque on the fourth floor dedicated to him.

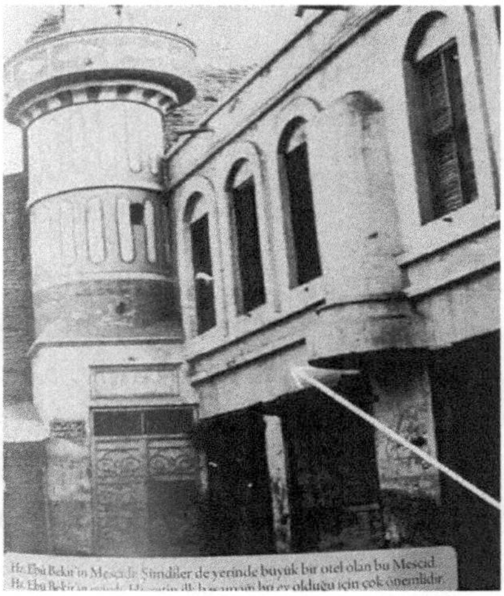

Abū Bakr Masjid built by the Ottomans.

When the decision to assassinate the Prophet ﷺ had been made by the Quraysh, Jibrīl ؑ was sent down to the Prophet ﷺ to reveal to him the plot and to give him his Lord's permission to leave Mecca. Having been given the command for migration, the Prophet ﷺ called at the house of Abū Bakr ؓ at noon when the burning sun had forced the people indoors. He disclosed that migration to Madinah had indeed been ordered. After telling Abū Bakr ؓ of the plan, the Prophet ﷺ went back to his home. That night, the Prophet ﷺ slipped past the assassins surrounding his house and made his way to the house of Abū Bakr ؓ. The two of them left Mecca hastily before the beginning of Fajr *ṣalāh* as they first journeyed to Jabal Thawr.

Mecca Towers, where House of Abū Bakr was located.

Close up of Masjid Abū Bakr in the hotel.

Story: From the House of Abū Bakr to the Cave of Secrets

Shaykh Muhammad Hisham Kabbani

The importance of Hijrah is not to go in the desert to seek a *dalīl*, a guide. Why does the Prophet ﷺ need a *dalīl*? But he took one in order to teach us: we need a guide, a teacher, a master, a shaykh to reach the Prophet ﷺ. You cannot reach barefoot in the desert, or your feet will burn. You need someone to guide you. This life is worse than the desert. So how can you travel all this distance without a guide, without a master, without a shaykh?

So, the Prophet ﷺ dressed Sayyīdinā ʿAlī ؓ with all these secrets when he left him in his bed. Now he wanted to dress Sayyīdinā Abū Bakr: he went to his house, took him and left.

Prophet Muhammad ﷺ, the one who read the following verse and threw sand (in the faces of the enemies, which prevented them from seeing him):

وَجَعَلْنَا مِن بَيْنِ أَيْدِيهِمْ سَدًّا وَمِنْ خَلْفِهِمْ سَدًّا فَأَغْشَيْنَاهُمْ فَهُمْ لاَ يُبْصِرُونَ

And We have put a bar in front of them and a bar behind them, and further, We have covered them up; so that they cannot see.[197]

Was he not able to throw it in the face of the enemy when they came after him? Allah ﷻ said, "Go to the cave, O Believers, O Human Beings, and Allah ﷻ will spread His Mercy on you." Go to the cave means go back to your spirituality, go back to your heart. Go back to the cave of the Ummah. The cave hides the needy ones, the cave is Sayyīdinā Muhammad ﷺ, he is the cave of the Ummah.

[197] Sūrat YāSīn, 36:9.

فَأْوُوا إِلَى الْكَهْفِ

Run to the cave[198]

He wanted to show Sayyīdinā Abū Bakr aṣ-Ṣiddīq ❀ the real cave. He wanted to spread his mercy. He gave Sayyīdinā 'Alī, now he wants to give to Sayyīdinā Abū Bakr. He went to a cave. Was Allah unable to prevent the enemy from seeing? But no, the plan was not like that. The plan has to be as Allah planned ❀. That is why you don't plan for yourself anything, leave everything to Allah. When you leave everything to Allah everything will come out good for you. When you leave things to your Creator, all will come good.

We are *ṭarīqah* people. We are trying to follow the way of the Prophet ❀. We cannot say "yes, we followed", but we are trying. So, what did the Prophet ❀ do in Ghāri Thawr? The Prophet ❀ entered and Sayyīdinā Abū Bakr aṣ-Ṣiddīq ❀ put his leg down for the Prophet ❀ to put his head to rest. As the Prophet ❀ was resting, a snake came from the hole. Sayyīdinā Abū Bakr aṣ-Ṣiddīq ❀ saw it and was thinking the snake is hungry, "Let the snake eat me and then my Prophet ❀ will be safe."

If people don't give up themselves, they aren't going to get heavenly knowledge. If we are not going to give up backbiting and bad character, we will not achieve.

So Sayyīdinā Abū Bakr ❀ put his leg in the hole through which that snake was coming, and the snake began to eat from the leg of Sayyīdinā Abū Bakr. When a snake eats, it is not like other animals, like the biting of a lion; it takes everything inside and crushes everything, crushing bones and crushing the meat. Yet, out of his love for the Prophet ❀, Sayyīdinā Abū Bakr ❀ did not feel any of that. He was worrying, "When that snake finishes eating me, it will eat my Prophet!" At that thought, a tear came from his eye and dropped on the blessed face of the Prophet ❀.

The Prophet ❀ woke up and said, "O Abū Bakr do not worry, Allah is with us." Sayyīdinā Abū Bakr said, "O Prophet of Allah ❀, I know that Allah is with us, but a snake is eating my leg and when it finishes, I am worried it will come and eat you." Sayyīdinā Muhammad ❀ looked and

---

[198] Sūratu 'l-Kahf 18:16.

the snake backed up. Then the Prophet ﷺ took his saliva and put it on Abū Bakr aṣ-Ṣiddīq's leg and it was miraculously restored to what it was before. Then the Prophet ﷺ said to the snake, "Don't you know that Allah ﷻ has forbidden snakes to eat the flesh of prophets and *ṣiddīqs,* veracious ones? The snake said, "O Prophet ﷺ, I was alive for thousands of years and I heard of your name, and throughout this time I was yearning to see you. Then you came here and aṣ-Ṣiddīq's leg was blocking me from seeing you." The Prophet ﷺ said, "Okay, come out." And that snake looked at the Prophet ﷺ and then gave the *Shahādah* and died.

Look at the wisdom in that event. That snake wanted to see the Prophet ﷺ, and Sayyīdinā Abū Bakr was to be tested. At the end, Sayyīdinā Abū Bakr ؓ gave himself to Prophet ﷺ as Sayyīdinā ʿAlī ؓ gave his life to Sayyīdinā Muhammad ﷺ. So, the Prophet ﷺ then dressed Sayyīdinā Abū Bakr with *ʿUlūm al-Āwwalīn wa 'l-Ākhirīn,* Knowledge of the Firsts and the Lasts.

That is why we see that 41 *ṭarīqahs* take from that knowledge of the Prophet ﷺ, 40 coming from Sayyīdinā ʿAlī ؓ and one coming from Sayyīdinā Abū Bakr ؓ. That is the need to give oneself in Islam, submission.

Story: A Vast Ocean Inside the Cave

Hajjah Amina Adil

MOUNTAIN OF THAWR, THE WAY TO THE CAVE.

The Holy Prophet ﷺ stroked the snake that had bitten Sayyīdinā Abū Bakr aṣ-Ṣiddīq's ؓ foot. The snake was the color of saffron and gave off a beautiful scent. The Prophet ﷺ said to it, "Promise me that you will not bite anyone belonging to my nation from now on." The snake gave its word, and the Prophet ﷺ prayed for its progeny to become numerous and for its scent to remain with it until the Day of Judgment. To this very day this snake is found frequently in Mecca and its body gives off a lovely scent. No one hurts it, and it harms no one.

At the entrance to the cave a rock dove had made her nest, and a spider had woven its web across the entrance. A wind arose and spread dust over everything, giving it the appearance of having been undisturbed for a thousand years. The Lord Almighty ordered the angels Jibrīl ؑ and Mikā'īl ؑ to go look after His Prophet ﷺ. When they got there, they met the spider that was weaving its web. "What are you doing?" they asked it. "I am concealing the Holy Prophet ﷺ," answered the spider. "How do you think you can hide him," the angels laughed, "your web is not even able to keep out the wind, one gust and it is blown away."

The spider replied, "O Jibrīl, this web is not like any of my own webs, this web I am spinning upon the Command of the Almighty; try it out if you like." So, the mighty angel Jibrīl ﵇ whose single scream makes cities crumble tried with all his force to tear the web of the little spider, but try as he might, he could not snap a single thread of its silk.

The pursuing search parties following the footprints came very close to the cave, but seeing the nesting dove and the spider's web, they said to the guide who had led them there, "We took you to be a clever person, but now you seem to be the silliest of us all. Had anybody entered this cave, do you really think this bush would be covering the entrance, and this spider's web remain unbroken? And what about the nesting dove sitting on its eggs? Would it not have flown away and abandoned its nest?" They had come so close that Abū Bakr ؓ could see their feet. He began to weep. "They have come for us," he said. The Holy Prophet recited:

إِذْ أَخْرَجَهُ الَّذِينَ كَفَرُوا۟ ثَانِىَ اثْنَيْنِ إِذْ هُمَا فِى الْغَارِ إِذْ يَقُولُ لِصَاحِبِهِ لَا
تَحْزَنْ إِنَّ اللَّهَ مَعَنَا

...When the unbelievers drove him forth, the second of two,
when the two were in the Cave, when he said to his
companion, "Sorrow not, surely God is with us."[199]

But Abū Bakr ؓ continued to tremble, and he said, "O Messenger of Allah, if I had one thousand souls at my disposal, they should all be your ransom. But what if they were to kill you? What should then be left in this world of any worth? The Muslims will be forsaken and destitute." The Holy Prophet ﷺ then answered him, pointing at the wall of the cave, "O Abū Bakr ؓ, look here." When he looked, he saw a door there, and it was open. Through the open door he could see an ocean so vast its farther shore was not in sight. But on the shore near them lay a boat. The Prophet ﷺ then said, "If they come to get us, we will simply board that ship and sail away. Allah Almighty will shut that door, and they will never reach us, in all eternity."

---

[199] Sūratu 't-Tawbah, 9:40

With these words, the Holy Prophet ﷺ made Abū Bakr feel at ease. The Holy Prophet ﷺ and Abū Bakr ؓ remained in this cave for three days and nights. On the morning of the fourth day which was Thursday, the first day of Rabīʿ al-Āwwal, they mounted the camels that their servant Amir had brought, along with the Bedouin guide who was to lead them to Madinah. They set out on the journey.

MOUNT THAWR

“*He had no more than*
one Companion;
they two were
in the cave,
and he said
to his Companion,
'Have no fear,
for Allah is with us!'
Then Allah sent down
His Tranquility
upon him,
and strengthened him
with soldiers
that you did not see.”

Holy Qur'an, Sūrat at-Tawbah, 9:40

INSIDE VIEW OF THE CAVE OF THAWR.

Jabal Thawr is the mountain containing the cave in which the Prophet ﷺ and Abū Bakr ؓ sought refuge for three days and nights from the Quraysh. This occurred when they secretly left Mecca to emigrate to Madinah. With the Quraysh so close to discovering their hiding place, Abū Bakr ؓ became very tense about the Prophet's ﷺ safety. The Prophet ﷺ reassured him, "How can you be apprehensive about two with whom is a third, especially when the third one is Allah?"

For Real Companionship, You Must Enter the Cave

Shaykh Muhammad Hisham Kabbani

Sayyīdinā Shāh Naqshband ق, the *Īmām* and Sulṭān of this *ṭarīqah* always defines his meetings with a title before he begins: *ṭarīqatunā aṣ-ṣuḥbah wa 'l-khayru fi 'l-jam'īyyah*, "Our way is companionship, and the best is in the gathering. It means, if there is no companionship, in reality, there is no relationship. So, he wants to make sure whenever he opens a *majlis*, to say, "Our way is companionship," as Allah ﷻ mentioned *ṣuḥbah* in the Holy Qur'an. That person in particular that Allah ﷻ mentioned is the Companion of the Prophet ﷺ, Sayyīdinā Abū Bakr aṣ-Ṣiddīq ؓ:

إِلاَّ تَنصُرُوهُ فَقَدْ نَصَرَهُ اللّهُ إِذْ أَخْرَجَهُ الَّذِينَ كَفَرُواْ ثَانِيَ اثْنَيْنِ إِذْ هُمَا فِي الْغَارِ إِذْ يَقُولُ لِصَاحِبِهِ لاَ تَحْزَنْ إِنَّ اللّهَ مَعَنَا فَأَنزَلَ اللّهُ سَكِينَتَهُ عَلَيْهِ وَأَيَّدَهُ بِجُنُودٍ لَّمْ تَرَوْهَا وَجَعَلَ كَلِمَةَ الَّذِينَ كَفَرُواْ السُّفْلَى وَكَلِمَةُ اللّهِ هِيَ الْعُلْيَا وَاللّهُ عَزِيزٌ حَكِيمٌ

If you help him not, still Allah helped him when those who disbelieve drove him forth, the second of two, when they (the Prophet and Abū Bakr) were in the cave, and he said to his companion, "Be not sad (or afraid), for surely Allah is with us." Then Allah sent down His peace upon him, and strengthened him with forces which you saw not, and humbled to the depths the word of the unbelievers. But the Word of Allah is exalted to the heights: for Allah is Exalted in Might, Wise. [200]

That verse has been revealed in the cave when they were migrating from Mecca to Madinah; they were passing through that cave and were going there to rest. There, Sayyīdinā Abū Bakr aṣ-Ṣiddīq ؓ became sad, which is why Allah ﷻ revealed that verse to the Prophet ﷺ. It means, if you want to have real companionship with Allah ﷻ and His Prophet ﷺ and with

---

[200] Sūratu 't-Tawbah, 9:40.

the *mashaykh,* then you have to go to the cave. That *ṣuḥbah,* companionship, cannot be found anywhere, not in the park, not at home. You must find it in the cave!

Who is that cave? As Allah ﷻ said to *Aṣ-ḥāb al-Kahf,* the Companions of the Cave:

فَأْوُوا إِلَى الْكَهْفِ يَنشُرْ لَكُمْ رَبُّكُم مِّن رَّحمته ويُهَيِّئْ لَكُم مِّنْ أَمْرِكُم مِّرْفَقًا

Betake yourselves to the Cave: Your Lord will shower His mercies on you and disposes of your affair towards comfort and ease.[201]

O People of the Cave, O the people who were running, either they were three or five or seven, and their dog was with them. No one knows their number except Allah ﷻ. Allah was telling them to run to the cave. That cave is *al-Kahf al-Muhammadīyya,* the Muhammadan Cave. That means "run to the Prophet ﷺ!" He is the Boat of Safety that can carry everyone from these storms in the ocean; his boat will sail in that stormy ocean.

وَخَلَقْنَا لَهُم مِّن مِّثْلِهِ مَا يَرْكَبُونَ

And We have created for them similar (vessels) on which they ride.[202]

This *āyah* means, "From the example of that, we have created an 'imitational' boat they can ride on." Like today people go on a boat: that boat is an imitation of the real boat that takes you through that ocean from one shore of safety to another shore of safety. And no one can take you to pass from one side of *dunyā* to the other side of *dunyā* except Sayyīdinā Muhammad ﷺ.

When you run to that cave, which is the *as-Safīnat al-Muhammadīyya,* the Muhammadan Ship, or the *al-Kahf al-Muhammadīyya,* the Muhammadan Cave, you cannot enter if you are not a companion, because you have to enter and go all the way. Not everyone can go on a boat and enter, they

---

201 Sūratu 'l-Kahf, 18:16.

202 Sūrah YāSīn, 36:42.

will not let him in. So, no one can jump on the Muhammadan Boat except those who are accepted by Sayyīdinā Muhammad ﷺ.

How can we become companions of the Prophet ﷺ? Not companions like the Sahabah of the Prophet ﷺ, but you can inherit from them; you can be the imitational one. In that cave, the reality of *talqīn,* to put on your tongue the secret of this order, was established. It means you have been called to the presence of the Prophet ﷺ in that cave. Grandshaykh ق said that the Prophet ﷺ ordered Sayyīdinā Abū Bakr aṣ-Ṣiddīq ؓ to bring all the souls in the Naqshbandi Order; all the souls of the Naqshbandi Disciples were in Ghāri Thawr, the Kahf al-Muhammadīyya, where Allah ﷻ called Sayyīdinā Abū Bakr, "*Ṣāḥib,* the Companion".

ĪMĀM SAHIB MAHAMOUDOU IN FRONT OF GHĀRI THAWR, HAJJ 2011.

If the father is *ṣāḥib* what about the children? The children will be *aṣḥāb,* companions. So, they called all the souls of the Naqshbandis, and if they attended any Naqshbandi *dhikr,* they were certainly stamped as a Naqshbandi and were present in that cave. When you enter into that cave, are you not going to see everyone there?

Who was there? Sayyīdinā Muhammad ﷺ! So, anyone who saw the Prophet ﷺ and believed in him and said, "*lā ilāha illa 'Llāh Muḥammadun Rasūlullāh,*" can he go to Hellfire? There, everyone was called with Sayyīdinā Abū Bakr aṣ-Ṣiddīq ؓ along with the *Īmām* of the Khatm al-Khawajagan, Sayyīdinā Abdul Khāliq al-Ghujdawānī ق, to lead them in the *khatm* and to really see the Prophet ﷺ. That is why Sayyīdinā Shāh

Naqshband ق said in every *ṣuḥbah,* "Our *ṭarīqah* is *ṣuḥbah,* companionship," which means, our *ṭarīqah,* the Naqshbandi Ṭarīqah, has already been with the Prophet ﷺ in the cave with Sayyīdinā Abū Bakr aṣ-Ṣiddīq ؓ; they have already acquired and inherited the secret of Sayyīdinā Abū Bakr aṣ-Ṣiddīq ؓ in the *ṣuḥbah* with the Prophet ﷺ. That is enough to guide them all the way from *dunyā* to *Ākhirah,* and they will not leave this *dunyā* without seeing the Prophet ﷺ.

May Allah ﷻ keep us always with the *ṣuḥbah* of our *shuyūkh,* with the *ṣuḥbah* of Sayyīdinā Abū Bakr aṣ-Ṣiddīq ؓ, of all Sahabah ؓ, especially with Sayyīdinā ʿUmar ؓ, Sayyīdinā ʿUthman ؓ, Sayyīdinā ʿAlī ؓ, Sayyīdinā Ḥasan ؓ, Sayyīdinā Ḥusayn ؓ, with all , who are descending from the Prophet ﷺ at every moment, with the *ṣuḥbah* of our shaykh, Shaykh Nazim ق and with the *ṣuḥbah* of Grandshaykh ʿAbdAllāh ق. Just now Shaykh Nazim ق wanted me to tell you that truly you are all in that *ṣuḥbah* of the Prophet ﷺ and you will never be away from it! *Fātiḥah.*

STORY: THE *BAYA*ʿ THAT TOOK PLACE IN GHĀRI THAWR

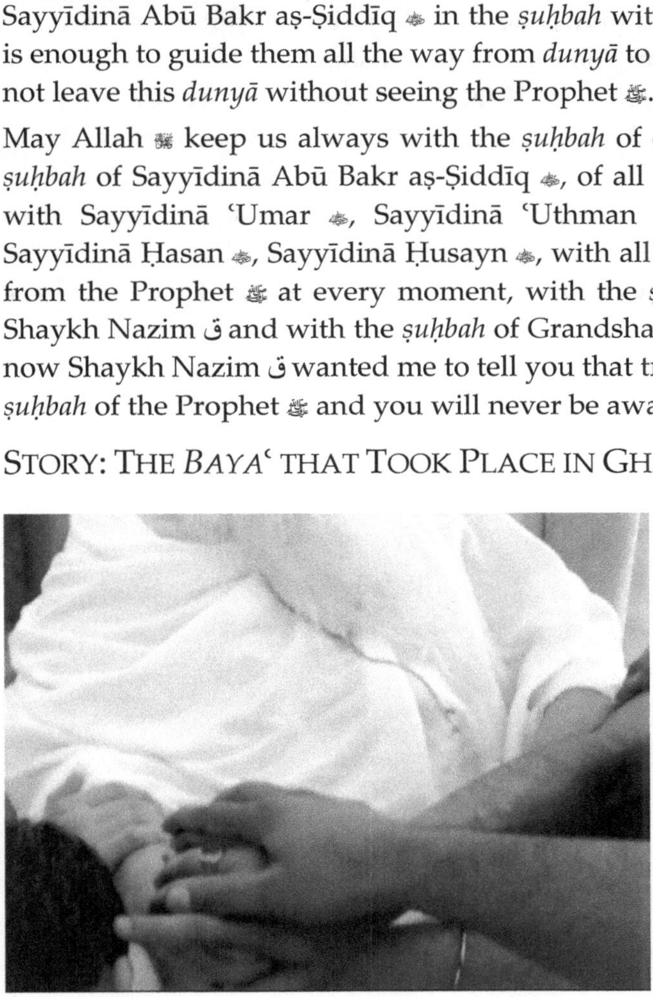

There was a *baya*ʿ that took place in a vision. I was with Grandshaykh ق and Shaykh Nazim ق. I saw him taking me to Ghāri Thawr, the cave in which the Prophet ﷺ hid with Sayyīdinā Abū Bakr aṣ-Ṣiddīq ؓ on the way to Madinatu 'l-Munawwarah, *ʿalā sākinihā afḍal aṣ-ṣalāt wa 's-salām. Allāhumma ṣalli ʿalā Sayyīdinā Muhammadin wa ʿalā āli Sayyīdinā Muhammad.* He said to me, "I want you to take a real *baya*ʿ." Grandshaykh ق usually didn't give *baya*ʿ; he didn't give it to anyone except two people: Shaykh Nazim ق and Shaykh Ḥusayn ق. All other representatives never had *baya*ʿ and were never allowed to give *baya*ʿ. Now Shaykh Nazim ق, with the mercy that he is carrying, is giving *baya*ʿ to everyone. That is the wisdom: to spread that everywhere in *dunyā*.

Grandshaykh ق said, "O my son! Now I want you to take the real *baya*ʿ in front of me." At that moment, 124,000 *Awlīyā* appeared. Grandshaykh ق said, "Put your hand under their hands and I will put mine." Shaykh Nazim ق placed his hand on top and Grandshaykh's hand was on top of all of them. Then the spirits of 124,000 prophets appeared and they put their hands on top, and then Sayyīdinā Mahdī ﷺ put his hand on top of theirs. Then, the Prophet ﷺ put his hand, *ʿalayhi ʿafḍalu 'ṣ-ṣalātu wa 's-salām, yā Sayyīdī, yā Rasūlullāh, shafaʿatak yā Ḥabību 'Llāh*! Then Grandshaykh ق recited Āyat al-Bayaʿ in front of all these *Awlīyāullāh,* Sayyīdinā Mahdī ﷺ, the Prophet ﷺ and all the prophets. That is real *baya*ʿ

MASJID AL-JINN

> “*Say (O Muhammad!):*
> *It has been revealed to me that*
> *a group of Jinn listened and said,*
> *'Verily, we have heard a marvelous Qur'an.*
> *It guides unto righteousness,*
> *so we have believed in it.'*”

Holy Qur'an, Sūrat al-Jinn, 72:1-2

MASJID AL-JINN NEAR JANNAT AL-MUʿALLA CEMETERY.

Masjid al-Jinn, also known as Masjid Haras, is built on the place where the Prophet recited the Qur'an to a group of Jinn.

ʿAbdAllāh bin Masʿūd ﷺ narrates, "While in Mecca, the Prophet ﷺ once said to the Sahabah ﷺ 'Whoever wishes to see what the Jinn are all about should come along'. Besides myself no one else came. When we reached the place in the Maʿla district of Mecca, the Prophet ﷺ used his foot to draw a circle on the ground. He then instructed me to sit inside the circle. After proceeding a little further, the Prophet ﷺ started reciting the Qurʿan. It then happened that Jinn started to arrive in troops as they gathered there. So many came that I could not even see the Prophet ﷺ nor hear him. The Prophet ﷺ then continued talking with a group of them until Fajr.[203]

---

[203] Tafsīr ibn Kathīr.

Story: If You Don't Believe, We Will Show You!

Shaykh Muhammad Hisham Kabbani

There is a story by Īmām Abū Ḥāmid al-Ghazālī ﷺ, of whom everyone has heard and read from his most famous book, Iḥyā ʿUlūm ud-Dīn. He was also a *mufti* of *mu'min* Jinn, and he published the book Al-Awfāq, much of which is about preventing unbelieving Jinn and *shayāṭīn* from attacking you.

One time, Īmām Ghazālī ﷺ asked his followers, "What are you hearing about scholars today?" They said, "Az-Zamakhsharī does not believe in Jinn." So, he wanted to convince az-Zamakhsharī —who had written many books of *tafsīr*—that Jinn do exist. This time az-Zamakhsharī was in the process of writing a new *tafsīr* of the Holy Qur'an and he had reached halfway when Īmām Ghazālī ﷺ asked a Jinn to bring that book to him. When it brought the book, he copied the book entirely with scribes in the same way it was written, then he ordered the Jinn to return the original to az-Zamakhsharī's table.

Afterwards, he invited az-Zamakhsharī to his house and brought out the copy of his book. When az-Zamakhsharī saw it, he said, "No one except me saw my book! I wrote it and hid it, and your book is exactly like mine, every word you wrote I have already written in my book! How did you do that?" Īmām Ghazālī ﷺ said, "*Yā* az-Zamakhsharī! I cannot claim this book, but rather I ordered one of my Jinn friends to take yours and bring it here, then I copied it." After that az-Zamakhsharī started believing in Jinn. The Jinn world exists, and they can interact with human beings, which is why Allah ﷻ said in the Holy Qur'an:

قُلْ أُوحِيَ إِلَيَّ أَنَّهُ اسْتَمَعَ نَفَرٌ مِّنَ الْجِنِّ فَقَالُوا إِنَّا سَمِعْنَا قُرْآنًا عَجَبًا

يَهْدِي إِلَى الرُّشْدِ فَآمَنَّا بِهِ وَلَن نُّشْرِكَ بِرَبِّنَا أَحَدًا

Say, "It has been revealed to me that a company of jinns listened (to the Qur'an). They said, 'We have really heard a wonderful recital! It gives guidance to the right, and we have believed therein. We shall not join (in worship) any (gods) with our Lord.'"[204]

Jinn live together in large groups, not like us. As Grandshaykh ق said, millions of Jinn can easily fit in a small space as that is how Allah ﷻ created them. So, Allah ﷻ said a large group of Jinn were listening to the Holy Qur'an as the Prophet ﷺ recited it (at the location of Masjid al-Jinn in Mecca) and they believed and were guided to Islam.

There are pious people or *ʿulama,* such as Īmām Abū Ḥāmid al-Ghazālī ؓ, who can use *mu'min* Jinn to help and benefit human beings, just as there are *mushʿawadhīn,* witches and charlatans that do black magic by using *kāfir* Jinn to harm people. However, Allah ﷻ said in the Holy Qur'an:

فَلَمَّا قَضَيْنَا عَلَيْهِ الْمَوْتَ مَا دَلَّهُمْ عَلَى مَوْتِهِ إِلَّا دَابَّةُ الْأَرْضِ تَأْكُلُ

مِنسَأَتَهُ فَلَمَّا خَرَّ تَبَيَّنَتِ الْجِنُّ أَن لَّوْ كَانُوا يَعْلَمُونَ الْغَيْبَ مَا لَبِثُوا فِي

الْعَذَابِ الْمُهِينِ

Then, when We decreed (Solomon's) death, nothing showed them (the Jinn) his death except a little worm of the earth, which kept (slowly) gnawing away at his staff. So, when he fell down, the jinn saw plainly that had they known the Unseen,

---

[204] Sūratu 'l-Jinn, 72:1-2.

they would not have tarried in the humiliating Penalty (of their task).[205]

Sayyīdinā Sulaymān عليه السلام was using the Jinn to build his shrine and he leaned on his stick under his chin observing them. They didn't know he had died until a worm ate through his stick and his body fell down. They worked for him in fear for another ten years, thinking he was alive when in fact he was dead. Then, as Allah ﷻ said in the *āyah,* the Jinn discovered that they cannot know the *ghayb,* Unseen. They can know what's going on between you and other people, but such things are *dunyā* matters that are not *ghayb,* only *Ākhirah* matters are *ghayb.*

[205] Sūrah Sabā', 34:14.

JANNAT AL-MUʿALLA CEMETERY

“ *When the Prophet ﷺ arrived at al-Ḥajūn,*
he was sad and grieved.
He stayed there for as long as
Allah ﷻ willed him to stay.
Upon his return, he was happy and said,
'I asked my Lord, Mighty and Sublime,
to bring my mother back to life.
Allah ﷻ did that and then took her back.'
Allah revived both of
Sayyīdinā Muhammad's ﷺ parents
and they both testified to his prophethood! ”

Sayyidah Āʿyesha ☙

Blessed tomb of Sayyidah Khadijah ﵂ in Jannat al-Muʿalla in its original form.

Jannat al-Muʿalla, also known as al-Ḥajūn, is the main cemetery in Mecca, housing the graves of many prominent individuals including Sayyidatinā Khadijah ﵂, wife of the Prophet ﷺ, their two sons, as well as many Companions, scholars and righteous people.

It lies to the north of the Masjid al-Ḥarām, near Masjid al-Jinn, the Mosque of the Jinn, in Mecca. Also buried here are the Prophet's ﷺ grandfather, ʿAbdul Muṭṭalib, his uncle, Abū Ṭālib, father of Sayyīdinā ʿAlī ﵁, and great-great-grandfather of the Prophet ﷺ, ʿAbd Manaf.

Jannat al-Muʿalla Cemetery in Mecca before 1925, during the Ottoman period. Photograph: HA Mirza.

Ask to Die in Holy Lands

Shaykh Muhammad Hisham Kabbani

JANNAT AL-MUʿALLA.

Time is passing, no soul knows in which land it is going to die and where it will be buried. You can die anywhere, and the Angel of Death will come to you wherever you are.

كُلُّ نَفْسٍ ذَآئِقَةُ الْمَوْتِ وَإِنَّمَا تُوَفَّوْنَ أُجُورَكُمْ يَوْمَ الْقِيَامَةِ فَمَن زُحْزِحَ عَنِ النَّارِ وَأُدْخِلَ الْجَنَّةَ فَقَدْ فَازَ وَما الْحَيَاةُ الدُّنْيَا إِلاَّ مَتَاعُ الْغُرُورِ

Every soul shall have a taste of death and only on the Day of Judgement shall you be paid your full recompense, your full reward. Only he who is saved far from the Fire can be admitted into the Garden of Paradise will have attained the purpose of life, for the life of this world is nothing but goods of deception.[206]

[206] Sūrat Āli-ʿImrān, 3:185.

We understand the literal meaning of that *āyah*, *"Every soul shall have a taste of death,"* the taste of death will either be sour or sweet. When thinking about the soul being pulled out by Sayyīdinā Malak al-Mawt ﷺ, the Angel of Death, our mind always goes to the sour taste. He comes and calls you by Allah's Order and you immediately respond, you cannot say "no". You go with him wherever he goes, like a magnet, one group goes to Hellfire, punishment, and one goes to Jannah, Paradise.

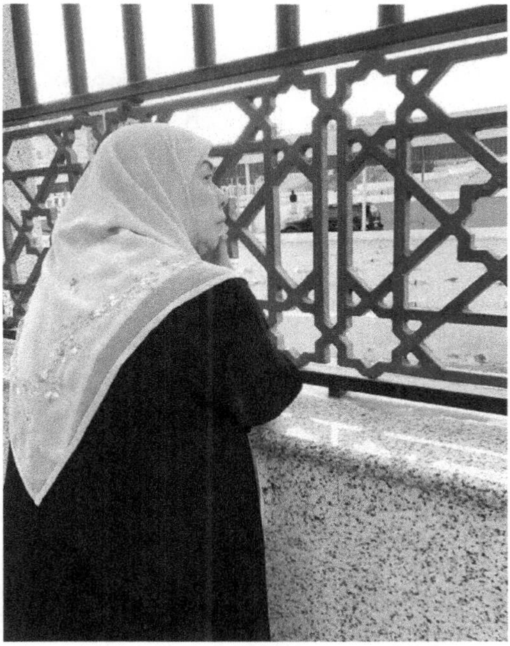

HAJJAH NAZIHA VISITING JANNAT AL-MUʿALLA, ʿUMRAH 2020.

We ask that Allah ﷻ takes our soul in a Muslim place, like Mecca, Madinah, Quds or Sham, these four places. There are over one hundred *aḥadīth* on the virtues of Sham. On the Day of Resurrection, Allah's Throne will come over Sham. When we were young, we never thought about death, but when you grow up, you begin to feel it and think about it. You are going to die in a place that is not in your hands, but in Allah's Hands.

Grandshaykh ق said that the virtues of Sham is such that when a Muslim or *mu'min* dies in a foreign country, angels will carry him to be buried in Sham, Mecca, Madinah or Quds Sharīf. The angels will carry you to one of those holy places by Allah's Order. We ask Allah ﷻ to take our soul in these areas and if not, angels transfer us there by His Order! We ask Allah ﷻ to take our soul to a place where there are *Awlīyāullāh*.

In one of his lectures, Grandshaykh ق said, "It is Sunnah for everyone to know where they will be buried." So, in our lifetime, we must decide where we will be buried. If you die away from the place you wish to be buried, angels will take you there. Remembering death is important, and

Prophet ﷺ used to lay on his right-side remembering death for a moment at Fajr time.

All these *ʿulama* went (passed away) and are replaced with new ones who are now hiding themselves because of too much *zhulma,* darkness; they cannot appear because the people will attack them, as certainly, if people attacked Prophet ﷺ and all prophets, they will attack anyone!

The summary is to have a burial place. Dhul-Kifl ﷷ, who is mentioned in the Holy Qur'an, is buried in Qāsiyūn in that small graveyard where fifty or sixty are buried. Grandshaykh ق advised us to buy our graves there when we were young and crazy, so immediately we tried to get a grave in that antique cemetery from Ottoman times. We asked the one responsible and he got us three places: one for my brother Shaykh Adnan, someone else, and me. You can see the signs there; someone is buried there and next to it is my brother's.

When you read a *duʿā,* you can send it to your own grave and angels will carry us to that grave when we die. It is a Sunnah to remember death, because *"Every soul shall taste of death."*[207]

Everyone will taste death, and people think immediately that death is *ʿadhāb,* punishment, but rather it is waking up. Īmām Ghazālī ق said, "When you die, it is an awakening because you can then see," but now our eyes are closed. We hope that Allah ﷻ keeps us together in *dunyā* and *Ākhirah* based on the love of Prophet ﷺ and love of *Awlīyāullāh.*

When I look at my life, I see so many mistakes, but with good intentions. We all make mistakes, *kullunā khaṭā'ūn,* that is why Allah ﷻ ordered us to make *istighfār*. The Prophet ﷺ said to Sayyidah ʿĀ'ishā ؓ:

مِن حُوسِب عُذِّب

(Yā ʿĀ'ishā!) Who will be judged will be punished for sure.[208]

Whoever wishes to be judged will be punished. So, this group and others like it include young people, who come to learn more *Sharīʿah* and spirituality. Elsewhere, young people like going to clubs to dance or they

---

[207] Sūrat Āli-ʿImrān, 3:185.

[208] Bukhārī.

go to sports events, but people here and in other places are sitting and learning, and Allah ﷻ will give them a sweet taste (at death).

We are counting our days, we do not know when that day to give our souls back will come, and we ask Allah ﷻ to take our souls on Islam. That is why I am thinking to move back to the Middle East or here. *Inshā-Allāh* wherever it is written, you cannot change it. *Lā nafsin tardī ghayri yamūt,* you don't know. Someone from within you is talking to you and reminding you of death every 24 hours.

Sayyīdinā ʿUmar ؓ hired a Ṣaḥābi ؓ to sit at his door like a bodyguard, but his only job was to remind Sayyīdinā ʿUmar of death every Fajr, "*Yā ʿUmar, lā tansa 'l-mawt.*" One day Sayyīdinā ʿUmar called him and said, "I don't need you anymore, because I have one white hair in my beard that will continuously remind me of death." You don't know where or when you will leave, or if you will leave good children behind. We ask Allah ﷻ to give us the sweetness of death, not the sourness.

For Muslims, Mālik al-Mawt ؑ, the Angel of Death, has "Allah" written on his hand and the soul will jump directly on that. May Allah ﷻ make us like that. We ask for forgiveness from Allah ﷻ, from Prophet ﷺ and from *Awlīyāullāh.*

There is not too much to smile or laugh about in *dunyā*. Sahabah ؓ were busy with work, *dhikr,* remembrance of Allah ﷻ, *ṣalāwāt,* and remembrance of *Awlīyāullāh.*

اللَّهُمَّ صَلِّ عَلَى سَيِّدِنَا مُحَمَّدٍ الْفَاتِحِ لِمَا أُغْلِقَ و الْخَاتِمِ لِمَا سَبَقَ نَاصِرِ الْحَقِّ

بِالْحَقِّ وَ الْهَادِي إِلَى صِرَاطِكَ الْمُسْتَقِيمِ وَعَلَى آلِهِ حَقَّ قَدْرِهِ وَ مِقْدَارِهِ الْعَظِيمِ.

O Allah! Bless our Master Muhammad ﷺ, who opened what was closed and who is the Seal of what went before, he who makes the Truth victorious by the Truth, the guide to Your Straight Path, and bless his household as is the due of his immense position and grandeur.

Wa min Allāhi 't-tawfiq, bi ḥurmati 'l-Ḥabīb, bi ḥurmati 'l-Fātiḥah.

Abū Ṭālib ⸙ Breathed His Last as a Muslim!

Shaykh Nazim Adil al-Haqqani

In unknown deserts one boy was born. He was an orphan. His name was Muhammad ﷺ, *Sayyid al-Awwalīn wa 'l-Ākhirīn, Ḥabību Rabbi 'l-ʿĀlamīn wa khalīfat ul-Ḥaqq*, Master of the First Ones and the Last Ones, Beloved of the Lord of the Worlds, and Caliph of Allah, the Truly Existent One! When his mother was pregnant, his father passed away. He was an orphan in the womb of his holy mother, and after a while he was born. And he was only 5 or 6 years old when his mother passed away.

He was in such a position, with no father and no mother, but Allah Almighty made some people to look after him, his uncle, Abū Ṭālib ⸙! Abū Ṭālib is *sayyid*, a chief, a master. All *Awlīyā* were witnesses that he said, "*Lā ilāha illa 'Llāh Muḥammadun Rasūlullāh!* You are Rasūlullāh ﷺ, the heavenly one over all prophets. You are *Ḥabību 'Llāh, Rasūlullāh, Nūr ʿArshillāh!*" and then he breathed his last.

There are so many discussions among ʿ*ulamas*, and we are not listening. There is so much *qīl wa qāl*, "This one said this and this one said that." We are not making *qīl wa qāl* discussions. We have been granted something else for Abū Ṭālib ⸙, for his *Īmān*, his last breathing and finished.

THE BLESSED GRAVE OF LADY MAYMŪNA رضي الله عنها

> *Sayyīditinā Maymūna* رضي الله عنها
> *is very generous*
> *and always gives*
> *when you come to her.*

Shaykh Muhammad Hisham Kabbani ق

Enclosure of the grave of Mother of the Believers, Sayyidah Maymūna bint al-Harith ؓ, 'Umrah 2020.

The Grave of Maymūna bint al-Ḥārith ؓ, the wife of the Prophet ﷺ, is located in Saraf, a town 20 kilometres north of Mecca. She was buried underneath the tree where she got married to the Prophet ﷺ. She had been recently widowed when the Prophet ﷺ married her at Sarif, a place lying on his journey to Mecca when he was in *iḥrām*, on his way for *'Umrah* in Dhul-Qa'dah, 7 A.H.

The grave of Sayyidah Maymūna bint al-Ḥārith ؓ.

The Prophet ﷺ had intended to start living with her when in Mecca after performing *'Umrah*, but as the Quraysh did not allow him to enter Mecca, he called her over to him in the same place on his return journey. Many years later, she came to Mecca for *'Umrah*. On her way back to Madinah, she wasn't feeling well so she asked to stay there and passed away in the same place as where she got married (at the age of 81).

Story: Charity Will Prolong Your Life and Remove Afflictions

Shaykh Muhammad Hisham Kabbani

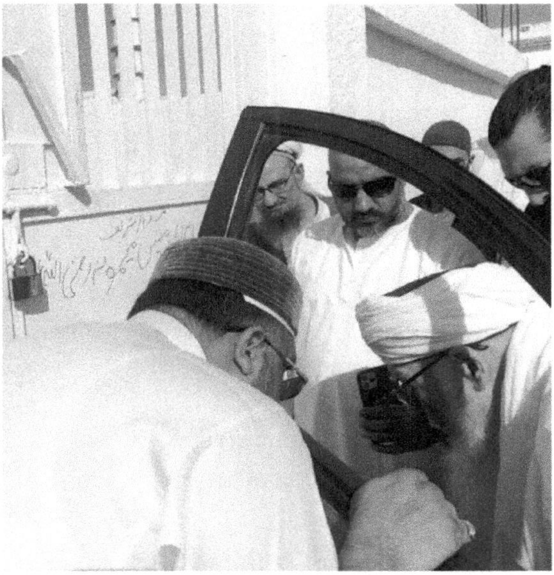

SHAYKH HISHAM KABBANI VISITING THE GRAVE SAYYIDAH MAYMŪNA BINT AL-ḤĀRITH ﵂, ʿUMRAH 2020.

Shaykh Nazim ق used to tell this story often. There was a king of many Arab countries at that time, who always went to hunt in the desert. One day they went hunting and the guide in the desert lost the way and he did not know the way to come back. The king and he and his soldiers did not know how to return home.

Night fell, and they slept in the desert, but they had nothing. The next day also, they became very thirsty but didn't find any water. Finally, far away in the desert they found a small tent and asked each other, "Is this a tent or a mirage?" They said, "No, it is a tent." They sent one person to check, and he found a tent with an old lady sitting there making *dhikrullāh*. There was nothing in the empty desert, so how was one lady sitting there? The king went with people, and they said, "Can you offer us some water?" They saw a big barrel made of clay filled with water. The clay makes the water very fresh, and you feel it in your mouth. I remember when we used to go for *ʿUmrah* or Hajj in the 1960s, not like today; then they brought water on donkeys carrying it to where we were living. In any case, she said, "What will he give me if I give him water?"

In this *dunyā,* if you take, you also have to give. If you don't give then don't ask, as you are not eligible for anything. Only with people who are generous can you take without giving (like Sayyidah Maymūna ﵂, the wife of Prophet ﷺ).

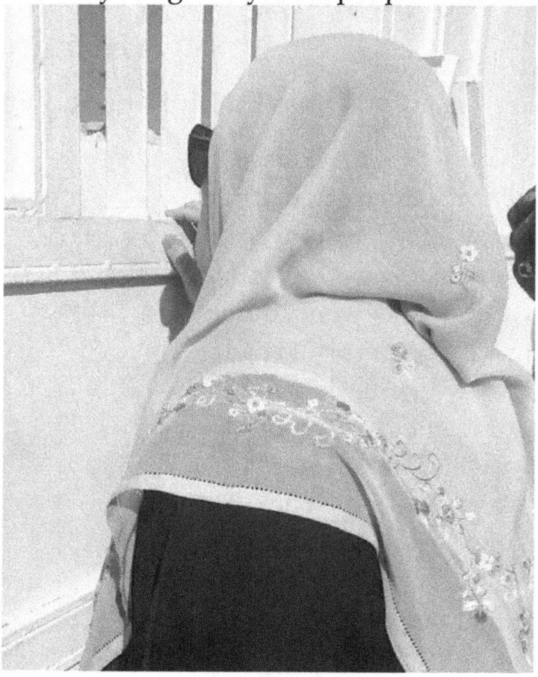

HAJJAH NAZIHA ADIL VISITING THE GRAVE SAYYIDAH MAYMŪNA BINT AL-HARITH ﵂, 'UMRAH

So, she said, "What will he give me?"

The king said, "I will give you money."

She said, "I don't need your money, I'm in the desert. I do not want it. I want the most precious thing you have. Give me that and I will give you water."

He said, "Okay, the most precious thing I have is my horse."

She said, "What am I going to do with a horse? I am not in need of it."

He said, "You can come and go with it."

She said, "You go with it, use it and get out of this misery, this problem."

He looked at her as a king and found himself as nothing in front of that lady.

Then she said, "Look, you are a king in your kingdom, but here in the tent I am the queen; you must listen to what I say as you have no kingdom here, this is my kingdom!"

He was shaking, because no one can say something like that to a king. He began to think that this lady is something different.

She said, "Look, this water that you are looking at, I know you will give all your life to get it or else you are going to be dead in this desert. So, what is your kingdom going to benefit you?"

So, he said, "Okay, what do you want from me?"

"I want all of your kingdom and don't leave anything out! Give me everything and I will save you from death."

What is his answer going to be? Even a child will know the answer!

He said, "Give me the water and I will give you all my kingdom!"

She replied, "Swear to Allah that you will give me your entire kingdom for that water."

He said, "I promise you in front of Allah ﷻ that I give you my entire kingdom, for I am not a king, so give me that water so I can live!"

Allah gave life to human beings as an *amāna,* trust, which is very precious, so you have to save it. Don't give excuses to yourself; follow the system and keep that *amāna* that Allah gave to you intact.

She said, "Are you accepting to give me everything?"

He said, "Yes."

She said, "Okay, this is a cup of water to save your life."

He took the water and said, "*Alḥamdulillāhi Rabbi 'l-ʿĀlamīn.*"

She said, "Your king sold his kingdom for one cup of water!"

"Your *dunyā* isn't worth the wing of a mosquito," as the Prophet ﷺ said. Your health, your trust that Allah gave you, is what you need to keep intact. So, what do you have to do? The Prophet ﷺ said, and I am repeating it a hundred times, everyone must hear it:

الصَّدَقَة تُرَدّ الْبِلَا وَتَزِيد الْعُمْر .

Charity extends life and removes afflictions.

Ṣadaqah on your behalf, when you give in Allah's Way, Allah stretches your life and cures you from sickness. Give *ṣadaqah fī sabīli 'Llāh,* for Allah's Sake, don't let your hand tremble (in doubt), but give what you can.

This house is empty; there is no furniture here but still we can use it, so don't think it is gone. Allah made you to take out the furniture, as an example, to make all these good people come to have lunch, to take burdens from you and honor this house. So, give in Allah's Way for your health! You spend millions on doctors and hospitals, but you don't spend *ṣadaqah* on your health.

The Prophet ﷺ is aṣ-Ṣādiq al-Āmīn, the Truthful and Trustworthy One.

وَالنَّجْمِ إِذَا هَوَى مَا ضَلَّ صَاحِبُكُمْ وَمَا غَوَى وَمَا يَنطِقُ عَنِ الْهَوَى إِنْ هُوَ إِلَّا وَحْيٌ يُوحَى

By the star when it goes down, your companion is neither astray nor being misled. Nor does he say (aught) of (his own) desire. It is no less than inspiration sent down to him.[209]

He ﷺ said, "Give, and Allah will give you more and give you good health." May Allah ﷻ give health and cure and long life to all of you in the way of Allah ﷻ and in the love of Prophet ﷺ! *Allāhumma innī ballaght, Allāhumma fash-had,* "O Allah! Bear witness, I have conveyed the message." I conveyed the message. If you want to hear, if you want to accept, it is up to you. If you don't want to accept, don't come later and say, "O! I have this and that problem." Whatever is needed has been given, and it is now your responsibility to execute the advice.

May Allah forgive us.

bi ḥurmati 'l-Ḥabīb, bi ḥurmati 'l-Fātiḥah

[209] Sūratu 'n-Najm, 53:1-4.

MASJID AL-BAYAʿ

“ *I had the honor to be*
with Allah's Messenger ﷺ
on the night of ʿAqabah
when we pledged
our allegiance to Islam
and it was dearer to me
than my participation
in the Battle of Badr,
although Badr was more popular
amongst people
as compared with that
(i.e. the ʿAqabah Pledge). ”

ʿAbd Allah bin Kaʿb bin Mālik ؓ

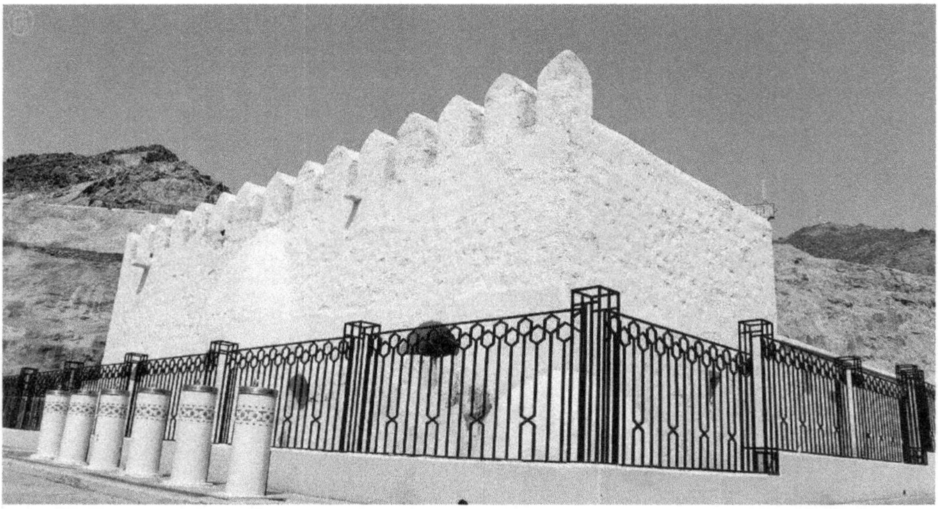

MASJID AL-BAYAʿ.

Masjid al-Bayaʿ, also known as Masjid al-ʿAqabah, is situated near Mina and it is the site where two crucial pledges of allegiance were made by the Anṣār of Madinah, which led to the migration of the Prophet ﷺ to the city of Madinah.

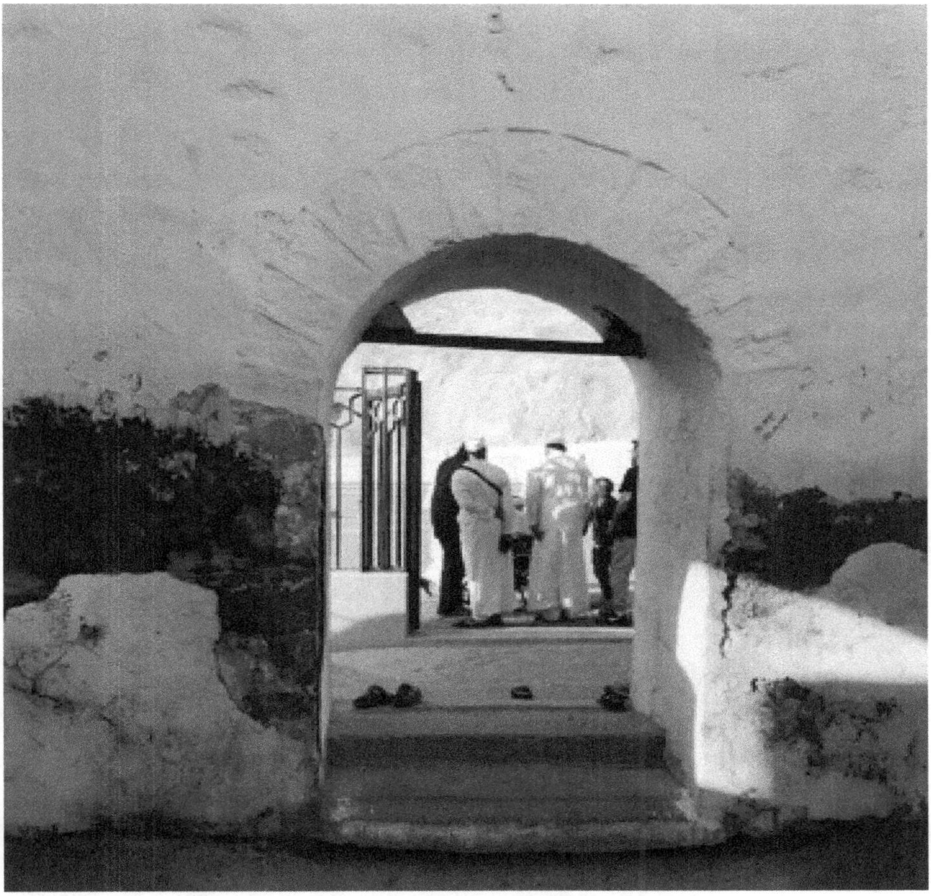

SHAYKH HISHAM ENTERING MASJID AL-BAYAʿ.

Story: The Secrets of the Visit to Masjid al-*Baya*ʿ

Shaykh Muhammad Hisham Kabbani

I saw Grandshaykh, may Allah bless him, and Shaykh Nazim ق say to me, "Hisham, the time is coming; we will take you to see!" and it was not a dream. I saw the Prophet ﷺ standing waiting for me. As soon as I arrived (to this masjid), I looked and saw that it was a *nafaq*, a tunnel. I was on one end of the tunnel and there was someone on the other side of the tunnel dressed in white clothes. It is well known to *Awlīyā* who that person is. They took my hand and we entered into that big tunnel, which has a beginning but no end. The end is in the hand of Mahdī عليه السلام. They said, "This is our way and this is our life." They gave us something that was given to Aṣ-ḥāb an-Nabī ﷺ, the Companions of the Prophet ﷺ. They give them different tunnels according to what they have done in the time of the Prophet ﷺ.

For us to be given something from them, they took us on an unknown trip, and it was a trip to something very important that every Muslim likes to see. They took us to the *maqām* (station) of *Āhlu 'l-Baya'* (the People of the Pledge) in the time of the Prophet ﷺ. That is where Sahabah ؓ give *baya'* to the Prophet ﷺ.

إِنَّ الَّذِينَ يُبَايِعُونَكَ إِنَّمَا يُبَايِعُونَ اللَّهَ يَدُ اللَّهِ فَوْقَ أَيْدِيهِمْ فَمَن نَّكَثَ فَإِنَّمَا
يَنكُثُ عَلَى نَفْسِهِ وَمَنْ أَوْفَى بِمَا عَاهَدَ عَلَيْهُ اللَّهَ فَسَيُؤْتِيهِ أَجْرًا عَظِيمًا

Lo! Those who swear allegiance unto you (O Muhammad), swear allegiance only unto Allah. The Hand of Allah is above their hands. So, whosoever breaks his oath, breaks it only to his soul's hurt; while whosoever keeps his covenant with Allah, on him will He bestow immense reward.[210]

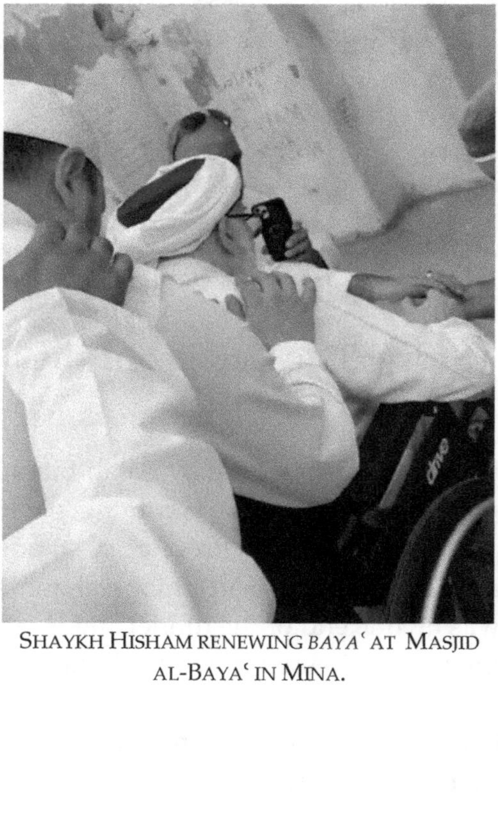

SHAYKH HISHAM RENEWING *BAYA'* AT MASJID AL-BAYA' IN MINA.

Radīnā billāhi rabban, wa bil-islāmi dīnan, wa bi Sayyīdinā wa Nabīyyīnā Muḥammadun ṣall-Allāhu 'alayhi wa sallam Rasūlan wa Nabīyyan wa bil-Qurāni kitāban w'Allāhu 'alā mā naqūlu wakīl, w'alḥamdulillāhi rabbil-'Ālamīn. Wa qabilnā bi Sayyīdinā ash-Shaykh Muhammad Nazim al-Haqqani shaykhan lanā w'Allāhu

[210] Sūratu 'l-Fatḥ, 48:10.

ʿalā mā naqūlu wakīl. Allāhu Allāhu Allāhu Ḥaqq! Allāhu Allāhu Allāhu Ḥaqq! Allāhu Allāhu Allāhu Ḥaqq!

We went into that *maqām*, and it turned out to be a place that Sahabah ﷺ used to give *bayaʿ* to the Prophet ﷺ. So, they said, "Do *bayaʿ* here, it is open for you!" and the people who were with me did *bayaʿ* with Grandshaykh ق and Mawlana Shaykh Nazim ق, from whom we take *bayaʿ*, and we are supported by them. Then we made the *duʿā* of *Āhl al-Bayaʿ*.

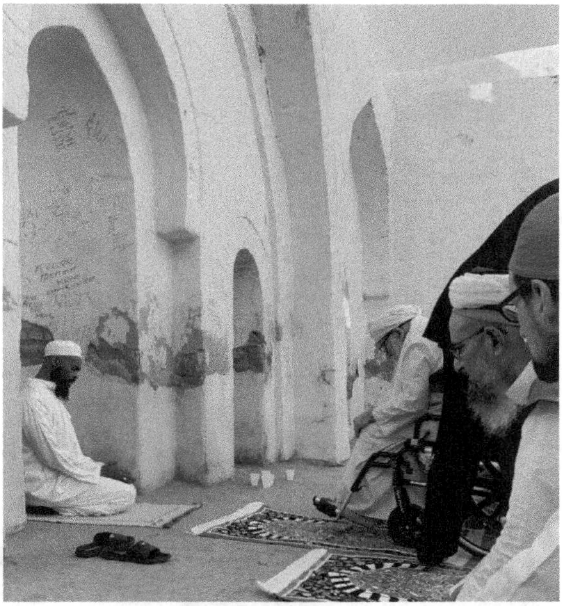

SHAYKH HISHAM AND *MURĪDS* MAKING MAKING *DUʿA* AFTER *SALĀH* AT MASJID AL-BAYAʿ.

It was not a small event. It is a huge event to those who can see. As for those who cannot see, even if they do *bayaʿ* all day they still cannot see. However, to *Āhl as-Sunnah wa 'l-Jamaʿah*, and to *Āhl an-Naqsh*, the Sahabah ﷺ wrote in our hearts by means of spiritual power "*Āhl as-Sunnah wa 'l-Jamaʿah;*" the *maqām* of *Āhl as-Sunnah wa 'l-Jamaʿah* was written. So that spiritual power that *Āhl as-Sunnah wa 'l-Jamaʿah* was able to take from *Awlīyāullāh* and the sign of it is that you are coming here, because you are part of it.

So, we are from *Āhl as-Sunnah wa 'l-Jamaʿah* and we are from Naqshbandis. We are peaceful people. Every moment we stay here, a new opening opens. A lot of things have been shown and according to the level of the people, they were given these powers. This has been a grant, and this has been supported and is a grant from Heavens. May Allah ﷻ pour into our hearts! When we take the *bayaʿ*, it means we accepted, and when we accepted, at that time that opening opened. Do not think that they are not aware of what we are doing, they are behind it, supporting us. You are sitting and getting that (bounty), and you are getting tired, but for them it is not tiring.

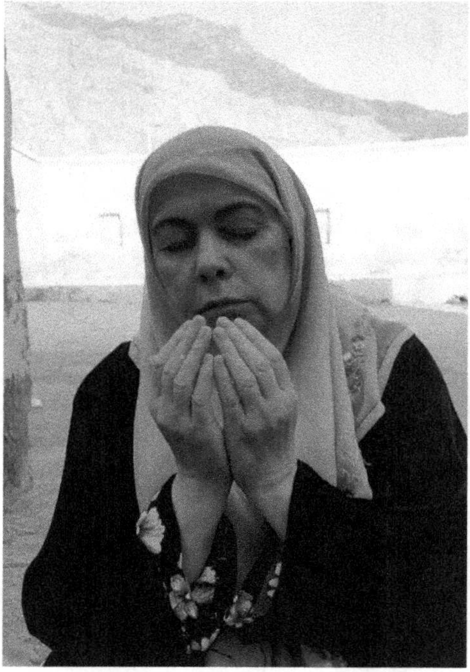

HAJJAH NAZIHA MAKING *DU'A* AT MASJID AL-BAYA'.

For *Awlīyāullāh*, they can see that we are tired, but that tiredness is important to clean you from all kinds of sins, and now you are all as if newly born, especially Jakarta people and Malaysia people, and Singapore people, and all the Middle East area. I am speaking to the hearts. It will be *naqsh* on the hearts. *Alḥamdulillāh*, I have been taken to be inheritor of Grandshaykh ق and Shaykh Nazim ق. They have taken my heart to the presence of the Prophet ﷺ. I did not want to open this, but I was asked to open this reality. Grandshaykh ق was taken from *dunyā* and Shaykh Nazim ق (inherited) when Grandshaykh ق was going to die, now as inheritor of *shuyūkh*, I have been taken to be away from the presence of people, and it was not enough, so they asked of me another twenty days (after completing forty). So, we will continue to be here near Sayyīdinā Muhammad ﷺ.

Hajjah Naziha ق also did her best and she completed every 2-3 days one *Khatm*, so she made like twenty *Khatms* of the Qur'an. This was her job, because by reciting the Holy Qur'an you elevate the people of *ṭarīqah* around the world. They gave her that position, but she was not aware of it, now she is aware of it. So, they took my soul as inheritor of the Prophet ﷺ and of Grandshaykh 'AbdAllāh ق and of Shaykh Nazim ق and they opened from *Asrār al-Qur'an fī Baḥr al-Kamāl*, Secrets of the Qur'an in the Ocean of Perfection, *fī Baḥar al-Mūsā'ada*, in the Ocean of Assistance for *Āhl as-Sunnah wa 'l-Jama'ah*, and there is more that will not open until later. *Alḥamdulillāh* for this.

FAREWELL *ṬAWĀF*

"*The Hajj company*
then entered Mecca,
performed the Ṭawāf al-Widaʿ,
the parting circumambulation,
drank of the water of the Zamzam Well
from the hand of Ibn ʿAbbās ﵁
and thus completed the rites of the Hajj.
Then the Holy Prophet ﷺ *returned to Madinah.*
When the city of Madinah came into view,
the Prophet ﷺ *felt such joy*
and elation at its sight
that he cried out with a loud shout:
Lā ilāha illa-Llāh wahdahu lā sharīka lah
lahu 'l-mulku wa lahu 'l-ḥamd
yuḥīyy wa yumīt wa hūwa ʿalā kulli shayin qadīr,
'There is no god but Allah, the One and Only,
who has no partners; in His possession is all there is,
and to Him is due all praise;
and it is He who has power
over all things!'"

Hajjah Amina Adil ق

Leaving the Blessed Land, Mecca

Shaykh Nazim Adil al-Haqqani

ṬAWĀF AL-WIDA', FAREWELL ṬAWĀF, HAJJ 2011.

Everything pertaining to this world is impermanent, constantly in a state of transition. Therefore, it is only natural that I am here addressing you today and elsewhere tomorrow. Don't let this condition sadden you, for in reality, transition is God's mercy to man. Don't wish even for good times to last forever, for you wouldn't be able to bear permanence; you would just get fed up.

Know that the discontinuation of any desirable state or condition is the catalyst for gaining an even deeper appreciation of what is good. Longing for the attainment of the spiritual realities of which you have caught a glimpse is the means to their attainment. Is there any morsel tastier than that upon which the fast is broken?

This is the reason that Allah Almighty created the world as it is. The signs of the Heavens take their turns inspiring our souls. The rising sun brightens our day, but just when we would start to get fed up with it, lo and behold, it bows out and the soft light of the moon enchants us with its many forms: appearing first as a delicate crescent, then waxing gradually to its full and waning. If it never waned, no one would be able to appreciate the awe-inspiring immensity of the starlit Heavens.

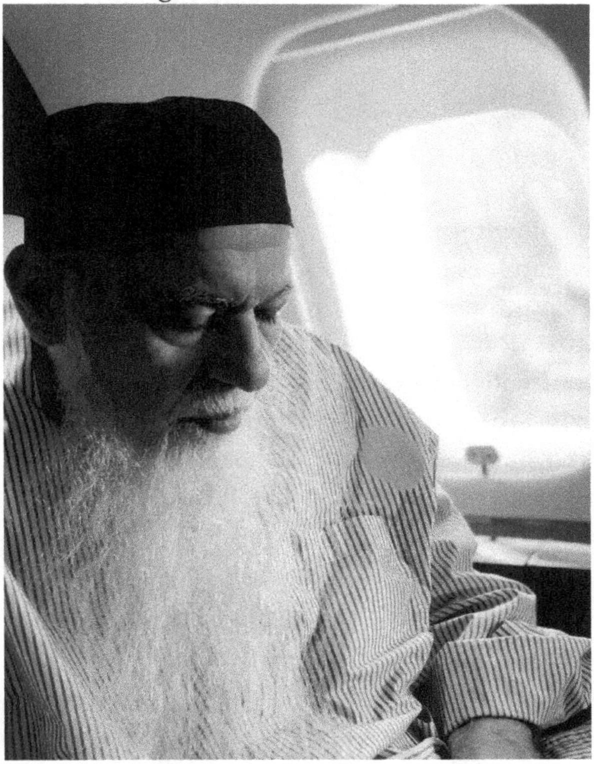
SHAYKH HISHAM RETURNING HOME FROM *'UMRAH*, 2020.

The threadbare pilgrim may cross snowy mountain passes and sun-scorched deserts barefoot, or even on his hands and knees in order to reach Mecca. When he finally arrives, he is struck dumb by the awesome majesty of the Holy Ka'bah. Tears stream down his face as he clings to its door, pouring out his heart and soul to his Lord, and the Lord fulfills his heart's innermost desire in accordance with the longing that drove him to suffer freezing wind and scorching sun.

Longing brought the pilgrim to the House of the Lord, but the pilgrim's dedication to his Lord will not be served by his staying in Mecca on and on, but by returning to his country with the cherished memories of his pilgrimage inspiring his faith. Should he choose to remain in Mecca he runs the risks of gradually becoming callous and hardened to the sight of the Ka'bah like the inhabitants, who never had a Mecca as their distant sought-after goal, who crossed no deserts to attain it, but who may, rather, cross through the Holy Mosque as a shortcut to get from one part of the market to another, barely casting a glance at the magnificent Ka'bah.

Once a disciple used to attend his shaykh's discourses only occasionally, although he lived in the vicinity of the shaykh's dargah. The shaykh asked him, "Why do you attend so infrequently?" The clever disciple answered, "Because I don't like being asked to attend less frequently."

The sun, the moon, the stars, the Holy Ka'bah, the beauty of nature or architecture, or the face of a beloved person: all these sights may inspire us, may remind us of a great truth that is alive in our hearts, but of which we are yet heedless. But don't become enamored of the signs to such an extent that they become ends in themselves, and you cease to follow the directions they seek to impart to you. The object is not a heavenly body that will set, a symbol which may become commonplace nor a face that will age or turn away from you. When Abraham was yet a seeker of truth, at a stage of bewilderment on his road to truth, he became enamored of the sun, moon and stars, but as each set he said, "My love is not for those that disappear!"

Love is eternal, and the transitory nature of all things pertaining to this world is a sign of truth, a sign that shows us by means of contrast. Real spiritual love, love of God and love of Mankind for the sake of God is the only truth, the only thing in this world that is permanently and constantly sweet. Physical separation from someone you love, in accordance with the rule that pertains to the physical, may create a longing that will cause love to increase, may augment the bliss of reunion, but on the spiritual level that love is constant, is never interrupted by distance nor by time. Your beloved may be on the moon, and you may be in bliss at the thought of reunion, but if love is unrequited, that is not sweet separation but a bitter pill. The extinction of love is pitch darkness. You may regard the sunset as beautiful, but how would you feel if it were setting forever?

Love is the water of life. God created Ādam 舗 from clay and water. If it were not for water the clay would hold no shape. Divine Love is what binds our souls together. That is why people become so miserable when they feel unloved. It is a feeling that something essential is missing from one's life, that life itself is incomplete, and in the face of this ache people set out in search of love with the desperation of a man dying of thirst!

Story: All of Mecca Cried for Shaykh Abū Muhammad Qāsim ق

Shaykh Muhammad Hisham Kabbani

Grandshaykh ʿAbdAllāh ad-Dāghestānī (the thirty-eighth and thirty-ninth shaykhs in the Naqshbandi Golden Chain, respectively) narrated to us the following story:

> The year in which Abū Muhammad Qāsim ؓ was to leave this world, on the third of Ramadan he went on pilgrimage. When he arrived to al-Qudayd, where pilgrims usually stop, Allah ﷻ opened to his vision to behold the angels descending from Heaven and ascending in countless numbers. They would come down, visit the place, and then go back up. As he saw these angels carrying the blessings that Allah ﷻ was sending down with them, it was as if that light and concentrated power was being poured into his heart directly, filling it with sincerity and God-consciousness.
>
> As soon as this vision occurred, he fell asleep. In a dream he saw Abū Bakr aṣ-Ṣiddīq ؓ coming to him. He said, "O my grandfather, who are these heavenly beings that are descending and ascending and who have filled my heart with God-consciousness?"
>
> Abū Bakr aṣ-Ṣiddīq ؓ answered, "Those angels you see ascending and descending, Allah ﷻ has assigned for your grave. They are constantly visiting it. They are obtaining blessings from where your body is going to be buried in the earth. To reverence you, Allah ﷻ ordered them to come down and to ask blessings for you. O my grandson, don't be heedless about your death; it is coming soon, and you are going to be raised to the Divine Presence and leave this world."
>
> Qāsim ؓ immediately opened his eyes and saw his grandfather in front of him. He said, "I just saw you in the dream." Abū Bakr aṣ-Ṣiddīq ؓ replied, "Yes, I was ordered to meet you." "That means I am going to leave this world," answered Qāsim ؓ. "Yes, you are going to leave the world and accompany us to the hereafter," said our master Abū Bakr aṣ-Ṣiddīq ؓ.

"What kind of deed do you advise me to do in the last moments I am on Earth?" asked Qāsim ♦ of his grandfather. Abū Bakr aṣ-Ṣiddīq ♦ answered, "O my son, keep your tongue moistened with *dhikrullāh* and keep your heart ready and present with *dhikrullāh*. That is the best you can ever achieve in this world."

Then Abū Bakr ♦ disappeared and Qāsim ♦ began *dhikr* on his tongue and in his heart. He continued to Mecca and witnessed the standing at Mount 'Arafat (which occurs each year on the 9th of Dhul-Hijjah). In that year many saints, both men and women, were spiritually present at 'Arafat, and Qāsim bin Muhammad bin Abū Bakr aṣ-Ṣiddīq ♦ met with them.

As they were standing, they all heard the Plain of 'Arafat and its mountain crying mournfully. They asked Mount Arafat, "Why are you crying this way?" and Mount 'Arafat replied, "I and all the angels are crying, because today this earth is going to lose one of its pillars."

They asked, "Who is that pillar that the earth is about to lose?" Mount 'Arafat replied, "Abū Muhammad Qāsim is going to leave this world, and the world will no longer be honored with his steps, and I will no longer see him on my plain, where all pilgrims come, and I will miss him. That is why I am crying in this way. Not only from myself, but his grandfather Muhammad ﷺ, and his grandfather Abū Bakr ♦, and his grandfather 'Alī ♦, and the whole world is crying. They say the death of a scholar is the death of the world."

At that moment the Prophet ﷺ and Abū Bakr aṣ-Ṣiddīq ♦ were spiritually present on 'Arafat, where they were crying. Prophet ﷺ said, "With the death of Qāsim, great corruption will appear on Earth, for he was one of the pillars able to prevent it."

Previously, that mournful crying of Mount 'Arafat only occurred when the Prophet ﷺ passed away from this world, then when Abū Bakr ♦ passed, then when Salman ♦ passed, and when Qāsim ♦ passed. One of the saints, Rābī'a al-'Adawīyya, met Qāsim ♦ in the spiritual assembly of saints and he said, "Every dry thing and living thing, I heard them crying. Why, O Rābī'a, did this happen? I never experienced such crying in my life. Do you know its cause?" She replied, "O Abū Muhammad, I also was not able to discern the nature of that crying, so you must ask your grandfather, Abū Bakr ﷺ."

Abū Bakr ﷺ appeared spiritually to them, saying, "That crying from every point on this earth is because you are leaving this worldly life, as I informed you on your pilgrimage." Then Qāsim ﷺ raised his hands and prayed to Allah ﷻ, "Since I am passing away from this life now, forgive whoever stood with me on Mount Arafat!" Then they heard a voice saying, "For your sake, Allah ﷻ has forgiven whoever stood with you on Mount Arafat on this Hajj." At that moment Allah ﷻ revealed to Qāsim's heart unlimited Gnostic knowledge.

Then he departed from Mount ʿArafat and said, "O Mount ʿArafat, don't forget me on Judgment Day. All saints and all prophets stood here and so I ask you not to forget me on Judgment Day." That huge mountain replied, "O Qāsim," in a loud voice which everyone could hear, "Don't forget me on the Judgment Day. Don't forget me. Let me be part of the intercession of the Prophet ﷺ."

At that moment Qāsim ﷺ left Mount ʿArafat and arrived at Makkatu 'l-Mukarramah, at the Kaʿbah. There he heard crying coming from Allah's House that kept increasing as he approached, and everyone heard it. That was the voice of the Kaʿbah, crying for the passing of Qāsim ﷺ from this world. And it was coming like a flood, a flood of tears pouring forth from the Kaʿbah, flooding the entire area with water.

Allah's House said, "O Qāsim! I am going to miss you and I am not going to see you again in this world." Then the Kaʿbah made 500 circumambulations around Qāsim ﷺ out of respect for him. Whenever a saint visits the Kaʿbah, it responds to that saint's greetings saying, *"Wa ʿalayka 's-salām yā walī-Allah,"* "and upon you be peace, O Friend of Allah."

Then Qāsim ﷺ said farewell to *Ḥajar al-Aswad*, the Black Stone, then to Jannat al-Muʿalla, the cemetery in which Khadījatu 'l-Kubrā ﷺ, first wife of the Prophet ﷺ, is buried, and then to all of Mecca. He then left and went to al-Qudayd, a place between Mecca and Madinah, on the 9th of Muharram, where he passed on to the next life.

HEAVY RAINFALL DESCENDING ON THE HOUSE OF ALLAH AFTER THE PASSING OF SULTAN AL-AWLIYA, SHAYKH NAZIM ADIL AL-HAQQANI ق, THE FORTIETH MASTER OF THE NAQSHBANDI GOLDEN CHAIN, ON MAY 7, 2014.

Obligations of Hajj According to the Four Schools

ḤANAFĪ	SHAFIʿĪ	MĀLIKĪ	ḤANBALĪ
Iḥrām.	*Iḥrām.*	*Iḥrām.*	*Iḥrām.*
Spending a day at ʿArafah	Spending a day at ʿArafah.	Spending a day at ʿArafah.	Spending a day at ʿArafah.
Saʿī between Ṣafā and Marwah.	*Saʿī* between Ṣafā and Marwah.	*Saʿī* between Ṣafā and Marwah.	*Saʿī* between Ṣafā and Marwah.
Circumambulation. *Ṭawāf al-Ifāḍah* which is done at the *Yawm an-Naḥr* - the day of sacrifice - on returning from Minā. (*Iḥrām* is a prerequisite for the validity of *ṭawāf.*)	Circumambulation. *Ṭawāf al-Ifāḍah* which involves seven rounds of the Kaʿbah.	Circumambulation. *Ṭawāf al-Ifāḍah* which involves seven rounds of the Kaʿbah.	Circumambulation. *Ṭawāf al-Ifāḍah* which involves seven rounds of the Kaʿbah.
	Clipping some of the pilgrim's hair or shaving it all.		
	Close sequence of most rites of Ḥajj, e.g. *iḥrām* must proceed all other rites and standing at ʿArafah must proceed *ṭawāf*.		

RESTRICTIONS OF IḤRĀM

Sexual intercourse and all matters leading to it such as kissing, caresses or talking with one's spouse about intercourse or related sexual matters.
Violating the limits ordained by Allah and disobeying His orders.
Disputing, arguing or fighting with servants, companions or others.
Wearing any sewn clothes which fit the body

It is forbidden for the *muḥrim* to wear clothes dyed with a scented material that lingers with him wherever he goes. He is forbidden from using perfume on body, clothes or hair.

Abū Ḥanīfa and ath-Thawrī held that a *muḥrim* may contract a marriage but he is forbidden to consummate it.

There is a consensus among the scholars that, in the state of *iḥrām*, the *muḥrim* is forbidden to clip his nails without any genuine excuse.

It is forbidden for a *muḥrim* to cover his head with any normal headcover.

There is consensus among the scholars that hunting is forbidden to the *muḥrim* even if he does not actually slaughter the animal

SUMMARIZED STEPS OF HAJJ

On the pre-noon of the eighth Dhul-Ḥijjah enter into *iḥrām* from your place and perform ghusl (total washing) if it is possible and put on the *iḥrām* cloths and repeat the *Talbīyah.*

Set out and stay at Minā to pray Ẓuhr, ʿAṣr, Maghrib, ʿIshā and Fajr prayers. Every prayer comprising of four *rakʿats* is to be shortened to two *rakʿats* only.

At ʿArafah perform Ẓuhr and ʿAṣr obligatory prayers in combination for travelers; each prayer shortened to two *rakʿats*. Stay there until sunset and implore God frequently facing the Qiblah.

When the sun sets, march from ʿArafah to Muzdalifah. Once at Muzdalifah you should pray Maghrib, ʿIshā and Fajr prayers. Stay there to implore God until sunrise. If you are weak and are not able to walk and mingle with the crowd, you may go to Minā at late night. However the 49 stones must be collected by you or someone on your behalf.

When the sun is about to rise, walk from Muzdalifah to Minā; when you arrive at Minā, do the following:

A: Stone Jamarat al-ʿAqabah which is the Stoning Site located nearest to Mecca. You have to throw seven pebbles, one by one, pronouncing Takbīr (*Allāhu Akbar*!) at every throw and say:

raghman li 'sh-Shaytan riḍan li 'r-Raḥmān 3 times, *bismillāh Allāhu akbar*!	رغماً لِلشَّيْطَانِ رضاً لِلرَّحْمَنِ 3 مَرَّات بِسْمِ اللهِ اللهُ أَكْبَرُ.

In opposition to Satan, seeking God's good pleasure and satisfaction; God is greater!

B: Slaughter a sacrificial animal, eat from its meat and distribute the rest to the poor. The slaughtering of a sacrificial animal is obligatory on the one doing Ḥajj Tamattuʿ or Ḥajj Qirān (combined *ʿUmrah* and Ḥajj).

C: Shave or shorten the hair of your head. Shaving is recommended (women should shorten their hair equal to a fingertip length). The order of the three above-mentioned acts is: first, throwing the pebbles, second, slaughtering the sacrificial animal and third to shave or shorten the hair of the head. There is no harm if the order is interchanged. After completion of the above mentioned three acts, you can put on your normal clothes and do all the acts prohibited during the Ḥajj with the exception of sexual intercourse.

Then go to Mecca with the intention to perform *Ṭawāf al-Ifāḍah* (*Ṭawāf al-Ḥajj*) and to perform *saʿī* between Ṣafā and Marwah (Saʿī al-Ḥajj).

When you reach Mecca, do circumambulation (*ṭawāf*) of the Kaʿbah seven times starting from the corner of Ḥajaru 'l-Aswad (the Black Stone) and finishing by it. One then prays two *rakʿats* behind Maqām Ibrahīm, if possible.

After the performance of two *rakʿats*, go to the hillock of Ṣafā to perform *saʿī* seven times commencing from Ṣafā and ending at Marwah.

After completion of *ṭawāf* and *saʿī*, go back to Minā in order to spend the two nights of 11th and 12th of Dhul-Ḥijjah. By completion of *Ṭawāf al-Ifāḍah*, every act prohibited for the pilgrim during the Ḥajj time now becomes lawful including sexual intercourse.

On the days of 11th and 12th of Dhul-Ḥijjah, after the sun declines, throw the pebbles at the three Stoning Sites (*Jamarahs*). Start with the furthest from Mecca and then the middle one and finally Jamarat al-ʿAqabah. Throw seven pebbles at each Stoning Site and pronounce the *Takbīr* every time a stone is thrown. After throwing at the first and the middle Stoning Site, implore God facing the Qiblah; it is a must that throwing of the stones in these two days (i.e. 11th and 12th) be after *zawāl* (noon).

When you complete throwing the pebbles on the 12th of Dhul-Ḥijjah, you may go out of Minā before sunset. If you want to delay going out it is better to spend the night of the 13th of Dhul-Ḥijjah at Minā and repeat throwing pebbles at the three Stoning Sites after the sun reaches its noon peak (*zawāl*) as before.

If you want to go back home, you have to perform a Farewell Circumambulation (*Ṭawāf al-Widaʿ*) (seven turns around the Kaʿbah). There is no *Ṭawāf al-Widaʿ* enjoined on a woman in the post-partum state or one in her menses.

ʿ*UMRAH* – SUMMARY OF STEPS

ʿ*Umrah* technically means paying a visit to Ka'bah, performing circumambulation (*ṭawāf*) around it, walking between Ṣafā and Marwah seven times (*sāʿī*). A performer of ʿ*Umrah* puts off his *iḥrām* by having his hair shaved or cut.

If you want to perform ʿ*Umrah*, make the intention (*niyyah*) for ʿ*Umrah*, first perform *ghusl* (shower). Next put on the *iḥrām* clothes. Pray two *rakʿats Sunnatu 'l-iḥrām*. Then pronounce the *Talbīyah*.

When you reach Mecca, do circumambulation (*ṭawāf*) of the Kaʿbah seven times for ʿ*Umrah* starting from the corner of *Ḥajar al-Aswad* (the Black Stone) and finishing by it. One then prays two *rakʿats* behind Maqām Ibrahīm, if possible.

After the performance of two *rakʿats*, go to the hillock of Ṣafā to perform *saʿī* seven times commencing from Ṣafā and ending at Marwah.

After completion of *saʿī* you may shorten your hair. By this, your ʿ*Umrah* is complete and you may disengage from *iḥrām* clothes and put on normal clothes.

HAJJ AND ʿ*UMRAH* – DETAILED STEPS

Here we present details of some but not all aspects of the rites of Ḥajj and ʿ*Umrah* for which the shaykhs of the Naqshbandi Way have given particular recitations and or methodologies, to be observed in addition to all the normal steps performed by the pilgrim in following his or her particular *madhhab* and the guide assigned to his or her group.

PREPARATION FOR ḤAJJ

Imam Nawawī said according to the consensus of scholars it is from the *adab* of Ḥajj, that the essential intention of Ḥajj is to repent. Such repentance has the following conditions:

1. to leave all manner of sins;
2. to never return to these sins;
3. to regret the sins you have committed;
4. to ask forgiveness of anyone you have harmed, upset or made angry. If you owe someone money but you are unable pay them back at the time, you should inform them of your intention to make Ḥajj and give them a faithful promise to repay them in the future.
5. to write a will, since one does not knows if he will return from Ḥajj alive;
6. to use only money from licit means (*ḥalāl*) to go for Ḥajj, as God said:

"O you who believe! Give of the good things which ye have (honourably) earned, and of the fruits of the earth which We have produced for you, and do not even aim at getting anything which is bad, in order that out of it ye may give away something, when you yourselves would not receive it except with closed eyes."[211]

Abu Hurayra ‎ reported God's Messenger ‎ as saying:

> *O people, God is Good and He therefore, accepts only that which is good. And God commanded the believers as He commanded the Messengers by saying: "O Messengers, eat of the good things, and do good deeds; verily I am aware of what you do."*[212] *And He said, "O those who believe, eat of the good things that We gave you."*[213] *He then made a mention of a person who travels far and wide, his hair dishevelled and covered with dust. He lifts his hand towards the sky (to makes supplication), "O Lord, O Lord," whereas his diet is unlawful, his drink is unlawful, and his clothes are unlawful and his nourishment is unlawful. How then can his supplication be accepted?*[214]

The meaning of this is that when going for Ḥajj, you must only use only licit means and leave all that is forbidden and repent from it, as God ordered: "O ye who believe! Turn to God with sincere repentance."[215]

The pilgrim visits his family, neighbors and friends, informs them he is leaving and asks them to pray for him.

One states the intention to go for Ḥajj before the 8th of Dhul-Ḥijjah, or before arriving at the location (*al-Mīqāt*) for dressing in the *iḥrām*, whichever comes first. Intention should normally be made before starting one's trip, or at least one hour by plane from arrival at Jeddah. If coming by land from outside the Ḥijāz, it is recommended to make intention before setting out.

Before you enter into travel, take a shower and pray two *rakʿats niyyatu 'l-Ḥajj*, according to the Prophet ‎ who said, "The best that a servant can put behind him when he travels to take care of his family, are two *rakʿats* that he prays before he sets forth on his travel; they which will be like his deputy during his absence [calipha]."[216]

---

[211] Sūratu 'l-Baqarah, 2:267.

[212] Sūratu 'l-Mu'minūn, 23:51.

[213] Sūratu 'l-Baqarah, 2:172.

[214] Muslim.

[215] Sūratu 't-Taḥrīm, 66:8.

[216] Ibn Abī Shaybah from Miqdād (*mursal*).

If more than two are travelling together should choose one among them as a leader, according to the hadith:

If three are travelling let them choose one as leader.[217]

Make intention to undertake a great deal of supplication (*duʿā*) and to give generously in the way of God for the poor, for the Prophet ﷺ said:

Spending (on others) in Ḥajj is like giving in the way of God: one dirham is rewarded seven hundred-fold."[218]

IḤRĀM

TYPES OF IḤRĀM

For men, *iḥrām* consists of two pieces of white, un-sewn and plain cloth; for women no special form of dress is required.

There are three types of *iḥrām*:

1. *Ifrād* (single)
One intends only the Ḥajj and maintains *iḥrām* up to the Day of Sacrifice. No offering is required from the *mufrid*.

2. *Qirān* (combined)
One intends the Ḥajj and *ʿUmrah* combined. *ʿUmrah* is done and Ḥajj is followed immediately in the same *iḥrām*. Only after pelting the Jamrat al-ʿAqabah, and shaving the hair for men or trimming the hair (men and women) can the pilgrim take off *iḥrām*. The condition is to slaughter an animal, or if one is unable, to fast three days during Ḥajj and seven upon returning home.

3. *Tamattuʿ* (interrupted)
One intends *ʿUmrah* and Ḥajj separately. One performs *ʿUmrah* in *iḥrām*, then return to a normal state and dress and remains like that until the *Yawm at-tarwīyya*, which is the 8th of Dhul-Ḥijjah, when he again dresses in *iḥrām* from the *Mīqāt* with the intention of Ḥajj and performs the Ḥajj. After fulfilling the Ḥajj rituals, one should offer a sacrificial animal.

INTENTION

Correct intention is crucial when putting on *iḥrām* for Ḥajj or *ʿUmrah*. The intention is made based on the type of Ḥajj/*ʿUmrah* being performed.

---

[217] Ibn Mājah from Abū Hurayra.

[218] Narrated by Āḥmad from Ibn Buraydā.

1. *Ḥajj Ifrād*
One intends:
Allāhuma innī nawaytu al-Ḥajja, fa-yassirhu lī wa taqabalhu minnī.

نِيَّةِ الْحَجِّ:

اللَّهُمَّ إِنِّى نَوَيْتُ الْحَجَّ فَيَسِّرْهُ لِى وَتَقَبَّلُهُ

مِنِّى

O God I intend to make the pilgrimage so make it easy for me and accept it from me.

2. *ʿUmrah*
For *ʿUmrah* alone one intends:
Allāhuma innī nawaytu al-ʿUmrata, fa-yassirhā lī wa taqabalhā minnī.

نِيَّةِ الْعُمْرَةِ:

اللَّهُمَّ إِنِّى نَوَيْتُ الْعُمْرَةَ فَيَسِّرْهَا لِى وَتَقَبَّلْهَا

مِنِّى

O God I intend to make the lesser pilgrimage so make it easy for me and accept it from me.

3. *Qirān*
For Ḥajj and *ʿUmrah* combined one intends:
Allāhuma innī nawaytu al-ʿumrata wal-Ḥajja, fa-yassirhumā lī wa taqabalhumā minnī.

نِيَّةِ الْحَجِّ وَالْعُمْرَةِ:

اللَّهُمَّ إِنِّى نَوَيْتُ الْحَجِّ وَالْعُمْرَةِ فيسرهما لِى

وتقبلهما مِنِّى

O God I intend to make both the lesser pilgrimage and the greater pilgrimage so make them both easy for me and accept them both from me.

One then says:
Nawaytu 'l-arbāʿīn, nawaytu 'l-ʿitikāf, nawaytu 'l-khalwah, nawaytu 'l-ʿuzlah, nawaytu 'r-riyāda, nawaytu 's-sulūk, lillāhi taʿalā.

نَوَيْتُ اَلْأَرْبَعِين، نَوَيْتُ اَلِاعْتِكَاف نَوَيْتُ

اَلْخَلْوَة نَوَيْتُ اَلْعُزْلَة، نَوَيْتُ الرِّيَاضَة نَوَيْتُ

السُلُوك، لِلَّه تَعَالى.

For the sake of blessing (*barakah*) I intend the forty (days of seclusion); I intend isolation; I intend discipline (of the ego); I intend to travel in God's Path; for the sake of God, the Exalted.

I am intending to perform Ḥajj on behalf of myself and my family and on behalf of the entire Nation of the Prophet ﷺ. If God with His Favor, honors me by accepting my Ḥajj, I gift the rewards of this worship (*faḍīlat*), to the Prophet ﷺ, to all 124,000 prophets and messengers, to the Sahabah, to the saints, to Imām Mahdī and to my Shaykh. I am sharing all the rewards that He is granting me in His Mercy with the entire Nation of the Prophet ﷺ, without leaving one person behind.

TALBĪYAH التلبية

Recite three times:
Labayk allāhumma labayk, labayka lā sharīka laka labayk.
Then:
Inna al-ḥamda w'an-ni'mata laka wal-mulk, lā sharīka laka labayk.

لَبَّيْكَ اللَّهُمَّ لَبَّيْكَ، لَبَّيْكَ لَا شَرِيكَ لَكَ لَبَّيْكَ، إِنَّ الْحَمْدَ وَالنِّعْمَةَ لَكَ وَالْمُلْكَ لَا شَرِيكَ لَكَ.

At Your service O my God, at your service. At Your service, there is no partner to You, at Your service. Verily all praise, and all bounty belongs to You, as does the Kingdom. There is no partner to You, at Your service.

Then sit and recite the Naqshbandi Adab up to the first *Ihdā*.

ABANDONING ANGER AND SMOKING

Then from that time onwards, do not speak unnecessarily. Two things must be avoided at all costs during Ḥajj: anger and smoking. Anger must be abandoned completely. Know that that there will be a lot of testing to see if you have truly eliminated anger. Know that God, His Angels, the Prophet ﷺ and the inheritors of the Prophet ﷺ the *Awlīyā* and the *Abdāl* are observing you. Even on the last moment of your pilgrimage, you might face a disliked situation that incites your anger, so you must be careful. If your anger emerges; if you complain or fight, your Ḥajj will be brought to nought, so beware of anger.

Anger in Ḥajj is utterly unacceptable. If you sense that you are likely to get angry, do not go for Ḥajj, but rather work to eliminate this bad characteristic from yourself.

Avoid smoking.

CONDUCT OF TRAVEL ادب السفر

As soon as you enter the vehicle of travel recite:
100x *Bismillāhi 'r-Raḥmāni 'r-Raḥīm. Dhālika taqdīru 'l-'Azīzi 'l-'Alīm.*[219]

(100 مرة) بِسْمِ اللهِ الرَّحْمنِ الرَّحِيمِ. ذَلِكَ تَقْدِيرُ الْعَزِيزِ الْعَلِيمِ

In the name of God the Beneficent, the Merciful. That is the decree of (Him), the Exalted in Might, the All-Knowing.

---

[219] 36:38.

From that time on, occupy the time on your journey with whatever comes to your heart of *dhikr*, praise of the Prophet ﷺ, reading Quran, reading Dalā'il al-Khayrāt or making any kind of glorification (*tasbīḥ*) until you reach your destination.

When one approaches Madīnah (if flying, this is about an hour and a half before arriving at Jeddah), you pay respect towards the Prophet ﷺ by praising and seeking his intercession to accept you to be from his Ummah, and to facilitate your Ḥajj and your Visitation (*Ziyārah*) to him. Then call upon the Men of God (*Rijālullāh*) of Mecca and Madīnah to support you in that intention, as mentioned in the hadith that the Prophet said:

> *If one of you loses something or seeks help or a helper (ghawth), and he is in a land where there is no-one to befriend, let him say: "O servants of God, help me! (yā ʿibād Allāh, aghithūnī), for verily God has servants whom he does not see.*[220]

Praise the Prophet ﷺ excessively one hour before landing, five hundred or one thousand times continuously until you reach your first entry point or destination in Ḥijāz.

When you reach the entry point (the airport at Jeddah or the border, if coming by land), you will go through some formalities after which your guide will take you to either Mecca or Madīnah depending on your date of arrival.

CONDUCT OF ARRIVAL IN MECCA

When you arrive in Mecca, proceed directly to the accommodations assigned to you, whether it be a hotel room, a room in a house or any other form of lodging. Do not fight with other members of your Ḥajj group by demanding special treatment or accommodations, but rather go directly to whatever accommodations have been assigned to you or is available.

If you are tired rest. Then shower (*ghusl*), pray two *rakʿats*, then proceed to Masjid al-Ḥarām for making *ʿUmrah*, if you are doing *Ḥajj tamattuʿ*. Intend to make your *ʿUmrah* immediately after you enter Masjid al-Ḥarām.

---

[220] Abū Yaʿlā, Ibn al-Sunnī, and Ṭabarānī in al-Muʿjam al-kabīr. Al-Haythamī said in Majmaʿ al-zawāʾid (10:132): "The men in its chain of transmission have been declared reliable despite weakness in one of them."

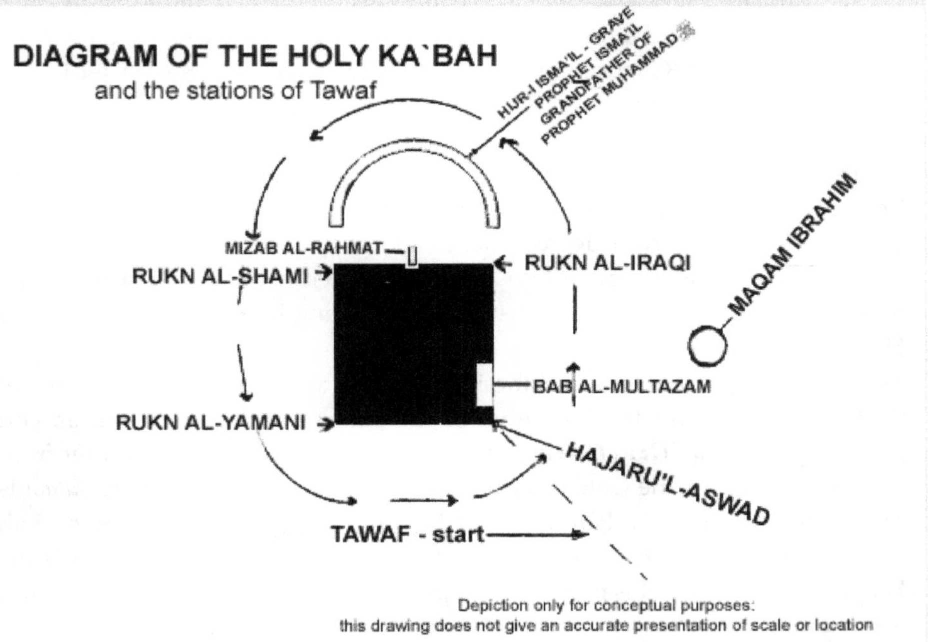

Before entering the Sanctuary (*ḥaram*), recite a greeting for the Kaʿbah:

GREETING KAʿBAH — تَحِيَّةُ الْكَعْبَة.

Allāhumma anta 's-Salām wa minka 's-salām wa ilayka yāʿūdu 's-salām, fa ḥayyinā Rabbanā bi 's-salām, wa adkhilnā 'l-jannata bi luṭfika wa karamika wa jūdika dāraka, dār as-salām. Tabārakta Rabbanā wa tāʿalayta, yā Dhā 'l-Jalāli wa 'l-Jamāli wal-Baqā'i wa 'l-ʿAẓamati wa 'l-Ikrām. Kulluna laka ʿabdun. Wa aḥaqqu mā yaqūl al-ʿabd Allāhumma lā māniʿa limā āaʿṭayta, wa lā muʿṭiya limā manʿata wa lā rādda limā qaḍayta, wa lā yanfaʿu dhā 'l-jaddi minka 'l-jaddu. Rabbī lā ḥawla wa lā quwwata illa billāhi 'l-ʿAlīyyi 'l-ʿAẓīm.

اللَّهُمَّ أَنْتَ السَّلَامُ وَمِنْكَ السَّلَامُ وَإِلَيْكَ يَعُودُ السَّلَامُ فَحَيِّنَا رَبَّنَا بِالسَّلَامِ وَأَدْخِلْنَا الْجَنَّةَ بِلُطْفِكَ وكرمك وَجُودك دَارك دَارِ السَّلَامِ. تَبَارَكْتَ رَبَّنَا وَتَعَالَيْتَ يَا ذَا الْجَلَالِ وَالْجَمَالِ وَالْبَقَاءِ وَالْعَظَمَةِ الْإِكْرَامِ. كُلُّنَا لَكَ عَبْدٌ، وَأَحَقُّ مَا يَقُولُ الْعَبْدُ اللَّهُمَّ لَا مَانِعَ لِمَا أعطيتَ وَلَا مُعْطِيَ لِمَا مَنَعْتَ وَلَا رادَّ لِمَا قَضيتَ وَلَا يَنْفَعُ ذَا الجدّ مِنْكَ الْجَدُّ رَبِّي لَا حَوْلَ وَلَا قُوَّةَ إِلَّا بِاَللهِ العَلِيّ العَظيم.

O God! You are Peace and from You comes Peace. Blessed and lofty are You, O Lord of Majesty and Bounty. There is no god but God, He is One, no partner has He. His is the Kingdom and His is all praise, and He is over all things Powerful. We have heard and obeyed. Your forgiveness, O our Lord! And to Thee is the end of all journeys. All of us are servants to You, and the most true of what a servant may say is: O God! No one can disallow the one to whom You are giving, and there is no giver, to the one whom You have denied. And there is no refusing Your decree. Riches and good fortune will not profit the possessor thereof with You (for nothing will profit him but acting in obedience to You). My Lord, there is no power and no strength save in God, the Most High, the Great.

That is greeting for Mecca and the Kaʿbah. You ask the spiritual servants of God, His angels and the inheritors of the Prophet ﷺ to direct you as you perform your Ḥajj/ *ʿUmrah*. When you enter, it is recommended to enter from the Bāb us-salām – the Gate of Peace. Bābu 's-Salām is below where *adhān* is called, as you enter the Ḥaram, there is a line of sight direct to the Kaʿbah where you recite greetings to the Kaʿbah, raising your two hands towards the Ḥajaru 'l-Aswad or if it is possible to approach it without scuffling, one should do so and kiss it, otherwise raise both hands towards it and say:

Face the *Ḥajar al-Aswad* and say:
Bismillāh Allāhu Akbar (3 times) بِسْمِ اللهِ اللهُ أَكْبَرُ (3 مرات)
As-salāmu ʿalayki yā Kaʿbatallāh السَّلَامُ عَلَيْك يَا كَعْبِه اللّ

Peace be upon you, O Kaʿbah of God.

As-salāmu ʿalayka yā Baytallāh السَّلَامُ عَلَيْك يَا بَيْتِ اللهِ.

Peace be upon you, O House of God.

If God wants, you will hear the Kaʿbah return the greeting to you, as many saints hear. If you have not yet reached that level, the Kaʿbah will return your greeting but you will not hear anything.

ṬAWAF AL-QUDŪM

Before *ʿUmrah* or Ḥajj, the *Ṭawāf al-qudūm* is required (*wājib*).
First make intention, depending on whether doing Ḥajj or *ʿUmrah*:

Intention (Ḥajj) نَوَيتُ طَوّف الْقُدُوم.
Nawaitu ṭawāf al qudūm.

I intend the preliminary circumambulation.

Intention (*ʿUmrah*) نَويتُ طَوَافِ الْعُمْرَةِ.
Nawaitu Ṭawāf al-ʿumrāh.

I intend the circumambulation of the lesser pilgrimage.

Raise hands towards the Black Stone and say:
Bismillāh, Allāhu Akbar three times.

بِسْمِ اللَّهِ اللَّهُ أَكْبَرَ (3 مرات).

During circumambulation *talbīyah* is not done, until after complete *sā'ī*.

When in front of the door of the Ka'bah say:
Allāhumma inna 'l-bayta baytuk, wa 'l-ḥaramu ḥaramuk, wa 'l-amnu amnuk wa hadhā maqāmu 'l-'ā'idha bika min an-nār.

أَمَامَ بَابِ الْكَعْبَةِ:

اللَّهُمَّ إِنَّ الْبَيْتَ بَيْتُكَ وَالْحَرَمَ حَرَمُكَ وَالْأَمْنَ أَمْنُكَ وَهَذَا مَقَامُ الْعَائِذِ بِكَ مِنْ النَّارِ

O God, this house is Your House, this sacred territory is Thy sacred territory, this security is Your Security, and this is the place for one who seeks protection with You against the hell fire.

(ii) At the corner of the second wall by the opening of the *ḥijr* (semi-circular wall):
Allāhumma innī 'aūdhu bika mina 'sh-shakki wa 'sh-shirki wa 'sh-shiqāqi wa 'n-nifāqi wa sū 'il-akhlāqi wa sū 'il-munqalabi fī 'l-āhli wa 'l-māli wa 'l-walad.

(ب) إِمَام بَاقِى الْجِدَارُ مِنْ بَابِ الْكَعْبَةِ:

اللَّهُمَّ أَعُوذُ بِكَ مِنْ الشَّكِّ وَالشِّرْكِ وَالشِّقَاقِ وَالنِّفَاقِ وَسُوءِ الْأَخْلَاقِ وَسُوءِ الْمُنْقَلَبِ فِى الْأَهْلِ وَالْمَالِ وَالْوَلَدِ.

O God I take refuge in You from doubt, from ascribing partners to You, from discord, hypocrisy, evil traits, and bad turns of fortune in family, property and children.

(iii) While passing the second wall, in front of the drainspout of Mercy (Mīzāb ar-Raḥmah): *Allāhumma azillanī fī ẓillika yawma lā ẓilla illā ẓilla 'arshik. W'asqinī bi-kā'si Sayyīdinā Muḥammadin ṣallallāhu 'alayhi wa sallam, sharbatan hanī'atan ma-rī'atan lā aẓmā'u b'adahā abadan yā Dhā 'l-Jalāli wa 'l-Ikrām.*

(ج) عِنْدَ الْجِدَارِ الثَّانِى:

اللَّهُمَّ أَظِلَّنِى فِى ظِلِّكَ يَوْمَ لَا ظِلَّ إِلَّا ظِلُّ عَرْشِكَ وَاسْقِنِى بِكَأْسِ سَيِّدِنَا مُحَمَّدٍ صَلَّى اللَّهُ عَلَيْهِ وَسَلَّمَ شُرْبَهُ هُنَيْئَةً مَرْئِيَّةً لَا أَظْمَأُ بَعْدَهَا أَبَدًا، يَا ذَا الْجَلَالِ وَالْإِكْرَامِ.

O God, put me under Your Shadow on the day when there will be no shadow except the shadow of Your Throne and give me to drink from the cup of our master Muhammad ﷺ a delicious and sating drink after which I shall never get thirsty, O You who is full of Majesty and Bounty.

(iv) When crossing the third wall between the third corner and the Yamānī Corner (and according to whether it is during the Ḥajj or the ʿUmrah):
Allāhum 'ajʿalhu Ḥajjan mabrūrā/(ajʿalhā ʿumratam-mabrūra) wa dhanban maghfūran wa sāʿīyan mashkūrān wa tijāratan lan tabūra yā ʿAzīzu yā Ghafūr.

(د) عِنْد الْجِدَار الثَّالِث حَسَب الْحَجِّ أَوْ الْعُمْرَة:

اللَّهُمَّ اجْعَلْهُ حَجًّا مَبْرُورًا(أو عُمْرَة مبرورة)وَذَنْبًا مَغْفُورًا وَسَعْيًا مَشْكُورًا وَتِجَارَةً لَنْ تَبُورَ يَا عَزِيزُ يَا غَفُورُ

O God, make that this be a Ḥajj/*ʿUmrah* which is accepted, with (my) sin which is pardoned, an accepted work, a commerce which is not lost, O Thou the Powerful, the Forgiving.
When one reaches the Yamānī Corner do not kiss it, but touch it if possible and then kiss one's hand.

(v) While crossing the fourth wall:
Rabbanā ātinā fī 'd-dunyā ḥasanatan wa fī 'l-ākhirati ḥasanatan wa qinā ʿadhāba 'n-nār.

(هـ) عِنْد الْجِدَار الرَّابِع:

رَبَّنَا آتِنَا فِى الدُّنْيَا حَسَنَةً وَفِى الْآخِرَةِ حَسَنَةً وَقِنَا عَذَابَ النَّارِ.

O our Lord, give us good in this world and good in the Hereafter, and protect us from the punishment of the hell fire.

Once one reaches the Black Stone a single round (*ṭawāf*) has been completed. It is Sunnah for men to trot in the first three rounds and to bare their right shoulders, except in the Farewell *Ṭawāf*. However if this means leaving any women without menfolk to accompany, this should not be done, or some men should remain with the women.

After completing the circumambulation until you finish seven turns (*ṭawāf*), reciting what you are able of the above invocations then you go to *Bāb al-Multazam* and make *duʿā* there. If it is difficult due to crowds, do not fight, but step back and go to Maqām Ibrāhīm and from far away make the invocation. Then pray two *rakaʿats* at Maqām Ibrāhīm. It is often not possible for ladies to pray there, so they should pray two *rakaʿats* in the ladies section.

SAʿĪ

Then you go to do *saʿī*. At this portion of *ʿUmrah*/Ḥajj one should keep in mind the struggle of Lady Hajar, searching desperately for water for her baby, the Prophet Ismaʿīl ﷺ.

CONDUCT OF SAʿĪ

أَدَب السَّعْى.

Begin saying:
Bismillāhi 'r-Raḥmāni 'r-Raḥīm
In the name of God, the Beneficent, the Merciful.

بِسْمِ اللهِ الرَّحْمنِ الرَّحيمِ

Then invoke God (*duʿā*):
Yā Rabbī, Yā Allāh, I am making *saʿī* I am seeking the means of support through the Prophet ﷺ and the inheritors of his spiritual states, the saints. O God, if You favor me by accepting my *ʿUmrah*/Ḥajj, all the rewards that I receive I will share with all your servants on this earth.

After completing *saʿī*, present your *ʿUmrah*, or Ḥajj to the Presence of the Prophet ﷺ, by saying, "*Yā Rasulullāh*, I performed that *ʿUmrah*/Ḥajj by trying to follow your footsteps, I am requesting that it be accepted and be changed from imitational to real worship and that you O Prophet of God, present it to the Presence of God."
You then ask from God whatever you want for this life and the hereafter.

You return to your lodging if you are making *ʿUmrah*.
In the case of Ḥajj at-Tamattuʿ, after completing the *ʿUmrah*, the pilgrim trims his or her hair, showers, and changes into everyday clothes.
These steps complete the *ʿUmrah* portion of the Ḥajj at-Tamattuʿ. All restrictions of the *iḥrām* are temporarily lifted. The pilgrim waits until the 8th of Dhul-Ḥijjah to start the rites of Ḥajj and return to *iḥrām*.

INTENTION AND IḤRĀM FOR ḤAJJ TAMATTUʿ

If doing Ḥajj at-Tamattuʿ, on the 8th of Dhul-Ḥijjah, the pilgrim pronounces a new intention (*nīyyah*) at the place to perform Ḥajj. There is no need to go to the *Mīqāt* for this. The pilgrim changes into Iḥrām in the prescribed manner and proceeds to Minā soon after the Fajr Prayers.
Then perform the rites of Ḥajj, by going to ʿArafah , Minā and Muzdalifa and Minā and observing all the details following one's Ḥajj guide.

STANDING AT 'ARAFAH

It is no crime in you if ye seek of the bounty of your Lord (during pilgrimage). Then when ye pour down from (Mount) 'Arafah, celebrate the praises of God at the Sacred Monument, and celebrate His praises as He has directed you, even though, before this, ye went astray.[221]

There is consensus among Muslim scholars that spending the Day of 'Arafah is the most important part of Ḥajj.

'Abd ar-Raḥmān bin Ya'mur ⚘ reported:

The Prophet ﷺ ordered an announcer to proclaim, "Ḥajj is 'Arafah ...."

> *Standing as much as possible is very much recommended, especially around the plains of Jabal ar-Raḥmah (Mount of Mercy) where the Prophet ﷺ delivered his last sermon.*

In another hadith, Jābir ⚘ reported that the Prophet ﷺ said:

> *....And there is no day better in the sight of Allah than the Day of 'Arafah. On this day Allah, the Almighty and the Exalted, descends to the nearest heaven, and He is proud of His slaves on the earth, and says to those in Heaven, "Look at My servants. They have come from far and near, with hair dishevelled and faces covered with dust, to seek My mercy, even though they have not seen My chastisement." Far more people are freed from the Hell-fire on the Day of 'Arafah than on any other day.*

On that day the pilgrims should spend most of their time reading the Qur'an, making remembrance of God (*dhikr*), supplication (*du'ā*), praising the Prophet (*ṣalawāt*) ﷺ, and most importantly asking Allah for forgiveness.

STONING THE JAMARĀT

One pelts the Stoning Sites on the four days of Eid. On the first day you throw seven stones at the Jamarat al-'Aqabah only. On the remaining three days you must throw 21 stones altogether each day, seven at each Jamarah, one-by-one pronouncing the formula below. Some people take the stones and throw them altogether - this is not accepted. Similarly, it is unacceptable to use your slippers or other objects to stone the sites.

Ladies can appoint someone to throw stones for them if the Stoning Sites are very crowded.

---

[221] Sūratu 'l-Baqarah, 2:198.

CONDUCT OF STONING

أَدَب الرَّجْم

Take one pebble at a time and with each one say:
Raghman li 'sh-shayṭān, riḍan li 'r-Rahman, 3 times, *Bismillāh, Allāhu Akbar.* And then throw it at the Jamarah.

رغماً لِلشَّيْطَان رضاً للرحمن 3 مَرَّات، بِسْمِ اللهِ اللهُ أَكْبَرُ .

In opposition to Satan, seeking God's good pleasure and satisfaction; In opposition to Satan, seeking God's good pleasure and satisfaction; God is greater!

STAY AT MINA

During one's stay at Minā, the pilgrim should engage in much remembrance (*dhikr, tasbīḥ*), praise of the Prophet ﷺ (*ṣalawāt*), recitation of Qur'an, invocation (*du'ā*) and supererogatory prayers, for God said:

> *Then pass on at a quick pace from the place whence it is usual for the multitude so to do and ask for Allah's forgiveness. For Allah is Oft-forgiving, Most Merciful. So when you have accomplished your holy rites, celebrate the praises of Allah, as you used to celebrate the praises of your fathers; yea, with far more Heart and soul.*[222]

And:

> *Celebrate the praises of Allah during the Appointed Days. But if any one hastens to leave in two days, there is no blame on him, and if any one stays on, there is no blame on him, if his aim is to do right. Then fear Allah, and know that ye will surely be gathered unto Him.*[223]

And:

> *O you who believe! Remember Allah with much remembrance. And glorify His praises morning and evening.*[224]

ṬAWĀF AL-WADA'

This is the *ṭawāf* of farewell, which is unrelated to either the 'Umrah or Ḥajj. One makes this before leaving with the intention not to return.

---

[222] Sūratu 'l-Baqarah, 2:199-200.

[223] Sūratu 'l-Baqarah, 2:203.

[224] Sūratu 'l-Aḥzāb, 33:41-42.

This concludes the essential conduct of Ḥajj. Keep in mind this contains only a summarized version of the Ḥajj rites. The main intent here is to present the spiritual aspects of the intention and recitations at various point in the pilgrimage. However, to observe the Ḥajj correctly it is essential to follow the instructions and details that your Ḥajj guide directs you to do.

DAILY ṬAWĀF

When you enter the Sacred Mosque, it is preferred to make a *ṭawāf* as it is the greeting for the Kaʿbah (*Taḥīyyatu 'l-Kaʿbah*). Use the same steps mentioned above, leaving out the wording *"al-qudūm"* from the intention. If it is not possible to do the *ṭawāf*, pray first, and when it is less crowded make *ṭawāf* if you are able.

When you leave the Sacred Mosque, it is not necessary to make *ṭawāf*.

SHOPPING AND DAILY ACTIVITY

During pilgrimage it is permitted to shop, but one should not spend excessive time doing so. Similarly, excessive time should not be spent in restaurants and coffee shops. Rather, keep oneself busy in praying, remembrance (*dhikr*) and praise of the Prophet (*ṣalawāt*) ﷺ.

HOLY PLACES OF VISITATION IN MECCA

JANNAT AL-MUʿALLA

Also known as al-Hājūn, this is a general cemetery in existence from before the time of the Prophet ﷺ and in which his first wife, the Mother of the believers (*Umm al-mu'minīn*) Sayyida Khadījat al-Kubrā ؓ is buried. Buried there too are many member of the Family of the Prophet ﷺ, his Companions, Successors, Successors of the Successors, saints and scholars. The Prophet ﷺ used to visit it frequently. It is the second holiest graveyard after al-Baqiʿ in Madīnah.

Those buried here include:

Grave of ʿAbd Manāf: Great, great-grandfather of the Holy Prophet ﷺ

Grave of Hāshim: Great-grandfather of the Holy Prophet ﷺ

Grave of ʿAbd al-Muṭṭalib: Grandfather of the Holy Prophet ﷺ, who raised him in his early childhood.

Grave of Sayyidah Āmina bint Wahb: Mother of the Holy Prophet ﷺ who died when he was only 5 years old. According to another source, Sayyidah Āmina is buried in Abwā (between Mecca and Madīna).

Grave of Sayyīdinā ʿAbd Allāh ibn ʿAbd al-Muṭṭalib: The blessed father of our Holy Prophet ﷺ, who died and was buried in Madīna. Later his body was disinterred and found to be intact. It was transferred to Mecca and buried in Jannat al-Muʿalla.

Grave of Abū Ṭālib: The uncle of the Prophet ﷺ who raised him after the passing of his grandfather ʿAbd al-Muṭṭalib. He was father of ʿAlī ibn Abī Ṭālib, Jaʿfar and ʿAqīl ﷺ.

Grave of Sayyidah Khadīja ﷺ: First wife of the Holy Prophet ﷺ and mother of his daughters.

Grave of Sayyīdinā Qāsim ﷺ: son of the Holy Prophet ﷺ who died in his infancy.

SUPPLICATION AT ʿARAFAT

Shaykh Muhammad Hisham Kabbani

[The *duʿā* made at ʿArafat after *Khatm al-Khawajagān*, Hajj 2011.]

SHAYKH HISHAM READS THE *DUʿA* OF ʿARAFAH, HAJJ AL-AKBAR 2011.

Any gathering here, in this area particularly, is equal to 100,000 gatherings for the sake of Allah ﷻ anywhere else. This *dhikr* is equal to 100,000 *dhikr* gatherings. The *dhikr* we made at Kaʿbah is also equal to 100,000. *Inshā-Allāh,* all those who came with us from anywhere around the world under Mawlana's name, and those who are not here, are dressed with the blessings of Hajj al-Akbar. The Prophet ﷺ prayed Ẓuhr and ʿAsr combined in Masjid Namirah, which we just did earlier, and then after that he would come here and make his *duʿā*. So, we do the *duʿā* now and then we are finished.

O Allah! We are coming to you with the *duʿā* of ʿArafat, so do not turn us away from Your door disappointed:

لَا إِلَهَ إِلَّا الله وَحْدَهُ لَا شَرِيكَ لَهْ. لَهُ المُلْكُ وَلَهُ الحَمْدُ يُحْيِى وَيُمِيتُ وَهُوَ حَيٌّ لَا يَمُوتُ بِيَدِهِ الخَيْرِ وَهُوَ عَلَى كُلِّ شَىْءٍ قَدِيرْ.

There is no god but Allah, only Him, without any partners. To Him belongs the dominion and praise. He gives life and death. He is the Eternally Living who never dies. In His hands is all good and He is All-Powerful over all things.

اللَّهُمَّ إِنَّكَ وَفَّقْتَنِي وَحَمَلْتَنِي عَلَى مَا سَخَّرْتَ لِي حَتَّى بَلَّغْتَنِي بِإِحْسَانِكَ إِلَى زِيَارَةِ بَيْتِكَ وَالْوُقُوفِ عِنْدَ هَذَا الْمَشْعَرِ الْعَظِيمِ اقْتِدَاءً بِسُنَّةِ خَلِيلِكَ وَاقْتِفَاءً بِآثَارِ خِيرَتِكَ مِنْ خَلْقِكَ سَيِّدِنَا مُحَمَّدٍ صَلَّى اللهُ عَلَيْهِ وَسَلَّمَ.

O Allah, You have facilitated and carried me through all that You have given me until You delivered me through Your Bounty to visit Your House and stand at the threshold of this great ritual, following the way of Your Khalīl, Friend and adhering to the relics of the Best from Your Creation, our Master Muhammad ﷺ.

وَإِنَّ لِكُلِّ ضَيْفٍ قِرًى وَلِكُلِّ وَفْدٍ جَائِزَةً وَلِكُلِّ زَائِرٍ كَرَامَةً وَلِكُلِّ سَائِلٍ عَطِيَّةً وَ لِكُلِّ رَاجٍ ثَوَابًا وَلِكُلِّ مُلْتَمِسٍ لِمَا عِنْدَكَ جَزَاءً وَلِكُلِّ رَاغِبٍ إِلَيْكَ زُلْفَةً وَلِكُلِّ مُتَوَجِّهٍ إِلَيْكَ إِحْسَانًا

Indeed, every guest deserves a fire of hospitality; every delegation has a reward; every visitor is shown a generosity; everyone with a need is given; everyone seeking is rewarded; everyone desiring what You have will be rewarded; everyone wanting You is given nearness and everyone who directs themselves towards You is shown beauty.

وَقَدْ وَقَفْنَا بِهَذَا الْمَشْعَرِ الْعَظِيمِ رَجَاءً لِمَا عِنْدَكَ فَلَا تُخَيِّبْ إِلَهَنَا رَجَاءَنَا فِيْكَ يَا سَيِّدَنَا يَا مَوْلَانَا يَا مَنْ خَضَعَتْ كُلُّ الْأَشْيَاءِ لِعِزَّتِهِ وَعَنَتْ الْوُجُوهُ لِعَظَمَتِهِ.

And here we are: we have stood at the threshold of this great ritual seeking what You have, so do not disappoint, O our Lord, our hope in you! Our Master, our Guardian, the One to whose majesty all things have bowed, and to whose greatness all faces have been lowered!

اللَّهُمَّ إِلَيْكَ خَرَجْنَا وَبِفَنَائِكَ أَنَخْنَا وَإِيَّاكَ أَمَّلْنَا وَمَا عِنْدَكَ طَلَبْنَا وَلِإِحْسَانِكَ تَعَرَّضْنَا وَلِرَحْمَتِكَ رَجَوْنَا وَمِنْ عَذَابِكَ أَشْفَقْنَا وَلِبَيْتِكَ الحَرَامِ حَجَجْنَا.

O Allah, for Your sake we have left our homes, at Your court we have submitted. You are our hope. What You have we have sought, to Your Generosity we have exposed ourselves, for Your Mercy we hope, from Your Punishment we have sought refuge, and to Your Holy House we have come as pilgrims.

يَا مَنْ لَيْسَ مَعَهُ رَبٌّ يُدْعَى وَلَا إِلَهٌ يُرْجَى وَلَا فَوْقَهُ خَالِقٌ يُخْشَى وَلَا وَزِيرٌ يُؤْتَى وَلَا حَاجِبٌ يُرْشَى يَا مَنْ لَا يَزْدَادُ عَلَى السُّؤَالِ إِلَّا كَرَمًا وَجُودًا وَعَلَى كَثْرَةِ الحَوَائِجِ إِلَّا تَفَضُّلًا وَإِحْسَانًا.

O You alongside whom there is no other lord to be called upon, another god to be sought, nor above whom is there a creator to be feared, nor a minister to be approached, nor a middleman to be bribed! O You who only increases in generosity and beneficence the more he is asked, and who only grants more in beauty and bountifulness as needs increases!

يَا مَنْ ضَجَّتْ بَيْنَ يَدَيْهِ الأَصْوَاتُ بِمُخْتَلَفِ اللُّغَاتِ يَسْأَلُونَكَ الحَاجَاتِ وَسَكَبَتْ الدُّمُوعُ بِالعَبَرَاتِ وَالزَّفَرَاتِ مُلِحِّينَ بِالدَّعَوَاتِ فَحَاجَتِي إِلَيْكَ يَا رَبِّ مَغْفِرَتُكَ وَرِضَاءٌ مِنْكَ عَلَيَّ لَا سَخَطَ بَعْدَهُ وَهُدًى لَا ضَلَالَ بَعْدَهُ وَعِلْمًا لَا جَهْلَ بَعْدَهُ وَحُسْنَ الخَاتِمَةِ وَالعِتْقَ مِنَ النَّارِ وَالفَوْزَ بِالجَنَّةِ.

O You between whose hands all the voices, in their different languages, have elevated. They ask You their needs, and tears have been shed with expressions, exhalations, insistent in supplications. My need for You our Lord is Your Forgiveness. I seek a contentment from You after which there is no anger, a guidance after which there is no misguidance, a knowledge not followed by ignorance, a good ending, salvation from the fire and attaining Paradise.

وَأَنْ تَذْكُرَنِى عِنْدَ الْبَلَاءِ إِذَا نَسِيَنِى أَهْلُ الدُّنْيَا وَوَارُونِى التُّرَابَ وَانْقَطَعَ عَنِّى الأَحْبَابُ وَتَقَطَّعَتْ بِىَ الأَسْبَابُ يَا عَزِيزُ يَا وَهَّابُ يَا أَرْحَمُ الرَّاحِمِينْ.

I ask that You remember me during calamities, when people of this world will forget me, and when dust will surround me, loved ones will depart from me and all causes are cut off from me, O Exalted One, Giver of Gifts, the Most Merciful of the Merciful!

اللَّهُمَّ إِنَّكَ تَرَى مَكَانِى وَتَسْمَعُ كَلَامِى وَتَعْلَمُ سِرِّى وَعَلَانِيَتِى وَلَا يَخْفَى عَلَيْكَ شَىْءٌ مِنْ أَمْرِى، أَنَا الْبَائِسُ الْفَقِيرُ الْمُسْتَغِيثُ الوَجِلُ الْمُشْفِقُ الْمُقِرُّ الْمُعْتَرِفُ بِذَنْبِهْ.

O Allah! You see my place, hear my speech, know my secret and outward. Nothing from my affair is hidden from You. I am the miserable one, the impoverished one, the one seeking Your Salvation, the humbled one who acknowledges and admit his sins.

أَسْأَلُكَ مَسْأَلَةَ الْمِسْكِينِ وَابْتَهِلُ إِلَيْكَ اِبْتِهَالَ الْمُذْنِبِ الذَّلِيلِ وَأَدْعُوكَ دُعَاءَ الْخَائِفِ الضَّرِيرِ دُعَاءَ مَنْ خَضَعَ لَكَ عُنُقَهُ وَذَلَّ لَكَ جَسَدُهُ وَفَاضَتْ لَكَ عَيْنَاهُ وَرَغِمَ لَكَ أَنْفُهُ لَا تَجْعَلْنِى بِدُعَائِكَ رَبِّ شَقِيًّا وَكُنْ بِى رَؤُوفًا رَحِيمًا يَا خَيْرَ الْمَسْؤُلِينَ وَيَا خَيْرَ الْمُعْطِينْ .

I ask You in the manner of the weak and direct myself to You in the manner of the lowly sinner. I supplicate to You the supplication of the one who is fearful and wounded and one who submitted their neck to You, as well as their body, and one whose eyes have overflowed for You and lowered their honor for You. Do not make me arrogant in supplicating to You, and be gentle and merciful with me, O Best of those who are asked and Best of Givers.

رَبِّ اِهْدِنَا بِالْهُدَى وَزَيِّنَا بِالتَّقْوَى وَاغْفِرْ لَنَا فِى الآخِرَةِ وَالأُولَى. اللَّهُمَّ اجْعَل فِى قَلْبِى نُوراً وَفِى لِسَانِى نُوراً وَعَنْ يَمِينِى نُوراً وَعَنْ يَسَارِى نُوراً وَمِنْ فَوْقِى

نُوراً وَمِنْ تَحْتِي نُوراً وَمِنْ أَمَامِي نُوراً وَمِنْ خَلْفِي نُوراً وَاجْعَلْ فِي نَفْسِي نُوراً وَاعْظِمْ لِي نُورا.

Our Lord, guide us with guidance, ornament us with piety and forgive us in the Hereafter and this life. O Allah, make in my heart a light, in my tongue a light, on my right a light, on my left a light, above me a light, below me a light, in front of me a light, behind me a light. Make in my soul a light and make my light greater.

رَبِّ اشْرَحْ لِي صَدْرِي وَيَسِّرْ لِي أَمْرِي. اللَّهُمَّ إِنِّي أَسْأَلُكَ الهُدَى وَالتَّقْوَى وَالعَفَافَ وَالغِنَى. اللَّهُمَّ لَكَ الحَمْدُ كَالَّذِي تَقُولُ وَخَيْراً مِمَا نَقُولْ. اللَّهُمَّ إِنِّي أَسْأَلُكَ رِضَاكَ وَالجَنَّةَ وَأَعُوذُ بِكَ مِنْ سَخَطِكَ وَالنَّارِ وَمَا قَرَّبَ إِلَيْهَا مِنْ قَوْلٍ أَوْ فِعْلٍ أَوْ عَمَلْ.

O Allah, expand my chest for me and ease my affair for me. O Allah, I ask You guidance, piety, bashfulness and sufficiency. O Allah, all praise is due to You as You have said, and better than what we say. O Allah, I ask you Your Contentment and Paradise and seek refuge in You from Your Anger and Hellfire and whatever brings us closer to it of statements, actions, or deeds.

اللَّهُمَّ اجْعَلْهُ حَجًّا مَبْرُوراً وَذَنْباً مَغْفُوراً وَعَمَلاً صَالِحًا مَقْبُولا. رَبَّنَا أَتِنَا فِي الدُّنْيَا حَسَنَةً وَفِي الآخِرَةِ حَسَنَةً وَقِنَا عَذَابَ النَّارْ. إِلَهِي لَا قُوَّةَ لِي عَلَى سَخَطِكَ وَلَا صَبْرَ لِي عَلَى عَذَابِكَ وَلَا غِنَى لِي عَنْ رَحْمَتِكَ وَلَا قُوَّةَ لِي عَلَى البَلَاءِ وَلَا طَاعَةَ لِي عَلَى الجُهْدْ.

O Allah, make this an accepted pilgrimage, a forgiven sin, a righteous and accepted action. O our Lord, grant us in this world goodness, in the Hereafter goodness and protect us from the Fire. O Allah, I have no power over Your Anger, nor any patience amidst Your Punishment, any sufficiency from Your Mercy, any power during calamities or any obedience through my own strength.

أَعُوذُ بِرَضَاكَ مِنْ سَخَطِكَ وِمِنْ فُجَاءَةِ نِقْمَتِكَ يَا أَمَلِى وَيَا رَجَائِى يَا خَيْرَ مُسْتَغَاثٍ يَا أَجْوَدَ المُعْطِينَ يَا مَنْ سَبَقَتْ رَحْمَتُهُ غَضَبَهُ يَا سَيِّدِى وَمَوْلَاىَ يَا ثِقَتِى وَرَجَائِى وَمُعْتَمَدِى.

I seek refuge through Your Contentment from Your Anger, and Your sudden tests. O my Hope and Destination, O the Best of those who is sought and Most Generous of givers. O You whose Mercy has surpassed His Anger. O my Master and Guardian, my Trust and Hope and Dependence.

اللَّهُمَّ يَا مَنْ لَا يَشْغَلُهُ سَمْعٌ عَنْ سَمْعٍ وَلَا تَشْتَبِهُ عَلَيْهِ الأَصْوَاتُ يَا مَنْ لَا تَغْلُطُهُ المَسَائِلُ وَلَا تَخْتَلِفُ عَلَيْهِ اللُّغَاتُ يَا مَنْ لَا يَبْرُمُهُ إِلْحَاحُ المُلِّحِينَ وَلَا تُعْجِزُهُ مَسْأَلَةَ السَّائِلِينَ أَذِقْنَا بَرْدَ عَفْوِكَ وَحَلَاوَةَ مَغْفِرَتِكَ يَا أَرْحَمَ الرَّاحِمِينْ.

O Allah, who is not preoccupied by any hearing from any other hearing, nor do voices become confusing for Him. O You who is not overwhelmed by the abundance of seekers or burdened by the questions of questioners, let us taste the coolness of Your Clemency and sweetness of Your Forgiveness, O Most Merciful of the merciful.

اللَّهُمَّ إِنِّى قَدْ وَفَدْتُ إِلَيْكَ وَوَقَفْتُ بَيْنَ يَدَيْكَ فِى هَذَا المَوْضِعِ الشَّرِيفِ رَجَاءً لِمَا عِنْدَكَ فَلَا تَجْعَلْنِى اليَوْمَ أَخْيَبَ وَفْدِكَ فَأَكْرِمْنِى بِالجَنَّةِ وَمُنَّ عَلَىَّ بِالمَغْفِرَةِ وَالعَافِيَةِ وَأَجِرْنِى مِنْ النَّارِ وَادْرَأْ عَنِّى شَرَّ خَلْقِكْ.

O Allah, I have come to You and stood between Your Hands in this honored place and time, seeking what you have, so do not make me today the most disappointed of your visitors, but be generous towards me with Paradise, and be bounteous upon me with forgiveness and good health, and save me from the Fire. Keep the most evil from among Your Creation away from me.

اِنْقَطَعَ الرَّجَاءُ إِلَّا مِنْكَ وَأُغْلِقَتِ الْأَبْوَابُ إِلَّا بَابُكَ فَلَا تَكِلْنِى إِلَى أَحَدٍ سِوَاكَ

فِى أُمُورِ دِينِى وَدُنْيَاىَ طَرْفَةَ عَيْنٍ وَلَا أَقَلَّ مِنْ ذَلِكَ وَانْقُلْنِى مِنْ ذُلِّ الْمَعْصِيَةِ

إِلَى عِزِّ الطَّاعَةِ وَنَوِّرْ قَلْبِى وَقَبْرِى وَأَعِذْنِى مِنَ الشَّرِّ كُلِّهِ وَاجْمَعْ لِى الْخَيْرَ كُلَّهُ يَا

أَكْرَمَ مَنْ سُئِلَ وَأَجْوَدَ مَنْ أَعْطَى.

All hope has been cut save from You, all doors have closed save Yours, so do not leave me to other than You for a blink of an eye, or less than that, in the affairs of my religion and life. Move me from the humility of sins to the honor of obedience. Illuminate my heart and grave and protect me from all evil and gather for me all goodness, O Most Generous of those who are asked and Bounteous of those who give.

اللَّهُمَّ بِنُورِكَ اهْتَدَيْنَا وَبِفَضْلِكَ اسْتَغْنَيْنَا. وَفِى كَنَفِكَ وَإِنْعَامِكَ وَعَطَائِكَ

وَإِحْسَانِكَ أَصْبَحْنَا وَأَمْسَيْنَا. أَنْتَ الْأَوَّلُ فَلَا شَىْءَ قَبْلُكَ وَالْآخِرُ فَلَا شَىْءَ بَعْدَكَ

وَالظَّاهِرُ فَلَا شَىْءَ فَوْقُكَ وَالْبَاطِنُ فَلَا شَىْءَ دُونَكَ نَعُوذُ بِكَ مِنَ الْفَلَسِ وَالْكَسَلِ

وَعَذَابِ الْقَبْرِ وَوَسْوَسَةِ الصَّدْرِ وَشَتَاتِ الْأَمْرِ وَفِتْنَةِ الْغِنَى.

O Allah, through Your Light we have been guided, and through Your Bounty we have become sufficient. In Your Protection, Bounty, Gifts and Generosity we have reached our mornings and nights. You are the First before whom there is no other, and the Last after whom there is no other. You are the Outward above whom there is no other, and the Inward, more inward than whom there is no other. We seek refuge in You from bankruptcy, laziness, the punishment of the grave, devilish whispers in the chests, distractions, the test of wealth.

وَأَسْأَلُكَ مُوجِبَاتِ رَحْمَتِكَ وَعَزَائِمَ مَغْفِرَتِكَ وَالْغَنِيمَةَ مِنْ كُلِّ بِرٍّ وَالسَّلَامَةَ مِنْ

كُلِّ إِثْمٍ وَالْفَوْزَ بِالْجَنَّةِ وَالنَّجَاةَ مِنَ النَّارِ.

We ask You those things that bring Your Mercy and most exalted of Your Forgiveness, to obtain every worthy piety and salvation from every sin, to attain Paradise, be saved from the Fire.

اللَّهُمَّ يَا عَالِمَ الخَفِيَّاتِ وَيَا سَامِعَ الأَصْوَاتِ يَا بَاعِثَ الأَمْوَاتِ يَا مُجِيبَ الدَّعَوَاتِ يَا قَاضِىَ الحَاجَاتِ يَا خَالِقَ الأَرْضِ وَالسَّمَوَاتِ أَنْتَ اللهُ الَّذِى لَا إِلَهَ إِلَّا أَنْتَ الوَاحِدُ الأَحَدُ الفَرْدُ الصَّمَدُ الوَهَّابُ الَّذِى لَا يَبْخَلُ وَالحَلِيمُ الَّذِى لَا يَعْجَلُ.لَا رَادَّ لِأَمْرِكَ وَلَا مُعَقِّبَ لِحُكْمِكَ رَبَّ كُلِّ شَىْءٍ وَمَلِيكَ كُلِّ شَىْءٍ وَمُقَدِّرَ كُلِّ شَىْء.

O Allah, who knows all that is hidden, who hears the voices, who resurrects the dead, answers the supplications, fulfills needs, and creator of the Earth and Heavens! You are Allah, there is no god but You, the One, Singular, Unique, Everlasting, Giver of Gifts who is never stingy, the Clement who never hurries. There is no obstacle for Your Command and nothing follows Your Rules. You are the Lord of all things, the King of all things and One who measures all things.

أَسْأَلُكَ أَنْ تَرْزُقَنِى عِلْمًا نَافِعًا وَرِزْقًا وَاسِعًا وَقَلْبًا خَاشِعًا وَلِسَانًا ذَاكِرًا وَعَمَلًا زَكِيًّا وَإِيمَانًا خَالِصًا وَهَبْ لَنَا إِنَابَةَ المُخْلِصِينَ وَخُشُوعَ المُخْبِتِينَ وَأَعْمَالَ الصَّالِحِينَ وَيَقِينَ الصَّادِقِينَ وَسَعَادَةَ المُتَّقِينَ وَدَرَجَاتَ الفَائِزِينَ يَا أَفْضَلَ مَنْ قُصِدَ وَأَكْرَمَ مَنْ سُئِلَ وَأَحْلَمَ مَنْ عُصِى.

I ask You to sustain me with beneficial knowledge, expansive sustenance, a fearful heart, a remembering tongue, a pure deed, sincere faith, and grant us the presence of sincere ones, the fear of present ones, the deeds of righteous ones, certainty of truthful ones, happiness of pious ones and ranks of victorious ones. O Best of those who are intended and Most Generous of those who are asked and Most Clement of those who are disobeyed!

مَا أَحْلَمُكَ عَلَى مَنْ عَصَاكَ وَأَقْرَبُكَ إِلَى مَنْ دَعَاكَ وَأَعْطَفُكَ عَلَى مَنْ سَأَلَكَ لَا مَهْدِيٌّ إِلَّا مَنْ هَدَيْتَ وَلَا ضَالٌّ إِلَّا مَنْ أَضْلَلْتَ وَلَا غَنِيٌّ إِلَّا مَنْ أَغْنَيْتَ وَلَا فَقِيرٌ إِلَّا مَنْ أَفْقَرْتَ وَلَا مَعْصُومٌ إِلَّا مَنْ عَصَمْتَ وَلَا مَسْتُورٌ إِلَّا مَنْ سَتَرْتَ

How forgiving are You towards those who disobey You? How near are you to those who ask You? How gentle are You with those who seek You? No one is guided save the one whom You guide, and no misguided one save the one whom you allow to be misguided. There is no rich save the one whom you have made wealthy and no impoverished save they whom You have made impoverished. There is no protected one save those whom You have protected, no safeguarded save those whom You have safeguarded.

أَسْأَلُكَ أَنْ تَهَبَ لَنَا جَزِيلَ عَطَائِكَ وَالسَّعَادَةَ بِلِقَائِكَ وَالمَزِيدَ مِنْ نِعْمَتِكَ وَآلَائِكَ وَأَنْ تَجْعَلَ لَنَا نُوراً فِي حَيَاتِنَا وَنُوراً فِي مَمَاتِنَا وَنُوراً فِي قُبُورِنَا وَنُورًا فِي حَشْرِنَا وَنُوراً نَتَوَسَّلُ بِهِ إِلَيْكَ وَنُوراً نَفُوزُ بِهِ لَدَيْكَ فَإِنَّا بِبَابِكَ سَائِلُونَ وَلِلِقَائِكَ رَاجُونْ.

I ask You to grant us the best of Your Bounty, the happiness to meet You, more of Your Beneficence and that You make for us a light in our lives, deaths, graves, resurrection, and a light through which we can intercede to You, and a light through which we become victorious in Your Presence. For we are seekers at Your Door, hopeful in meeting You!

اللَّهُمَّ اجْعَل خَيْرَ عُمْرِي آخِرَهُ وَخَيْرَ عَمَلِي خَوَاتِمَهُ وَخَيْرَ أَيَّامِي يَوْمَ لِقَائِكْ.

اللَّهُمَّ ثَبِّتْنِي بِأَمْرِكَ وَأَيِّدْنِي بِنَصْرِكَ وَارْزُقْنِي مِنْ فَضْلِكَ وَنَجِّنِي مِنْ عَذَابِكَ يَوْمَ تَبْعَثُ عِبَادِكَ فَقَدْ أَتَيْتُكَ لِرَحْمَتِكَ رَاجِيًا وَعَنْ وَطَنِي نَائِبًا وَلِنُسُكِي مُؤَدِّيًا وَلِفَرَائِضِكَ قَاضِيًا وَلِكِتَابِكَ تَالِيًا وَلَكَ دَاعِيًا وَمِنْ قَسْوَةِ قَلْبِي شَاكِيًا وَمِنْ ذَنْبِي خَاشِيًا وَلِنَفْسِي ظَالِمًا وَبِجُرْمِي عَالِمًا

O Allah, make the best of my life its last, the best of my deeds its last, the best of my days those when I meet You. O Allah, make me firm upon Your Commands, and aid me with Your Victory and grant me from Your Bounty. Save me from Your Punishment on the day that You resurrect Your Servants, for I have come to You, seeking Your Mercy, leaving behind my home, fulfilling my rituals, completing your obligations, reciting Your Book, supplicating to You, lamenting the hardness of my heart, fearful of my sins, transgressing against myself, fully aware of my transgressions.

دُعَاءَ مَنْ جُمِعَتْ عُيُوبُهُ وَكَثُرَتْ ذُنُوبُهُ وَتَصَرَّمَتْ آمَالُهُ وَبَقِيَتْ آثَامُهُ وَانْسَكَبَتْ دَمْعَتُهُ وَانْقَطَعَتْ عُدَّتُهُ دُعَاءَ مَنْ لَا يَجِدْ لِذَنْبِهِ غَافِرًا غَيْرُكَ وَلَا لِمَأْمُولِهِ مِنَ الخَيْرَاتِ مُعْطِيًا سِوَاكَ وَلَا لِكَسْرِهِ جَابِرًا إِلَّا أَنْتَ يَا أَرْحَمَ الرَّاحِمِينَ. وَلَا حَوْلَ وَلَا قُوَّةَ إِلَّا بِاللهِ العَلِيِّ العَظِيمْ.

I supplicate as one whose faults have gathered, sins have increased, hopes have decreased, sins have remained, tears have flowed, means have ended. I supplicate as one who finds no one to forgive his sins save You, and no one to grant him goodness save You, no one to mend his brokenness save You, O Most Merciful of the merciful, and there is no power or means save through Allah, the Most High and Greatest.

اللَّهُمَّ لَا تُقَدِّمْنِى لِعَذَابِكَ وَلَا تُؤَخِّرْنِى لِشَىْءٍ مِنْ الفِتَنْ. مَوْلَاىَ هَا أَنَا أَدْعُوكَ رَاغِبًا وَأَنْصُبُ إِلَيْكَ وَجْهِى طَالِبًا وَأَضَعُ لَكَ خَدِّى مَهِينًا رَاهِبًا

O Allah, do not bring me closer to Your Punishment and do not leave me for any tribulations. O my Guardian, here I am calling You and seeking You. I put my face towards You, beseeching You, and I leave my cheek down for You in humility and fearfulness.

فَتَقَبَّلْ دُعَائِى وَاصْلِحْ الفَاسِدَ مِنْ أَمْرِى وَاقْطَع مِنْ الدُّنْيَا هَمِّى وَحَاجَتِى وَاجْعَل فِيمَا عِنْدَكَ رَغْبَتِى وَاقْلِبْنِى مُنْقَلَبَ المَذْكُورِ عِنْدَكَ دُعَاؤُهُمْ القَائِمَةُ حُجَّتُهُم وَالمَغْفُورُ ذَنْبُهُم المَبْرُورُ حَجُّهُم وَالمحْطُوطُ خَطَايَاهُم المَمْحُوُّ

سَيِّئَاتُهُم الرَّاشِدُ أَمْرُهُم مُنْقَلَبَ مَنْ لَا يَعْصِى لَكَ أَمْرًا وَلَا يَأْتِى بَعْدَهُ مَأْثَمًا وَلَا يَحْمِلُ بَعْدَهُ وِزْرًا.

So, accept my supplication, fix what is faulty in my affair, cut off my burdens and needs from this world and make what I desire that which You have. Turn me in the way of those who are remembered in Your Presence, with established proofs, forgiven sins, accepted pilgrimage and whose sins are erased, whose affairs are set straight. Turn me as one who will not disobey any of Your Commands, nor bring forth any more sins, nor carry any more burdens!

مُنْقَلَبَ مَنْ عَزَّزْتَ بِذِكْرِكَ لِسَانَهُ وَطَهَّرْتَ مِنْ الأَدْنَاسِ بَدَنَهُ وَاسْتَوْدَعْتَ الهُدَى قَلْبَهُ وَشَرَحْتَ بِالإِسْلَامِ صَدْرَهُ وَأَقْرَرْتَ بِرِضَاكَ وَعَفْوُكَ قَبْلَ المَمَاتِ عَيْنَهُ وَغَضَضْتَ عَنْ اِلمَآثِمِ بَصَرَهُ وَاسْتَعْمَلْتَ فِى سَبِيلِكَ نَفْسَهُ.

Turn me as one whom You have honored their tongue through Your Remembrance, and purified their body from filth, placed guidance in their heart, expanded their chest with Islam, made firm their eyes with Your Contentment and forgiveness before death, and directed their gazes away from sins, used their souls in Your Way.

وَأَسْأَلُكَ أَنْ لَا تَجْعَلَنِى أَشْقَى خَلْقِكَ لِلمُذْنِبِينَ عِنْدَكَ وَلَا أَخْيَبَ الرَّاجِينَ لَدَيْكَ وَلَا أَحْرَمَ الآمِلِينَ لِرَحْمَتِكَ وَلَا أَخْسَرَ المُنْقَلِبِينَ مِنْ هَذَا المَوْقِفِ العَظِيمِ مَوْلَاىَ رَبَّ العَالَمِينَ.

I ask You that You do not make me the most miserable of Your sinful Creation in Your Presence, nor the most disappointed of those who are hopeful in Your Presence, nor the most deprived of those seeking Your Mercy, nor those most bereft of those who turn away from this great station, O my Guardian, the Lord of the Worlds!

اللَّهُمَّ وَقَدْ دَعَوْتُكَ بِالدُّعَاءِ الَّذِى عَلَّمْتَنِيهِ فَلَا تَحْرِمْنِى الرَّجَاءَ الَّذِى عَرَّفْتَنِيهِ يَا مَنْ لَا تَنْفَعُهُ الطَّاعَةُ وَلَا تَضُرُّهُ المَعْصِيَةُ

O Allah, I have called upon You with the supplication that You have taught me, so do not deprive me of the hope that You have made known to me. O You who does not benefit from acts of obedience nor is he harmed by disobedience!

وَمَا أَعْطَيْتَنِى مِمَّا أُحِبُّ فَاجْعَلْهُ لِى عَوْنًا فِيمَا تُحِبُّ وَاجْعَلْهُ لِى خَيْراً وَحَبِّبْ طَاعَتَكَ لِى وَالعَمَلَ بِهَا كَمَا حَبَّبْتَهَا إِلَى أَوْلِيَائِكَ حَتَّى رَأَوْا ثَوَابَهَا وَكَمَا هَدَيْتَنِى لِلإِسْلَامِ فَلَا تَنْزَعْهُ مِنِّى حَتَّى تَقْبِضَنِى إِلَيْكَ وَأَنَا عَلَيْه.

What you have given me of those things that I love, make it for me an aid to fulfill what You love. Make it for me goodness and make obeying You beloved to me as well as practicing it, as You have granted Your Saints, until they perceived its reward. As you have guided me to Islam, do not deprive me of it until You take me back to You while I am adhering to it.

اللَّهُمَّ حَبِّبْ إِلَيَّ الإِيمَانَ وَزَيِّنْهُ فِى قَلْبِى وَكَرِّهْ إِلَيَّ الكُفْرَ وَالفُسُوقَ وَالعِصْيَانَ وَاجْعَلْنِى مِنَ الرَّاشِدِينْ. اللَّهُمَّ اخْتِمْ بِالخَيْرَاتِ آجَالَنَا وَحَقِّقْ بِفَضْلِكَ آمَالَنَا وَسَهِّلْ لِبُلُوغِ رِضَاكَ سُبُلَنَا وَحَسِّنْ فِى جَمِيعِ الأَحْوَالِ أَعْمَالَنَا يَا مُنْقِذَ الغَرْقَى يَا مُنْجِيَ الهَلْكَى يَا شَاهِدَ كُلِّ نَجْوَى يَا مُنْتَهَى كُلِّ شَكْوَى يَا قَدِيمَ الإِحْسَانِ يَا دَائِمَ المَعْرُوفِ يَا مَنْ لَا غِنَى لِشَيْءٍ عَنْهُ وَلَابُدَّ لِكُلِّ شَيْءٍ مِنْهُ .

O Allah, make faith beloved to me and make it an ornament in my heart. Make disbelief, transgressions, and disobedience hateful to me and make me from those rightly guided one. O Allah, seal with goodness our lives and fulfill our hopes with Your Bounty, facilitate our ways to reach Your Contentment, beautify in every state our actions, O You who saves the drowning ones, the Savior of those destroyed, O Witness of every supplication, and Destination of every need, O Ancient in bounty, Continuous in gifts. O You of whom no one is sufficient, everyone needs.

يَا مَنْ رِزْقُ كُلِّ شَيْءٍ عَلَيْهِ وَمَصِيرُ كُلِّ شَيْءٍ إِلَيْهِ إِلَيْكَ رُفِعَتْ أَيْدِى السَّائِلِينَ وَامْتَدَّتْ أَعْنَاقُ العَابِدِينَ نَسْأَلُكَ أَنْ تَجْعَلَنَا فِى كَنَفِكَ وَجُودِكَ وَحِرْزِكَ وَعِيَاذِكَ وَسِتْرِكَ وَأَمَانِكْ.

O You to whom belongs all our wealth, to whom returns all our destinies. To You are raised the hands of seekers, and to You have been lowered the necks of worshippers. We ask You to make us in Your Protection, Bounty, Guardianship, Salvation, Safe-guardianship and Security.

اللَّهُمَّ إِنَّا نَعُوذُ بِكَ مِنْ جَهْدِ البَلَاءِ وَدَرْكِ الشَّقَاءِ وَسُوءِ القَضَاءِ وَشَمَاتَةِ الأَعْدَاءِ وَسُوءِ المَنْظَرِ وَالمُنْقَلَبِ فِى الأَهْلِ وَالمَالِ وَالوَلَدْ .

O Allah, we seek refuge in you from the struggle of calamities, ways of misery, an evil return and mockery of enemies, the bad ending in our families, wealth and children.

اللَّهُمَّ لَا تَدَعْ فِى مَقَامِنَا هَذَا ذَنْبًا إِلَّا غَفَرْتَهُ وَلَا هَمًّا إِلَّا فَرَّجْتَهُ وَلَا غَائِبًا إِلَّا رَدَدْتَهُ وَلَا كَرْبًا إِلَّا كَشَفْتَهُ وَلَا دَيْنًا إِلَّا قَضَيْتَهُ وَلَا عَدُوًّا إِلَّا كَبَبْتَهُ وَلَا خُلَّةً إِلَّا سَدَدْتَها وَلَا فَسَادًا إِلَّا أَصْلَحْتَهُ وَلَا مَرِيضًا إِلَّا عَافَيْتَهُ وَلَا حَاجَةً مِنْ حَوَائِجِ الدُّنْيَا وَالآخِرَةِ لَكَ فِيهَا رِضًا وَلَنَا فِيهَا صَلاحٌ إِلَّا قَضَيْتَهَا. فَإِنَّكَ تَهْدِى السَّبِيلَ وَتَجْبُرُ الكَسِيرَ وَتُغْنِىَ الفَقِيرْ.

O Allah, do not leave for us in this station a sin save that You forgive it, a burden save that You alleviate it, an absent one save that You return them to us, a calamity save that You make it disappear, any debt save that You fulfill it, an enemy save that You destroy, friendship save that You complete it, a corruption save that You rectify it, anyone sick save that You cure, any need from the needs of this world or the Hereafter which has Your Contentment and our benefit save that you fulfill it, for

You are the One who guides to the right way, mend the broken ones, and suffice the impoverished!

اللَّهُمَّ إِنَّهُ لَابُدَّ لَنَا مِنْ لِقَائِكَ فَاجْعَلْ عِنْدَكَ عُذْرَنَا مَقْبُولاً وَذَنْبَنَا مَغْفُورًا

وَعَمَلَنَا وَسَعْيَنَا مَشْكُورا. أَصْبَحَ وَجْهِى الْفَانِى مُسْتَجِيرًا بِوَجْهِكَ الْبَاقِى الْقَيُّومِ

ذِى الْعِزَّةِ وَالْجَبَرُوتِ. اللَّهُمَّ لَا يَمْنَعُنِى مِنْكَ أَحَدٌ إِذَا أَرَدْتَنِى وَلَا يُعْطِينِى أَحَدٌ

إِذَا حَرَمْتَنِى فَلَا تَحْرِمْنِى بِقِلَّةِ شُكْرِى وَلَا تَخْذُلْنِى بِقِلَّةِ صَبْرِى .

O Allah, we will definitely meet You, so let our excuse be accepted in Your Presence, our sins forgiven, our deeds and rituals accepted. My disappearing face has arisen seeking Your Subsistent Countenance, Everlasting with Exaltedness and Might. O Allah, no one can stand between me and You if you want me, and no one will give me if You deprive me. So do not deprive me due to my lack of gratitude and do not disappoint me due to my lack of patience.

اللَّهُمَّ اجْعَلِ الْمَوْتَ خَيْرَ غَائِبٍ نَنْتَظِرُهُ وَالْقَبْرَ خَيْرَ بَيْتٍ نُعَمِّرُهُ وَاجْعَلْ مَا

بَعْدَهُ خَيْرًا لَنَا مِنْهُ. رَبِّ اغْفِرْ لِى وِلِوَالِدَىَّ وَلِأَبْنَائِى وَلِإِخْوَتِى وَلِأَخَوَاتِى

وَلِإِخْوَانِى وَأَهْلِ بَيْتِى وَذُرِّيَتِى وَلِلْمُؤْمِنِينَ وَالْمُؤْمِنَاتِ وَالْمُسْلِمِينَ وَالْمُسْلِمَاتِ

الْأَحْيَاءِ مِنْهُم وَالْأَمْوَاتِ.

O Allah, make death the best of those absent ones for which we await, and make the grave the best abode in which we will live and make whatever comes after it better for us than it. O my Lord, forgive me, my parents, my children, brothers, sisters, my household, my descendants, all believing men and women and Muslim men and women, those living and dead.

اللَّهُمَّ إِنِّى أَسْأَلُكَ إِيمَانًا يُبَاشِرُ قَلْبِى وَيَقِينًا صَادِقًا حَتَّى أَعْلَمَ أَنَّهُ لَا يُصِيبُنِى

إِلَّا مَا كَتَبْتَ لِى وَرَضِّنِى بِقَضَائِكَ وَأَعِنِّى عَلَى الدُّنْيَا بِالْعِفَّةِ وَالْقَنَاعَةِ وَعَلَى

الدِّينِ بِالطَّاعَةِ وَطَهِّرْ لِسَانِى مِنَ الكَذِبِ وَقَلْبِى مِنَ النِّفَاقِ وَعَمَلِى مِنَ الرِّيَاءِ
وَبَصَرِى مِنَ الخِيَانَةِ فَإِنَّكَ تَعْلَمُ خَائِنَةَ الأَعْيُنِ وَمَا تُخْفِى الصُّدُورُ.

O Allah, I ask you for a faith that directly enters my heart, a truthful certainty so that I know that nothing befalls me save that which you have decreed for me. Make me content with Your Decree and aid me upon this world through bashfulness, contentment and in my religion through obedience. Make my tongue pure from lying, my heart from hypocrisy, my deeds from arrogance, my gaze from treason for You know the treason of eyes and what chests hide.

رَبَّنَا آتِنَا فِى الدُّنْيَا حَسَنَةً وَفِى الآخِرَةِ حَسَنَةً وَقِنَا عَذَابَ النَّارِ وَاغْفِرْ لَنَا
وَلِوَالِدِينَا وَلِوَالِدَيَّ وَالِدِينَا وَذُرِّيَّتِنَا وَأَخَوَاتِنَا وَأَهْلِنَا وَالحَاضِرِينَ وَالغَائِبِينَ مِنَ
المُسْلِمِينَ أَجْمَعِينَ بِرَحْمَتِكَ يَا أَرْحَمَ الرَّاحِمِينَ وَصَلَّى اللهُ عَلَى سَيِّدِنَا مُحَمَّدٍ
وَعَلَى آلِهِ وَصَحْبِهِ أَجْمَعِينَ"

O our Lord, grant us in this world goodness and in the Hereafter goodness and save us from the punishment of the Fire. Forgive us, our parents, the parents of our parents, our descendants, siblings, families, all those present and absent from among the Muslims, through your mercy, O Most Merciful of the merciful. May Allah send His Prayers and Salutations upon our Master Muhammad, His Family and Companions altogether. Al-Fātiḥah.

تم بحمد الله

Printed in the USA
CPSIA information can be obtained
at www.ICGtesting.com
JSHW020111250524
63336JS00001B/5

9 781938 058653